SECOND EDITION

AUTHENTIC CLASSROOM MANAGEMENT

Creating a Learning Community and Building Reflective Practice

BARBARA LARRIVEE

California State University, San Bernardino

Boston ■ New York ■ San Francisco
Mexico City ■ Montreal ■ Toronto ■ London ■ Madrid ■ Munich ■ Paris
Hong Kong ■ Singapore ■ Tokyo ■ Cape Town ■ Sydney

Senior Editor: *Arnis E. Burvikovs*
Series Editorial Assistant: *Megan Smallidge*
Marketing Manager: *Tara Whorf*
Editorial–Production Service: *Omegatype Typography, Inc.*
Manufacturing Buyer: *Andrew Turso*
Composition Buyer: *Linda Cox*
Cover Administrator: *Joel Grendon*
Electronic Composition: *Omegatype Typography, Inc.*

For related titles and support materials, visit our online catalog at www.ablongman.com.

Between the time Website information is gathered and published, some sites may have closed. Also, the transcription of URLs can result in typographical errors. The publisher would appreciate notification where these errors occur so that they may be corrected in subsequent editions.

Library of Congress Cataloging-in-Publication Data

Larrivee, Barbara.
    Authentic classroom management : creating a learning community and building reflective practice / Barbara Larrivee.—2nd ed.
        p. cm.
    Includes bibliographical references and index.
    ISBN 0-205-38088-3
    1. Classroom management.   I. Title.

LB3013.L294 2005
371.102'4—dc22

2004040114

Printed in the United States of America

10   9   8   7   6   5   4   09   08   07   06   05

CONTENTS

CHAPTER FOUR

Keeping Communication Channels Open   92

CHAPTER FIVE

Managing a Learning Community: Collaborative Participation   138

CHAPTER SIX

Managing by Rewards and Consequences   184

More can be done to improve education by enhancing the effectiveness of teachers than by any other single factor affecting students and educational outcomes (Marzano, 2003; Wright, Sanders, & Horn, 1997). An effective teacher is effective in three important arenas: designing the curriculum to facilitate learning, using the most effective instructional methods and strategies, and managing the learning environment to maximize productive learning time.

CLASSROOM MANAGEMENT: A CRITICAL INGREDIENT FOR ACHIEVING STUDENT OUTCOMES

Research has documented the profound impact an individual teacher can have on student achievement. Furthermore, effective teachers are effective with students at all achievement levels regardless of the degree of heterogeneity in their classes. The converse is also true: Ineffective teachers achieve inadequate progress with all their students regardless of their prior level of academic achievement (Haycock, 1998; Marzano, 2003; Sanders & Horn, 1994; Wright, Sanders, & Horn, 1997).

Classroom management is a critical ingredient in the three-way mix of effective teaching strategies, which includes meaningful content, powerful teaching strategies, and an organizational structure to support productive learning. In fact, based on a comprehensive review of research, classroom management has been rated number one in terms of its impact on student achievement (Wang, Haertel, & Walberg, 1993).

Because today's classroom represents increasing diversity among students, a teacher's management style has to accommodate and adjust to this greater range of differences in ethnicity, socioeconomic status, and developmental levels. This text presents teachers with a wide variety of approaches that can be effective in certain situations with certain students, as well as decision-making criteria to determine when, how, and why specific interventions are likely to be more or less responsive to the varying needs of students.

IMPLICATIONS OF THE STANDARDS MOVEMENT

The Elementary and Secondary Education Act (ESEA) as amended by the No Child Left Behind (NCLB) Act of 2001 offers some hope for reallocating more resources to those students most in need. At the same time, it also poses many challenges to achieving its intended results.

These new provisions call for some sweeping revisions. Underscoring these new provisions are mandates that enforce accountability for student outcomes; give greater flexibility to states both in allocation of funds and development of standards; require use of research-based programs, methods, and materials; and offer choice for parents. Low-performing schools must engage in professional development and restructuring that is research driven, utilizing effective school and classroom practices.

The NCLB Act, under Title IV, allows schools to use federal money for drug and violence prevention programs and activities, both after school and integrated within the general curriculum. It also allows for teacher training to incorporate character building into lessons and activities, opening the door for teaching emotional literacy under the umbrella of "character education" supported by this legislation.

Although this legislation on the surface attempts to ensure that every child, particularly those most likely to be at risk of school failure, receives a quality education, there are mixed messages inherent in its conception, one of which is its calling for a comprehensive plan for providing a school environment that is "safe and conducive to learning" that adopts a zero-tolerance policy. This approach is not only counter to much research but also appears to be at odds with the 1997 amendments to the Individuals with Disabilities Education Act (IDEA) requiring proactive problem solving rather than reactive punishment of misbehavior. Many students who exhibit violent or persistently disruptive behavior have an emotional or other type of disability and according to IDEA are entitled to a *functional behavioral assessment* (a proactive alternative to using disciplinary approaches) or *manifestation determination* (a mandatory determination prior to an expulsion as to whether the behavior is a result of the child's disability). A zero-tolerance approach is likely to lead to more suspensions and expulsions overall, but especially for students with disabilities. IDEA calls for building classroom and schoolwide positive behavior support systems and strategies, rather than using control and punishment tactics.

Research has shown that school practices, such as ineffective instruction leading to academic failure and punitive school discipline and classroom management practices, may actually contribute to the development of antisocial and potentially violent behavior. Programs and approaches proved to be successful in improving school climate and overall student behavior provide for systematic instruction in social skills (e.g., character education), curricular restructuring and adaptation to better align with the needs of students, early identification of and intervention for children who exhibit problematic behavior patterns, and positive discipline systems. This text advocates practices that support these approaches.

STANDARDS FOR PROFESSIONAL DEVELOPMENT

Increasing pressure is being levied on teachers to be accountable for students' reaching imposed standards of performance. Rushed to cover content and raise test scores, teachers may prioritize efficiency over quality and expediency over creativity. The teacher accountability measures in place at both the state and federal levels make it more likely that teachers will use management strategies, styles of talk, and interaction patterns that are actually counterproductive to a "no child left behind" philosophy.

Although the language throughout both state and national standards for teacher training and continued professional development is laced with references to teachers developing as reflective thinkers in order to better meet the needs of an increasingly diverse student population, an environment of looming threat created by mandated standards of teacher accountability undermines realization of thoughtful reflection on teaching practices.

The National Council for Accreditation of Teacher Educators (NCATE) includes in its standards for professional development that teachers "reflect on practice and make necessary adjustments." Most state standards are likewise calling for teachers to become reflective practitioners who continually evaluate the effects of their choices and actions on students. It remains to be seen whether these two divergent sets of standards, that is, mandated teacher accountability and reflective decision making, can have a point of convergence.

ASSUMPTIONS ABOUT THE TEACHING AND LEARNING PROCESS UNDERLYING THIS TEXT

This approach to classroom management is markedly different from existing texts both in its focus and learning approach. It is predicated on the assumption that effective classroom/behavior management requires teachers to develop both a reflective stance and a learning stance. In adopting a reflective stance, teachers examine classroom practices for their relevancy and efficacy for producing broad learning outcomes that encompass developing academic as well as emotional literacy. In the process of constantly challenging their own practices, new dilemmas surface, initiating a new cycle of planning, teaching, observing, and reflecting. The passageway to arriving as a reflective practitioner is uncharted territory. This book offers a compass to point developing teachers in the right direction as they plot their own course.

In taking a learning stance, teachers build three capacities: the capacity of self-efficacy, the capacity of ongoing inquiry, and the capacity of perpetual problem solving. When teachers have self-efficacy they believe in their capacity to create personal solutions to problems. When teachers develop the habit of ongoing inquiry they challenge assumptions that they and others are making. They are never satisfied that they have all the answers and continually seek new information, thereby continuously accessing new lenses through which they may view their practice and alter their perspectives. When teachers accept problems as natural occurrences and become perpetual problem solvers, they use problems as opportunities to cocreate better solutions, build relationships, and teach students new coping and self-management strategies.

LEARNING FOCUS

Development of dynamic and effective classroom management strategies involves the creation of interactive learning formats that facilitate both the understanding of underlying theoretical concepts and the integration of those concepts into classroom practice. The content, format, and structure of this book are designed to move teachers beyond a knowledge base of discrete skills to a stage where they integrate and modify skills to fit specific contexts, and eventually, to a point where the skills are internalized, enabling teachers to invent new strategies.

To facilitate classroom application, implementation activities follow the presentation of each concept. Specific activities include structured individual and group problem-solving tasks, analysis of classroom practices, case studies, and role plays. These tasks provide a vehicle to enhance and personalize concept understanding, implementation, and integration. Two types of learning tasks are provided:

Learning Practice Task (LPT). Directed learning tasks that provide practice with the concepts and strategies presented. These are completed individually, with a learning partner, or in a collaborative learning group.

Critical Reflection on Practice (CROP). Structured activities to encourage critical reflection on classroom practices and self-reflection on teaching behaviors, interaction patterns, and communication styles.

These reflective learning activities, or tasks, are especially suitable for web-based teaching and learning. Utilizing online course management tools such as discussion board forums, chat rooms, and threaded discussions can enhance the depth of reflection and self-analysis. By structuring iterations of response and feedback teachers can achieve higher-order reflection on classroom practices and interventions used with their students.

The focus is on providing teachers with opportunities to develop new skills and implement more effective strategies within the context of examining their own values and belief systems. The material presented is structured to provide opportunities for teachers to reflect on their current behavior, develop an awareness of the influence of their own actions on student behavior, and come to personal realizations regarding desired behavior change.

Research on adult learning theory clearly supports the principle that teacher trainees need to be self-motivated and accept ownership in order to change teaching practices. Sustainable change occurs only when those directly responsible for addressing the problem are involved in the design and implementation of the change strategy (Knowles, 1975, 1992). Meaningful change takes place over time and at a personal rather than systemic level.

Current theories of professional development add to these notions the belief that learning is enhanced when teachers (as learners) are provided with *mediating structures,* or processes that mediate or draw personal connections between existing knowledge and new knowledge. Mediating structures allow teachers to construct personal meaning that informs their teaching practice. Learning occurs when teachers tap into their own realms of experiences and reflect on these experiences relative to the new theoretical construct being presented.

Every teacher makes the choice to seek growth or resist growth as a learner. If the choice is to stop learning, then students' learning will atrophy as well, and the major satisfaction of teaching will be lost. The position taken in this book is that every teacher seeks perpetual growth—what Maslow referred to as self-actualization, or the striving to become the best that one can be.

SPECIAL FEATURES OF THIS TEXT

This text promotes a multidimensional perspective for managing classrooms while integrating the process of becoming a reflective practitioner. In particular, this text

- Is designed specifically to support the more independent, reflective nature of online learning with directed learning tasks structured for independent learning
- Incorporates reflective learning exercises as a means for enhancing and personalizing concept understanding, implementation, and integration
- Embeds a process for developing reflective practice relative to managing classroom circumstances, decision making, and problem resolution
- Emphasizes providing teachers with opportunities to develop new skills and implement more effective strategies within the context of examining and challenging their own attitudes, values, beliefs, and assumptions
- Encourages reflection on classroom practices, teaching behaviors, interaction patterns, and communication styles
- Focuses on creating a learning community based on respectful and authentic communication to invite student cooperation and develop student problem-solving capacity
- Fosters a thoughtful, purposeful, and deliberate way of relating to students

NEW TO THIS EDITION

- Greater emphasis on developing tools, habits, and practices to build reflective practice
- Enhancing students' emotional literacy
- Expanded coverage on helping students develop self-management skills, such as problem solving and anger management

- A new chapter on addressing more troubling behavior (e.g., aggression, violence, bullying)
- Strategies geared more to inclusive settings
- Increased emphasis on building a learning community
- More strategies for stress management for students and teachers
- Alternatives to punishment to move beyond consequences
- Contextual or functional behavioral assessment procedures for determining the purpose of challenging behavior
- Responding below the surface, considering communicative intent and underlying unmet needs

ACKNOWLEDGMENTS

I would like to thank the following reviewers of this edition: Kay Burke, Skylight, and Patricia A. Pintar, St. Mary-of-the-Woods College.

INTRODUCTION

Demands of Today's Classroom

Classroom management and discipline are a topics of concern to everyone—teachers, parents, administrators, teacher trainers, as well as the community at large—as the incidence of violence becomes more prevalent among school-age children. For the past decade, NEA's annual surveys consistently report that teachers rank classroom management as their number one concern. And, as teachers experience disruptive student behavior with increasing frequency and severity, they report that their classrooms are increasingly more difficult to manage. Many surveys also report an alarming increase in students' concerns for their safety.

The response to these concerns in many school districts has been reactionary—instituting top-down, unilateral bureaucratic dictums of restrictive zero-tolerance policies to maintain law and order. Schools have built fences, installed weapon detectors, and stationed security forces on school grounds and armed guards at school entrances. Increasingly, schools look and function like prisons.

Given this scenario, teachers often find themselves having to deal with increasingly strict disciplinary procedures for students who disobey school policies. Such policies tend to erode individual teacher efforts to provide a real sense of security, both physical and emotional.

To many, the term *classroom management* is synonymous with *discipline,* or a teacher's ability to control their students' behavior. Thus, the teacher's role is to keep students "in line" and "on task," with little attention paid to the interface with quality instruction or meaningful relationships. For others, classroom management means instilling self-discipline and a set of values that are the foundation for a democratic society. In accordance with this goal, the teacher's role is to help their students internalize the values of respect, honesty, tolerance, and compassion to become responsible citizens.

CHANGING STRUCTURE OF AMERICAN SOCIETY

More and more, schools are battlegrounds for a society in crisis. Following are some relevant and alarming statistics.

Moments in America for All Children

Every 1 second	a public high school student is suspended.
Every 9 seconds	a high school student drops out.
Every 20 seconds	a child is arrested.
Every 44 seconds	a baby is born into poverty.
Every 1 minute	a baby is born to a teen mother.
Every 4 minutes	a child is arrested for drug abuse.
Every 8 minutes	a child is arrested for a violent crime.
Every 2 hours and 20 minutes	a child or youth under 20 is killed by a firearm.

(continued)

Moments in America for All Children *(continued)*

Every 3 hours	a child or youth under 20 is a homicide victim.
Every 4 hours	a child or youth under 20 commits suicide.

Source: Moments in America for All Children. *Children's Defense Fund, The State of America's Children Yearbook 2001.* Washington, DC: Children's Defense Fund, 2001.

Statistics indicate that the challenges faced by youth today are greater than those of previous generations.

Violence

- Although overall crime victimization rates have decreased since 1993, U.S. adolescents are twice as likely as adults to be victims of serious violent crimes, including aggravated assault, rape, robbery, and homicide (Forum on Child and Family Statistics, 2002).
- In 1999, youths ages 12–18 were victims of about 2.5 million crimes at school, including 186,000 serious violent crimes (National Center for Educational Statistics, 2001).
- Students ages 12–18 experienced 2.5 million incidents of violence at school in 1999; of these, 186,000 were serious violent crimes such as aggravated assault, rape, robbery, and sexual assault (U.S. Department of Education and Justice, Bureau of Justice Statistics, 2001).
- In a study of child homicide in 26 industrialized nations, America led the sampled nations by a very wide margin, accounting for 73 percent of all the reports of murdered children. In the United States, adults kill children and children kill other children at rates ten times higher than in Western Europe and Japan and five times higher than in Canada, New Zealand, and Australia (Bleich, Ingersoll, & Devine, 2000).
- Each year, more than 3,000 youths under age 20 are killed, and more than 18,000 are injured by firearms in the United States (David and Lucille Packard Foundation, 2002).
- U.S. children under age 15 are twelve times more likely to die from gunfire than children in twenty-five other industrialized countries combined (Children's Defense Fund, 2001).

Poverty

- The number of children living in poverty is 14.7 million, or nearly 21 percent of all children. The U.S. child poverty rate is the highest in the developed world (Children's Defense Fund, 2001).
- The child poverty rate is highest for African American (30 percent) and Latino (29 percent) children. The child poverty rate for white children is 13 percent (9 percent in 2000). The poverty rate for children under age 6 follows a similar pattern: 35 percent (33 percent in 2000) for African American children under age 6, 33 percent (29 percent in 2000) for young Latino children, and 15 percent (10 percent in 2000) for young white children. White children experienced the highest increase in child poverty from 2000 to 2001 (National Center for Children in Poverty (NCCP) based on the U.S. Census Bureau, *March Current Population Surveys,* 1976–2002).

Child Abuse

- About 3 million reports of possible maltreatment are made to child protective service agencies each year, and the actual incidence of abuse and neglect is estimated to be three times higher than the number reported to authorities. Of 870,000 substantiated reports in the year 2000, 63 percent of child victims suffered neglect, 19 percent were physically abused, 10 percent were sexually abused, and 8 percent were psychologically maltreated (U.S. Department of Health and Human Services, 2002).

- One in four girls and one in eight boys will be sexually abused before they are 18 years old (U.S. Department of Health and Human Services, 2002).
- Child fatalities are the most tragic consequence of maltreatment. Approximately 1,200 children died of abuse or neglect in 2000 (U.S. Department of Health and Human Services, 2002).
- Homicide is one of the top five causes of death among children under age 12, and nine young people under the age of 20 are victims of homicide every day in the United States (Children's Defense Fund, 2001).

Substance Abuse and Addiction

- Thirty percent of high school seniors, 25 percent of tenth graders, and 13 percent of eighth graders report heavy drinking, that is, at least five drinks in a row at least once in the previous two-week period (Forum on Child and Family Statistics, 2002).
- More adolescents are experimenting with drugs at a younger age, with many having their first experiences with drugs prior to age 15.
- Illicit drug use is reported by 26 percent of high school seniors, 23 percent of tenth graders, and 12 percent of eighth graders, with males more likely to use illicit drugs than females in each grade (Forum on Child and Family Statistics, 2002).
- African American youths have lower rates of illicit drug use, as well as alcohol use, than do white and Hispanic youths, with 19 percent of African American, 25 percent of Hispanic, and 27 percent of white students reporting illicit drug use in the past month (Forum on Child and Family Statistics, 2002).
- Hispanic teenagers' use of alcohol, marijuana, or other illegal drugs rose by nearly 50 percent from 1991 to 1997 (Coles, 2000).

Teen Pregnancy

- Each year, about 1 million teenage girls in the United States become pregnant (Alan Guttmacher Institute, 1999).
- The U.S. teen pregnancy rate is more than twice as high as that in other industrialized countries, even though U.S. teenagers do not exhibit significantly different patterns of sexual activity (National Campaign to Prevent Teen Pregnancy, 2001).

Suicide

- Overall, approximately 1 million young people attempt suicide each year in the United States, and estimates indicate that this number is increasing (Hoyert, Anas, Smith, Murphy, & Kochanek, 2001).
- Between 1980 and 1995, suicide rates of African American male youth increased from 2.1 to 4.5 per 100,000, an increase of 114 percent, whereas for white male youth the increase was only 5.4 to 6.4 per 100,000 (National Center for Injury Prevention and Control, 2001).
- For every teenager who actually commits suicide, 100 more attempt it (Portner, 2000a).

Depression

- The prevalence of major depression in adolescence is between 15 percent and 20 percent (Cicchetti & Toth, 1998).

An increasing number of students are already severely troubled even before they enter school. Because of changes in family structure and the weakening of the family support system essential for children's normal development, many children are at risk for what has been termed *broken cords*—the failure to develop healthy human attachments.

The message in these statistics is alarming: Large numbers of U.S. youth are at risk—for school failure, substance abuse, psychological and emotional disorders, abuse and neglect, teenage pregnancy, and violence. When these young people come to school, their problems come with them. This means that teachers have to deal with issues that were unimaginable in an earlier era, issues that require knowledge and skills far beyond those needed merely to be an effective instructor (Weinstein, 2003).

Accommodating Increasing Diversity

Teachers face an ever-present challenge to meet the needs of all students in a diverse society moving toward a global community. In most large U.S. cities, so-called minority students actually have majority representation. All indications are that the current trend will be expanding to an even greater extent in our immediate future.

Those who make the career choice to enter and remain in the teaching profession will need to master skills that go far beyond their ability to teach academic content. Given the scope and intensity of the needs of today's students, it is evident that the teaching function, while necessary and important, is not nearly sufficient to define the inclusive and complex array of skills necessary to render a teacher effective.

Teachers face greater instructional and management challenges as they strive to accommodate increasing diversity of student learning styles and behavior patterns. With growing support for inclusive classrooms, teachers will continue to be called on to enhance their classroom and behavior management skills to effectively address the wider range of educational, psychological, and emotional problems students are experiencing.

The onus falls on teachers to create a more responsive educational climate to better serve all students, especially those currently at risk of school failure and alienation. For teachers to be successful in today's classroom, they will need to integrate large-group management skills, individual behavior management interventions, counseling techniques, strategies for developing students' social and coping skills, and effective communication skills. Educating all learners primarily in inclusive classrooms requires a model of effective classroom management that goes beyond managing instruction and ensuring student compliance.

CURRENT MODEL FOR CLASSROOM MANAGEMENT

The model of effective classroom management currently in practice stems largely from research conducted in the 1970s and 1980s that has come to be known as teaching effectiveness research. This research identified teaching skills, strategies, and styles associated with high levels of student achievement and produced, subject to some variability due to subject area, grade level, and student composition, substantial consensus about the kinds of teaching strategies that seem to promote high levels of student achievement and involvement with learning tasks (Brophy, 1979; Brophy & Evertson, 1974; Brophy & Good, 1986; Gage, 1978; Gersten, Woodward, & Darch, 1986; Medley, 1977; Rosenshine, 1979; Rosenshine & Berliner, 1978; Rosenshine & Stevens, 1984; Slavin, Karweit, & Madden, 1989).

One popular set of instructional methods attempting to capture the results of this research is direct instruction, calling for teachers to direct instruction, solicit specific student responses, and closely monitor student on-task behavior during independent work (Brophy, 1987; Crocker & Brooker, 1986; Good & Brophy, 2003; Rosenshine & Stevens, 1986).

Not surprisingly, this instructional approach also produced relatively low levels of student disruption and management difficulties. Subsequent research identified specific strategies and procedures effective teachers used to produce efficiently functioning classrooms. This line of research resulted in recommendations for teachers based on explicitly teaching students classroom routines and practices for accomplishing learning tasks (Anderson, Evertson, & Brophy, 1979; Emmer, Evertson, & Anderson, 1980; Evertson, Anderson, Anderson, & Brophy, 1980; Evertson & Emmer, 1982). Within this framework, classroom management is tantamount to effectively "managing instruction."

However, it is important to note that this research-based approach to classroom management was established during an era in which the predominant instructional model was one of the teacher providing direct instruction and students working independently. Brophy (1988) characterized this approach as the "whole-class instruction/recitation/seatwork" approach. In this instructional orientation, the teacher primarily provides direct instruction, carefully structures student response patterns, closely monitors student feedback, and keeps students on task during seatwork activities, largely completed independently.

Within this instructional framework, the primary intervention model for addressing student behavior is the behavioral paradigm. Student behavior is managed by consequences–rewards when possible, punishment when necessary.

The traditional classroom has evolved since the emergence of this model. The current movement away from teacher-directed classrooms to classrooms in which students are active participants in their learning requires a new model of what effective classroom management should look like. Effectively managing classrooms where students are interactive participants requires a shift away from teacher control and student compliance patterns of interaction. Placing students in such interactive roles in which the predominant work style is no longer independent but cooperative requires students to develop autonomy from the teacher.

EMERGING BELIEFS ABOUT QUALITY TEACHING AND CLASSROOM MANAGEMENT

What constitutes effective classroom management needs to be reexamined in light of emerging beliefs about quality teaching. Major curricular changes that provide greater emphasis on curricular integration, teaching for meaning, interactive dialogue, socialization, and collaboration require fundamental changes in the way teachers interact with students and call for different teacher discourse patterns. This shift is characterized by a move from teacher-directed lessons to participatory learning, from predetermined learning outcomes to less-defined learning outcomes, from uniform assessment of performance to varied assessment of mastery of concepts, from sequenced curriculum to integrated curriculum, from teacher solicitation of specific student responses to interactive dialogue, and from the teacher questioning students to reciprocal teaching.

The teacher role is changing from controlling learning to deliberately facilitating learning. The student role is changing from passive recipient of teacher-directed instruction to interactive participant, often functioning in a variety of collaborative modes with peers. This transformation is guided by assumptions about teaching and learning which move us from the belief that students learn from paying attention to the teacher and repetition and rote memory, to the belief that students construct their own meaning and have responsibility for their own learning. These changing classroom demands call for classroom management and interaction styles that better align with emerging metaphors of teacher as social mediator and learning facilitator.

Historically, conceptions of good teaching have evolved from primarily good discipline in the 1960s, efficient and careful monitoring of student work in the 1970s, increasing levels of student on-task engagement in the 1980s, emphasis on how to enhance learning in the 1990s, to development of lifelong learners for the new millennium. The trend represents a gradual redistribution of control and responsibility for learning from teachers to students. Hence, there needs to be a corresponding shift in emphasis in models of classroom management and student–teacher interaction styles to accompany the academic shift from teacher control to development of greater student autonomy (Bullough, 1994; Freiberg, 1999; Kamii, Clark, & Dominick, 1994; Larrivee, 1997; Marshall, 1992; McCaslin & Good, 1992, 1998; Randolph & Evertson, 1994).

Popular approaches to classroom management based on the behavioral model are antithetical to school reform initiatives and espoused educational goals. A curriculum designed to produce self-motivated, active learners is undermined by classroom management practices that encourage mindless compliance. Preparing students to wait to be told what to do fails to prepare them for the increasingly complex world they will live in. Classroom management should do more than produce obedient followers; it should promote self-management and self-discipline by encouraging self-awareness, self-reflection, and critical inquiry—those qualities that are fundamental for a democratic society.

Current beliefs about quality teaching practices place greater emphasis on participatory learning, higher-order thinking, and the social construction of knowledge. These learning processes are consonant with those of a democratic teaching style. Changing classroom demands call for classroom management and interaction styles that better align with the teacher as leader. Yet the predominant model remains deeply rooted in the behavioral approach, relying on the use of extrinsic rewards and punishment, praise, and teacher evaluation of appropriate behavior and acceptable work.

A management system based on rigid rules that acclimates students to passivity and compliance undercuts the potential effects of an instructional system designed for purposeful, self-regulated learning in which meaning is coconstructed. The student roles implied by these goals call for students to display thoughtfulness, initiative, collaboration, and sustained metacognitive awareness in regulating their own learning efforts (Brophy, 1999). Traditionally emphasized behavioral management models, especially those designed to train students to follow standardized routines and respond automatically to cues, are not well suited to preparing students to fulfill the more demanding role of functioning as members of a learning community engaged in the joint construction of knowledge.

When one defines community as a cohesive group committed to shared values and relationships that foster interdependence, such relationships, based on mutual commitments, render much of traditional management and control tactics moot. Through the dialogue teachers create with students and the authority structures they employ, they play a critical role in modeling freedom of expression and autonomy. Management models that best serve a democratic learning community reflect the premise that individual rights are sacred and yet must be balanced against equally compelling societal needs, making the impact of one's actions on others in the community an overriding consideration (McEwan, 1998).

Management versus Leadership: Bossing or Leading?

The very use of the term *classroom management* connotes a relationship of authority in the classroom carrying with it assumptions about power and purpose. As McLaughlin (1994) notes, the term *classroom management* accurately reflects a "preoccupation with scientific efficiency and bureaucratic political control at the school level." Management is a relationship based on authority; leadership is a noncoercive relationship of influence (Rost, 1991). Managers have a relationship of authority over their subordinates. Glasser (1998a) makes a clear distinction between the teacher role as manager, or as he refers to this role, as boss, and the teacher role as leader.

Comparison of Characteristics of a Boss and a Leader

BOSS	LEADER
Drives	Leads
Relies on authority	Relies on cooperation
Says "I"	Says "We"
Creates fear	Creates confidence
Knows how	Shows how
Creates resentment	Breeds enthusiasm
Fixes blame	Fixes mistakes
Makes work drudgery	Makes work interesting

Leaders go beyond stopping behavior to guiding and showing students what to do. The teacher who leads is more reflective, helpful, and responsive to students.

Leadership requires a clear vision of what a classroom could become. The leader translates this vision into goals and expectations that reflect mutual purposes. Shared leadership is based on assumptions that students will exercise self-direction and self-control in service of what they are committed to. Effort is motivated by achieving, not solely by external rewards or threats of punishment.

Authority versus Power

Authority is the right teachers have to make decisions that affect the choices available to students. It is the right vested in them as teachers. Power is how they use it. Teachers use their authority when they assign work to students. Power is what they use to get students to complete their assignments.

Avoiding the Dualistic Trap

A teacher does not have to choose between drill sergeant and doormat. Effective classroom management is not an either/or proposition. Teachers can and should be both supportive and confrontive. They can find a healthy balance between support and challenge.

GUIDING ASSUMPTIONS ABOUT EFFECTIVELY MANAGING TODAY'S CLASSROOM

The following assumptions about what constitutes effective classroom management are the guiding tenets for the development of the ideas advocated in this book.

1. Effective classroom management calls for teachers to develop as reflective practitioners who resist establishing a classroom culture of control in favor of creating an authentic learning community.
   - Building the habit of reflective practice allows teachers to see beyond the filters of their past and the blinders of their expectations to respond more appropriately to classroom situations and circumstances.
   - Effective classroom management cannot be prescribed with an intervention formula. The path cannot be preplanned; it must be lived.

2. Effective classroom management begins with teacher self-awareness, self-control, and self-reflection, not with the students.
   - Unless teachers engage in reflection and ongoing inquiry, they stay trapped in unexamined judgments, assumptions, and interpretations.
   - Teachers' responses to the various types of behavior students exhibit in the classroom say much about how secure and competent they feel as teachers. If teachers have self-efficacy, that is, confidence in their potential to be effective, then they successfully solve problems, maintain healthy relationships with students, and employ strategies that humanize rather than dehumanize students.
   - Teachers' emotional responses to students' behavior are sometimes based on their own emotional healing that needs to take place.

3. Effective classroom management supports a climate for teaching and learning that validates and accommodates the psychological, emotional, sociocultural, and academic needs of both teachers and students.
   - More students are coming to school neglected, rejected, abused, hungry, and ill prepared to learn and function adequately within the constraints of the classroom setting. Many students have not had the opportunity to learn the prosocial skills needed to work productively with their classmates; social and emotional needs often override academic needs.
   - In daily classroom life, the behavior of individual students will sometimes make teachers uncomfortable, angry, or even furious. These feelings are inevitable and teachers need to balance their own feelings and reactions with their responsibility to serve as role models for their students. The challenge for teachers is to respond appropriately in spite of such feelings—not to deny or invalidate them. Effectively communicating negative emotions is an important teaching function.

4. Effective classroom management is a reflective, purposeful, and caring way of interacting with students.
   - Teachers must face deeply rooted personal attitudes concerning human nature, human development, human potential, and human learning in their interactions with students.
   - Teachers possess tremendous power to have far-reaching influence on their students. They can be sources of humiliation or inspiration. They can hurt or heal. They can destroy or build.

5. Effective classroom management models democratic values.
   - The classroom is a microcosm of our society and should instill a set of democratic values founded on the principles of tolerance, acceptance, respect, and compassion.

- The teacher's role is to help students internalize these values and learn that freedom is tied to responsibility.
- In a spirit of equal opportunity for all, teachers have the responsibility to invite, encourage, and engage the participation of all their students.

6. Effective classroom management is much more than a compilation of skills and strategies. It's a deliberate philosophical and ethical code of conduct.
   - Without tying management and disciplinary procedures to beliefs about the teaching and learning process and assumptions about, and expectations for students, teachers will have only fragmented techniques—stabs in the dark.
   - If teachers latch onto techniques for handling student behavior without examination of what kinds of responses to students would be congruent with their beliefs, aligned with their designated teaching structures, and harmonious with their personal styles, they will have just a bag of tricks.

CHAPTER ONE

Becoming a Reflective Practitioner

Classroom management is much more than an accumulation of skills and strategies. Without tying management and disciplinary decisions to personal beliefs about teaching, learning, and development, a teacher will have only the bricks. The real stuff of managing the classroom is the mortar—what holds the bricks in place and provides a foundation. Learning to manage a classroom environment effectively goes beyond taking on fragmented techniques for keeping students on task and handling their behavior.

Being effective in the classroom setting requires that the teacher remain fluid and able to move in many directions, rather than stuck only being able to move in one direction as situations occur. Today's classroom is dynamic and complex. More students are coming to school ill prepared to learn and work productively. To combat increasing student alienation and meet the scope and intensity of the academic, social, and emotional needs of today's students, those entering the teaching profession will need to find ways to create authentic learning communities. These changing demands call for teaching styles that better align with emerging ways of defining the teacher's role as social mediator, learning facilitator, and reflective practitioner (Larrivee, 2000a).

ON BECOMING A REFLECTIVE PRACTITIONER

Others have made a distinction between technical reflection and other types of reflection (Hatton & Smith, 1995; Larrivee, 2000a; Sparks-Langer & Colton, 1991; Zehm & Kottler, 2000). Technical reflection is vital to planning and delivery of appropriate learning experiences for students. This is the kind of thinking teachers use to make pedagogical decisions about learning environments, content selection, and teaching methods. The position taken here is that technical reflection is merely analytical thinking, and is insufficient to define reflective practice.

Developing as a reflective practitioner requires building three capacities: the capacities for continual examination of teaching practices, critical inquiry, and self-reflection. Ongoing consideration of the efficacy and utility of established teaching practices develops insight for contemplating alternatives and taking action to improve practice. Critical inquiry involves the conscious consideration of the ethical implications and consequences of classroom practices on students. Few teachers get through a day without facing ethical dilemmas. Even routine evaluative judgments of students' work is partly an ethical decision, in that lack of opportunity to learn as well as impact on self-concept are ever-present considerations. Self-reflection adds the dimension of deep examination of personal values and beliefs, embodied in the assumptions teachers make and the expectations they have for students. These three capacities define the distinguishing attributes of reflective practitioners. Reflective teachers "turn back on" or call into question the assumptions, premises, or presuppositions underlying their beliefs and practices. The taken-for-granted is reconsidered to inform a more deliberate and conscious course of action.

Typically, the term *reflection* has been used to define a way of thinking that accepts uncertainty and acknowledges dilemmas, while ascribing less significance to the role of self in the reflective process (Dewey, 1963, 1938; King & Kitchener, 1994; Sparks-Langer & Colton, 1991; Zehm & Kottler, 2000). In his writings (1938, 1963), Dewey asserted that the capacity to reflect is initiated only after recognition of a problem or dilemma and the acceptance of uncertainty. The dissonance created in understanding that a problem exists engages the reflective thinker to become an *active inquirer,* involved both in the critique of current conclusions and the generation of new hypotheses. According to Dewey, reflective thinking requires continual evaluation of beliefs, assumptions, and hypotheses against existing data and against other plausible interpretations of the data. Resulting decisions always remain open to further scrutiny and reformulation.

The definition of reflection supported here attributes greater influence to the role of self-reflection, including challenging self-imposed limitations as well as idealizations. Being reflective brings commonly held beliefs into question. Beliefs are convictions we hold dearly, having confidence in their truth, while acknowledging that they are not susceptible to proof. Our beliefs shape our identity; thus, shedding a dearly held belief shakes our very existence. If a teacher tries to shed the belief that the teacher must be in control to be effective, it means revealing uncertainty and vulnerability.

Values steer how we behave on a daily basis to pursue educational goals and student outcomes. They also define the lines we will and will not cross. Values are our ideals; thus they are subjective and arouse an emotional response. Often in teaching, sets of values are in conflict, challenging the teacher to weigh competing values against one another and play them off against the facts available. For example, a teacher may value being consistent while simultaneously valuing treating students justly; however, there are times when to be fair is to be inconsistent.

Developing Reflective Practice

Teaching has been described as a "complex, situation-specific dilemma ridden endeavor" (Sparks-Langer & Colton, 1991). Becoming a lifelong learner is the foundation for improved teaching practice and requires developing the capacity to be reflective. The development of reflective practice is the pinnacle of professional competence. Reflective practice facilitates learning, renewal, and growth throughout one's career (Steffy, Wolfe, Pasch, & Enz, 2000).

The following are some ways reflective practice has been described in the literature.

- An inquiry approach to teaching that involves a personal commitment to continuous learning and improvement (York-Barr, Sommers, Ghere, & Montie, 2001)
- A willingness to accept responsibility for one's professional practice (Ross, 1990)
- The practice of analyzing one's actions, decisions, or products by focusing on one's process for achieving them (Killion & Todnem, 1991)
- The capacity to think creatively, imaginatively, and eventually self-critically about classroom practice (Lasley, 1992)

- A critical, questioning orientation and a deep commitment to the discovery and analysis of information concerning the quality of a professional's designed action (Bright, 1996)
- Use of higher-level thinking processes, such as critical inquiry and metacognition, which allow one to move beyond a focus on isolated facts or data to perceive a broader context for understanding behavior and events (Hatton & Smith, 1995)

Critical Reflection on Teaching Practice

Typically, critical reflection is considered a higher-order form of reflection, building on other dimensions of reflection.

Critical reflection adds the following focus:

- Examining underlying assumptions, biases, and values one brings to the educational process
- Consciously considering the ethical implications and consequences of practices on students and their learning
- Critically examining how instructional and other school practices contribute to social equity and to the establishment of a just and humane society
- Extending awareness beyond immediate instructional circumstances to caring about democratic foundations and encouraging socially responsible actions

At this level of reflection, the focus of teachers' deliberations is on examining the ethical, social, and political consequences of their teaching. Believing that classroom and school practices cannot be separated from the larger social, political, and ideological realities, critically reflective teachers strive to become fully conscious of the range of consequences of their actions. These teachers recognize that instruction is embedded within institutional, cultural, and political contexts and that these contexts both *affect* what they do and *are affected by* what they do.

Teachers who are critically reflective focus their attention both inwardly on their own practice, and outwardly on the social conditions in which these practices are situated. These teachers acknowledge that their teaching practices and policies can either contribute to, or hinder, the realization of a more just and humane society. Their emphasis is on thinking about issues of equity and social justice that arise in and outside of the classroom and on connecting their practice to democratic ideals.

They ask themselves questions like the following:

How might the ways I group my students affect individuals?

Are the ways I assess them potentially limiting the life chances of some of my students?

Do I have practices that differentially favor particular groups of students (e.g., males or females)?

How does the culture of my classroom compare to the cultures of the homes of my students?

Focus of Reflection

Reflection can focus on several types of examination of classroom practices, behaviors, and beliefs.

Technical Reflection. Examines the strategies and methods used to teach

Reflection on Practice. Examines general practices, such as organizing the classroom, structuring the school day, establishing task structures and routines, determining assessment strategies, interacting with students, and building relationships with parents

Self-Reflection. Examines how one's personal beliefs and values, expectations and assumptions, family imprinting, and cultural conditioning impact students and their learning

Critical Reflection. Examines the moral, ethical, and social equity aspects of practice

Avoiding the Reflexive Loop

Argyris (1990) pointed out how our beliefs are self-generating, and often untested, based on conclusions inferred from our selected observations. In other words, from all the data available to us, we select data by literally choosing to see some things and ignore others. He coined the term *reflexive loop* to describe the circular process by which we select data, add personal meaning, make assumptions based on our interpretations of the selected data, draw conclusions, adopt beliefs, and ultimately take action. We stay in a reflexive loop where our unexamined beliefs affect what data we select.

Self-reflection involves a deep exploration process that exposes our unexamined beliefs, assumptions, and expectations and makes visible our personal reflexive loops. Becoming a reflective practitioner calls teachers to the task of facing deeply rooted personal attitudes concerning human nature, human potential, and human learning. Experience is culturally and personally sculpted. Experience is not pure—everything is contextually bound. We develop mental habits, biases, and presuppositions that tend to close off new ways of perceiving and interpreting our experiences (Argyris, 1990; Brookfield, 1995; Burbules, 1993; Knowles, 1992; Senge, 1990; Sokol & Cranston, 1998).

Being Authentic

Authenticity is also a dimension of being a reflective practitioner. As people become more aware of the beliefs and assumptions that drive them, they become aware of the dissonance between what they say and what they do. With that awareness comes the capacity to change and become more authentic. To be authentic begins with being honest with yourself.

Based on the human brain's capacity to learn, the gateway to accessing more of one's potential lies in the emotions (Caine & Caine, 1997). Walking through that gateway means facing oneself. This journey through one's own fears, limitations, and assumptions is essential for becoming more authentic.

Authenticity is acting without pretense. Brookfield (1995) describes authenticity as being alert to the voices inside your head that are not your own, the voices that have been deliberately implanted by outside interests rather than springing from your own experiences. The opposite of authenticity is defensiveness. Authentic people, although not denying their fears, erect minimal barriers and have little to hide. They communicate a powerful sense of inner authority. Being authentic means not depending on others for your sense of well-being, not having to appear in control, to look good, or refrain from rocking the boat.

Being Authentic Means . . .
You trust and know who you are.
You know both your strengths and weaknesses.
You are always learning and changing.
You say what's on your mind.
All your emotions are experienced and displayed.

You're clear about your motives.
You challenge others' inauthenticity.
You have nothing to lose that is worth keeping.

Essential Practices for Becoming a Reflective Practitioner

The process of becoming a reflective practitioner cannot be prescribed. It is a personal awareness discovery process. While it's not possible to prescribe a linear process or define a step-by-step procedure, there are actions and practices that are fundamental to developing as a reflective practitioner. The following three practices are essential.

1. Solitary reflection
2. Ongoing inquiry
3. Perpetual problem solving

The first creates an opening for the possibility of reflection while the others allow for a way of developing teaching practice that accepts uncertainty, recognizes contextual bounds, and considers multiple plausible causal explanations for events and circumstances.

Solitary Reflection. Making time for thoughtful consideration of your actions and critical inquiry into the impact of your own behavior keeps you alert to the consequences of your actions on students. Teachers also need reflective time to consider the inevitable uncertainties, dilemmas, and trade-offs involved in everyday decisions that affect the lives of students. Any effort to become a reflective practitioner involves negotiating feelings of frustration, insecurity, and rejection. Taking solitary time helps teachers come to accept that such feelings are a natural part of the teaching process.

It's important to engage in systematic reflection by making it an integral part of your daily practice. Keeping a reflective journal is one vehicle for ensuring time is set aside for daily reflection. You might also want to take a few quiet moments in your classroom at the end of the day.

Ongoing Inquiry. This practice involves unending questioning of the status quo and conventional wisdom by seeking your own truth. Becoming a fearless truth-seeker involves being open to examining the assumptions which underlie your classroom practices. It's a process of identifying and connecting patterns to form personal conceptions for understanding the complexity of what you observe and experience.

Engaging in ongoing critical inquiry is enhanced when you enlist collegial support. The support can be in the form of a support group, a "critical friend," or a mentor. The function of the support group or person is not only to empathize with your dilemmas but also to point out incongruencies in practice and fallacies in thinking.

Perpetual Problem Solving. Becoming a perpetual problem solver involves synthesizing experiences, integrating information and feedback, uncovering underlying reasons, and discovering new meaning. Your *modus operandus* is solving problems, not enforcing preset standards of operation. The classroom is a laboratory for purposeful experimentation. A practice or procedure is never permanent. New insights, understandings, and perspectives can bring previous decisions up for reevaluation and consideration. When teachers perpetually seek better solutions, they adjust the power dynamics to turn power *over* into power *with* learners.

Faithfully engaging in these three practices helps teachers recognize their repetitive cycles and reflexive loops which limit their potential for tolerance and acceptance—the vital elements for effectively managing classrooms composed of students from different cultural and social backgrounds who have diverse beliefs and values. Reflective practitioners find a means to catch themselves when they try to unjustly impose their values or dismiss students' perspectives without due consideration.

Reflective teachers infuse their practice with a sense of excitement and purpose as they continually forge new ground. While they learn from the past, they thrive in the present. These teachers know that much of what occurs can't be predicted, but they also know that they are not victims of fate. Not to be reflective puts teachers in danger of what Freire (1993) calls "magical consciousness," viewing life in the classroom as beyond their control subject to whimsical blessings and curses.

There are many pathways to becoming a reflective practitioner, and each teacher must find his or her own path. Any path a teacher chooses must involve a willingness to be an active participant in a perpetual growth process requiring ongoing reflection on classroom practices. The journey involves finding a means of infusing your personal beliefs and values into your professional identity. It results in developing a deliberate code of conduct that embodies who you are and what you stand for. Reflection is not only a way of approaching your teaching, but it's also a way of life. The more you explore, the more you discover. The more you question, the more you access new realms of possibility.

Reagan, Case, and Brubacher (2000) suggest that becoming a reflective practitioner has much in common with the process of becoming "Real" as the Skin Horse explained it to the Rabbit in the children's book *The Velveteen Rabbit* (Williams, 1981, pp. 14–16). Just as becoming Real takes time and happens after a toy has lost its hair and become shabby, so becoming a reflective teacher involves time, and inevitably a bit of wear and tear. Yet every teacher should strive to become a reflective practitioner, knowing that only by making the effort to become reflective can one really become a good teacher, just as every toy knows that being loved by a child is the only way to become Real.

Incremental Fluctuations on the Route to Becoming a Reflective Practitioner

The route to becoming self-reflective is plagued by incremental fluctuations of irregular progress, often marked by two steps forward and one step backward. There are necessary and predictable stages in the emotional and cognitive rhythm of becoming a reflective practitioner (Berkey, Curtis, Minnick, Zietlow, Campbell, & Kirschner, 1990; Brookfield, 1995; Kasl, Dechant, & Marsick, 1993; Keane, 1987; Larrivee, 1996; Usher & Bryant, 1989). The sense of liberation at discarding a dearly held assumption is quickly followed by the fear of being in limbo. This state leads to a longing for the abandoned assumption and a desire to revert to the familiar, to keep the chaos at bay. Old ways of thinking no longer make sense, but new ones have not yet gelled to take their place and you are left dangling, in the throes of uncertainty. This uncertainty is the hallmark for transformation from which new possibilities will emerge.

This inner struggle is a necessary and important stage in the reflective process. To break through your familiar cycles, you need to allow yourself to feel confused and anxious, not permanently, but for a time. Fully experiencing this sense of uncertainty is what allows you to come to a deeper personal understanding, leading to a shift in your way of thinking and perceiving. If you can weather the storm, you emerge with a new vision.

Developing Awareness and Self-Reflection by Journal Writing

Journal writing is a reflective process that allows you to become more aware of your contribution to the experiences you encounter. This process of systematic self-reflection enables you to become more insightful and better attuned to your wants and needs. Journaling can provide the clarification necessary for you to gain, or regain, a sense of meaning and purposefulness in your teaching. Finding personal meaning is the key to preventing burnout.

Journals can be instrumental in helping you unleash your creative powers as well as reduce daily tension. Making regular journal entries helps you remain clear and intensely aware of what is going on in both your inner and outer worlds. Most of all, a journal is a place where you can talk to yourself. The act of maintaining and reviewing a journal over time can serve as a therapeutic tool.

Journal writing develops self-discipline. Attitudes about teaching and interacting with students are the result of attitudes and experiences gained over time. By making journal entries you can look more objectively at your behaviors in the classroom.

Having a record of your thoughts, feelings, concerns, crises, and successes provides a window of the past and a gateway to the future. When maintained over time, it can serve as a database offering both a historical perspective and information about patterns of thought and behavior.

Journals can serve several important purposes for teachers. They can provide a safe haven for

- Dumping all your daily frustrations
- Storing your most private thoughts and feelings
- Working through internal conflicts and solving problems
- Recording significant events and critical incidents
- Posing questions, naming issues, and raising concerns
- Identifying cause and effect relationships
- Noting strategies that work and those that don't and seeing patterns over time
- Celebrating joys
- Experimenting with new ways of thinking and acting
- Tracing life patterns and themes

A journal can also be a place to set goals for yourself. Committing yourself in writing can be the impetus it takes to move you toward what is really important to you. Keeping a journal can help you map out where you want to be in your teaching 1, 5, 10 years from now.

Journal writing is also an excellent tool for examining personal biases and prejudices that may unwittingly play out in your interactions with students whose backgrounds are significantly different from your own. Although you may not be conscious of inappropriate responses to students on the basis of culture, race, gender, or social class, there may indeed be areas where you unknowingly behave in insensitive ways. Making journal entries would allow you to look more objectively at your behaviors toward students from a variety of diverse settings.

The following questions can serve as a guide to beginning the process of making journal writing an integral part of developing the habit of critical reflection.

- What type of schedule would be manageable for you to keep a journal?
- When and where would you make entries?
- Would you do free-form reflection?

- Would you categorize entries?
- Would your entries be crisis or problem related?
- How would you use your journal to guide inquiry and decision making?

CRITICAL REFLECTION ON PRACTICE: DAILY REFLECTION

Activity Directions: One way to build reflection into practice is to take some time at the end of the school day and before you go home to reflect on the day. Based on what is important to you and the values you want to uphold in your classroom, write a few personal daily reflection questions. Below are some sample daily reflection questions.

1. Did I speak respectfully to all of my students?
2. Did I use fair and just discipline procedures?
3. Did I remain open to unusual or unexpected student responses?
4. Did I try to teach and reach all of my students?
5. Did I take time to interact with each student?

My personal daily reflection questions:

_____

_____

_____

_____

REFLECTIVE QUESTION
How can you make reflection an integral part of your daily practice?

CRITICAL REFLECTION ON PRACTICE:
REFLECTING ABOUT A TEACHING PRACTICE

Activity Directions: Read the case study below. Then respond to the questions posed.

Mr. Clark had known for quite some time that a few of his particular teaching strategies weren't working very well. He had been teaching an elementary level special day class for 5 years and was beginning to think that he could do a better job. He wanted students to work together in his classroom, and he believed that when students learned together all of them could benefit.

For the last year, he had tried a variety of ways to gather his students into cooperative learning groups. He knew he had a knack for getting the students to feel like the classroom was theirs and that they were all part of "one big family," but when it came down to translating that feeling in specific learning situations, the achievement always seemed to elude him. So he signed up for a class on effective instruction. He learned that some of the research on collaborative learning indicated that: (a) the teacher needed to plan the group work to align with the particular learning goals of the lesson in addition to a concern for the social interaction among group members; (b) the teacher needed to identify what kinds of group talk would serve as evidence that learning was being achieved during the group sessions; and (c) the teacher should exercise caution when entering the group setting so as not to disturb the dynamics already in place.

(continued)

CRITICAL REFLECTION   Continued

Mr. Clark realized that he had to be much more strategic in his structuring of the groups to accomplish the learning goals he had for his students. Consequently, he changed the way he approached and structured group time with his class.

1. Describe a situation similar to Mr. Clark's in which new information or research caused you to make a significant change in a teaching practice.
2. What information, knowledge, or research findings would you like to have about a teaching method you are currently using or would like to use?

REFLECTIVE QUESTIONS
What is an aspect of your teaching that you would like to see working better?
What would you like to see that's not happening now?

DEVELOPING THE PRACTICE OF SELF-REFLECTION

By developing self-reflection, teachers become more cognizant of the interdependence between teacher responses to students and student responses to teachers. Through self-reflection, teachers become increasingly aware of how they are interactive participants in classroom encounters, rather than innocent bystanders or victims. By developing the practice of self-reflection teachers learn to

1. Slow down their thinking and reasoning process to become more aware of how they perceive and react to students, and
2. Bring to the surface some of their unconscious ways of responding to students.

Self-reflection involves developing the ability to look at a situation and withholding judgment while simultaneously recognizing that the meaning you attribute to it is no more than your interpretation filtered through your cumulative experience. When you are able to acknowledge this, reality takes on a different meaning. When you can say, "This is my experience, and this is the meaning I attribute to what I am experiencing," you acknowledge that each person's reality is uniquely defined. Self-reflection encompasses reflection, deliberation, awareness, and insight turned inward, so you continually discover new dimensions of yourself. This complex process is not prescriptive in nature; rather it is a process that allows insights to surface which serve to challenge your familiar behavior patterns. It is more a way of knowing than one of knowing how.

For teachers to understand their professional lives and continue to develop their professional work, they need to understand the formative as well as the continuing experiences and influences that have shaped and continue to shape their perspectives and practices. A teacher cannot become a reflective practitioner without both developing the capacity for self-reflection and making time for reflection on practice. That means questioning not only what you do but also who you are.

Similarly, Cole and Knowles distinguish between *reflective inquiry* and *reflexive inquiry*, describing the latter as tantamount to self-reflection as defined here.

Reflective inquiry is an ongoing process of examining and refining practice, variously focused on the personal, pedagogical, curricular, intellectual, societal, and/or ethical contexts associated with professional work, perhaps, but not necessarily, from a critical perspective. Underpinning all such reflective inquiry is the idea that assumptions behind all practice are subject to questioning. *Reflexive inquiry*, on the other hand, is reflective inquiry situated within the context of personal histories in order to make connections between personal lives and professional careers, and to understand personal (including early) influences on professional practice. In other words, reflexive inquiry takes into account the personal history-based elements of contextual understanding, emphasizing the foundational place of experience in the formulations of practice in a way that reflective inquiry does not. Reflexive inquiry, unlike some forms and interpretations of reflective inquiry, is rooted in a critical perspective. Such a critical perspective is characterized by interrogation of status quo norms and practices, especially with respect to issues of power and control. (Cole & Knowles, 2000, p. 2)

They also suggest that the meaning of *reflexive* be thought of in terms of the properties of prisms and mirrors, which reflect and refract light. These objects change the direction in which light rays travel, sometimes even bending them back on themselves, causing them to move in directions opposite from their original path. Reflexive practices associated with teaching have somewhat similar qualities. Being reflexive is like having a mirror and transparent prism with which to view practice. Examinations of practice, with an eye to understanding and improving it, sometimes lead to complete turnabouts in thinking. The ideas and thoughts bent back through reflexive inquiry may derive from a whole range of experiences and interactions throughout one's life inside and outside classrooms and schools, as students and as teachers. In a reflexive stance, making sense of both prior and current educational experiences within the context of present practice may shed new, perhaps brighter, light on understandings of teaching.

Our Screening Process: Examining
Our Personal Filtering System

Developing the practice of self-reflection allows you to recognize that what you see goes through a series of internal, interpretive filters reflecting your belief system. Perception is subjective—it is not pure and it can be distorted. When a student acts out, one teacher sees a cry for help, another a personal attack. It is our interpretation of the student's behavior, or the meaning we attach to the behavior, that determines how we will respond. Through self-reflection we can learn to see beyond the filters of our past and the blinders of our expectations.

The meaning we attribute to our experiences is influenced by various factors that effectively screen out some responses while letting others through. This screening process leads to differing perceptions of circumstances and events, resulting in different interpretations and, subsequently, in different responses. When we critically examine our screens, we can become more aware of how our screens may be filtering out potentially more effective responses to classroom situations and students' challenging behavior.

Our actions are governed by multiple screens which can be envisioned as a series of interpretive filters (see Figure 1.1). Each level of screen serves to eliminate some potential responses while allowing others to filter through. Our past experiences, beliefs, assumptions and expectations, feelings and mood, and our personal agendas and aspirations can either serve to limit or expand the repertoire of responses available to us in any situation. Beliefs about students' capacity and willingness to learn; assumptions about the behavior of students, especially those from different ethnic and social backgrounds; and expectations formulated on the basis of our value system can potentially be sources for responding inappropriately to students.

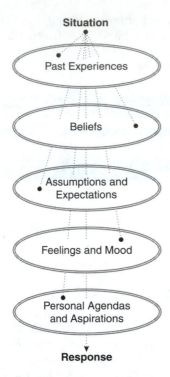

FIGURE 1.1   Personal Filtering System

Certain responses can be eliminated by being screened through our past experiences. For example, the sight of a snake can conjure up a multitude of differing reactions on a continuum from absolute terror to curiosity to pleasure, based on what our experiences have been. Additional potential responses are ruled out, or in, on the basis of the beliefs we hold. Our beliefs can be affirming or defeating, expansive or limiting, rational or irrational. The assumptions that we make and the expectations that we have can make more responses available, or unavailable, to us. Our feelings, both those directly related to the immediate situation and those resulting from other experiences, can either serve to screen out responses or to avail us to additional responses. And, finally, the agenda we set for ourselves and the aspirations we have act as still another filter. We may become driven by our personal goals and lose sight of what we stand for. For example, we might be so concerned about keeping our job that we go against our own values to keep the classroom quiet because that's what the principal values.

The way we respond is determined by this personal filtering system. This filtering system serves as a subjective mediating process. At the simplest level, there is an immediate reflexive response with no thought process occurring. A reflexive reaction, like removing your hand from a hot burner, is a reaction without conscious consideration of alternative responses. This type of response is often referred to as a "knee-jerk" response connoting that the response is automatic. Often we operate on "automatic pilot," closed off from entertaining a continuum of responses. When we do this in the complex classroom environment, we run the risk of responding to students in intolerant and disrespectful ways, which can easily escalate, rather than deescalate, student reactions.

Bringing your personal screens into awareness expands the intermediate thought process between a situation and your resulting reaction. By bringing a greater portion of the mediating process into awareness, you can increase your range of possible responses to the often difficult classroom situations you face daily.

As an example, consider your typical response to being criticized by a student. Suppose your reflexive reaction is to automatically offer a defense to the criticism. Let's say you usually come in with a "but . . . " rather than merely "taking in" the criticism or exploring it further. Becoming aware of your own resistance and asking yourself questions like, "Why am I being defensive?" or "What am I defending?" or "Why do I need to be right?" or "Why do I need to have the last word?" would represent challenging your screening process at the *assumptions-and-expectations* layer. By challenging your usual way of reacting, you thereby allow a greater range of responses to filter through your interpretive screen.

Our cumulative layers of screens can lead to responding to situations in conditioned and rigid ways. To have the greatest freedom of choice and the capacity to respond uniquely to each classroom situation encountered calls for constantly examining your choices to see how your personal screens are influencing your ability to respond in unconditioned ways. As you take time to challenge your screens and consider alternate responses to reoccurring classroom situations, you become open to more possibilities and no possible response is automatically ruled out or in.

- - - - - - - -

CRITICAL REFLECTION ON PRACTICE: CHALLENGING YOUR PERSONAL SCREENING PROCESS

Activity Directions: To examine how your filtering screens may result in limiting responses to students, follow the steps below.

1. Think of an area in your teaching where one of the five filters from the diagram is "clogged," keeping you from a more open response. Is it a bad past experience, a limiting belief, an expectation for how students should act?
   Clogged filter area:

   _____

   _____

   _____

   Describe the specific aspect of the filter area:

   _____

   _____

   _____

2. What types of responses are more likely because of this clogged filter?

   _____

   _____

   _____

3. What other ways of responding are being screened out?

   _____

   _____

   _____

4. List specific classroom actions you can begin to take to curtail your reflexive response.

   _____

   _____

   _____

(continued)

CRITICAL REFLECTION   Continued

5. Select one typical response that you want to begin challenging. Write a self-question that will help you.

_____

_____

_____

REFLECTIVE QUESTION

What can you do to remind yourself to become more aware of how your filters are screening out potentially more effective responses to students?

EXAMINING CORE BELIEFS, ASSUMPTIONS, AND EXPECTATIONS

Examining core beliefs is a critical aspect of self-reflection. A core belief is a fundamental belief about human nature, development, or learning. Our beliefs are adopted based on conclusions _inferred_ from our observations and interpretations, and they often remain largely untested. Developing the practice of self-reflection involves observing our patterns of behavior and examining our behavior in light of what we truly believe. This process can be envisioned as flowing through several levels, from the level of core beliefs to the level of specific actions. Similar to a model developed by Shapiro and Reiff (1993) to examine the congruence between core beliefs and job performance, this process has four levels: philosophical, framework, interpretive, and decision making (see Figure 1.2).

Philosophy of life is the backdrop for all other levels and activities. The philosophical level embodies core beliefs and includes values, religious beliefs, ways of knowing, life meanings, and ethics.

Level two represents our way of providing an organizational framework for these basic beliefs and includes the theories we espouse, such as theories of human development and human behavior, theories of motivation and learning, theories of organizational development, and chaos theory. It is our framework for attaching meaning to what's happening. These underlying principles serve as the basis for how we organize what we have learned and experienced.

The next level is how we interpret these underlying principles into our general approach to daily practice. This is where we link our beliefs and theories into a way of behaving. Our daily practice is an overriding stance, a pervasive attitude for how we approach life and the situations we encounter. It's a frame of mind.

From our attitude about daily practice evolves our momentary actions. It is our way of making real our ideals and translating them into thoughts, behaviors, and actions. This last level represents the translation into moment-by-moment decision making.

Core Belief	A fundamental belief about human nature
	■ Each student is doing the best that he or she can at any given moment.
Underlying Principle	A principle that organizes our experiences and beliefs or our framework for interpreting experiences
	■ We are all wounded by our unmet needs in childhood and our life experiences. Our wounds

lead us to act in protective, and sometimes hurtful, ways toward ourselves and others.

Daily Practice   Linking of beliefs with a general plan of action
- If I hold this core belief and understand that behavior is often driven by unmet needs, I will act in a way that accepts the student's limitations and refrains from judging the student.

Strategies and Moves   Linking of beliefs with moment-to-moment decisions
- If I accept the student's behavior without judgment, then I will choose a behavior acknowledging that the student is not acting against me, rather to get unmet needs met.

Aligning Core Beliefs with Classroom Practice

Following is an example of a core belief that is potentially affirming and one that is potentially limiting. For each type of belief, possible underlying principles, daily practice, and specific strategies are described. Some potential questions for reflection are also offered.

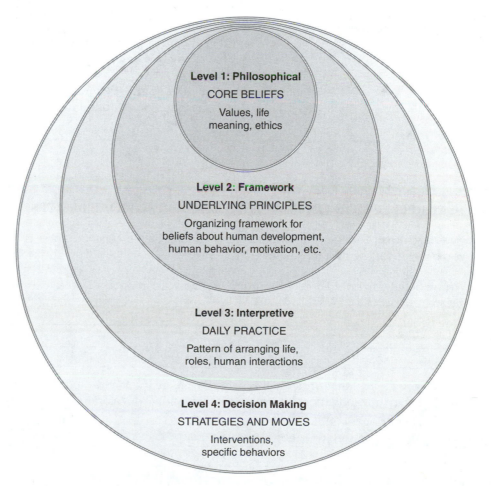

Level 1: Philosophical

CORE BELIEFS

Values, life meaning, ethics

Level 2: Framework

UNDERLYING PRINCIPLES

Organizing framework for beliefs about human development, human behavior, motivation, etc.

Level 3: Interpretive

DAILY PRACTICE

Pattern of arranging life, roles, human interactions

Level 4: Decision Making

STRATEGIES AND MOVES

Interventions, specific behaviors

FIGURE 1.2   Multilevel Process for Self-Reflection

Affirming Core Belief	**Every student can be successful in my class.**
Underlying Principle	Students have different learning styles and intelligences that need to be addressed.
Daily Practice	Organize lessons to support multiple learning styles.
Specific Strategy	Allow students to select from three alternatives how they will demonstrate that they have learned the major concepts in the science unit on light.
Reflective Questions	■ Have I given up on any students in my class because I have a limiting belief about their potential to learn? ■ Do all students in my class have daily opportunities to be successful?

Limiting Core Belief	**Every student should show respect for the teacher.**
Underlying Principle	Adults have the best interests of children in mind.
Daily Practice	Have the following classroom rule: Treat everyone with respect.
Specific Strategy	When a student is disrespectful to me have him or her write 10 times, "I will treat my teacher with respect."
Reflective Questions	■ Have some of the students in my class experienced adults who do not have their best interest in mind? If so, have they had an opportunity to learn respectful behavior? ■ In what ways might I be modeling disrespect? ■ Am I showing respect for all my students, or just those I think "deserve" it?

■ ■ ■ ■ ■ ■ ■ ■ ■ ■ ▬▬▬▬▬▬▬▬▬▬▬▬▬

CRITICAL REFLECTION ON PRACTICE: EXAMINING CORE BELIEFS

Activity Directions: To examine whether your actions in the classroom are congruent with what you believe, follow the steps below.

1. Write a belief you hold about education, students, classrooms, schools, learning, or human nature.

   Core Belief: _____

   _____

   _____

2. List the principle(s) that underlie this belief. What are the theories of human development, human behavior, motivation, learning, or organizational development that frame this belief?

   Underlying Principle(s): _____

   _____

   _____

3. List specific ways of approaching classroom practice and the situations you encounter that support this belief.

Daily Practice: _____

_____

_____

4. List specific classroom actions and behaviors that are consistent with this belief.
   Specific Strategies: _____

_____

_____

5. List any of your classroom behaviors and practices that are not in alignment with this core belief.

_____

_____

REFLECTIVE QUESTION
What do you need to do to better align your moment-to-moment choices with this core belief?

Often, reflection simultaneously with our actions is difficult because of the multiple demands we have to juggle in the classroom. For example, focusing our attention on completing a lesson may distract from paying attention to the way in which we interact with students. Thus, self-reflection often requires a perspective of a metaposition, a looking back after the action has taken place.

The self-reflective process raises our level of consciousness and this increased awareness provides an opportunity to spot incongruence or imbalance. Effective classroom management necessitates continual examining and revisiting of our core beliefs and assessing our actions against these beliefs.

Developing the practice of self-reflection keeps us coming back to our core beliefs and evaluating our choices in accordance with these beliefs. Change is an emergent process, requiring that we learn to become increasingly more aware. That consciousness is the source of our capacity to grow and expand, opening up to a greater range of possible choices and responses to classroom situations and individual student behaviors.

Challenging Your Beliefs

In order to change, you have to challenge the underlying beliefs that drive your present behavior. If you merely try to change a behavior without attacking the belief that drives the behavior, the change is not likely to last long. However, the channel to changing beliefs is not direct; it is through perpetually examining your assumptions, interpretations, and expectations.

Your beliefs about the roles of the teacher and the learner, the nature and purposes of learning, and the teaching and learning environment best suited to these purposes will shape your management decisions. These beliefs disclose your operating principles related to how you view student potential, motivation, development, and growth. The following belief statements represent some possible beliefs that teachers may have.

- I believe students learn best in an intellectually challenging yet structured learning environment.
- I believe students misbehave when they feel defeated and become discouraged and are not able to find constructive outlets for their frustrations.
- I believe students will strive in a classroom environment where individual differences are accommodated and where they enjoy each others' company.

■ ■ ■ ■ ■ ■ ■ ■

CRITICAL REFLECTION ON PRACTICE: ALIGNING BELIEFS AND PRACTICES

Activity Directions: To help you articulate some of your core beliefs about learning and examine practices that may not match your beliefs, complete the following:

1. Complete each statement.

   I believe my students learn best when I _____

   I believe my students learn best when they _____

2. For each of your core belief statements list some classroom practices and strategies that support the belief.

   _____

   _____

   _____

   _____

3. For each of your core belief statements list some classroom practices and strategies that are questionable when aligned with the belief.

   _____

   _____

   _____

   _____

4. Devise some alternative strategies that would be more in line with the belief.

   Alternative strategies: _____

   _____

   _____

REFLECTIVE QUESTION
What questionable practice concerns you the most?

Challenging Limiting Expectations

Teacher beliefs are revealed in the expectations they have for students. There is much research to suggest differential teacher responses to students on the basis of their expectations. These expectations can, and often do, serve as self-fulfilling prophecies, when they are acted on with classroom interaction patterns that are discriminatory (Rosenthal & Jacobson, 1968). Limiting expectations can be based on gender, race, culture, social status, disability, or academic deficits, to name some. There is also research to suggest the teacher's mediating role in the attitudes that students develop toward their classmates as well (Larrivee, 1991).

There is a considerable body of research on the differing ways teachers treat and respond to low-achieving students versus high-achieving students. Good and Brophy (2002) list some of the following teacher behaviors that might communicate low expectations for low-achieving students. Teachers tend to do the following.

- Wait less time for low-achieving students than for high-achieving students to answer questions before giving the answer or going to another student.
- Give low-achieving students the correct answer rather than offer clues or rephrase the question.
- Call on low-achieving students less often.
- Ask low-achieving students only easy questions.

- Expect less academic work from low-achieving students.
- Make fewer efforts to improve the performance of low-achieving students.
- Accept and use the ideas of low-achieving students less.

CRITICAL REFLECTION ON PRACTICE: LIMITING EXPECTATIONS

Activity Directions: Use the example of a particular student who is low-achieving to answer the following questions.

1. Describe the student's academic behavior.

_____

_____

_____

2. Now, read over your description. Does it reveal any limiting expectations? If so, list.

_____

_____

_____

3. Which of the specific behaviors that communicate low expectations do you find yourself displaying with this student?

_____

_____

_____

4. Are there any other behaviors you are engaging in with this student that might be communicating low expectations?

_____

_____

_____

5. How does your experience relate to the research findings reported here?

_____

_____

_____

6. What is one thing you want to change when responding to this student?

_____

_____

_____

REFLECTIVE QUESTION
What message is the student getting about your expectation for his or her performance?

Teacher Self-Efficacy

Teachers' notions of self-efficacy can also play a part in perpetuating their behavior toward certain types of student behavior. Self-efficacy refers to the teacher's perceived ability to be effective, find reasonable solutions to problems, and maintain a belief in their own capacity to effect positive change (Bandura, 1977, 1997; Caine &

Caine, 1997). When teachers see students' actions as threatening their need for control and as intentional misbehavior, they are often pessimistic about their likelihood of producing positive results or any improvement (Brophy & Evertson, 1981).

Hence, teachers' notions of self-efficacy related to their lack of success with students exhibiting such behavior contributes to a sense of powerlessness in being able to effect change. That, in turn, often leads to a continuing pattern of ineffective, even increasingly more hostile, teacher responses.

In contrast, even frequent misconduct does not necessarily impair the teacher–student relationship if it is not disruptive or aggressive, provided the student responds well to the teacher's intervention. Apparently, even if they present behavior problems, students who defer to teachers' authority and respond positively to their interventions are treated with teacher concern and assistance, whereas students who fail to respond appropriately to teacher interventions are treated with rejection and hostility. These findings indicate an interdependence between the teacher's perceived effectiveness, and resulting interaction pattern, and individual student's responses to teacher attempts to curtail inappropriate behavior.

Research findings support the contention that teachers tend to respond with rejection and an orientation toward control and punishment when students are disruptive or threaten the teacher's authority or control (Brophy & Evertson, 1981; Brophy & Good, 1974; Brophy & McCaslin, 1992). Teachers have been found to be especially rejecting and punitive when misbehavior is threatening rather than merely irritating. Students who persistently defy teachers' authority with sullenness or open hostility experience teacher rejection and punishment. Teachers react quite negatively to hostile–aggressive and especially defiant students and to any students who display a surly or insolent attitude. Responses typically depict negative expectations and are characterized by restricted language, often confined to terse demands for behavior change with little emphasis on shaping more desirable behaviors or improving coping skills. Demands are often accompanied by threat or punishment but seldom by rationales or offers of incentives for improved behavior.

Teachers' negative emotional response can trigger a need for control. When student behavior elicits feelings of frustration, irritation, or anger, teachers are more likely to respond with power assertion than to engage in problem-solving negotiations. On the other hand, teachers tend to respond supportively and attempt to help when student problems are purely academic or related to student anxiety or difficulty in coping with the demands of school. Similarly, responses to problems viewed as student-owned, where students are frustrated by people or events that do not include the teacher, are characterized by extensive talk designed to provide support and instruction, with frequent emphasis on long-term goals such as improving students' self-evaluations or teaching them coping techniques.

■ ■ ■ ■ ■ ■ ■ ■ ■

CRITICAL REFLECTION ON PRACTICE: SELF-EFFICACY

Activity Directions: Follow the steps listed.

1. Describe your emotional response to a student for whom your intervention tactics have been mostly ineffective.

   _____

   _____

2. What specific comment(s) do you find yourself making when you feel threatened?

   _____

   _____

   _____

3. What specific comment(s) do you find yourself making when you fear losing control?

_____

_____

_____

4. What are the physical effects you experience when dealing with this student?

_____

_____

5. What are the mental effects you experience when dealing with this student?

_____

_____

6. How would you classify your usual comments (e.g., demands, threats, criticisms)?

_____

_____

7. How does your experience relate to the research findings reported here?

_____

_____

_____

REFLECTIVE QUESTION
What do you want to pay more attention to when dealing with this student?

GUARDING AGAINST TEACHER BURNOUT: CULTIVATING TEACHER RENEWAL

Teachers are particularly susceptible to burnout because of the high degree of dedication and commitment required, making burnout a definite occupational hazard for those in the teaching profession.

Teacher Burnout Factors

One of the most common contributors to teacher stress and burnout is student misbehavior. Research has repeatedly documented the relationship of teacher perceptions of student behavior problems to stress levels (Abel & Sewell, 1999; Bibou-Nakou, Stogiannidou, & Kiosseoglou, 1999; Boyle, Borg, Falzon, & Baglioni, 1995; Brock, 1999; Brophy, 1996; Brouwers & Tomic, 2000; Friedman, 1995; Kijai & Totten, 1995; Travers & Cooper, 1996). Those in helping professions, such as teaching, often fall prey to burnout as a "consequence of caring," or the emotional response to the chronic strain of dealing with others. Maslach (1982) describes the following eight characteristics of burnout.

- Reluctance to discuss work with others
- High incidence of daydreaming to escape current plight
- Attitude of cynicism and negativity toward constituents
- Loss of excitement and interest in daily activities
- Emotional exhaustion and feelings of being spent, having nothing more to give
- Decreased effectiveness in job performance
- Blaming others for unhappiness
- Feeling powerless to change the situation

Friesen, Prokop, and Sarros (1988) offer three main reasons teachers experience burnout: (1) emotional exhaustion, (2) depersonalization, and (3) lack of personal accomplishment. Emotional exhaustion stems from trying to do too much keeping up with a workload that is overwhelming. Depersonalization takes place when teachers develop negative attitudes toward those they work with and become cynical and critical. Burned-out teachers feel a lack of personal accomplishment, becoming disillusioned because they are not satisfying their own needs for challenges, recognition, and appreciation.

Of particular relevance to beginning teachers, Gold (1988) found that those most likely to experience burnout are young and inexperienced. These teachers tend to be ambitious and driven, are likely to be loners who are unable to express feelings, and have a propensity to be depressed. Certain personality characteristics predispose some teachers to greater risk of stress and burnout: being driven, ambitious, competitive, and impatient; needing to be perfect; not feeling in control of emotions (see Mills, Powell, & Pollack, 1992).

Gmelch (1983) coined the term *rustout* to describe a type of professional burnout that afflicts teachers in the form of waning enthusiasm. Rustout is operating when teachers temporarily or permanently cease to be enthusiastic learners. Seeing oneself as a perpetual learner promotes risk taking, inventing, exploring, and extending—all vital to sustaining excitement about learning. When the desire to keep learning withers, the teacher merely goes through the motions of teaching.

Teachers are also prone to the effects of excessive stress, which if unattended can result in rustout or burnout. Because of the daily unrelenting pressures and demands on teachers from others as well as self, teaching is among the most stressful professions (Blase & Kirby, 1991; Farber & Miller, 1981; Lortie, 1975). Because teachers answer to so many different people, a number of external factors also contribute to burnout. In addition to dealing with students who can be trying and difficult, teachers have irate parents to contend with. The imposing structure of school itself leads to constraints of time and scheduling, as well as the lack of opportunity to collaborate with peers, contributing to a feeling of isolation.

Whereas a new job has energizing effects with the excitement of learning new things and mapping out a new territory, as the job becomes familiar, enthusiasm and energy wane. According to Langer (1989), burnout sets in when two conditions prevail: Certainties start to characterize the workday, and demands of the job make workers lose a sense of control. If, in addition, an organization is characterized by rigid rules, problems that arise feel insurmountable because creative problem solving seems too risky. When bureaucratic work settings are of the "we've always done it this way" mentality, burnout is common.

Taking Steps to Inoculate Yourself against Teacher Burnout

It is not inevitable that such demoralizing feelings will someday infect every teacher's professional life and destroy idealism. Although feeling demoralized periodically throughout one's career is normal and predictable, teachers can take steps to insulate themselves and keep from surrendering to burnout. As Zehm and Kottler (2000) remind us, burnout doesn't happen all of a sudden; rather it results from an insidious form of self-neglect, a slow deterioration that eventually corrodes the edges of a teacher's compassion.

If teachers recognize the sources of stress and how it affects their perceptions of themselves, their work, their students, and their colleagues, they will be less likely to succumb to potential stressors. Being more aware of the conditions that induce stress, teachers can notice sooner the symptoms of distress and begin to take specific steps to counteract the effects of stress. Teachers will need vehicles to dissipate stress. When feelings of frustration, hopelessness, and isolation cause teachers to feel overwhelmed, it's easy to fall into habits that can exacerbate stress, such as excessive caffeine as a pick-me-up, overeating, skipping meals, or avoiding exercise due to fatigue. Early career teachers will need to prepare themselves for the challenges they will face by equipping themselves with the resources and tools to vigorously counteract the potential destructive effects of burnout.

Believing in what you are doing and deriving personal satisfaction from doing it is one of the best "stress-busters." To guard against the potentially debilitating effects of on-the-job stress, the following strategies are critical.

Ongoing Growth and Development.   Become a lifelong learner. Improve your own teaching skills. Teachers who are burned out feel they no longer make a difference with their students. You can have an impact, and you can improve yourself and your classroom. Feelings about yourself in general, but in particular feelings of competency and control in the classroom, lend a sense of importance and significance to your work.

Be More Authentic.   Being genuine and sharing your concerns, fears, and emotions with colleagues as well as students will do much to keep your spirits high. The school culture often promotes the idea that teachers should be able to solve their own problems and should not voice their issues and concerns. This creates a subversive climate in which critical issues are "undiscussable."

Develop a Sense of Belonging to Your School Community.   Most teachers are isolated from one another due to the sheer workload involved in teaching. Furthermore, teacher talk often dwells on the undesirable aspects of the job and the shortcomings of colleagues and administrators. Cynicism and pessimism are a common reaction to the stress of teaching. Feeling part of a caring community helps diminish a feeling of solitude while providing a forum for being recognized and appreciated.

Being in a supportive environment promotes satisfaction, enjoyment, and affiliation. When you create a sense of connectedness among your colleagues, you expand your opportunities for authentic discourse. By getting to know each other, you learn each other's strengths as well as limitations. When colleagues respect differences among their peers, they begin to view these differences not as liabilities but as assets. Assessing, utilizing, indeed capitalizing on the unique strengths of individual teachers can contribute to the overall resources of the school community to meet the needs of a diverse student population. Because feeling overwhelmed and hopeless are major contributors to burnout, it is important for teachers to become resources for each other to counteract such feelings. They can even help each other. For example, a teacher who deals effectively with large groups and teacher-led lessons can "trade" teaching a science topic for an individual teacher conference with a "problem" student.

Teachers can also create work incentives by reinforcing themselves. One school started a "secret admirer" club. At the beginning of the year, all staff members drew a name and became that person's secret admirer (Froyen & Iverson, 1999), and twice each month they exchanged thoughtful "gifts." The gift might be a solicited note from an appreciative parent, an invitation from a student to share a special box lunch, or a basket of fruit. You can see how tailoring these gifts to the unique preferences and "soft spots" of an individual teacher can do much to boost morale. By providing these gifts on different schedules, some teacher is regularly expressing gratitude. The teacher's lounge is buzzing with talk about kind deeds, keeping everyone more attuned with the special gifts each person brings to teaching. The elements of mystery, excitement, anticipation, special attention, and personalized affection make this program especially rewarding. The point is, teachers can be proactive and ingenious in creating a spirit of mutual support and encouragement.

Have Access to a Support System.   It is important to build a support system to provide comfort and compassion as well as understanding, direction, and redirection when necessary. In the normal school structure, teachers have little opportunity to provide emotional support for each other or to share experiences. There is great consolation in knowing your peers have the same struggles and agonize over better solutions to common problems. Recurring problems can erode self-perceptions of ability to find adequate solutions to problems that plague teachers on a day-to-day basis, leading to a preoccupation with negative aspects of self and work.

One vehicle for supplanting negative attitudes and self-appraisals with encouragement is a support group. Support groups can be an uplifting experience, and they can provide a buffer against burnout (Dunham, 1984; Holt, Fine, & Tollefson, 1987; Jenkins & Calhoun, 1991). A support group is an informal group of peers who meet on a regular basis to provide an opportunity for unstructured communication and socialization. The group can be composed of teachers at one school site, within a district, or across districts, such as same-grade teachers or colleagues taking the same class or workshop. It provides a welcome time-out from structured group meetings. Here you can vent emotions and frustrations, give and receive constructive and purposeful criticism, and develop strategies to improve work situations and relations.

A support group is a place where you feel safe and accepted enough to allow yourself to be vulnerable, admit mistakes, and ask for help. Such a group can be rejuvenating and keep you from getting stuck in destructive habits to deal with the stress of teaching. Your peers can help you sift through the maze and acknowledge the good you are doing as well as see how you might be contributing to your own demise. Benefits of support groups include greater realization and appreciation of the unique abilities and talents of both yourself and your peers.

Enhance Your Communication Skills.   Better communication skills can also serve to reduce stress. Having more effective ways to articulate your feelings, frustrations, wants, needs, and desires will help you find the courage to express yourself. Positive and affirming interpersonal relationships are at the heart of feeling good about yourself and what you do. Later chapters in this book address skills for initiating and responding more effectively to both everyday experiences as well as more confrontive encounters.

CRITICAL REFLECTION ON PRACTICE: DEALING WITH STRESS

Activity Directions: Follow the steps below to begin paying more attention to your stress level.

1. Keep a diary of your daily activities for one week.
2. Then go back and reflect on the level of stress you felt on each of those days.
3. Use your entries to make connections between more or less stress and differences in "quality of life" experiences for those days.
4. What did you learn from this activity?

REFLECTIVE QUESTIONS
What are some cause-and-effect relationships you want to be more aware of?
What seems to serve as a stress buffer for you?

Learning Stress Management Strategies

Stress management occurs on two levels: prevention and coping. Stress inoculation involves preventative measures that attempt to minimize stress, so that you are "inoculated" against the harmful effects of stress-producing situations. Strategies can be (1) physiological, dealing with the direct effect on the body, such as diet, exercise, or relaxation; (2) cognitive, or increasing your awareness of, and redirecting, your thinking and internal talk; or (3) behavioral, such as time management. A more in-depth description of these strategies is provided in Chapter 7. In Chapter 8, some specific techniques are provided for use with students.

Some techniques available to help manage stress produce a direct effect on the body. Such techniques help you deal with the physical reactions the body has to stress. We all need some type of physiological coping strategy. Physiological stress coping skills that release the relaxation response include diaphragmatic ("deep") breathing, progressive relaxation techniques, meditation, and visualization techniques. Progressive relaxation produces a deeper and longer-lasting state of relaxation than diaphragmatic breathing (Cautela & Groden, 1978; Lucic, Steffen, Harrigan, & Stuebing, 1991; Watson & Thorp, 2002). It involves alternately making your muscles tense and then relaxed. The idea is to learn the difference between these two states, so that you can better recognize tension in your body and use progressive relaxation techniques to achieve relaxation.

Managing Stress at the Mental Level.   When faced with a problem, you basically have two choices—change the situation or change your reaction to the situation. Often you can't change the situation, but you can change how you emotionally respond, by using tension-releasing strategies to help you experience some relief and cope more effectively. You can learn to reframe, reposition, and restructure classroom situations and work circumstances by monitoring your self-talk and altering limiting self-appraisals of events and situations.

Beliefs and attitudes materialize in the form of internalized self-talk. You continually talk to yourself throughout the day and throughout the hours you're in school, and you talk to yourself as you're interacting with students. Often with a student who poses a problem, your internal talk is about how impossible the student is. Try stepping back and listening in on your internal talk for a few seconds, and you will notice the kind of running commentary you have about the student.

Your mind is typically engaged in anxiety-producing thoughts which trigger the fight-or-flight response keeping your body in a state of arousal. Your body's other response is the relaxation response, a state of lowered arousal which diminishes many adverse symptoms brought on by stress. It is your perspective on things, your mental appraisal of external events, that determines your emotional tone and, hence, your level of stress. The secret to effectively regulating stress is to learn to cultivate the ability to monitor and regulate harmful thought patterns (Ellis, 1974; Ellis & Bernard, 1984; Ellis & Harper, 1975; Harvey, 1988). Control in this sense means that you are aware of and can exercise choices that direct you away from patterns that create anxiety and stress toward patterns that lead to satisfaction and coping.

Many methods and techniques are available to handle stress at the mental or cognitive level. Meditation is a popular strategy, but any strategy that creates an internal stillness that stops the endless flow of noise and interference constantly parading through your mind can precipitate the relaxation response. The idea is to create an observation point from which you can begin to notice your thoughts and then let go of your old dialogues.

It is important to have a way to access the body's relaxation response. You need to find ways to catch yourself in the act of constructing your familiar stories, so you can make the shift from thought to awareness of what is immediately happening. In its normal state, your mind is preoccupied with an inner dialogue, which is an endless stream of thinking, providing commentary on your experiences. Our mind is a realm of metaphors, myths, and movies. The repetitive stories you tell yourself about how things should be serve to perpetuate automatic ways of interpreting your experiences. These stories serve the function of putting your immediate experiences into your past experience framework, continuously replaying the past.

Your self-created storylines can wreak havoc in the classroom by creating a mental picture of how things ought to be—stories such as "It's impossible to teach this class the way they behave"; or "These kids just don't want to learn"; or "I should be able to control all the students in my class." These stories provide the backdrop for the expectations you have for your classroom and can set you up for disillusionment, loss of a sense of vision, and, ultimately, burnout.

The vast majority of self-talk is learned. It is learned from families, friends, and society. If self-talk is learned, then you can learn to use different self-talk. Your old patterns of responding create a groove in your mind, making it difficult to take a different route. The path of critical inquiry involves examining the filters through which you see and interpret the world and disputing, altering, and acting against your familiar internal verbalizations. It is possible to accomplish considerable change in your way of behaving through learning to rechannel your thoughts. If you fail to break out of your destructive thinking patterns, you stay trapped behaving automatically.

The goal is not to be worry free, rather to keep the harmful effects of cumulative stress at bay. A certain level of discomfort is healthy and leads to taking necessary action. Also, stress is a subjective response to potentially stressful events. Different individuals function more or less effectively with differing amounts of stress. Some teachers seem to be able to manage great amounts of stress, whereas others become overwhelmed with modest amounts. Joseph (2001) in his book *Stressfree Teaching* offers "The Ten Commandments for Reducing Stress."

The Ten Commandments for Reducing Stress
Thou shalt not be perfect or even try to be.
Thou shalt not try to be ALL things to ALL people.
Thou shalt not leave things undone that ought to be done.
Thou shalt not spread thyself too thinly.
Thou shalt learn to say "No."
Thou shalt schedule time for thyself and thy support network.
Thou shalt switch off and do nothing—regularly.
Thou shalt be boring, inelegant, untidy, and unattractive at times.
Thou shalt not feel guilty.
Thou shalt not be thine own worst enemy but thine own best friend. (p. 120)

■ ■ ■ ■ ■ ■ ■ ■ ■

CRITICAL REFLECTION ON PRACTICE: INOCULATING YOURSELF AGAINST STRESS

Activity Directions: Answer the following questions to get a better handle on school-related stress.

1. Write a general statement about your ability to handle stress.

_____

_____

_____

2. What school or classroom events or situations do you find most stressful?

_____

_____

_____

3. Considering your personal qualities and your own idiosyncrasies, what aspects of the job of teaching are likely to be stress-producing for you?

_____

_____

_____

4. Of the potential sources of personal and job-related stress discussed, which are you most susceptible to?

_____

_____

_____

REFLECTIVE QUESTION

What can you do to make yourself less vulnerable to, or to inoculate yourself against, the sources of stress that are potentially most debilitating to you?

Guarding against Setting Unattainable Expectations

In addition to the anxiety created by the often unreasonable demands of today's classroom, a teacher's own dissatisfaction with self adds to the feelings of helplessness. Sometimes teachers fail to discriminate between the actual demands of teaching and their own self-imposed demands. Idealism, dedication, and commitment can result in unreasonable and virtually unattainable expectations. Your own limiting assumptions about a problem, or a student perceived as a problem, can drive behavior in unproductive directions.

The pressure to conform to a picture of the perfect teacher lies at the root of much self-induced stress. Your own thoughts and feelings undermine more effective behavior. Such limiting beliefs are expressed in self-verbalizations. As a stress inoculation strategy, you can learn to replace negative thought patterns with affirming ones. Two especially destructive ways of thinking about problems and issues are (1) all-or-none and (2) catastrophic thinking.

All-or-None Thinking

Ms. Morris doesn't like me, so none of the teachers here likes me.
My principal let me down. I'll never trust him again.

Catastrophic Thinking

I messed up again. I can't do anything right.
Why even try? It won't do any good—she's a hopeless case.

Combating Commonly Held Teaching Myths. Some beliefs can be especially devastating for teachers to try to measure up to. When teachers set unattainable standards for themselves, they are headed for disillusionment at the very least.

The following I-should statements represent some commonly held teaching myths.

I should

■ Like and care for all students equally
■ Have no preferences or prejudices
■ Be consistent in my actions with students
■ Remain calm and collected at all times
■ Hide my true feelings and place students' feelings above mine
■ Be able to readily solve all problems
■ Cope with all situations without anxiety, stress, or conflict
■ Run my classroom so that there is no confusion, uncertainty, or chaos

CRITICAL REFLECTION ON PRACTICE: CHALLENGING TEACHING MYTHS

Activity Directions: For each of the eight teaching myths, write a corresponding belief that is more realistic and accepting of being human.

LIMITING BELIEF	ACCEPTING BELIEF
I should like and care for all students equally.	_____
I should have no preferences or prejudices.	_____
I should be consistent in my actions with students.	_____
I should remain calm and collected at all times.	_____
I should hide my true feelings and place students' feelings above mine.	_____
I should be able to readily solve all problems.	_____
I should cope with all situations without anxiety, stress, or conflict.	_____
I should run my classroom so that there is no confusion, uncertainty, or chaos.	_____

REFLECTIVE QUESTION
Which of these I-should statements is the most important for you to challenge?

TEACHER BURNOUT AND RENEWAL CYCLES

Curwin and Mendler (1988) described a phenomenon they labeled the "discipline-burnout cycle." When teachers respond ineffectively to student misbehavior, typically using either denial or attacking tactics, their response leads to continuation or worsening of the student's behavior, causing tension and frustration. Faced with not knowing what to do, the teacher either holds in the tension or yields to explosive outbursts. If the tension accumulates with no relief in sight, the teacher responds with either withdrawal or aggression.

When the cycle becomes repetitive, burnout sets in. "Burnout victims" suffer from both physical and mental side effects. Signs of imbalance due to burnout can take the form of preoccupation with negative thoughts, lack of motivation to go to work, fatigue, irritability, muscular tension, high blood pressure, or ulcers.

On the other hand, when the teacher's interventions result in appropriate student responses, it leads to the teacher's enhanced sense of self-efficacy. Believing that they are capable of finding reasonable solutions to the day-to-day problems they face helps keep teachers actively engaged and enthusiastic about their work. As teachers learn to use more effective interventions for both teacher-owned and student-owned problems, they become more confident of their own resources for solving problems. They stay in a renewal cycle.

One of the best buffers against undue stress and potential teacher burnout is to learn intervention strategies that get you the student responses you desire.

Figures 1.3 and 1.4 provide a graphic display of teacher burnout and renewal cycles.

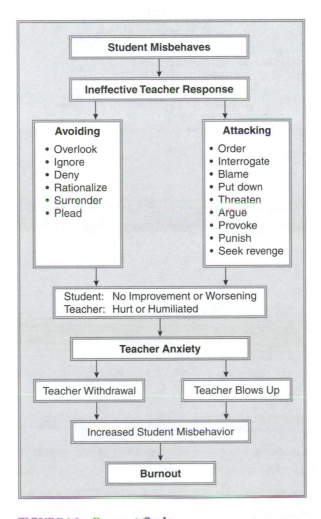

FIGURE 1.3   Burnout Cycle

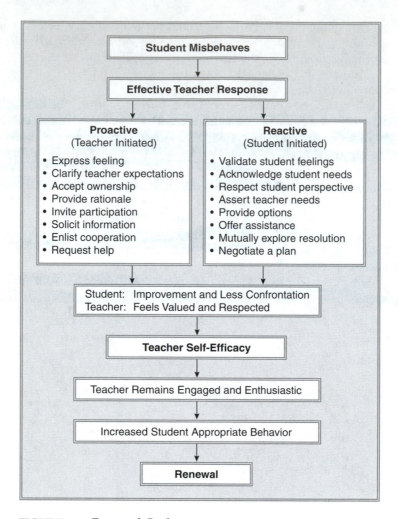

FIGURE 1.4   Renewal Cycle

CHAPTER TWO

A Multidimensional Approach to Classroom Management

Effective classroom management is inextricably tied to the quality of educational experiences in which students engage as well as the teacher's skill in organizing the class structure to facilitate efficient teaching and learning. In order to provide the necessary foundation, several conditions need to be sustained simultaneously. The following three conditions are integral to effective classroom management.

1. A stimulating and supportive setting for learning to occur.
2. Reasonable expectations established considering student characteristics and needs.
3. Opportunities for all students to receive recognition and experience success.

The teacher's ability to effectively orchestrate the learning environment to enhance the competence of all students is also clearly related to student behavior. In a setting in which students typically fail, students will be less motivated to follow the established rules and expectations. If students' sense of self-efficacy is not supported in positive ways, then again misbehavior is likely to occur. When students feel helpless and powerless they are less likely to comply with expected classroom norms.

THE BALANCING ACT: THE MANY FACES OF CLASSROOM MANAGEMENT

Developing a personal system of classroom management involves considering instructional factors, management issues, discipline strategies, and interpersonal relationships. Effectively managing the classroom setting requires balancing these multiple layers.

Several authors have delineated the multiple dimensions of classroom management from different perspectives—as levels, stages, and roles.

Charles (2002) refers to three levels of discipline, which he labels preventive, supportive, and corrective.

1. Preventive disciplinary steps are those taken to prevent misbehavior from occurring.
2. Supportive disciplinary measures are strategies that assist students in self-control by helping them get back on task.
3. Corrective disciplinary steps are called for when students misbehave and need to be corrected.

Grossman (2003) discusses the three stages of management.

1. At stage one, management is directed at organizing classroom routines and procedures to avoid behavior problems.
2. Stage two includes general strategies for solving behavior problems.
3. Stage three involves strategies primarily geared toward strengthening personal relationships.

Kounin (1970) talks about the three aspects of a teacher's role: instructor, manager, and person.

1. The role as instructor calls for teachers to provide appropriate instructional activities.
2. The role as manager stresses effective group management techniques.
3. The role as person is concerned with positive human interactions.

An important dimension of classroom management involves developing strategies for maintaining personal relationships with students. This includes building, sustaining, and restoring, when necessary.

12 General Principles of Effective Classroom Management

The following behavior management principles provide the foundation for maintaining an effective classroom. They represent key management concepts that are embellished to varying degrees in many of the models of discipline to be presented in subsequent sections. These recurring themes form the basis for establishing a healthy and productive teaching and learning environment.

1. Demonstrate caring.
2. Take charge—be in control of yourself.
3. Communicate regularly and clearly with students.
4. Establish enforceable rules and enforce them.
5. Hold high expectations for students.
6. Persistently confront unproductive behavior.
7. Invoke consequences in a calm manner.
8. Comment only on students' behavior, not personal traits.
9. Model desirable behavior.
10. Teach students to make appropriate choices.
11. Organize teaching activities to avoid boredom and wasted time.
12. Provide ample opportunities for students to experience success and receive recognition.

■ ■ ■ ■ ■ ■ ■ ■ ▄▬▬▬▬▬▬▬▬▬▬▬▬▬▬▬▬▬▬▬▬▬▬▬▬

CRITICAL REFLECTION ON PRACTICE: ANALYZING YOUR USE OF EFFECTIVE MANAGEMENT PRINCIPLES

Activity Directions: Follow the steps below.

1. List the two principles you most consistently follow.

_____

_____

2. List the two principles you least consistently follow.

_____

_____

3. List the one principle you most want to be more evident in your classroom.

_____

4. Decide on one specific behavior you could engage in to enhance adherence to the selected principle.

_____

_____

_____

_____

REFLECTIVE QUESTION
Which principle do you think is the most important for effectively managing a classroom?

Setting Reasonable and Ethical Expectations. Behavior management should not be thought of as a set of procedures to make students conform to a rigid, inflexible value system, or to force compliance. Any behavior management strategies utilized in the classroom should be for the purpose of facilitating the learning environment and bringing about meaningful learning, not merely to squelch noncompliant behavior. Before attempting to modify an individual student's classroom behavior, teachers need to assess how they have structured their classroom environment to support learning.

The following questions will help teachers reflect on their personal "classroom ecology."

Reflective Questions to Ask Yourself
- Do your classroom rules and procedures really benefit students, or are they primarily for your own comfort level and convenience?
- What type of behavior is annoying to you but essentially harmless to the learner and other students?
- Is the student's behavior irritating to you because it offends your personal values or sensitivities?
- What classroom freedom can be permitted without infringing on the rights of other students?
- Should silence be maintained while children are working, or should reasonable communication among students be permitted?

LEARNING PRACTICE TASK: INSTRUCTOR, MANAGER, AND PERSON

Activity Directions: Think of a class you really enjoyed and in which you were motivated to learn.

1. List five characteristics of this teacher or class.

_____

_____

_____

(continued)

LEARNING PRACTICE TASK   Continued

_____

_____

2. Then join with three other colleagues and share your list.

3. On a sheet of paper label three columns: Instructor, Manager, and Person.

4. Take the twenty characteristics listed by the four members of your group and place each under one of the three columns.
   - Place items that are primarily organizational and structural in nature under the Manager heading.
   - Place items that are primarily related to the teacher's effectiveness in teaching the content and following the lesson format under the Teacher heading.
   - Place items that are primarily related to the teacher's personal characteristics or interpersonal relationships under the Person heading.

5. Discuss what the results suggest.

6. Write three observations your group made.

_____

_____

_____

_____

_____

_____

■ ■ ■ ■ ■ ■ ■ ■ ■

LEARNING PRACTICE TASK: APPLYING KEY CONCEPTS FOR EFFECTIVE CLASSROOM MANAGEMENT

Activity Directions: Write a statement about what each of the twelve principles means to you and why the principle is important.

1. Demonstrate caring. _____

_____

_____

2. Take charge—be in control of yourself. _____

_____

_____

3. Communicate regularly and clearly with students. _____

_____

_____

4. Establish enforceable rules and enforce them. _____

_____

_____

5. Hold high expectations for students. _____

_____

_____

6. Persistently confront unproductive behavior. _____
_____
_____

7. Invoke consequences in a calm manner. _____
_____
_____

8. Comment only on students' behavior, not personal traits. _____
_____
_____

9. Model desirable behavior. _____
_____
_____

10. Teach students to make appropriate choices. _____
_____
_____

11. Organize teaching activities to avoid boredom and wasted time. _____
_____
_____

12. Provide ample opportunities for students to experience success and receive recognition.
_____
_____

SETTING THE STAGE: PREVENTIVE PLANNING

Successful teachers actually avoid many potential behavior problems by using effective teaching techniques, appropriately challenging students, promoting group accountability and cohesiveness, preventing potentially disruptive situations from occurring, establishing reasonable procedures and rules, modeling desirable behavior, satisfying students' basic needs, and maintaining good relationships with students.

For many students who behave inappropriately in spite of their teachers' best efforts at preventive planning, eliminating situational or contextual barriers, teaching students coping skills, or reasoning with them will often be all that is needed.

Preventive Planning by Effectively Managing Teacher-Led Activities

Many authors talk about preventive planning as the foundation for effective classroom management (Charles, 2002; Curwin & Messler, 1998; Grossman, 2003; Kounin, 1970; Jones, 1987; Redl, 1966). Preventive planning consists of teacher strategies that actually prevent management and discipline problems from occurring.

Several authors take the position that mastery of group management techniques will enable teachers to be free from concern about classroom management problems. They emphasize the teacher's role in smooth activity flow, primarily by keeping students on task and effectively managing teacher-led activities (Kounin,

1970; Redl & Wattenberg, 1959; Jones, 1987). Clear-cut directions, instructional clarity, careful sequencing of activities, and adequate student preparation for follow-up activities will do much for keeping the classroom running smoothly.

Kounin's Techniques for Group Management.   Kounin, like Gordon, believes many classroom problems are clearly teacher owned. He described several factors related to whole class instruction, interactive group activities, and smooth activity flow that characterize effective classrooms. When the lesson flow keeps students' attention without frequent interruptions, distractions, or diversions, there is less opportunity for off-task behavior and less competition for student attention from what is external to the lesson. On the other hand, by issuing vague and indefinite directions, presenting information out of sequence, backtracking, inserting extraneous information, moving from one topic to another without warning, making assignments without first checking for understanding, and giving assignments that do not align with the content development activities, teachers leave students floundering, leading to a greater tendency for students to go off task.

According to Kounin, the following factors prevent misbehavior: withitness, overlapping, smoothness, momentum, and maintaining group focus by ensuring attention to the task by monitoring response rates and through general accountability. By using specific techniques that maintain constant alertness to the sights and sounds of the classroom, teachers can attend to multiple events at the same time, manage lesson flow and transitions, keep all students alert, and insulate lessons from distractions from student intrusions or external interruptions.

Kounin's categories for maintaining group focus are especially helpful for teachers to prevent student off-task behavior. Below are examples of these techniques.

TECHNIQUE	DESCRIPTION	EXAMPLE
Group alerting	Engages attention of whole class while individuals are responding	Using designation such as thumbs up for agreement
Encouraging accountability	Lets students know everyone's participation is expected	Pairing with a partner and explaining a concept to each other
High participation formats	Involves students other than those directly responding to teacher question	Writing a question about the concept being studied to be put in a pool for later whole class discussion

When teachers provide lesson continuity by thinking more about the whole than the lesson pieces and react promptly to problems, they will often be able to use simple, unobtrusive measures (e.g., eye contact, quiet correction) that don't interfere with ongoing activities or distract students from the task.

Jones's Techniques for Group Management.   Jones, like Kounin, focuses on prevention by calling on teachers to look at their ability to manage groups, lessons, and the overall classroom environment. His main emphasis is on managing group behavior to reduce disruptions and increase cooperative behavior. Jones identifies three clusters of skills that help to prevent misbehavior when it occurs: (1) using body language to set and enforce limits; (2) using formal and informal incentives;

and (3) providing efficient help for students. According to Jones, teachers should know exactly what they want done and have routines in place for accomplishing tasks that are simple and effective. In addition, teachers should use incentives to get students to be at the right place at the right time with the right materials doing the right thing.

Having a good structure, including rules, routines, standards of appropriate behavior, and positive student–teacher relations, avoids many problems. When students misbehave despite good structure, he advises limit setting that clearly communicates that the teacher is in charge at all times and means business, expecting and teaching students to assume responsibility, and using an incentive system of gaining and losing positive consequences (favored over punishment).

Redl's and Wattenberg's Techniques for Group Management. Like Kounin and Jones, Redl and Wattenberg stress surface management techniques for general managing of groups, but they add a mental hygiene component. They adapted their work with students with emotional problems for use in regular classrooms. Their focus is on managing students without resorting to negative consequences and accommodating the classroom environment to students' emotional needs. Like others concerned with students' unmet needs, they stress taking the conscious and unconscious motivation of students into consideration. They recommend techniques for managing surface behavior of students and preventing dangerous or disruptive behavior in nonpunitive ways.

Redl and Wattenberg advocate that the teacher must understand group processes in addition to individual differences, noting that the group is distinctly different from the individual. How teachers behave, as well as how they handle the misbehavior of one student, affects the way their students behave. Furthermore, group behavior in the classroom is influenced by how students perceive the teacher. In translating their psychodynamic concepts into classroom practice, the authors provide insight into both the psychological and social forces that affect student behavior, both individually and within a group. They suggest that teachers need to identify the various roles the student may play, such as leader, clown, fall guy, or instigator, to provide the student with a sense of belonging to the group.

According to Redl and Wattenberg, teachers maintain group control by (1) addressing the problem before it becomes serious; (2) helping students to regain control; (3) teaching students the underlying causes of misbehavior and helping them to foresee probable consequences; and (4) rewarding good behavior and punishing negative behavior.

Some Teacher-Owned Group Management Problems. Teachers often condition students to misbehave by their actions and policies. Cangelosi (1999) notes the following ways teachers condition students.

- When a teacher demonstrates awareness of off-task behavior but does not make an effective effort to lead students to redirect off-task with on-task behavior, students surmise that the teacher is not serious about expecting them to be on task.
- When a teacher tells students how to behave without taking any action to lead them to follow what is said, students are conditioned not to bother to listen.
- When the teacher repeats demands for students to be on task over and over without compliance until finally the teacher gets angry and upset, it conditions students not to listen until the teacher becomes upset.

If the teacher is confronted with off-task behavior and is not, at the moment, in the position to apply a strategy that has a reasonable chance of working, then the teacher should delay a response until the teacher can implement a suitable strategy.

Some types of teacher commands or directives can actually lower the rate of student compliance, such as chain commands or vague commands delivered as questions. Several authors suggest ways for teachers to give directives to students that are more likely to get students to comply (Barkley, 1987; Morgan & Jenson, 1988; Forehand & McMahon, 1981).

- Be specific and direct by phrasing requests and directives in descriptive terms, using language that can be clearly understood, so students know exactly what is expected.
- Get the student's attention and pause until eye contact is established.
- Give only one directive at a time.
- Avoid chain commands such as "Take out your math books, turn to page 56, do the odd-numbered problems, check your answers, and then report to me."
- Pause for sufficient time following the directive (a minimum of five seconds) for the student to respond. During this period don't reissue the directive or issue a new one, argue, prompt, or try to coerce the student.
- For noncompliance within the allotted time, repeat the directive only once.
- When giving directives to individual students, it is preferable to be in close proximity to the student and to speak to the student quietly.

When setting the stage for their classroom, the following questions will help teachers consider classroom structure variables.

Reflective Questions to Ask Yourself
- Are there long periods of nonfunctional time?
- Are there many unexpected changes in schedules, procedures, and routines?
- Are the assigned tasks made relevant to students?
- Are the classroom activities stimulating and thought provoking?
- Is each student given ample opportunity to experience success?
- Are there too many failures?
- Is there too much emphasis on competition?
- Is there more criticism than encouragement?
- Are students encouraged to strive for improvement, not perfection?

Summary

Although being able to manage group functions is certainly a necessary set of skills, it's only part of a total management system. There is much more to managing today's classroom than getting the classroom to function like a well-oiled machine with everything regulated for students. This approach has the drawback of the potential for teachers to lose sight of other essential elements of the student–teacher relationship.

Teachers need to create a balance between overdirecting students and leaving them too much on their own without providing a structure. Emphasizing group management techniques tends to tip the scale in favor of overdirecting.

Highlighting the instructional efficiency aspect as the major route to effective classroom management creates a tendency to move from a functional dimension directly to applying consequences for misbehavior and rule infractions. This sequence virtually eliminates the middle ground—what to do between relatively minor infractions and the teacher taking charge. In addition to group management structures, teachers also need to develop structures for helping students take responsibility before they revert to applying consequences.

A teacher's capacity for reflection is a key element in the ongoing challenge to balance the three interfacing roles of instructor, manager, and person. The teacher must balance regulating student behavior, to maintain an environment conducive to teaching and learning, with potentially stifling student creativity, decision-making power, and problem-solving autonomy. The ability to balance the teacher's inner comfort with setting and upholding reasonable expectations for students is another critical dimension.

DECIDING TO INTERVENE

The reflective mind-set relative to classroom and problem behavior management involves an open-minded stance, recognizing that there are many ways to view a particular circumstance, situation, or event. When considering intervention, the reflective teacher

- Acknowledges beliefs and limiting assumptions that may affect perception of the problem
- Is fully cognizant of the interaction between teacher responses to students and student responses to the teacher
- Engages in ongoing inquiry to identify behavior patterns
- Recognizes the communicative intent of student behavior
- Considers multiple alternative explanations of student behavior

The question of when a teacher should intervene is an important classroom management decision. Determining when to intervene involves three considerations: first, whether an intervention is warranted; second, at what point to intervene; and third, whether it would be most effective or efficient to intervene immediately or delay an intervention. Determining if and when to intervene involves consideration of the following.

- Whether the teacher owns the problem
  Teacher-owned problems are problems that interfere with teacher needs, such as maintaining an orderly environment or having students be respectful, both to the teacher and to classmates.
- At what point intervention is warranted
  When teachers fail to set limits or intervene when first necessary, they can develop counteraggressive feelings toward students when misbehavior has escalated.
- Whether immediate or delayed intervention would be most effective
  Sometimes immediate intervention can be counterproductive when the student is in a disturbed state or the teacher is at a critical point in a lesson activity.

Determining When to Intervene

Several authors offer guidelines for making the best choice. Gordon (1989) suggests that teachers learn to determine who owns the problem; Redl (1966) suggests specific situations in which intervention is necessary; Grossman (2003) suggests that teachers consider the classroom context in determining whether intervention should be immediate or delayed.

Prior to determining when to intervene, the teacher first has to determine whether a problem is teacher owned. The teacher owns a problem when it either actually or potentially interferes with the teacher's legitimate needs. Unacceptable student behaviors that have tangible negative effects on teachers cannot be ignored and call for teachers to assume an active posture and deal with the behavior.

When teachers identify a student behavior as unacceptable, they have several options available to them. In attempting to modify unacceptable behavior, teachers have three variables to work with: the student, the environment, and their own behavior. They can

- Confront the student directly and attempt to modify the behavior
- Modify the learning context, by altering the task, their expectation, or the learning situation
- Modify their own reaction or response to the behavior

The following example illustrates these choices.

Ms. Peters is repeatedly interrupted by Brian, who seems to be unable to go ahead with an assignment without constant checking and reinforcement. This is unacceptable to Ms. Peters, so she owns the problem. What can she do?

1. She can confront Brian, sending some message that will cause him to stop interrupting. [Modify the student.]
2. She can provide the student with an alternative way for checking other than directly with the teacher. [Modify the environment.]
3. She can say to herself, "He's just a dependent student and he'll outgrow it soon," or "He obviously needs more reassurance than the others." [Modify the self.]

These are not clear-cut distinctions, and often more than one or all three variables might be involved in the most effective solution to a classroom problem. In this example, the teacher might pair some nonverbal cue to the student with designating a willing classmate to answer the student's frequent questions.

When teachers make a conscious choice to try to modify student behavior that they consider unacceptable, they usually send a confrontative message. This message often has negative effects on students and fails to bring about the desired results. According to Gordon, most teachers have simply never considered the potential impact of their messages on students. Typically, the messages teachers send when confronting students fall into three general categories.

1. Power play, or telling students what to do
2. Put-down, or personal assault
3. Guilt trip, or trying to shame students

More effective confrontive strategies are presented in Chapter 8.

Situations Warranting Immediate Interventions.   Redl also offers criteria for determining when to intervene. Teachers often are not sure whether they should interfere when faced with a particular student behavior. When teachers fail to set limits or interfere until they are overcome with negative feelings toward a student, they are likely to use an intervention that is too severe. Redl suggests nine situations in which immediate intervention is warranted (Fagen & Hill, 1977). In these situations, student behavior needs to be regulated immediately. These situations require an on-the-spot reaction that will contain the problem behavior, without regard to underlying causes or motives. Such techniques are referred to as *surface management* techniques and will be discussed in the next section. The nine situations are listed below, along with an example of each.

9 Situations Warranting Immediate Intervention	Example
1. Reality dangers	Fighting
2. Psychological protection	Calling another student a derogatory name

3. Protection against too much excitement   A game getting out of hand
4. Protection of property   Destroying a desktop
5. Protection of an ongoing program   Disruption of a group activity
6. Protection against negative contagion   Tapping on desk with pencil
7. Highlighting a value area or school policy   Smoking in school bathroom
8. Avoiding conflict with the outside world   Setting rules of conduct on a field trip
9. Protecting a teacher's inner comfort   Noise exceeding teacher's level of tolerance

---

Reality Dangers.   Adults are usually more reality oriented than students and have had more practice predicting the consequence of certain acts. If students are playing a rough game, fighting, or playing with matches, and it appears as if they might injure themselves, then the teacher moves in and stops the behavior.

Psychological Protection.   Just as in the case of being physically hurt, the teacher should protect the student from psychological injury. If a group is ganging up on a student or using derogatory racial nicknames, then the teacher should intervene. The teacher does not support or condone this behavior and the values it reflects.

Protection against Too Much Excitement.   Sometimes a teacher intervenes in order to avoid the development of too much excitement, anxiety, or guilt. For example, if a game is getting out of hand and continues another 10 minutes, the student may lose control and feel very unhappy about this behavior later. Once again, the teacher should intervene to stop this cycle from developing.

Protection of an Ongoing Program.   Once a class is motivated in a particular task and the students have an investment in its outcome, it is not fair to have it ruined by one student who is having some difficulty. In this case, the teacher would intervene and ask the student to leave or move next to the student in order to ensure that the enjoyment, satisfaction, and learning of the group is not impaired.

Protection against Negative Contagion.   When a teacher is aware that tension is mounting in the classroom and a student with high social power begins tapping the desk with a pencil, the teacher might ask the student to stop, to prevent this behavior from spreading to the other students and disrupting the entire lesson.

Protecting a Teacher's Inner Comfort.   It is important for a teacher to recognize his or her personal idiosyncrasies and realize when he or she might be overreacting to a student's behavior. On the other hand, it's better to try to stop the behavior than do nothing and inwardly reject the student. Protecting a teacher's inner comfort necessitates creating a balance between personal idiosyncrasies and reasonable expectations for students. This is a critical decision point in determining whether intervention is appropriate.

When to Delay Intervention.   Grossman (2003) has identified some specific situations that warrant either immediate or delayed intervention. Some situations require immediate intervention, such as when the behavior is dangerous, destructive, or contagious. It is also important to step in right away when the behavior could get worse or the behavior is self-perpetuating. Behavior problems that are likely to intensify if not corrected should be nipped in the bud. For example, an argument between two students verging on a real fight needs to be stopped immediately. Likewise, misbehavior that is intrinsically rewarding, such as cutting ahead in line, needs to be stopped before students receive any reinforcement for their actions.

Sometimes it is preferable to delay intervention rather than respond immediately to student misbehavior. Grossman provides the following examples of situations in which immediate intervention can be counterproductive.

1. *When the teacher does not have all the facts.* When you overhear someone say something nasty to another student, although you might get angry, it could be that the other student provoked the response. In this case, it may be better not to correct the first student, since you may have an incomplete understanding of the situation. Here you would want to wait to deal with it until you know all the circumstances.

2. *When the timing is wrong.* In the following situations, it may not be the right time to intervene. When the immediate circumstances will not allow you to deal with the problem effectively, it may be preferable to postpone dealing with a problem until a more convenient time.

- *Insufficient time.* If a student misbehaves at dismissal time, you may have to wait if you want to discuss the behavior at length. A simple statement such as "We'll have to discuss what you just did tomorrow morning" will suffice to let the student know that you are planning to handle it.
- *Disruptive effects of intervening.* If you are at a point in a lesson when it would be too disruptive to stop and handle a behavior problem, you might want to briefly signal your disapproval to the student and deal with it in a more constructive manner at a less disruptive time.
- *When students are too sensitive to be exposed publicly.* If dealing with students' behavior publicly might embarrass them, wait until you can talk to them in private.
- *When students are too upset to deal with their behavior rationally.* When students are extremely angry, it will be more effective to discuss their behavior with them after they have calmed down. Students are not likely to be receptive to teacher intervention when they are in an emotionally charged state.

■ ■ ■ ■ ■ ■ ■ ■ ■ ▬▬▬▬▬▬▬▬▬▬▬▬

LEARNING PRACTICE TASK: IDENTIFYING AND PRIORITIZING PROBLEM BEHAVIORS

Activity Directions: Think of yourself as the teacher in each situation described below. You are to make three determinations for each situation: first, whether or not there is a problem; second, who owns the problem (i.e., the teacher owning the problem means that the teacher would intervene to deal with the problem); and third, whether the particular problem would be of high or low priority for action. If you determine there is no problem in the situation, there is no need to fill in the other two columns. Code your responses as follows: Problem (Y), No Problem (N); Teacher Owns (T), Other Owns (O); High Priority (H), Low Priority (L).

	PROBLEM YES/NO Y/N	WHO OWNS TEACHER/OTHER T/O	INTERVENTION PRIORITY HIGH/LOW H/L
1. Several of your students are whispering loudly while you are giving instructions.	_____	_____	_____
2. Dennis tells you that he is having trouble with his friend and is too upset to do his work.	_____	_____	_____

3. Marvin glares at a classmate and threatens to punch him if he doesn't shut up.   _____   _____   _____

4. Harmony enters your room, drags herself to her seat, and puts her head down on her desk.   _____   _____   _____

5. A student has just handed in her homework late for the second time this week.   _____   _____   _____

6. Jessica has come up to you for the fourth time this morning complaining that her classmates are teasing her.   _____   _____   _____

7. You notice that the private reading area has been left a mess.   _____   _____   _____

8. Tanya keeps using obscene language in class, both to you and her classmates.   _____   _____   _____

9. A student is roaming around the room checking up on friends instead of doing the assignment.   _____   _____   _____

10. Juan has come in crying from recess for the third time this week.   _____   _____   _____

LEARNING PRACTICE TASK: IMMEDIATE OR DELAYED INTERVENTION EXERCISE

Activity Directions: Match each of the following situations or consequences with the most appropriate time to intervene. Use I for Immediate and D for Delayed.

_____ If student's behavior is likely to spiral

_____ If student may be embarrassed

_____ When lesson interruption may lead to group confusion

_____ If behavior may cause psychological damage to another student

_____ If there is potential for blaming innocent student(s)

_____ When student is too upset to be rational

_____ When teacher's inner comfort is violated

_____ If student's behavior can cause physical harm

_____ When student uses derogatory racial nickname

_____ When student's behavior disrupts class activity

Managing Surface Behavior

Many behavior problems can be controlled or circumvented by the use of instructional methods that take into consideration group dynamics, socialization needs, characteristics of the particular group, as well as individual learner characteristics. Effective instructional strategies give structure to the learning environment that prevents problems from occurring. When problems do occur, teachers need to clarify behavior expectations and assist students in acting in acceptable ways to prevent more serious problems from developing.

There are many times throughout the school day when disruptive behavior requires teacher intervention. Teachers need to have a variety of interventions at their fingertips in order to deal effectively with the inevitable, everyday minor disruptions, distractions, rule infractions, and off-task behaviors. Teachers need a repertoire, or a set of *surface management* techniques. Surface management techniques should serve several purposes. They should

1. Maintain the ongoing instructional program
2. Deter any minor student problem from becoming a major one
3. End disruptive behavior on the spot
4. Reduce student's stress
5. Maintain a positive student–teacher relationship, and
6. Be used before the teacher begins to harbor negative feelings

These techniques have also been referred to as *hurdle help* because they are designed to help students over rough spots, not as substitutes for well-planned instructional activities or as a total management plan. The goal is to provide situational assistance to help students cope with the instructional situation and stay on task or get back to the task. The term also connotes that these behaviors are normal and to be expected. Teachers need to have a systematic plan to deal with the many disruptive behaviors that routinely occur in the classroom, such as whispering, calling out, laughing, passing notes, doing other work, walking around, talking back, arguing, teasing, and name calling.

Surface management techniques are designed to deal with mild behavior difficulties that occur on a regular basis but have the potential to inhibit the smooth functioning of the classroom. Such overt student behavior needs to be addressed immediately, without regard (at the time) to underlying causes or motives. These techniques are meant to be short-term, surface-level strategies. The goals of surface management techniques are to effectively stop behaviors early before they escalate and to intervene in such a way that the teacher doesn't actually have to interrupt the lesson flow.

Techniques for Managing the Surface Behavior of Students.   The following techniques are designed to be used by teachers to maintain the surface behavior of students in the classroom. They are meant to be used in conjunction with a well-planned program based on the teacher's knowledge of each individual student's needs (Fagen & Hill, 1977).

Planned Ignoring. Much student behavior carries its own limited power and will soon exhaust itself if it is not fueled, especially if the behavior is done primarily to annoy the teacher. If it is not likely to spread to others, it is sometimes advisable for the teacher to ignore minor inappropriate behavior.

Signal Interference. Teachers use a variety of signals to communicate expected behavior to students. These nonverbal techniques include such things as eye contact, hand gestures, tapping or snapping fingers, coughing or clearing one's throat, frowns, and body postures. These techniques are usually most effective at the beginning stages of misbehavior.

Proximity Control. Merely standing near a student who is having difficulty can be effective. The teacher's presence serves as a source of comfort and protection and as a reminder for the student to control impulses. Standing close to a student is a gentle assertion of the teacher's authority.

Interest Boosting. If a student's interest in work is declining, and there are signs of boredom or restlessness, it may be helpful for the teacher to show an interest in the student. The teacher may engage the student in a conversation about a topic of interest. Stimulating the student's interest may provide the motivation to continue working and help the student view the teacher as a person who takes a personal interest.

Tension Decontamination through Humor. A funny comment is often able to defuse a tense situation. It makes everyone feel more comfortable.

Hurdle Help. Some students who experience difficulty with classroom assignments may seek help from the teacher or peers when appropriate. Other students skip over the difficulty and go on to work they can do. But some students stop working and don't know what to do next. They need to be able to overcome the obstacle that has them stopped. The teacher can be helpful in getting the student back on task by doing (or solving) the problem with the student, thus removing the hurdle and allowing the student to continue.

Restructuring the Classroom Program. Some teachers feel compelled to follow their class schedule rigidly. Other teachers are more flexible and sensitive to students' needs and concerns. Some middle ground seems most sensible. Discipline and structure are valuable, but not when they fly in the face of a general class need. Moderate restructuring based on affective as well as academic goals can be a very effective technique. Restructuring is appropriate when it is necessary to drain off high tension or emotion in the classroom. The technique is, as its name implies, simply a change of plan, format, task, or location based on a perceived need to drain off tension or high emotion in the classroom.

Direct Appeal to Values. A teacher can often appeal to a student's values when intervening in a problem situation. The teacher might

1. Appeal to the relationship of the teacher with the student, for example, *You seem angry with me. Have I been unfair with you?*

2. Appeal to reality consequences, for example, *I know you're angry, but if you break that aquarium, the fish will all die, and you'll have to replace it with your own money.*

3. Appeal to a student's need for peer approval, for example, *Your classmates will get pretty angry if you continue to interrupt them and correct them.*

4. Appeal to the student's sense of the teacher's power of authority, for example, Tell the student that as a teacher you cannot allow a behavior to continue, but that you still care about the student.

5. Appeal to the student's self-respect, for example, *I know you'll be upset with yourself if you tear up that paper you worked on all period.*

Removing Seductive Objects. It is difficult for the teacher to compete with certain objects. Sometimes removing seductive objects leads to power struggles. To avoid a power struggle, the teacher can take a strong interest in the object and politely ask to see it or handle it. Once in hand, the teacher has the option of returning it with a request for it to disappear for the remainder of the period or keeping it with a promise to return it at the end of the period.

Antiseptic Bounce. When a student's behavior has reached a point where the teacher questions whether or not the student will respond to verbal controls, it is best to ask the student to leave the room for a few minutes—perhaps to get a drink or deliver a message. In antiseptic bouncing, there is no intent to punish the student; the technique simply protects and helps the student and the group gain control over their feelings of anger, disappointment, or uncontrollable laughter. Unfortunately, many schools do not have a place the classroom teacher can send a student that the student will not think of as punishment.

Examples of Surface Management Techniques

PLANNED IGNORING
Several students enter the classroom acting very rowdy. I ignore their behavior at first. As soon as they settle down at their desks, I smile at them.

PROXIMITY CONTROL
During math class, Dennis frequently tries to distract others during independent work time. Today, when he begins poking the girl in front of him, I walk over and stand near her desk. He begins to work quietly.

TENSION DECONTAMINATION THROUGH HUMOR
Earlier we had made kites and now are flying them outside when one student's string breaks and his kite sails away. There is shocked silence, and I can see a face ready to cry. I quickly say, "Well, Ricky wins the High Flyer Award—he gets to choose the story this afternoon." Suddenly faces brighten, and there are no tears.

RESTRUCTURING THE CLASSROOM
During recess I overhear several students making unkind comments to a homeless person. During social studies class that day, we discuss the homeless situation in the United States. I have the students do research projects on the problem.

DIRECT APPEAL TO VALUE AREAS
One day Glen refuses to come to his small group when they are called together. I say, "Glen, the group will be pretty upset with you if you don't join us." He comes, joins in, and cooperates actively.

SIGNAL INTERFERENCE
Matt has very low self-esteem. Often he will belittle his own efforts. When he starts this behavior, I lower my glasses on my nose and gaze over them. He grins and usually stops his self-berating behavior.

INTEREST BOOSTING
Sammy daydreams a lot and is often quiet but off task. I've started talking to him for about 5 minutes each morning. He is now more interested in most class activities.

HURDLE HELP
Robin is having difficulty researching a social studies question. She is becoming frustrated and does not know what to do. I suggest a procedure for her to use and a place to look for the answer.

ANTISEPTIC BOUNCE
I have a student who often gets overly excited and becomes very loud. I sometimes find an excuse to send him out of the room to do an errand. When the student returns he is usually calmer.

REMOVING SEDUCTIVE OBJECTS
Anytime students bring objects from home to school, they have a basket (with their name) to put the object in until a designated time to share it with others.

LEARNING PRACTICE TASK: MANAGING SURFACE BEHAVIOR EXERCISE

Activity Directions, Part 1: Identify which of the following surface management strategies the examples below represent. In the space provided, write one of the ten strategies.

a. Planned ignoring
b. Signal interference

c. Proximity control
d. Interest boosting

e. Tension decontamination through humor
f. Restructuring the classroom program
g. Direct appeal to values

h. Removing seductive objects
i. Antiseptic bounce
j. Hurdle help

1. Change in plan, format, task, or location based on perceived need _____
2. Eye contact, snapping fingers, body posture _____
3. Seat student who often needs help close to teacher's desk _____
4. Have student leave room for a few minutes to defuse situation _____
5. Engage students in class discussion on an emotional incident that just occurred _____
6. Appraise student of reality consequences _____
7. Stand next to student who is having trouble _____
8. Show genuine interest in student's assignment _____
9. Gently touch student on shoulder _____
10. Engage student in conversation on a topic of interest to the student _____

Activity Directions, Part 2: For each of the following situations identify the appropriate surface management strategies.

SITUATION OR CHARACTERISTIC	STRATEGY
1. Does not embarrass student	_____
2. Used when student is frustrated by class assignment	_____
3. Used when behavior is likely to exhaust itself	_____
4. Does not identify student within the group	_____
5. Used when student shows signs of boredom, restlessness	_____
6. Used when behavior is not likely to spread	_____
7. Could be used to drain off tension	_____
8. Can use without interrupting classroom program	_____
9. Most effective at beginning stages of misbehavior	_____
10. Used not to punish but to protect student or help student get over the immediate situation	_____

ALTERNATIVES FOR MANAGING IN THE MULTICULTURAL CLASSROOM

Teachers have three major alternatives available to them. They can allow student behavior, intervene to try to change student behavior, or adapt the teaching–learning environment to accommodate students. Developing a personal management system involves three key decisions. A teacher will need to determine the following:

- What's allowed?
- For what student behaviors will I intervene?
- What accommodations are necessary to maintain a productive learning environment for all students?

Within each of these three primary alternatives there are three categories to consider, making a total of nine options available to the teacher. The following chart summarizes these.

Alternatives for Addressing Student Behavior

Allow	The teacher makes a conscious choice to allow the behavior.
	■ **Permit.** Allow behavior that is generally accepted for all class members.
	■ **Accept.** Accept unalterable aspects related to students' personality traits and cultural and social backgrounds.
	■ **Tolerate.** Tolerate behavior temporarily when students can't help themselves at the moment. Such situations include
	Learner's leeway—student is learning new concept or behavior
	Developmental stage—age-typical behavior likely to change as the student matures
	Illness, disability, or underdeveloped skill—behaviors students cannot control
	Situational stress or emotional state—behavior due to extenuating circumstances
Intervene	The situation requires that the teacher intervene and attempt to alter the situation.
	■ **Change.** Teach and model alternative behaviors.
	■ **Modify.** Deal with behavior without using authoritarian power or consequences.
	■ **Control.** Stop misbehavior for the moment by applying consequences.
Accommodate	The teacher takes primary responsibility for making adjustments to accommodate students' academic as well as emotional needs.
	■ **Adapt.** Make contextual and individual adaptations.
	■ **Support.** Provide personal and emotional support.
	■ **Prevent.** Develop procedures to avoid problems.

The following section delineates these alternatives in more detail.

Allow Behavior

Here the teacher makes a conscious choice to allow the behavior. This category includes permitting, tolerating, and accepting student behavior.

Permitting.   This is for behavior that is generally accepted for all members of the class. It includes specifying routine procedures, such as being able to get a drink, sharpen pencils, or get materials without teacher permission. Another example of permitting is having a specified policy in place, such as allowing students to go to the book corner after they complete their assignments.

Tolerating.   Tolerating problem behavior means accepting it temporarily. When teachers tolerate students' behavior problems, they may choose to allow students to misbehave, give up too soon, withdraw from the group, or pout or cry; they know that the students can't help themselves for the moment, so they tolerate the behavior temporarily. It might also be appropriate to tolerate misbehavior due to extenuating circumstances or the heat of the moment if students are unlikely to repeat the behavior. The following four conditions are situations in which toleration is warranted.

1. *Learner's leeway.* Whenever a student is learning a new concept, experimenting with ideas, or trying to win status in the group, the teacher expects that the student will make mistakes. Teachers often actually tell their students that they are not going to be upset when they err in trying to master new academic and social skills.

2. *Behavior that reflects a developmental stage.* Some behavior is age typical and will change as the student becomes more mature. Any attempts on the part of teachers to alter or inhibit this behavior will likely result in such negligible changes that it is usually not worth the inevitable fight.

For example,

- Students in the early grades are impulse ridden and motor oriented. Kindergarten teachers generally accept the fact that very little can be done about it except tolerate it. Such tolerance should not be confused with sanctioning it or permitting wild behavior.
- Students in the late third or early fourth grade, caught between group pressure and allegiance to the teacher, are notorious for tattling, for example, "Johnny pulled a leaf off your flower when you were in the hall."
- Other illustrations of age-typical behavior are the unscrubbed appearance of the preadolescent boy, the primping of sixth-grade girls, the secrets of preadolescent girls, and the sex language and behavior of adolescent boys.
- All adolescents sometimes feel the need to show their increasing autonomy and individuality to prove they can win with an adult, and this often leads to verbal confrontations. In their struggle to develop their own identities, they often reject adult characteristics. Such rejection may take the form of teasing or badmouthing, as in "Did you try to get your hair to look like that?" or "Did your mother pick out that dress for you?"

It's important to keep behaviors like these in developmental context and not participate in confrontations, because it is likely to make matters worse. A better response might be to poke fun at yourself to lessen the tension.

3. *Behavior that is symptomatic of an illness, disability, or undeveloped skill.* Behaviors that students engage in because they are incapable of doing otherwise will need to be tolerated. This is not to say that the teacher will not have to control some student behavior to prevent students from doing things that will harm themselves or others. Tolerance as well as control, when managing techniques don't work to stop harmful behavior, both may be necessary while the teacher tries to deal with the causes, not just the symptoms.

4. *Behavior that is related to situational stress.* This includes behavior that results from temporary stressors. These might include divorce, death or injury of a significant other or classmate, serious illness of a family member, or severing of an important relationship. Stressors might also be more fleeting emotional states resulting from a recent fight or conflict.

Accepting. When teachers accept the fact that students are who they are and have individual needs, teachers accommodate their demands, expectations, routines, and disciplinary techniques to the unalterable aspects of their students. This also includes adjusting their behavioral expectations to their students' culturally determined behavior patterns, as long as their behavior is not negatively affecting their learning or interfering with the rights of others.

Teachers also need to accept certain aspects of a student's personality, such as moodiness or temperament, again providing the particular behavior does not have a negative impact on the learning environment.

Accepting and Tolerating Compared. On the surface, accepting and tolerating look similar. In both cases teachers allow their students to behave in ways that sometimes differ from how the majority of students are expected to act. The difference is that teachers permanently accept the unchangeable aspects of their students' personalities or their cultural behavior patterns but tolerate only temporarily their alterable, yet presently problematic, behavior. For example, a teacher would choose to accept different discourse styles based on cultural background as a general code of conduct but only temporarily tolerate the moodiness of a student who lost a ring during lunch.

Intervene

When student behavior impinges on the rights of others, disrupts learning, or threatens the safety of the student or others, the teacher needs to intervene. Here the situation requires that the teacher use an intervention to attempt to alter the situation. This category includes changing, modifying, and controlling behavior.

Changing. These techniques aim to modify the attitudes, values, motives, beliefs, expectations, or the self-concepts of students, so that they won't have to behave in the same inappropriate way in given situations. Helping students develop coping and social skills are examples. Changing techniques require time, so the teacher may also pair these strategies with other short-term interventions. Changing techniques include teaching, modeling, and supporting students in learning alternative behaviors.

Modifying. The teacher attempts to modify a student's behavior, using means other than coercion. This involves managing students' behavior without resorting to consequences or using authoritarian power. Meeting the psychological needs of a student or responding to the communicative intent of the inappropriate behavior, rather than the symptom, also are included in this type of management.

Examples of this approach are diverting a student's attention, making a joke out of something a student might be taking too seriously, or speaking calmly to a student when the student is upset. Such techniques do not involve the use of consequences or direct control. Because changing students' behavior takes a considerable time commitment, teachers usually have to manage their students' behavior as well. Modifying refers to techniques that modify a situation enough to make it less likely that students will continue to exhibit inappropriate behavior. Modifying techniques aren't designed to change students, but to help students control their behavior. They may also be thought of as place holders, or strategies that do damage control or contain the situation. Strategies such as antiseptic bouncing, hurdle help, direct appeal to values, signal interference, and proximity control may also be used to modify behavior.

Controlling. Controlling management techniques involve using consequences and are concerned primarily with stopping inappropriate behavior. Teachers using consequences to manage students' behavior are using their power or authority. They reward students for behaving the way they want them to behave and punish them for behaving in inappropriate ways.

Intervening Techniques Compared. Controlling and modifying techniques handle misbehavior for the moment while changing techniques try to modify students' attitudes, motives, and self-concepts so they will not misbehave in the future. Convincing students likely to misbehave that they have to behave or they will be punished is an example of controlling students. Motivating students to want to behave appropriately is changing them. Ignoring the attention-seeking behavior of students who play the clown is modifying, whereas teaching them how to obtain attention in more acceptable ways is changing.

Accommodate

Here the teacher takes primary responsibility for making adjustments to accommodate students. The focus for change is primarily directed toward the instructional context. This may include adjusting expectations, procedures, or instructional format to accommodate individual differences in learning rate and style. Accommodations can be at the class level or the individual student level. This category includes preventing, supporting, and adapting.

Adapting. Both contextual and individual adaptations are included here. Some examples of adapting include defusing tension using humor, interest boosting, and restructuring the classroom program. At the individual student level, the teacher might adapt the length of a seatwork assignment without a break or an individual reading assignment to the shorter attention span of a student.

Supporting. Supporting techniques provide encouragement and emotional support for students. Here the intent is to provide personal support to help a student exercise self-control. It also includes a restorative aspect intended to restore positive relations.

Preventing. Preventing is proactive and involves developing classroom procedures that will avoid problems anticipated based on previous experience. Included here are planning for providing students with help when they are uncertain about assignments, and planning lesson flow and activities to accommodate different lengths of time needed for task completion.

Addressing Unproductive Student Behavior

Considering if, when, and how to intervene is a critical management decision. When deciding to intervene, you will need to address two fundamental questions:

- Will the intervention help the student learn better, not just eliminate the disruptive behavior?
- Will the intervention help the student learn a new way of behaving?

When you identify a student behavior as unacceptable, you have three variables to work with: yourself, the student, or the environment. You can choose to modify the student's behavior, the learning context, or your own response to the behavior. It is important to keep in mind that changing the student's behavior is not your only option and that combining modifying the student's behavior with changes in both your attitude and the learning environment is likely to produce maximum results.

Criteria for Assessing Your Intervention Pattern

Although there is no objective standard that can be applied to all interactions and responses to students and classroom situations, considering the following eight criteria can help you broaden your response options when addressing unproductive student behavior.

CRITERION	SELF-REFLECTIVE QUESTION
Escalating	Am I following a sequence beginning with an unobtrusive response and escalating progressively?
Respectful	Does my response maintain my dignity and treat students respectfully?
Contextual	Does my response take into account the effect of the instructional context and setting on the student's behavior?
Instructive	Do I provide students with guidance in accomplishing the desired behavior change?
Facilitative	Do I provide students with assistance in learning more appropriate ways to behave?
Reflective	Does my response consider how my reaction to the student may impact the student's behavior?
Responsive	Does my response consider that the student's behavior might be a reaction to a personal or academic need not having been met at the time?
Preventive	Does my response go beyond a single episode to anticipate and plan for the future?

To examine your typical responses to student misbehavior, it is important to reflect on the following questions.

Reflective Questions to Ask Yourself

- Did my response assist the student in assessing his or her own behavior?
- Did my response deescalate the student's behavior?
- Did my response allow an opportunity for the student to express thoughts or feelings?
- Did my response help the student develop a new strategy to use when a similar situation arises?
- Did the student leave the situation feeling supported and prepared to learn?
- Could I recommend that the student's parent(s) use a similar response?
- Would I want my supervisor to use a similar response regarding a behavior of mine that was a concern?

In deciding on an intervention, the teacher needs to weigh a range of contextual variables by considering the following questions.

Reflective Questions to Ask Yourself

- When a student misbehaves, am I thinking about how the student can be helped to learn better, or simply how the disruptive behavior can be eliminated?
- Is the intervention accompanied by a plan for the student to learn a new way of behaving?
- What types of student misbehavior can I control to a significant degree by restructuring expectations or classroom procedures?
- Do students have other ways of obtaining acceptance and recognition besides behaving appropriately?
- Is the intervention goal merely to gain the student's compliance for the moment?
- After an intervention, is the student typically angry? Passive–aggressive?
- After an intervention, does the student typically begin working again, or stop participating?
- Is the student–teacher relationship after an intervention enhanced, maintained, or eroded?
- Does the intervention help the student learn anything about his or her inappropriate behavior?

■ ■ ■ ■ ■ ■ ■ ■ ■

CRITICAL REFLECTION ON PRACTICE: ASSESSING YOUR INTERVENTION PATTERN

Activity Directions: Write several statements to describe each of the following aspects of your intervention pattern.

1. Behaviors that I choose to permit in my classroom:

_____

_____

_____

2. Behaviors that I consciously accept:

_____

_____

_____

3. Behaviors or situations that I decide to tolerate:

_____

_____

_____

4. I intervene in student behavior when:

_____

_____

_____

Working with a partner, compare and contrast your patterns. Then list some key similarities and differences.

SIMILARITIES   **DIFFERENCES**

_____   _____

_____   _____

_____   _____

REFLECTIVE QUESTION
Based on this exercise, what question(s) about your intervention patterns do you need to ask yourself?

INTERVENTION ESCALATION

To help build student autonomy, teachers need to give students more opportunities to manage their own behavior. When problems occur, teachers use intervention strategies that focus not on what they need to do *to* students, but rather on what they can do *for* students to help them make better choices. The following section describes ways teachers can intervene to deal with student behavior that is problematic and unproductive by supporting students in using self-control.

The idea of intervention escalation is to move systematically, sequentially, and progressively up the ladder of escalation. As shown in Figure 2.1, there are three

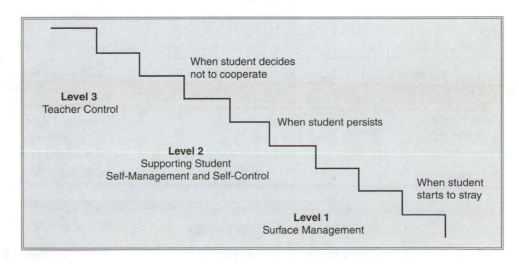

When student decides
not to cooperate

Level 3
Teacher Control

When student persists

Level 2
Supporting Student
Self-Management and Self-Control

When student
starts to stray

Level 1
Surface Management

FIGURE 2.1   Intervention Escalation: Moving Up the Staircase

levels of intervention at a teacher's disposal. Without specific intent to promote student self-management and self-control, teachers often move very quickly up the intervention ladder. Many teachers virtually skip Level 2 interventions, those most critical to helping students develop self-management. You should have several intervention options in your repertoire at each level. Your escalation pattern needs to strike a balance between moving too slowly, failing to assert your expectations, and moving too rapidly, not allowing students an opportunity to regulate their behavior on their own.

INTERVENTION ESCALATION CHARACTERISTICS	INTERVENTION OPTIONS	
Level 1 Interventions	*When student starts to stray*	
Maintain the lesson flow Deter a minor problem from escalating into a major one Are used before the teacher begins to harbor negative feelings	Planned ignoring Signal interference Touch State positive expectation Brief directive	Eye contact Proximity control Task engagement feedback Provide rationale Antiseptic bounce
Level 2 Interventions	*When student persists*	
Reduce student anxiety Keep students working productively Address motive underlying the misbehavior	Invite cooperation Express your needs I statement Simple request Request that student change behavior Ask what student needs Ask student to empathize with others' feelings Quiet correction Enlist group feedback Redirect with humor Provide hurdle help Acknowledge student's challenge Offer incentive Gentle reminder	Statement of value State your disappointment Impact statement Direct appeal to values Request that student make a better choice Ask student to make value judgment Ask student to consider others' needs Redirect by asking for help Redirect by restructuring task Provide personal support Accept student's feelings Appeal to future reward Suggest better alternative Rule reminder
Level 3 Interventions	*When student decides not to cooperate*	
Maintain positive relationship, restore if necessary Create window of opportunity Allow students to save face	Reminder of consequence Ask student to make choice Warning Thinking time Isolation Logical consequence Send to office Limited time suspension	Give range of choices Give either/or choice Separation Student conference Restoration In-school suspension Suspension

Intervention Escalation Levels

Listed previously are many types of interventions for dealing with student behavior as it becomes more serious. By intent, the list of options at Level 2 is the longest.

This is because supporting students in making a better choice is a core belief driving this approach to classroom management.

■ ■ ■ ■ ■ ■ ■ ■ ■ ■

LEARNING PRACTICE TASK: DEVELOPING YOUR LADDER OF ESCALATION

Activity Directions: Develop your own ladder of escalation by planning 10 steps of progressive escalation.

Step 1: _____

Step 2: _____

Step 3: _____

Step 4: _____

Step 5: _____

Step 6: _____

Step 7: _____

Step 8: _____

Step 9: _____

Step 10: _____

REFLECTIVE QUESTION

How do you want to expand your intervention options?

Student–Teacher Classroom Interaction Patterns: Are They Equitable?

Many teachers think that they treat all of their students the same. They think that they do not exhibit any favoritism. However, research has shown that the quality of student–teacher interactions sometimes contradicts the idea that all students are treated the same.

Research indicates that teachers tend to have more interactions relating to classroom behavior with low-achieving students and fewer interactions regarding learning activities. Consider the following questions and ask yourself whether you engage in any of these behaviors.

Reflective Questions to Ask Yourself

- Do you ask some students to analyze, synthesize, and evaluate answers to your questions whereas you ask others nonstimulating fact-type questions?
- Do you give students time to think about a question before expecting an answer, or do you ask the question and then move quickly to another student because you think that the first student will not be able to answer correctly?
- Do you give some students more encouragement or assistance after you have called on them?
- Do you merely give some students the answer to the question?
- Do you give briefer and less informational replies to questions to some students?
- Do you probe for deeper meaning behind only certain students' responses?
- Do you fail to tell some students their answer is incorrect?
- Do you actually praise some students for answers that aren't correct?
- Do you avoid eye contact with some students?

- Do you accept student answers to open-ended questions without judgment, or do you question the novel or nontraditional responses?
- Do you interact with the same students most of the time?
- Do you expect, tolerate, or demand different behavior from male students than you do from female students? If so, are these different standards justified?

Promoting Acceptance of Students from All Cultural and Social Backgrounds in Your Classroom

In order to ensure equity, you will need to be proactive in your planning of classroom practices and teaching–learning structures.

Reflective Questions to Ask Yourself

- During group work, do you ensure that students from different cultural and social backgrounds have the same responsibilities and duties as other students?
- What do you do to ensure that students from different backgrounds will participate in group work?
- What strategies do you use to raise the academic image of students from different cultures in the eyes of all students?
- What strategies do you use to bridge the gap between a student's culture and school?
- What strategies do you use that incorporate the cultural background and community of students?
- What resources, individual or group, from the community have you brought to class?
- Do your bulletin boards and overall classroom appearance reflect the culture(s) of your students' backgrounds?
- What methods do you use to enhance the self-esteem of students from different cultures?
- Do you try to accommodate the family structure of students from different social and cultural backgrounds?
- Have you considered the family discipline style of students from different cultural backgrounds in your management plan?
- Do you differentiate between behavior that is culturally based and behavior that is not? Do you respond accordingly?
- Are the behavior problems you identify more often attributed to one group?
- Have you considered the values of your students and their cultural backgrounds in setting standards? Are your behavioral standards in conflict with theirs?

■ ■ ■ ■ ■ ■ ■ ■

CRITICAL REFLECTION ON PRACTICE: ASSESSING YOUR INTERACTION PATTERN

Activity Directions: Follow the steps below.

1. Record the names of students called on during a period or for an entire day.

2. Then calculate the percentage of your students you called on. _____

3. What do the data tell you? Do you see a pattern?

_____

_____

_____

4. On another day, record all the names of students you interact with for inappropriate behavior.

5. Then calculate the percentage. _____

6. Compare these two lists. What does the comparison reveal?

_____

_____

_____

REFLECTIVE QUESTION
Is there anything you want to change about your interaction pattern?

Enhancing Student Status within Groups in the Classroom

Individual students have status within groups in the classroom (Cohen, 1994, 1998). This status can be related to gender, ethnicity, race, color, social class, knowledge, perceived ability, peer group membership, personality characteristics, or physical attributes. Such status can be a function of role status such as leader, clown, or bully. Status can also be inadvertently, covertly, or overtly *assigned* to certain students on the basis of gender, social status, or cultural background. Or that status might be a function of group members' attitudes about others' potential to contribute meaningfully to the learning task on the basis of their assessment of perceived ability or achievement level.

Carefully observing how students interact during assigned group learning tasks can furnish teachers with valuable information. Systematic observation provides a way to assess interaction patterns that could reveal biases that serve to impede some students' opportunities to learn. Such data can help teachers assess whether they need to intervene with a structure that offers greater potential for fair and just treatment of all members of the class, regardless of status or ability. This may involve teaching communication skills, developing problem-solving strategies, or creating awareness of inequities.

By proactively identifying students who are relegated to low status, teachers have the opportunity to restructure group norms to improve the status of these students. Low-status students could be ridiculed, ostracized, criticized, or ignored by other students. In the multicultural classroom, it is essential that teachers have a way to monitor interaction patterns and intervene when necessary to ensure unbiased treatment and opportunity to learn.

Assessing Interaction Patterns: The Moon Problem Exercise. The following structured experience developed by Hall (1971) is being used here as an attempt to simulate experiences your students may have during group learning tasks. The purpose of the exercise is to disclose how role perceptions are always operating in any group setting.

Guidelines for the Moon Problem Exercise
- It is not necessary to complete the exercise. The purpose of this activity is to provide a simulation for observing behavior during a problem-solving task.
- The participants should interact as naturally as possible.
- The observer should keep the focus of the feedback on the interaction and give objective, nonjudgmental feedback.

■ ■ ■ ■ ■ ■ ■ ■

LEARNING PRACTICE TASK: THE MOON PROBLEM EXERCISE

Activity Directions: You will be working in groups of five to seven for this activity.

1. Select one member to serve as an observer of the process. The observer will record information on the interaction pattern among the group members. After the structured activity, the observer will give specific feedback using the following questions to guide their observations and subsequent feedback to the group.
   - Who initiates the ideas?
   - Who complies with the ideas?
   - Who verbalizes the most in the activity?
   - Who controls the situation in the activity?
   - Who is silenced by other group members?
   - What do the physical movements tell you about the interaction?
   - What does other nonverbal behavior tell you about the interaction?
2. Once the groups and the observers have been established, engage in the activity for approximately 15 minutes.
3. Have the observers give feedback based on the specific behaviors they observed.

Note. Although the focus of the activity was the process, not the answers, the participants will most likely be curious about the right answers; hence the NASA solution is included.

■ ■ ■ ■ ■ ■ ■ ■

THE MOON PROBLEM EXERCISE

You are a member of a spaceship crew originally scheduled to rendezvous with a mother ship on the lighted surface of the moon. Due to mechanical difficulties, however, your ship was forced to land at a spot some 200 miles from the rendezvous point. During reentry and landing, much of the equipment aboard was damaged, and because survival depends on reaching the mother ship, the most critical items available must be chosen for the 200-mile trek.

Below are listed 15 items left intact and undamaged after landing. Your task is to rank them in terms of importance in allowing your crew to reach the rendezvous point. Place number 1 by the most important item, number 2 by the second most important, and so on through number 15, the least important.

UNDAMAGED EQUIPMENT	RANKING IMPORTANCE
Box of matches	_____
Food concentrate	_____
Fifty feet of nylon rope	_____
Parachute silk	_____
Portable heating unit	_____
Two .45 caliber pistols	_____
One case dehydrated milk	_____
Two 100-pound tanks of oxygen	_____
Stellar map (of the moon's constellations)	_____
Life raft	_____
Magnetic compass	_____
Five gallons of water	_____

Signal flares   ———
First-aid kit including needles   ———
Solar-powered FM receiver/transmitter   ———

There are no right or wrong answers to this exercise.

NASA SOLUTION TO THE MOON PROBLEM EXERCISE
This is the order in which these items have been ranked by NASA. Remember, there are no right or wrong answers. What is important is why you decided to rank the items the way you did.

1. Two 100-pound tanks of oxygen	*Fills respiration requirement*
2. Five gallons of water	*Replenishes loss by sweating, etc.*
3. Stellar map (of the moon's constellations)	*One of principal means of finding directions*
4. Food concentrate	*Supply daily food required*
5. Solar-powered FM receiver/transmitter	*Distress signal transmitter, possible communication*
6. Fifty feet of nylon rope	*Useful in tying injured together, help in climbing*
7. First-aid kit including needles	*Oral pills or injection medicine valuable*
8. Parachute silk	*Shelter against sun's rays*
9. Life raft	*CO_2 bottles for self propulsion across chasms, etc.*
10. Signal flares	*Distress call when line of sight possible*
11. Two .45 caliber pistols	*Self-propulsion devices could be made from them*
12. One case dehydrated milk	*Food, mixed with water for drinking*
13. Portable heating unit	*Useful only if party landed on dark side*
14. Magnetic compass	*Probably no magnetized poles, thus useless*
15. Box of matches	*Little or no use on the moon*

Using Structured Exercises with Students. This is an excellent activity in which to engage students to watch their interaction patterns. For this and similar activities, varying group composition will allow teachers to observe interaction patterns among many different combinations of gender, ethnicity, and ability during the group process. Systematic observation in such settings can provide teachers with valuable insight.

This exercise or similar activities can be used by teachers to assess how students in their classroom, especially those from different backgrounds, engage in group problem-solving tasks. Teachers can also use similar activities to gauge the social interaction between students from different cultural and social backgrounds and other students in group academic tasks. Activities like these can also help teachers identify an individual student's status within the group. Once low-status students are identified, the teacher can make concerted attempts to provide structures that will help enhance the status of these students. Some potential interventions and general strategies teachers can use include the following:

- Teach problem-solving strategies to limit decision making by power, status, aggression, and so forth.
- Give low-status students specific responsibilities.
- Assign roles to low-status students that will necessitate interacting with all students in the group.
- Provide task directions that call for all students to make contributions.
- Engage low-status students in learning activities in which they can exhibit or demonstrate their strengths or expertise.

Building a Democratic Learning Community

Developing the classroom as a learning community calls for teachers to attend to students' emotional and social needs concurrently with their academic needs. In such a teaching and learning climate, emphasis is placed on the quality of human interactions, both between teacher and student and student to student. Creating a classroom environment that breeds mutual tolerance and respect is the foundation for a caring learning community. Creating a classroom climate that honors participation, equity, and inclusiveness is the foundation for a democratic community.

COMMUNITY BUILDING IN SCHOOLS

Several arenas converged to give impetus to the concept of creating the school as a community of learners. Those include

- The effective schools research
- The concept of emotional intelligence (EQ) popularized by Goleman (1995)
- The demise of the traditional family support structure
- Increase in violence and alienation among youth
- A growing literature base on the importance of caring

All these avenues converge in support of the necessity to pay attention to the emotional, social, and psychological development of students. This belief guides the focus of this book.

The aspect of community with the greatest potential for achievement through a teacher's actions is that of *classroom as community*. The level of networking with the community to achieve a sense of community at the school level requires a community wide effort, clearly beyond the individual efforts of a single teacher. Hence, the focus here is on developing the classroom as community and the characteristics that need to be in place so that students develop a sense of belonging as a member of that community. At the heart of community is the principle that the people are as important as any information to be learned or techniques to be used.

Research Findings on the School as Community

The recent surge in popularity in the education literature for establishing the school as community grew out of several bodies of research, the major one being the effective schools research of the 1970s and 1980s. This line of research identified characteristics of schools that were considered effective primarily on the basis of achievement at the school level. From this literature base, a composite of desirable outcomes emerged to shape the concept of school as community (Purkey & Smith,

1983; Rowan, 1990), typically including mutually shared values, a common agenda highlighting academic standards, and emotional connections. This latter dimension was clearly related to the quality of interpersonal relationships and came to be labeled an *ethic of caring* (Grant, 1988; Halliger & Murphy, 1986; Lightfoot, 1984; Sizer, 1984). The concept of shared values and shared responsibility has come to be framed as a *democratic community.* The term caring, democratic community is used here to connote a merging of these two concepts.

Extending the concepts that were derived from this research, the next generation of research literature on the school as community sought to identify specific variables that contribute to a sense of community. In order to capture the key concepts that have emerged, the following chart summarizes the attempts to determine specific variables that contribute to the concept of community.

Identified Factors Defining Community

McMILLAN & CHAVIS (1986)	SERGIOVANNI (1994)	MEIER (1995)	BOYER (1995)	BRYK & DRISCOLL (1988)	BATTISTICH ET AL. (1995)
Sense of Community	**Democratic Community**	**Democratic Community**	**Community for Learning**	**Community Index**	**Democratic Community**
Influence	Democratic	Democratic, respect	Self-discipline, respect		Autonomy
Emotional connection/ membership	Caring	Trust, collaboration	Caring	Caring	Belonging
	Shared values, common purpose	Shared values	Shared purpose	Shared values	
		High standards for intellectual development	Curriculum coherence	Common agenda	Competence
Fulfillment of needs					

Utilizing the concept of sense of community, McMillan and Chavis (1986) and Sergiovanni (1994) synthesized existing research; each described several components of sense of community. Based on empirical research (correlational studies reanalyzing existing data), Battistich, Solomon, Kim, Watson, and Schaps (1995), and Bryk and Driscoll (1988) identified three clusters. Boyer (1995) and Meier (1995) operationalized the research literature to develop school-based models built on the concept of the school as a caring, democratic community.

As can be seen in the chart, four factors were common to several of these composite definitions for community. Two factors are at the student level: (1) a positive, caring, and connected relationship with others, and (2) the ability to influence their environment by both having an influence on and accepting group norms and values (achieved principally through being able to exercise choices, autonomy, and self-discipline). The consistency of the presence of these factors gives further momentum to the critical elements of bonding relationships (identified by all six of the data sources) and a democratic community that is based on mutual participation, responsibility, and acceptance of group norms (identified by five of the six data sources). The other two factors are at the school level: (1) mutually derived purpose, values, and curriculum agenda, and (2) high academic standards. Each of these factors was identified by four of the six sources.

The research findings indicate that community variables are usually related to affective outcomes assessed by attitudinal responses of teachers and students, but not necessarily to achievement outcomes. Only Bryk and Driscoll (1988) specifically identified academic achievement performance as a documented outcome; they found students achieved higher math scores when community variables were present. However, those who advocate for a caring community see caring as a goal in itself, not a means to an end.

Additionally, the general finding of the effective schools research was that a cluster of variables was more related to outcomes than a single aspect. This finding has evolved into the term *democratic community* being used as an all-encompassing term, merging the ideas of shared values, belonging, autonomy, and competence.

The School as Caring Community

The literature on the school as a caring community calls for equal status for caring and nurturing with other educational agendas (Beck, 1994; Boyer, 1995; Noddings, 1992; Sergiovanni, 1992). This literature is primarily philosophy based and espouses that teaching students to care is a primary goal, not just a means for accomplishing other academic goals. They espouse Dewey's (1938/1963) notion that school is *about life,* not preparation for life.

Some advocate that the school be designed to function as surrogate family, based on the underlying assumption that students today have fragmented home lives and require greater nurturance in the school setting. Because of the disconnectedness of the lives of many children outside of school and the lack of stable family relationships, many educators are advocating that the schools create a community within the school itself (Noddings, 1992; Sergiovanni, 1992, 1994). Recognizing the paucity of social, psychological, and emotional support systems available for many youth, they advocate that schools provide some of that missing support.

In addressing the concept of school as a caring community, authors emphasize the importance of emotional connections for schools to be successful with today's student population. They describe relationships within the school community as personal, committed, and familial. They also stress the importance of forging shared values and providing a sense of security and identity to both teachers and students (McLaughlin, 1991, 1993). Underlying the concept of school as a caring community is a commitment to shared values and relationships that foster interdependence. Others urge that school staffs redefine colleagueship in order to evolve into a professional community (Johnson, 1990; Sergiovanni, 1994). A professional community strives toward an ideal that includes exemplary practices in an atmosphere of friendship and caring.

With the traditional family structure and access to extended family waning, some educators are calling for schools to support families in meeting these needs by taking a more active role in nurturing students. They advocate that schools must become more nurturing places to better serve the emotional as well as the academic needs of students (Goodlad, 1990; Lieberman & Miller, 1984; Martin, 1992; McLaughlin & Talbert, 1990; Sergiovanni, 1994).

When one defines community as an organization committed to shared values and relationships that foster interdependence, such relationships, based on mutual commitments, render much traditional management and control tactics moot. Utilizing family as the metaphor for management, the terms *classroom management* and *discipline* don't begin to capture the teacher–student relationship. A relationship of family with shared responsibilities calls for the teacher to guide students; to facilitate their development; and to connect, confer, and collaborate with students.

As Bullough (1994) aptly states, when the focus is on building caring relationships, teachers participate with students "in their journey to make the world their own."

This line of research corresponds with those educators who take a more psychological stance for defining the goals of schooling by suggesting that the school provide for the basic needs of all human beings (Brendtro, Brokenleg, & Van Bockern, 1990; Dreikurs, Grunbwald, & Pepper, 1982; Erikson, 1980, 1991; Glasser, 1986; Rogers, 1969; Rogers & Freiberg, 1994). A fundamental need common to all models of healthy psychological development is the need to belong. Moreover, they suggest that the school should try to compensate for the devastating and debilitating effects of abuse, neglect, rejection, abandonment, and other psychological deprivation caused by lack of appropriate bonding at the early stages of development.

As Goleman (1995) pointed out, success in life is only partially attributed to intellectual capacity. Emotional intelligence is just as important. Being able to persist in the face of disappointment, handle frustration, control the desire for immediate gratification, and empathize and get along with others are also critical factors in one's success.

What Research Says about Student Resiliency

Another branch of related literature is that of students who are resilient. When students are resilient they develop a set of attributes that provide them with the strength and fortitude to confront the overwhelming obstacles they face in their life. Resilient students have the ability to rebound or recover from adversities that might have caused serious debilitating effects.

The literature on resilient children, those who thrive in spite of potentially devastating experiences, shows that what frequently makes the difference is one caring adult who gets involved in their lives; often that person is a teacher. This literature asserts that a sense of connectedness that comes from establishing the school as a caring community, even if direct links to academic performance can't be drawn, is important in itself because teachers have the proven potential to be the primary impetus and support for turning a child's life around.

Studying Asian American children living in adverse home conditions who were resilient and became successful adults, Werner and Smith (1992) found that these children most frequently mentioned a teacher as the person who really made a difference for them. Moskovitz (1983), studying Nazi concentration camp survivors, found that they attributed their resilience to their connection with warm, caring, and encouraging teachers. Another study identified a teacher as the primary source in helping children from a disadvantaged, urban neighborhood to overcome adversity and become successful adults (Pederson, Faucher, & Eaton, 1978).

Even when children grow up in the worst circumstances, some are able to thrive. What makes children resilient in the face of tremendous odds is often the dedicated commitment of a teacher. Teachers are consistently credited as significant protective factors in ameliorating the response to high risk factors and stressful life circumstances (Boyer, 1983; Cicchetti, 1989; Garmezy, 1984; Hawkins, Catalano, & Miller, 1992; Lynch & Cicchetti, 1992; Masten & Garmezy, 1985; O'Donnell, Hawkins, Catalano, Abbott, & Day, 1995; Werner, 1990; Zimrin, 1986). Caring teachers can be a child's salvation against all odds (Gootman, 2001).

HOW TEACHERS CREATE A SENSE OF COMMUNITY

Although the need for teachers to assume a role in meeting the social and emotional needs of children is clear, the form that role may take is less clear. After all, teachers are not parents, social workers, therapists, or counselors (Deiro, 1996).

Clearly, there are alternative paths to creating a classroom culture for emotional support and comfort.

Outstanding teachers who have significant impact on the lives of children and youth and are able to develop healthy bonds with students do so without necessarily becoming intimate, affectionate, or indulgent (Deiro, 1996; Gootman, 2001; Ladson-Billings, 1995). Teachers with very different personalities and with very different teaching styles can find ways to create a sense of community among their students. Research findings dispel three common myths related to being a caring teacher. The first is that caring is gender specific, based on the assumption that women are more effective nurturers than men. This has not been found to be the case, especially in Deiro's (1996) study. The second myth is that developing caring connections requires that the teacher touch students and show overt affection. Teachers need not be sweet, affectionate, or gentle; they can also be firm and professionally detached yet still be nurturing. The third misconception is that nurturing is synonymous with permissiveness. Caring is often associated with leniency and indulgence, even weakness, but those studying teachers who are able to make a difference in students' lives by making healthy connections often describe teachers as strict disciplinarians.

What emerges as the critical variable is treating students with dignity and respect. And there are diverse ways teachers can do this. Depicting caring and respect means listening to students, engaging in dialogue with them, showing interest in them, soliciting their opinions, valuing their ideas, and demonstrating a belief that they are capable. What is critical is that students perceive the teacher as caring; and that perception is created by a communication style that is respectful. (The next chapter provides some specific strategies for effective communication that is respectful.)

Deiro (1996) studied teachers who were able to build close and trusting connections to students. The teachers she studied were selected on the basis of having both excellent reputations among peers, students, and staff as teachers who develop caring connections with students and, simultaneously, having expert reputations for their ability to teach and expertise for their subject area. This set of criteria was used to ensure that the selected teachers nurture students in ways that do not compromise their primary teaching responsibility. The strategies listed below were derived from this qualitative study.

Create one-to-one time with students. These teachers remain accessible to students before and after school, between classes, during extracurricular activities, or during class periods by using a delivery style that maximizes individual or small-group contact.

Use appropriate self-disclosure. These nurturing teachers disclose personal information about themselves that is pertinent to the needs of the students while exercising discretion about what information to share.

Have high expectations of students while simultaneously conveying a belief in their capacities. These teachers establish and maintain high academic standards for their students while communicating a belief in their students' capacity to meet these expectations.

Network with parents, family members, friends, and neighbors of students. By creating intergenerational networks, they establish a common ground with common histories on which to build healthy connections.

Build a sense of community among students within the classroom. They encourage students to take risks in the classroom, make honest disclosures, and share personal information with classmates.

Use rituals and traditions within the classrooms. By developing rituals and traditions in which everyone participates, they help to build a sense of community by fostering a feeling of comfort and belonging.

Although these strategies are not the only role-appropriate methods for developing bonds with students, they represent a variety of ways secondary teachers, without compromising their primary responsibility for the cognitive development of students, bond successfully with them.

LEARNING PRACTICE TASK: WHAT CREATES A SENSE OF COMMUNITY?

Activity Directions: Working in groups of three to five, list characteristics that would make a group (e.g., family, school, neighborhood, or church) a "community." List specific factors that would have to be in place to create a sense of community.

1. _____   6. _____
2. _____   7. _____
3. _____   8. _____
4. _____   9. _____
5. _____   10. _____

DEVELOPING RITUALS AND TRADITIONS FOR COMMUNITY BUILDING

Rituals and traditions provide a familiar routine and create a common experience and serve to enhance teachers' connections with students. They may be incorporated into learning activities or used as noncurricular activities. Rituals are activities that are done the same way each time, such as having the last 10 minutes of every class period on Friday reserved for open discussion or beginning a social studies class with a current event introduced by a student. Traditions are customs, practices, or special events that are routinely acknowledged and honored, although they need not be honored the same way each time. In fact, by design they may be celebrated differently each time. Below are some examples of rituals teachers may establish.

As a daily ritual, one teacher at the beginning of her classes reads or has a student read a one-minute message from an inspirational reader. They read different messages about life, hope, and all kinds of human experiences, providing food for thought.

A junior high school teacher has her students periodically stand and yell at the end of class what she calls the PMA (positive mental attitude) cheer. When she asks them how their positive mental attitude is today, they answer: "Happy, healthy, feel fantastic, boy are we enthusiastic!"

To let students know it's okay to talk about their feelings and what's important to them, and to encourage them to talk about what's happening in their lives, one teacher saves time at the beginning or at the end of the week for talking about topics unrelated to the class focus, such as movies or current events in the news.

Such small rituals, in which everyone participates, help teachers develop close connections with students. A ritual teachers may want to institute is one that ends each day or class period on a positive note.

By finding opportunities to follow rituals and traditions and create special events and celebrations, teachers develop cultural norms that support community. When teachers help students learn the value of supporting one another in their trials and tribulations, they convey the notion that everyone has something worthwhile to say and reinforce the values of dignity and respect.

Teachers should create rituals that align with their teaching goals and subject area, while highlighting values they want their students to develop. A tradition already in place at the school can be adapted to fit a particular teacher interest or goal. Below are some examples.

Developing the Habit of Questioning

Asking questions encourages students to think beyond their own self-interest, consider the implications of their ideas and actions on others, and apply standards of fairness and justice.

- How would this action help, hurt, or affect others?
- Would this action help make the world a better place?
- How would you feel if you were on the other side?
- Is this just a matter of personal choice, or is it a question of right or wrong?

Creating the Ritual of "Calling the Circle"

This is a ritual that calls students together for the purpose of creating a safe haven for students to voluntarily express both negative and positive emotional experiences. They may express anger and frustration as well as joy and appreciation. Students are taught to honor the circle as a special time and space by doing a simple ritual to mark the beginning and end of the circle time. That simple ritual might be holding hands, taking several deep breaths, or reading a selection from a book or a poem.

The use of an object such as a talking stick or rock can also be incorporated during this time, so that everyone who wishes to can speak and be heard without interruption. The object is taken by the person who wishes to speak. The person holding the object speaks without interruption and then returns the object to the center when finished speaking.

The teacher may also want to create a saying that students can recite before the circle begins, for example, "We're here to listen thoughtfully to what each other has to say."

Morning Announcements

Some examples of morning announcement rituals include

- Acknowledging students who have demonstrated respect, thoughtfulness, authenticity, or emotional integrity
- Reciting a cheer or pledge that the class has created
- Telling a story or reading a poem, newspaper, or magazine article that delivers an important message
- Having a moment of silent reflection, unstructured or directed, to reflect on something in particular
- Having a daily quote containing a thought-provoking or inspiring message
- Thanking anyone for a kind deed
- Having a good news/bad news format
- Having a selected student deliver quote or thought-of-the-day

Schoolwide Opportunities for Rituals, Ceremonies, and Traditions

There are also many schoolwide opportunities for promoting community values with rituals, ceremonies, and traditions. Some of those include

- Awards ceremonies
- Appreciation days for support staff, teachers, and others
- Awareness days or weeks
- Value of the week or month
- Service days

Creating Community Spirit

Kirschenbaum (1995) offers some ideas for teachers to teach their students values that are also useful for building a community spirit. Some of these suggestions are listed below.

Appreciation time.   Daily or weekly ritual time for sharing appreciations. This is a time for students to appreciate one another, the teacher to appreciate students, and for students to appreciate the teacher for things done or said. Initially, teachers can provide a "sentence stem" to help students develop the habit and keep focused, such as

- "I appreciate . . . "
- "I feel really good when . . . "
- "The most helpful thing someone did for me this week was . . . "

Opinion time.   Set aside a particular time each week for the ritual of students speaking out on current topics. The teacher can make a greater ceremony by setting up a lectern. During this time any student may come up to the lectern and deliver an opinion or editorial on any topic they choose, or it can be confined to a particular topic area. This ritual inculcates the values of independent thought and respect for others' views.

Open forum.   Create a forum

- Where students listen to each other's dilemma and provide feedback
- Where students listen to each other without feedback
- Where students discuss events in their lives
- Where students talk about a specified question such as
  What's your favorite hobby?
  What do you do when you're feeling down?

Song.   At lower grade levels, teachers can have the tradition of the class singing a song at the beginning or end or at a regular time during the school day. These songs can have a particular theme to highlight a value area, such as friendship, helping others, family, or making the world better. This ritual can contribute to caring and cohesiveness of the class.

Applause.   Student applause or other nonverbal expressions of appreciation for designated things, such as when a student volunteers to do something less than desirable, performs a service to the class, or accomplishes a difficult task. By creating this type of ritual, students know that when they extend themselves, their classmates will be appreciative.

ACTIVITIES TO BUILD COMMUNITY AMONG STUDENTS

To build community, it is important to create opportunities for students to learn about one another and to discover the ways in which they are similar and different. Weinstein and Mignano (2003) offer the following suggestions.

- Have students create personalized CD covers with a title, an illustration, and twelve song titles that tell something important about themselves.

- Have students pair up and interview each other with a set of questions that the class has formulated. After the students have interviewed their partners, they introduce each other to the class. Then they write up their interviews, affix them to photographs that the teacher takes of each child, and post them on a bulletin board.
- Read *The Important Book* (1949) by Margaret Wise Brown. Then have each child make a banner proclaiming what is important about himself or herself and what is *most* important (e.g., "The important things about Juanita are that she loves to read, she can speak Spanish, she likes to skate, and she loves pizza. But *the most important thing is* that she loves to read").

Sapon-Shevin (1995) suggests the activity Find Someone Who, in which students must find one person in the class who fits a specific description (e.g., someone who has the same favorite television show or someone who went to Disney World this summer). This activity can be enhanced by including items related to race, cultural and linguistic background, or to disability and soliciting information in addition to a name. Some examples are

Find someone who grew up with an older relative. What's one thing that person learned from the older relative?

Find someone whose parents come from another country. What's one tradition or custom that person has learned from his or her parents?

Find someone who has a family member with a disability. What's something that person has learned about the person with a disability?

Sapon-Shevin (1999) describes several activities for students to disclose information about themselves.

Two Truths and a Lie (or Two Facts and a Fiction). Have students write down and then share three statements about themselves, two of which are true and one of which is a lie. For example, the teacher might write, "I once played the princess in *Once upon a Mattress*, and one night during a performance I fell from the top of fifteen mattresses and herniated a disk in my back," "I won third prize in the All-Alaska Logging Championship for the rolling pin toss," and "I trekked through Nepal on my honeymoon." Students guess which one is the lie, and then the teacher tells the truth. The activity can be done as a whole class or in small groups. In either case, because the activity allows students to select what to disclose about themselves, there is little chance of embarrassment. It also provides opportunities for students to discover common interests and experiences and to test assumptions and stereotypes.

Little-Known Facts about Me. Students write a statement about themselves that they think others won't know. The papers are folded, collected, and put in a box. Students take turns drawing a paper and reading the statement aloud. Everyone guesses who wrote the little-known fact.

Lifelines. Each student draws a line on a piece of paper and then marks six to ten points representing important events in their lives that they are willing to share (e.g., the birth of a sibling, the time they starred in the school play, when they moved to this school). Students then get into pairs and share their life stories. Members of each pair could also introduce each other to the rest of the class, referring to points on the lifeline.

Activities to Enhance Peer Acquaintance

It is important for teachers to engage students in peer-acquaintance activities at the beginning of the year to help develop a sense of security and become more actively engaged in learning tasks. In the following section, several such activities recommended by Jones and Jones (2004) are described.

Name Chain.   A name chain is an effective method for helping students learn each other's names. The following steps can make this activity run smoothly.

1. Have small groups of students sit in a circle.
2. Explain to students that each person will be asked to say his or her first name and tell the group one thing about himself or herself. For example, the student may tell the group something the student likes to do or something interesting that happened recently. Tell them that they will be asked to repeat each student's name and the statement he or she has made. They will begin with the person who spoke first and stop when he or she has given his or her name and has said something about himself or herself. The first student may say, "I'm Joe and I like to surf." The next would say, "That's Joe and he likes to surf. I'm Candy, and I have a new baby sister." The process continues until everyone in the circle has responded.

What's in a Name?   For this activity students are placed in groups of five or six. The activity involves sharing some things about the students' names. Ask students to give these facts about their names:

1. State your full name.
2. Tell how you got your name.
3. If you have one, give your nickname. Tell who calls you by this name.
4. Say what name you want used in the class.

After all groups have finished, one student in each group can volunteer to introduce each member of the small group to the entire class. They do so by giving the name each student wants to be called in the class.

Know Your Classmates.   Each student will need a sheet entitled Know Your Classmates containing a list of questions. Ask students to find a person in the class who fits each description listed on the sheet and to obtain the person's signature on the line in front of the description. To encourage students to interact with numerous peers, inform them that they cannot have the same person sign their sheets more than twice. The descriptions can be adapted to fit the specific interests of children at different ages and in different settings.

You may want to have your students generate lists of both things they want to know and may want to share.

The following is a sample Know Your Classmates format.

Name _____

Collect the signatures of the appropriate persons.

Classmate

_____   1. A person whose birthday is in the same month as yours.

_____   2. A person who has red hair.

_____   3. A person who has an interesting hobby.
                    What is it? _____

(continued)

_____ **4.** A person with freckles.

_____ **5.** A person whose favorite color is green.

_____ **6.** A person who loves to read.

_____ **7.** A person who is left-handed.

_____ **8.** A person who has a dog. The dog's name is _____

_____ **9.** A person who plays an instrument. What instrument? _____

_____ **10.** A person who traveled out of the state this summer. Where? _____

_____ **11.** A person who wants to play professional sports when he or she grows up. Which one? _____

_____ **12.** A person with more than four children in the family. How many? _____

Who's Like Me?   An adaptation of Know Your Classmates is to have students create their own individual lists composed of things about themselves. Their task is then to find others who are the same. The class is asked to share areas in which they found someone with a similar interest as well as report any topic they alone listed.

Interviews.   This activity will often foster new friendships. Lack of information about others can be a barrier to establishing new friendships. When children do not know their peers, they tend to make assumptions and may develop unfounded biases. As students interview each other, they learn new information about their peers, and this knowledge can promote diversified friendship patterns in the classroom.

Interviews in the classroom can be used in a variety of ways. One way is to introduce the interviewing process by having students list ten questions that would help them know a classmate better. Some examples of questions that might be asked by upper elementary students are

What are you proudest of?
Do you have any pets? If so, what are their names?
If you could go anyplace on a vacation, where would you go? Why?
Do you have any hobbies?

The teacher writes the questions the students generate on the board and tells students to each choose a person whom they do not know very well and, using the questions, learn as much as they can about that person. After about 10 minutes, each student is asked to draw their partner. These portraits as well as the information students gathered are later shared with the rest of the class.

A variation of this activity is to have each pair of students join with another pair to share the new information they have learned about their partners. The class then reconvenes, and each person shares four things about his or her partner with the class. Another interviewing technique has a student sit in a place of honor at the front of the classroom. The student is then asked questions by the other class members. A fourth interviewing approach has several students serve as reporters. They interview their peers, obtaining such information as where students were born, the number of members in their family, their favorite television show, a special hobby or pet, and their future goals. The teacher, with the help of the students, tabulates the information and either duplicates it and gives it to each student or makes a large chart for the classroom.

The byproduct of these interviewing activities is often new friendships and more open communication in the classroom. This atmosphere makes the classroom a more relaxed learning environment for students.

Guess Who? In this activity students write a brief autobiographical statement, including family background, hobbies, or extracurricular activities, which they do not sign. The teacher collects the statements, reads each description, and asks students to write the name of the individual they think wrote the description. The teacher can participate too. After all the descriptions have been read, the teacher rereads them and asks the authors to identify themselves. The students then indicate how many classmates they correctly identified.

A variation of this activity is to have students write poems or riddles about themselves. Then these poems are put into a box and each student draws a poem and reads it to the class. The class tries to identify the author of the poem. As a follow-up, the students may draw self-portraits that can be placed on a bulletin board with their poems below them.

T-Shirt. For this activity, students are provided with a sheet of paper with the outline of a T-shirt drawn on it. Students design a T-shirt that would help others know them better. When students have completed their designs, they share them in groups of four. After these groups have shared, students are asked to form new groups of four.

Activities to Promote Kindness

It's important to promote and recognize the prosocial behavior of students. For example, Beane (1999) suggests that teachers encourage kindness by having a *kindness box* for students to drop brief notes about acts of kindness they do or witness. Periodically, the teacher pulls out a note and reads it aloud. Other strategies include assigning students kindness pals, for whom they do random acts of kindness; having a kindness reporter, who watches for acts of kindness, briefly describes them in a notebook, and reports at the end of the week; and collaboratively writing *Our Big Book of Kindness*.

Related Definitions of Community

In all communities, members are bonded together for a common purpose, for the communal good of the group, as well as to meet their individual needs for belonging and acceptance. When people come together in a spirit of community, they embrace a collective concern for each other.

The principles of natural sustainable communities are the very same principles that sustain human communities (Capra, 1983). These basic principles of ecology are the principles of interdependence, partnership, and diversity. The principle of interdependence is our appreciation that we need each other. The principle of partnership is working together toward mutually valued goals. The principle of diversity is embracing diversity as a resource rather than a liability and appreciating differences.

Scott Peck (1987) defined community as a group of people who have learned to communicate honestly with each other, whose relationships go deeper than their masks of composure, and who have developed a commitment to rejoice together, to delight in each other, and to make others' conditions their own. The underlying principles here are those of open and honest communication, mutual vulnerability, significant commitment to each other, and collective responsibility for sustaining the community. These are at the heart of community building.

ATTRIBUTES OF A CARING, DEMOCRATIC COMMUNITY: RESPECT, AUTHENTICITY, THOUGHTFULNESS, AND EMOTIONAL INTEGRITY (RATE)

Establishing the foundation for a caring, democratic community begins with the way the teacher interacts with students and filters through to student-to-student interactions. The teacher serves as role model by living by the principles she espouses.

Creating such a community has two levels and involves teachers being both proactive and reactive.

1. Teachers demonstrate the value they place on the quality of relationships with students, by showing their commitment—of time, resources, and emotional energy.
2. Teachers monitor how students treat each other. They intervene, redirect, and challenge students when they violate community norms. (This requires that the teacher use assertion and confrontive skills discussed in detail in a later section.)

Concern for the welfare of the members of the community, open communication, and honest interactions define a caring community. In a caring community, members are thoughtful and respectful and are not afraid to be real, wrong, or vulnerable. Community members engage in direct and nonmanipulative dialogue that is accepting of each other's perspective. Students come to know each other and learn to value what each has to offer.

First and foremost, promoting a spirit of community requires that the teacher make the quality of relationships equally as important as the teaching–learning process. Transforming the classroom from a climate of competitiveness to a climate of caring relies on several personal attributes that contribute to feelings of connectedness, security, and belonging (Larrivee, 2000b). There are four critical attributes for teachers to promote among members of the community. The four fundamentals of a caring learning community are: respect, authenticity, thoughtfulness, and emotional integrity (RATE). As the acronym suggests, in a caring learning community, everyone rates. In the next section, these four critical attributes are discussed.

Respect

Respect is a less tangible concept. The key concept that underlies respect is acceptance. Teachers demonstrate acceptance by listening respectfully and honoring multiple voices. Oldfather (1993) coined the term *honored voice* to connote giving students a voice in the classroom and valuing what they have to say.

Respect is communicated through carrying on respectful dialogue with students, by not talking at students, but rather by talking with students. By listening to students' perceptions of life, caring about what they have to say, and thoughtfully responding to their ideas, teachers help honor their voices.

Respect is earned. You can gain it and you can lose it based on your deeds. Teachers communicate respect when they show regard for students' capacities to manage their own lives successfully. Dignity is the quality of being worthy of respect, a personal attribute of self-worth. Treating students with dignity means honoring their individual worth.

In respectful classrooms, differences are acknowledged and appreciated and everyone strives to listen to each other in search of common understandings. Students value what others have to offer and express what is important to them without the fear of judgment.

Teachers who respect their students also create trust, by being both trustworthy and trusting at the same time. They are willing to try to understand students' points of view and opinions. They are not afraid to discuss controversial issues; they speak the unspeakable, discuss the undiscussable.

Teachers who value respect know the rights of students and teachers are reciprocal. It's a two-way street: everyone's equal. The teacher is not above recrimination.

When students know that they can share concerns and difficulties with a teacher who will not stand in judgment but who will attempt to understand from the students' perspectives, it helps them understand more about their own experiences and their reactions to them.

When children have not been shown respect, they have trouble internalizing this value in ways that allow them to express it appropriately. In some neighborhoods, youngsters have seen or heard of so many killed in random violence, they come to feel disposable and expendable, without a future worth planning for. Young teens often confuse respect with fear and self-gratification and seek to intimidate others as a way of surviving. To respect others, one must have been shown respect. When you are treated with disrespect, over time you grow to feel worthless.

It is from the experience of being shown consideration and care that children learn to feel valued. Feeling valued is at the heart of self-respect. Rather than blame students for being disrespectful, teachers can show them how it feels to be respected.

The teacher's communication skills that contribute to being respectful are primarily the skills of acknowledging, encouraging, appreciating, and inviting (see Chapter 4).

Authenticity

Being authentic means being real. Teachers who are authentic do not act out assumed roles or roles others expect them to play. They know who they are and are clear about what they stand for. They have let down their masks and disguises. To use the colloquial expression, authentic teachers "walk their talk."

Teachers who are authentic speak the truth with care and thoughtfulness. They validate their right to the feelings they experience, respond honestly to students, and share what's really going on with them without trying to sugarcoat it. Authentic teachers aren't afraid to be wrong. They communicate to their students that it's okay for them to make mistakes and create a climate in which their students feel safe enough to also be authentic.

As teachers they use appropriate self-disclosure. Self-disclosure that is appropriate considers the context, the type of relationship, and the desired outcome of the communication. It's a judgment call, involving the ability to assess the depth of disclosure that is desirable or warranted in a particular situation.

In the classroom where authenticity is valued, both the teacher and the students share and express what they care about. Authentic teachers exude self-acceptance and self-confidence and inspire these qualities in their students. Being open and accepting of students and encouraging them to express a variety of feelings and opinions helps develop a sense of connectedness and emotional intelligence.

The specific communication skills for teachers to develop that align with authenticity are the skills of validating, self-disclosing, and accepting personal ownership and responsibility (see Chapter 8).

Thoughtfulness

The word *thoughtfulness* was purposefully chosen instead of the word *caring* to connote the concept that mutual consideration is what is called for in the large group structure of the classroom. We can't demand or dictate caring. Caring requires a special connection. Although teachers can exhibit caring in their relationships with students, it might be more appropriate to expect that students show tolerance and acceptance of their classmates, rather than expect a caring relationship with every-one. In the classroom setting, it may be more reasonable to strive for tolerance of individual differences, not necessarily caring the way it is normally defined. Caring may be reserved for those we choose to have more connected relationships with, such as family members and close friends.

In the thoughtful community, members know others in the community accept them as they are. Students cooperate by working together for a common purpose and collaborate to reach mutual goals. Students can rely on one another to be considerate of their needs, wants, desires, and fears.

The thoughtful teacher considers the emotional well-being of students in every classroom interaction. The skills that contribute to thoughtfulness on the part of the teacher are primarily listening skills, such as reflecting, paraphrasing, and clarifying (see Chapter 4).

Emotional Integrity

Having emotional integrity means communicating with emotional honesty. Emotional integrity is embedded in honest communication and mutual vulnerability. Teachers who have emotional integrity are aware of what is happening in the present moment and act on that awareness. They have the ability to be fully present and to share thoughts and feeling as they experience them. They also validate students' rights to express their feelings. They deal with emotions as they emerge. This keeps lingering resentment from settling in to erode the relationship.

Emotional integrity also means being proactive and confronting students' behavior by respectfully challenging them and calling students to accountability. The following examples of teacher talk exemplify emotional integrity.

Directly discussing with the student your perception of the state of the relationship at any moment: *I'm sensing an edge in your voice in your last comment. I'm wondering if you had a negative reaction to what I just said. I'd like to get some feedback before we go on.*

Challenging student: *Wait a minute, I'm really uncomfortable with the tone of this conversation, and I don't want to start this way.*

Calling student to accountability: *When you call me names, I get upset and want to attack you too, and I don't want to do that. I'd like you to speak respectfully to me.*

Being proactive and confronting students' behavior: *I'm disappointed in this class. Just yesterday we talked about the importance of respecting one another and how, if you have any problems with something someone does, you should talk it over with them, and if you can't work it out, you should come to me. So when there was a fight on the playground at recess, I was very upset because I think you can handle conflicts without trying to hurt each other.*

Although teachers may be aware of and sympathetic to students' feelings, they may not communicate that to students. Learning to explicitly validate students' feelings can help build bridges to students whose behavior teachers find difficult and can be the starting point for changing ways of responding to students.

Some teachers find it easier to share their positive feelings with students but not their sadness, hurt, or frustration. Others have no difficulty communicating such feelings but seldom communicate their positive emotions and reactions to students. Teachers tend to have a predisposition either to openly express more negative or more positive emotions with their students. It is important for teachers to consider whether they are predisposed to expressing either type of emotion more exclusively and to try to create more balance in their expression of emotions.

The behavior of students will sometimes cause teachers to be uncomfortable or angry. These feelings are natural, and teachers are entitled to have these feelings without also experiencing guilt or shame. Teachers also are entitled to express their feelings as long as they do so in a way that doesn't harm students. The teacher serves as a role model for students when negative emotions are appropriately displayed.

Constantly concealing your feelings or trying to act as if nothing bothers you can be as much a problem as expressing your feelings in inappropriate ways. The balance comes with emotional integrity. Not acknowledging and expressing your true feelings is emotional dishonesty. The idea is to express your feelings in a way that both reflects emotional honesty on your part and is helpful to your students. The goal is to express your feelings appropriately by modeling constructive outlets for your emotions while providing students with feedback regarding the impact of their behavior.

Trying to deny or suppress your feelings typically leads to lingering resentment. When resentment is left to fester, eventually it can lead to rejection of the student—a far worse option than dealing with your anger when it happens.

Teachers are human and they have strong feelings about what is important to them. The way they interact with students tells students what they value. Expressing anger and disappointment about a cheating incident shows students the value placed on honesty and integrity. Expressing a deep concern when some students are picking on another student communicates the value of kindness and respect. On the other hand, when teachers also call students unkind names or use sarcasm, students see the incongruence between what teachers expect from them and what teachers expect from themselves.

No teacher enters the classroom with a symptom-free personal history, nor a perfect psychological fit that works equally successfully with all students to whom he or she happens to be assigned. Each teacher's psychological makeup is better suited for dealing with some students, and necessarily not others. As Long (1996) aptly states, the teacher's journey begins by "digging through one's developmental past and uncovering those powerful and buried life events that have affected the teacher's attitudes and behaviors toward select students."

Reflective Questions to Ask Yourself.   Self-reflection is an essential tool for the democratic classroom. Understanding oneself is a prerequisite to understanding others. Below are some questions to pose that foster emotional integrity.

- What am I feeling?
- Am I feeling hurt? What is my hurt about?
- What is keeping me from expressing my feeling?
- Is it fear of rejection? Is it fear of disapproval?
- Is there something I need to say to a student? the class?
- What message is my behavior communicating to the student?
- What need might the student be trying to get met?

The specific communication skills for teachers to develop that align with emotional integrity are confrontation and assertion skills (see Chapter 8).

Promoting Emotional Integrity with Students.   The teacher not only demonstrates emotional integrity but also encourages students to express a variety of feelings and opinions. Learning to deal with their feelings and to look within for the motives of their actions helps students develop their emotional intelligence. It also creates a sense of connectedness to others. Teachers can also help students go beyond words like *angry* and *mad* to get to the feelings that lie below the surface, or to deeper feelings. This level of feeling communicates the students' vulnerability.

Getting to the emotion that lies behind what students are feeling and then expressing it honestly is integral to a classroom community that values emotional integrity. The following examples illustrate deeper level feelings.

Surface Feeling
I'm mad because you won't let me play.

I get angry when you ignore me.

Deeper, Vulnerable Level
I feel left out when I'm not allowed to join the game.

It makes me sad when I think no one likes me.

When the classroom community values emotional integrity, group members feel secure that their challenges will be acknowledged and considered. They also come to value having access to feedback from class members and see it as an opportunity to learn about themselves through the eyes of others.

LEARNING PRACTICE TASK: FUNDAMENTALS OF A CARING, DEMOCRATIC COMMUNITY

Activity Directions: Working in groups of three to five, for each RATE concept (respect, authenticity, thoughtfulness, and emotional integrity), brainstorm teaching practices, including specific teaching behaviors, classroom structures, and rituals teachers can implement to promote these in their classrooms.

Respect _____

_____

_____

_____

Authenticity _____

_____

_____

_____

Thoughtfulness _____

_____

_____

_____

Emotional Integrity _____

_____

_____

_____

Establishing and Sustaining a Sense of Community

Establishing and sustaining a sense of community has to be put in operational terms and played out in daily interactions and moment-to-moment decisions.

Teachers need to infuse the classroom with community-building experiences and create a safe place where students feel secure enough to disclose and share what has purpose and meaning for them. Cultivating the classroom as a community of learners depends on instituting policies, practices, and routines involving real connections with students that solidify student–teacher alliances.

Putting community building into practice includes

- Responding with acknowledgment and acceptance rather than defensiveness, judgment, or denial
- Creating a vehicle for open and ongoing dialogue with students
- Getting to know students and their backgrounds by taking an interest in students' life stories
- Infusing the classroom with community-building experiences embedded in methods, structures, and content learning
- Creating classroom norms that balance the growth of the individual and the well-being of the community

Building a sense of community involves orchestrating community-building activities at two levels. One level is teacher bonding with students and the other is nurturing thoughtful and considerate interactions among students. Relating with students as an ally involves fostering a sense of connectedness, building trust, and honoring multiple voices.

To sustain a learning community, teachers need to infuse the classroom with community-building experiences that help create a sense of safety and security. Creating a learning community involves developing practices such as

- Having a forum for ongoing dialogue with students
- Making personal connections during one-on-one time with students
- Developing rituals and traditions
- Sharing what's important to you
- Creating networks outside the school walls

Several personal attributes contribute to feelings of connectedness, security, and belonging. The following characteristics are important attributes to cultivate. In a caring learning community the teacher strives to be (1) respectful, (2) authentic, (3) thoughtful, and (4) emotionally honest.

Reflective Questions to Ask Yourself
- How do I demonstrate to my students that I value these attributes?
- What rituals and traditions do I want to infuse into daily practice that will build student-to-student connections?
- What practices do I want to incorporate into daily practice that will strengthen my connections with students?

A learning community does not emerge from a step-by-step formula. It is not enough for teachers to try to show authenticity and respect; they also need to be perceived by students as authentic and respectful. No matter how hard a teacher tries to connect with students, if students do not interpret what teachers do as authentic and respectful, bonds between teachers and students will not develop.

When teachers are committed to creating such learning communities, they

- Act authentically by speaking the truth with care and thoughtfulness
- Pay attention to what's being said without interpretation, judgment, or trying to rescue

■ Listen beneath the surface, remaining open to discovering something about themselves in the stories of their students

Acting in a spirit of community changes not only the community but each person as well. When the climate of the classroom is converted from "me against you" to "us against the world," the classroom becomes a safe haven. Transforming the culture of the classroom can create the buffer necessary to help insulate students from the often hostile world they live in. When teachers invite cooperation through the language of respect they create allies in their students and promote mutual acceptance, dignity, and emotional literacy.

LEARNING PRACTICE TASK: MAKING CONNECTIONS

Research has shown that teachers who are able to build close and trusting connections to students do the following: create one-to-one time with students, create networks with parents, family members, friends, and neighbors of students, build a sense of community among students within the classroom, and develop rituals and traditions within the classroom.

Activity Directions: Working with a peer, list some ways you could develop these aspects.

1. Create one-on-one time with students.

   _____

   _____

   _____

   _____

   _____

2. Create networks with parents, family members, friends, and neighbors of students.

   _____

   _____

   _____

   _____

   _____

3. Build a sense of community among students within the classroom.

   _____

   _____

   _____

   _____

   _____

4. Develop rituals and traditions within the classroom.

   _____

   _____

   _____

   _____

   _____

LEARNING PRACTICE TASK: DEMONSTRATING CARING

Activity Directions: Working in groups of three or four:

List all the ways you might ascertain from students whether they perceive you as caring.

_____

_____

_____

Some important characteristics of a caring community are (1) respectful listening, (2) honoring multiple voices, (3) self-disclosure and sharing what's important, (4) maintaining personal safety, and (5) building trust.

For each characteristic, list some ideas about how you can promote these principles.

1. Engage in respectful listening.

_____

_____

_____

2. Honor multiple voices.

_____

_____

_____

3. Support students in disclosing and sharing what's important to them.

_____

_____

_____

4. Maintain personal safety.

_____

_____

_____

5. Build trust.

_____

_____

_____

CHOICE AND VOICE: FUNDAMENTALS OF A DEMOCRATIC LEARNING COMMUNITY

Although teachers may operate from a primary power base, a total management plan calls for joining forms of influence and using power judiciously. The teacher needs to be able to move in and out of various modes of authority as deemed necessary. Maintaining a democratic learning community does not preclude the teacher's right to exercise more direct control as situations arise. The teacher needs to strike a balance between exercising too much control, which propagates student dependence, and not exercising enough control, thereby jeopardizing a safe and productive learning environment.

Teachers will need to consider what constitutes judicious authority and how and when they can enhance student autonomy through shared decision making, negotiation, and problem solving. In the democratic learning community, power over students is transformed into power with students. Adjusting the power–status dynamics to yield more power to students means giving students a voice in classroom practices.

The teacher can still maintain some control, yet give students a sense of power and freedom by giving them choices among acceptable options. Students have a choice, but the options offered are within defined parameters that the teacher deems appropriate to the learning goals. The following choices empower students to have some voice while still meeting the teacher's objectives.

Giving Students a Voice in Classroom Procedures

To increase students' involvement in general and procedural choices, allow their imput regarding

- The order in which students do their assigned classwork
- Where to sit, or whether they sit for certain activities
- Which field trip they would like to take
- Which community service project they would like to adopt
- Which classroom activities require silence
- When they need a break from their work

The same is true of ways to increase involvement in curriculum and learning task choices. Ask them

- Which book to read from a list of suggested books
- What to write about given some general guidelines
- Which of several suggested topics they would like to study
- How they would like to study the topics and in what order
- How to present a project (e.g., oral report, video, visual display, play, poem, song)

These options vary in the degree of control yielded to students. Teachers who are most comfortable managing the classroom by "keeping the lid on" can begin to involve students to a greater extent by turning over less significant decisions, such as where to go on a field trip. Eventually, they can work their way up to sharing decision-making power in more significant matters.

Teachers can begin to wean students from unilateral control by gradually increasing the degree of involvement and participation students have in decision making. Teachers can devise their own sequence for relinquishing more and more control to students. A sample continuum is presented below.

Gradual Increase in Student Involvement in Decision Making.   In this continuum, for example, teachers who are comfortable at the level of presenting students with a tentative decision and then getting student input can move to actually sharing with students their thinking process along with any dilemmas and trade-offs they have concerns about.

- Level 1. Teacher makes decision and announces to students what they will do.
- Level 2. Teacher makes decision and provides students with rationale for decision to enlist support.

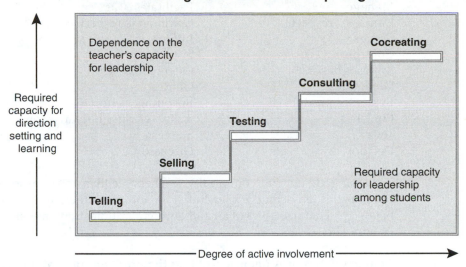

FIGURE 3.1   Management and Leadership Stages

- Level 3. Teacher presents tentative decision, subject to student input.
- Level 4. Teacher presents ideas and invites questions and comments prior to making a decision.
- Level 5. Teacher presents ideas and issues, solicits suggestions, and then makes a decision.
- Level 6. Teacher defines limits and asks students to make decision.
- Level 7. Teacher allows students to make decisions that are only confined by school policies.

Democratic Leadership.   Allowing students more active involvement in direction setting and decision making can be described as moving along a continuum of management stages from authoritarian to more democratic. Figure 3.1 is an example of a five-stage model.

Which stage best describes your management style?

Telling:	The teacher decides what should be, and the students have to follow.
Selling:	The teacher makes the decision, but wants the students to "buy in."
Testing:	The teacher shares ideas, and asks for students' reactions before making a decision.
Consulting:	The teacher solicits creative input from the students before making a decision.
Cocreating:	The teacher and students collaboratively decide.

Moving away from the traditional management role of providing rewards and punishments, delivering praise, and judging student behavior calls for a fundamental shift in the way teachers and students relate to each other. Changing the role of the teacher from manager to leader significantly transforms student–teacher interaction patterns. The climate dimensions of the teacher role in an authoritarian hierarchy are contrasted with those in a democratic learning community in the following list.

Authoritarian Hierarchy	Democratic Community
Manages	Facilitates
Demands respect	Commands respect
Orders	Invites
Controls	Supports
Imposes beliefs	Offers ideas
Dominates	Guides
Evaluates product	Encourages effort
Punishes	Acknowledges human error
Tells	Suggests
Decides	Discusses

In a caring, democratic community, teachers see themselves as leaders not bosses. They use a democratic leadership style and an authentic communication style. Below, the characteristics of an authentic communication style are contrasted with its opposite.

Characteristics of Authentic and Inauthentic Communication Styles

Authentic	*Inauthentic*
Honest	Dishonest
Direct	Indirect
Personal	Impersonal
Respectful	Disrespectful
Nonjudgmental	Judgmental

■ ■ ■ ■ ■ ■ ■ ■ ■

CRITICAL REFLECTION ON PRACTICE: HOW MUCH CHOICE AND VOICE DO YOUR STUDENTS HAVE?

Activity Directions: For each of the three areas, using a range of from 0 to 100 percent, indicate the current level of student choice–voice in your class.

AREA	CHOICE–VOICE CONTINUUM (%)
Curriculum and Learning	0 10 20 30 40 50 60 70 80 90 100
Procedure, Practices, and Routines	0 10 20 30 40 50 60 70 80 90 100
Expectations, Rules, and Consequences	0 10 20 30 40 50 60 70 80 90 100

REFLECTIVE QUESTION
What steps do you want to take to increase students' choice–voice in your classroom?

CRITICAL REFLECTION ON PRACTICE: BALANCING CONFORMITY WITH AUTONOMY

Activity Directions: Reflect on all the activities students experience and the requirements placed on students in your classroom. If you have more than one class, select one class for this activity. Then complete Steps 1 to 10.

Step 1   List all the rules, procedures, and activities that control students and require them to conform (e.g., line up, fold papers, have only four people at learning center at a time).

Step 2   List all the procedures and activities that allow students some choice and self-management (e.g., choose activity, get a drink without permission).

Step 3   Describe ways in which the choice and self-management list (Step 2) can be extended and still maintain learning and behavior goals.

Step 4   Which of the conformity requirements you listed in Step 1 can be eliminated or altered?

Step 5   What did this exercise tell you about how you promote student autonomy and support self-management?

Step 6   What did you learn about your management style from this exercise?

Step 7   Are you satisfied with the balance of control and freedom in your classroom?

Step 8   What did this exercise cause you to question about your current classroom policies and procedures?

Step 9   Write three to five questions you might raise regarding specific current practices.

Step 10   Write two to four questions that are self-reflective.

CHAPTER FOUR

Keeping Communication Channels Open

To transform the traditional classroom into a learning community, students need to feel secure, not only in terms of physical safety but also psychological security. Students need to feel free to express themselves, feel valued as group members, and accepted as individuals. In promoting equal opportunity for all, teachers have the responsibility to invite, encourage, and engage the participation of all their students. The dialogue teachers create with students plays a critical role in modeling styles of talk that manifest the language of acceptance, encouragement, and respect.

Fostering student self-evaluation requires that teachers restructure their discourse patterns and pay particular attention to the language they use when giving feedback to students. Teacher responses to students are sometimes judgmental. Certainly teachers must at times exercise control and serve in an evaluative and judgmental role, but there are many instances in which teachers can allow students to make their own judgments about the appropriateness of their behavior and the quality of their work. The process of evaluating and judging students inhibits acceptance.

This chapter presents styles of teacher talk more consonant with the goals of a caring democratic community, encouraging self-evaluation as well as self-reflection. Establishing the classroom as arena for critical conversation and respectful dialogue supports the development of values fundamental to a democratic society (Larrivee, 2002).

In addition to promoting community values, current beliefs about quality teaching practices that provide greater emphasis on interactive and collaborative work modes call for styles of teacher talk that involve more dialogue, both between teacher and student and among students. Placing students in a variety of collaborative roles with peers requires students to develop autonomy from the teacher.

THE POTENTIAL PERILS OF PRAISE AS A MANAGEMENT TOOL

Promoting a democratic classroom involves supporting students in learning self-management and self-control. With this end in mind, the traditional wisdom of teacher praise can be challenged on the grounds that praise conditions students to seek others' evaluation for accomplishments rather than develop responsibility for their own behavior (Larrivee, 1997).

Not only can the use of teacher praise be questioned because it undermines development of student autonomy as well as discourages freedom of expression and development of values fundamental to a democratic society, but also on the grounds that there is little evidence to support the espoused claims for the benefits of teacher praise even when the primary goal is not the development of self-regulated learners.

The three goals for delivering praise mentioned most frequently are enhancing performance or achievement of learning goals, promoting appropriate behavior or positive values, and helping students to feel good about themselves. As Kohn (1993) points out, research studies are remarkably scarce in support of these claims. In fact, most of the research serves to question the efficacy of the practice of teacher praise. Over the long run, praise in the form it is usually rendered by teachers not only fails to achieve any of these objectives, but it also often proves to be counterproductive.

Twenty Potential Perils of Praise

A multitude of issues concerning the use of praise have been raised in the research literature (Brophy, 1981, 1998; Brophy & Good, 1986; Deci, Koestner, & Ryan, 1999, 2001; Flink, Boggiano, Main, Barrett, & Katz, 1992; Kohn, 1993; Larrivee, 2002; Schwieso & Hastings, 1987). These issues include reducing interest in the learning task, lowering task performance, and sustaining minimal effort; generating disappointment and discouragement for those not receiving the praise; creating dependency; invoking resentment and setting up negative expectations; and promoting conformity while limiting creativity.

The following specific concerns have been raised about the potential pitfalls of teacher praise.

1. Praise creates a dependence on others for approval (Bennett, 1988; Dreikurs, 1968; Kohn, 1993; Rowe, 1974).
2. Praise can increase students' learned helplessness if they come to rely excessively on teacher approval in lieu of their own motivation (Deci & Ryan, 1985; Ginott, 1972; Lepper, 1983; Weiner, 1979).
3. When teachers praise students for behavior they want to encourage, the message students get is that poor behavior is what the teacher expects. Students often live up to such perceived negative expectations (Chandler, 1981; Farson, 1977; Gordon, 1974; Wolfgang & Brudenell, 1982).
4. Praise can discourage creativity if students become more concerned about pleasing their teachers or conforming to their teachers' expectations than on finding their own solutions to problems (Johnson & Johnson, 1987; Soar & Soar, 1975).
5. Praise can make some students fearful of the prospect of not being able to live up to expectations (Chandler, 1981; Dreikurs, Grunwald, & Pepper, 1982; Hitz & Driscoll, 1988; Kanouse, Gumpert, & Canavan-Gumpert, 1981; Madden, 1988; Wolfgang & Brudenell, 1982).
6. When praise is consciously employed as a technique for influencing students to choose some behavior deemed desirable by the teacher, students often perceive such praise as insincere, intended primarily to meet the teacher's needs (Boggiano, Main, & Katz, 1988; Brophy, 1998; Gordon, 1974, 1989; Pittman, Davey, Alafat, Wetherill, & Kramer, 1980; Ryan, 1982).
7. When students are praised every time they sit up straight, wait in line, listen, or engage in routine behaviors, they may perceive rewards as silly or irrelevant (Brophy, 1981, 1988).
8. Students who become accustomed to receiving frequent evaluative praise come to interpret the absence of praise as a negative evaluation. (Ginott, 1972; Gordon, 1974, 1989).
9. Praise given to one student, or a few, often is translated by the other students as negative evaluation of them (Ginott, 1972; Ollendick & Shapiro, 1984).
10. Teacher praise can generate disappointment for those students who don't receive it (Dreikurs, Grunwald, & Pepper, 1982; Hitz & Driscoll, 1988; Ollendick & Shapiro, 1984).

11. Praising certain students in front of their peers can be counterproductive if those students experience teacher attention in the form of praise as embarrassing rather than rewarding (Brophy, 1998; Caffyn, 1989; Long & Morse, 1996).

12. False praise given just to try to make students feel better can cause students to lose faith in themselves and become discouraged (Deci & Ryan, 1985; Hitz & Driscoll, 1988; Madden, 1988; Nafpaktitis, Mayer, & Butterworth, 1985; Natriello & Dornbusch, 1985).

13. The practice of profusely praising students who are low performing for trivial accomplishments can perpetuate their putting forth minimal effort (Brophy, 1981; Kast & Connor, 1988).

14. Praise given to students for minimal performance can actually worsen rather than improve students' functioning (Barker & Graham, 1987; Kast & Connor, 1988; Meyer, Bachmann, Bierman, Hempelmann, Plager, & Spiller, 1979; Rowe, 1974).

15. Students may doubt their own ability or lose confidence if they perceive that their performance does not warrant praise, leading them to have thoughts such as "She must really think I'm hopeless if she praises me for *that*!" or "How could he think *that* was good?" (Meyer, 1992; Meyer, Bachmann, Bierman, Hempelmann, Plager, & Spiller, 1979; Miller & Hom, 1997).

16. When a student is experiencing a problem, it is often accompanied by personal dissatisfaction. Praise when the student is in this state either goes unheard, makes the student feel that the teacher doesn't really understand, or provokes an even stronger defense of the student's low self-evaluation (Gordon, 1974; Long & Morse, 1996).

17. If the praise does not fit with the student's self-image, it can invoke resentment because the student may perceive it as an attempt at manipulation (Kanouse, Gumpert, & Canavan-Gumpert, 1981; Kohn, 1993).

18. When students feel that the praise is not sincere, but delivered to manipulate them into behaving in a certain way, it can undermine intrinsic motivation (Kast & Connor, 1988; Pittman, Davey, Alafat, Wetherill, & Kramer, 1980; Ryan, Mims, & Koestner, 1983).

19. When teachers use praise to tell students they are good because they know the right answer, students logically conclude that they are bad when they do not know the answer. This equating of knowledge with goodness is dangerous (Ginott, 1972).

20. Students grow to depend on praise, even demand it (Dreikurs & Cassel, 1972; Dreikurs, Grunwald, & Pepper, 1982; Gordon, 1974, 1989).

Effective Use of Praise

Depending on a student's prior experience with feedback and the way it is delivered, teacher praise may serve as a reinforcer, a punisher, or as a powerless antecedent that has no effect on either the alteration of inappropriate behavior or the continuation of desired behavior (Brophy, 1981). Furthermore, correlations between teachers' rates of praise and their students' achievement gains are low in magnitude and mixed in direction, suggesting that the most effective teachers are sparing rather than effusive in their praise (Brophy & Good, 1986). Several researchers have found that the quality of task engagement and of ultimate achievement tends to be higher when students perceive themselves to be engaged in activities for their own reasons rather than in order to please an authority figure, obtain a reward, or escape punishment (Deci & Ryan, 1985; Flink, Boggiano, Main, Barrett, & Katz, 1992; Lepper, 1983).

Brophy (1981) in his review of the research on teacher praise concluded that indiscriminate praise or mere frequency of praise is not positively related to student learning. However, providing feedback as to the correctness of student responses, with moderate levels of praise issued for quality responses, is positively related to student learning.

In order for praise to be effective, it should be

- Spontaneous rather than planned
- Sincere rather than insincere or rote
- Credible rather than given effusively for trivial accomplishments
- Specific rather than general, specifying the particular behavior being praised
- Contingent on performance that warrants recognition, rather than random

Effective use of praise is not related to its quantity but rather its qualitative use, that is, considering when and how to use it. As Kohn (1993) notes, teachers need to thoughtfully consider why and how they praise, and what effects praise has over time on those receiving it. Furthermore, it is important to note that not all children react the same way to praise. It will probably be interpreted differently depending on a child's background, experience, and personality. In fact, researchers have found that identical statements made by the same teacher produce different results for different students (Cannella, 1986; Kanouse, Gumpert, & Caravan-Gumpert, 1981).

For praise to have the positive impact on students teachers usually intend, it must be carefully construed. One condition for delivering effective praise is that it be realistic. If everything is *great, fantastic,* or *awesome,* these words lose their meaning as superlatives. Too much of the same pat phrase leads to satiation, and the praise dissolves into meaninglessness. An additional characteristic of effective praise is that it be credible rather than given for insignificant accomplishments. When teachers deliver praise not as part of a calculated attempt to manipulate students, but rather as a spontaneous and genuine reaction to student accomplishments, it can have intended effects (Brophy, 1998; Gordon, 1974). Honest, sincere, realistic praise that is not manipulative and stays focused on both the issue at hand and the student can be helpful (Gootman, 2001). In other words, effective praise is authentic.

A corollary issue is that teacher feedback needs to be matched to students' developmental levels. As students get older they become less extrinsically and more intrinsically motivated (Brophy, 1998; Grossman, 1990; Hartner, 1978; Meyer, Bachmann, Bierman, Hempelmann, Plager, & Spiller, 1979; Walker, 1979). By the time students are in the upper elementary grades they can reward themselves for behaving appropriately. At this age level they tell themselves that they are good students because they raise their hands and wait their turn. Upper elementary and secondary teachers should encourage students to reward themselves for good behavior. This means focusing comments more on providing students with factual feedback about how they are doing and their strengths and weaknesses, successes, and failures. By the time students are in secondary school, they have internalized standards they can use to evaluate their own accomplishments. Accordingly, teachers should reduce the amount of feedback they provide their students and instead encourage them to evaluate themselves. This calls for teachers to move away from strictly evaluative praise and move toward encouraging personal satisfaction and self-evaluation by calling on students to assess their performance by their own standards, values, and sense of accomplishment. This shift is illustrated in the following example of age-appropriate teacher feedback.

Primary Level:
Teacher Evaluation
You did a great job on the test.

Intermediate Level:
Personal Satisfaction
You must be very proud of getting nearly every answer correct.

Secondary Level:
Self-Evaluation
Your reading comprehension score was lower than your vocabulary score. Is that what you would have expected?

It is important to distinguish among the various forms of positive feedback. Praise as a verbal reward that attempts to control students and make them dependent on the teacher's approval is the form that is problematic, especially in pursuit of democratic principles. Praise consisting of words that positively evaluate students' work, behavior, or achievement conditions students to seek outside evaluation for their accomplishments rather than develop responsibility for their own actions and performance. However, if one defines praise more broadly including straightforward information about how well the student has done at a task, or encouragement that leaves the student feeling a sense of self-determination, then only some forms of praise need be avoided. The definition isn't what matters; The critical point is that some approving comments are not only acceptable but also desirable, whereas others are neither. Because the research on the pitfalls of praise is so compelling, it behooves teachers to take the necessary steps to avoid the potential detrimental effects of praise.

LEARNING PRACTICE TASK: CONSIDERING TEACHER PRAISE

Activity Directions: Based on the material presented on teacher praise, answer the following questions.

1. What are some of the potential dangers of teacher praise?

   _____

   _____

   _____

2. What is your own position on the use of teacher praise?

   _____

   _____

   _____

3. What do you want to reconsider relative to your thinking about teacher praise?

   _____

   _____

   _____

ALTERNATIVES TO PRAISE: AUTHENTIC RESPONSES TO STUDENTS

Transforming the classroom into a democratic community requires that the teacher support student self-evaluation, self-management, and self-reflection. Styles of talk that support such learning communities make two very important distinctions.

1. Teacher talk to students distinguishes between the deed and the doer.
2. Teacher talk to students distinguishes between a student's work and a student's worth.

When these two distinctions are made clear, the teacher communicates the fundamental principle of acceptance. The type of teacher talk that aligns with these distinctions is nonevaluative and nonjudgmental. It is the language of respect.

Distinguishing between the Deed and the Doer

Most of our responses to others, especially students, are judgmental. We judge a behavior to be positive or negative and respond accordingly in judgmental language such as "that's good" or "that's bad." Often teachers judge a behavior as good or appropriate based on their own comfort zone. They project their own intolerance for certain behaviors and consequently make a value judgment about the behavior of their students. More simply stated, because teachers don't like particular behaviors, they don't want students to practice them. They decide students shouldn't act that way, and they reject their behavior. Sometimes teachers may go even further and reject the student as well.

One alternative to using evaluative language when responding to students is to provide a simple description of the student's behavior, ensuring that the words chosen are neither judgmental nor likely to evoke a defensive response. When responding to inappropriate behavior, nonjudgmental descriptions of the student's behavior communicate that although you may disapprove of the behavior you don't reject the student. The following examples compare nonjudgmental descriptions of student behavior with judgmental statements about the student.

Nonjudgmental Description	Judgmental Statement about Student
This is the third time this week you've been late.	*You're being irresponsible.*
Your work hasn't been turned in for the past two days.	*You're just lazy.*

Clearly, nonjudgmental descriptions of a student's behavior are far more likely than judgmental statements about the student to solicit a dialogue in which the student takes responsibility for behavior. Toward this end, teachers need to learn more authentic ways to respond to students. Responding authentically to students uses the language of recognition, encouragement, and acceptance.

Recognition Rather than Personality Praise

Although the use of praise is usually heralded as a desirable way to build up students' self-concept, praising students who are troubled often has a negative effect. According to Long and Morse (1996), when working with students with low self-esteem and a history of failure, praise can have effects opposite of those intended. These students may think comments such as "you're great" and "you're the best" are not an accurate assessment. Instead of making the student feel better, these comments introduce additional stress and often lead to feelings of guilt. Such students may draw any of the following conclusions.

My teacher is a jerk and is lying to me.

I guess I had a lucky day. I happened to hit the bull's-eye today, but it will never happen again.

I'm not worthy of such praise, and I find it hard to take.

I'll have to show you I don't deserve such praise.

The authors recommend that teachers differentiate between what they label personality and descriptive praise, advocating for the latter. To align with the definition used here for praise, this concept is labeled recognition rather than descriptive praise. Recognition deals only with students' efforts and behavior without attaching any evaluation. The important impact is the positive message the student self-imposes after assessing the teacher's comment. Teachers telling students they are terrific is less helpful than students telling themselves they are competent and worthy. Such positive appraisals promote self-esteem and investment in learning.

> **Recognition:** "Jerome, I noticed you worked at your desk for fifteen minutes, and when you needed some help you raised your hand and waited until I could get to you."
>
> **Self-appraisal:** "I got right down to work and showed a lot of self-control today. Good for me!"

Nonjudgmental Rather than Judgmental Responses

Nonjudgmental responses facilitate the development of responsible behavior by granting students the responsibility for their behavior. Transforming from evaluative to nonevaluative responses will require a restructuring of classroom discourse. Although for some, self-reflection in the form of self-questioning will be all that it will take to curtail judgmental responses, for those whose judgmental behavior is more entrenched, it will take a more concerted effort.

Because evaluative responses are so ingrained, making the change to giving nonevaluative feedback to students will take a sustained effort to monitor responses to students. As a beginning step toward learning to replace judgmental responses with nonjudgmental responses, teachers may need to devise ways to actively practice new speaking patterns that involve specific self-prompting or cueing strategies for overtly monitoring the way they talk to students.

Personal Rather than Evaluative Feedback

Evaluative feedback is characterized by judgment and typically takes the form of "you are . . . ," "you are a . . . ," or "your . . . is . . . ." On the other hand, personal feedback makes a personal connection, communicating that you are aware of what's going on with the student and that you want to be supportive. It's feedback from the heart rather than the head. The following are some ways to respond that are personal, supportive, and nonjudgmental.

Nonjudgmental Response Options	Examples
Share personal position	*I sometimes have the same fears.*
	I'd be angry too.
	I remember how I felt when that happened to me.
Describe your own feeling about the student's behavior	*I was moved by how you were able to capture Jake's feelings.*
	I appreciate the way you expressed your feelings without blaming anyone.
Provide acknowledgment of student's emotional state	*It must be hard to accept that.*
	I know this is a difficult time for you.
Pose questions that help student consider others' perspective	*Have you considered other possible reasons for what he did?*
	How do you think he is feeling now?

Monitoring your verbal acceptance of behavior may also be helpful in situations in which you and a particular student are having problems. You could enlist a colleague or another student to record your verbal responses to the particular student. If you find your responses are typically judgmental (negative), you may want to try making acceptant responses and note the student's response.

Your students could also benefit from using acceptant responses with their peers. Students of all ages can be made aware of the difference between judgment and acceptance.

Distinguish between a Student's Work and a Student's Worth

Expressing dissatisfaction can be done either in a way that is facilitative and respectful or in a way that is obstructive and disrespectful, making it more difficult to maintain meaningful communication.

Teachers promote self-evaluation when they provide encouragement rather than praise; respond with acceptance, not judgment; and offer constructive interpretations rather than evaluative feedback or destructive criticism. By encouraging students to set their own standards and deal with their feelings, they learn to reflect on the motives of their actions.

When you want to help students solve problems or deal with difficult situations, your task is to build trust in their own capacity to deal effectively with their life situations. What you want to do is facilitate development of their own problem resolution, not provide a solution. Interacting with students in nonjudgmental ways allows new alternatives to surface and helps students become aware that they don't have to seek others' judgments; rather, they can make their own assessments. A fundamental premise for the separation of students' work and worth is that the teacher values process rather than end product. Making this distinction helps students feel accepted for who they are, not for what they can do.

Encouragement Rather than Praise

Praise consists of words that positively evaluate students' work, behavior, or accomplishments. Encouragement consists of words that convey teacher respect and belief in students' capabilities. Praise conditions students to seek outside evaluation for their accomplishments rather than develop responsibility for their own action and performance. Encouragement recognizes efforts, not necessarily achievements, and stimulates motivation from within, allowing students to become aware of their own strengths. Praise conditions students to measure their worth by their ability to please others; encouragement teaches students to evaluate their own progress and make their own decisions.

The dictionary distinguishes between praise and encouragement as follows.

PRAISE	ENCOURAGE
1. To express a favorable judgement of	1. To inspire with courage or confidence
2. To glorify, especially by attribution of perfection	2. To spur on; stimulate
3. An expression of approval	3. To give support to; foster

The following characteristics of encouragement clearly differentiate it from praise.

- Encouragement is available to all, not just to those who achieve at the highest levels.
- Encouragement decreases competition for limited rewards.
- Unlike praise, which diminishes in effectiveness as students mature, encouragement is equally effective at any age.

- Encouragement tells students that how they feel about themselves and their own efforts is what is important.
- Encouragement gives students the support they need to continue their efforts.
- Encouragement stimulates motivation from within.
- Encouragement allows students to become aware of their own strengths.
- Encouragement increases risk-taking behaviors and the possibility of students constructing new knowledge because its focus is on effort, not outcome.
- Encouragement increases the likelihood that students will develop an internal value structure.
- Encouragement supports cooperation and working to make everyone a winner.

Encouragement is grounded in the core belief that each student can be successful. When teachers use encouragement, they help students feel and believe that they are capable of taking charge of their own lives. Encouragement focuses on what students are doing, rather than on what they are not doing. Giving encouragement recognizes individual differences in the learning style, rate, and effort it takes to achieve desired results.

The purpose of encouragement is to provide a description of students' accomplishment that will enable them to understand what qualities made the accomplishment possible and worthwhile. It merely describes, leaving students to draw their own conclusions and take control of their own behavior. Encouragement does not evaluate or attempt to control students, rather it leaves an opening for student self-evaluation. When teachers use encouragement they give students the courage to contribute and participate fully by sending the message that everyone's contribution is important.

Praise versus Encouragement

When teachers use praise, *students learn to*	*When teachers use encouragement,* *students learn to*
Seek outside evaluation for their accomplishments	Be responsible for their own behavior
Measure worth by their ability to conform	Be self-confident
Measure performance by pleasing others	Evaluate their own and others' progress
Fear disapproval	Make their own decisions
Set unrealistic standards for themselves	Accept their own imperfections and those of others
Fear failure	Persevere with challenging tasks
Be competitive	Use talents and efforts for the good of all
Get ahead at the expense of others	Appreciate the successes of others

The Language of Encouragement.   When teachers respond with encouragement, they communicate that students are accepted as they are, that effort is recognized, that improvement is noticed, and that the process is as valuable as the end result.

The following remarks exemplify encouragement versus praise.

I noticed you got right to work and got the whole assignment done.

You used very descriptive words in your paragraph. It makes your writing more interesting.

I know you can do it.

You figured it out by yourself and stuck with it without giving up.

What did you learn from that mistake?

You have really spent a long time working on your project.

It looks like you put a lot of work into that paper.

You must be proud of the job you did on this.

I see you thought of a new way to put those together.

Your reading had so much expression. You really made the story come alive.

A common practice of teachers is to praise a student's innate talent or ability. Although it may influence a student in the short term, in the long run, it teaches that ability or lack of ability is the key indicator of success or failure (Bocchino, 1999; Mueller & Dweck, 1998). Praise should be gauged to fit the accomplishment with the amount and degree of praise commensurate with the extent of effort rendered. When they attribute success to luck, task difficulty, or innate ability, students believe they have little or no control over success or failure. The teacher's intent to help students attribute success to effort has a powerful effect on self-concept, feelings of pride, and perception of ability to succeed. Clearly linking effort to success increases the likelihood that students will rely on effort as they approach a new task. By recognizing the student's decision to expend effort and by encouraging that effort, the teacher reinforces the link between the outcome and the student's ability to affect that outcome. When teachers construe ability as an acquirable skill, deemphasizing competitive social comparison while emphasizing self-comparison of progress and personal accomplishments, they help build a sense of self-efficacy that promotes academic achievement (Bandura, 1993, 1997).

Ideally, students find satisfaction in their learning and the sense of purpose and accomplishment that ensues. Satisfactorily completing learning tasks is essentially its own intrinsic reward. Realistically, this happens only with more capable students who have the greatest opportunity to experience success and the resulting enhanced self-esteem. For many other students, there are few opportunities to experience success simply on the basis of their performance. For these students, the teacher's purposeful and sensitive use of encouragement can make a significant difference. Such encouragement may be in the form of extra teacher attention, support, and recognition, as well as acknowledgement of incremental gains in learning and performance.

■ ■ ■ ■ ■ ■ ■ ■

LEARNING PRACTICE TASK: PRACTICING ALTERNATIVES TO PRAISE

Activity Directions: For each of the five alternatives to praise listed below, write two examples.

1. Description of what you see.

   _____

   _____

   _____

2. Sharing of personal position.

   _____

   _____

   _____

(continued)

LEARNING PRACTICE TASK   Continued

3. Description of your own feeling evoked by the student(s).

_____

_____

_____

4. Honest acknowledgment of the student's situation or feeling.

_____

_____

_____

5. Question that helps the student consider others' perspectives.

_____

_____

_____

REFLECTIVE QUESTION
What will you need to do to begin using less praise and more nonjudgmental responses to students?

Responding to Students with Acceptance

In addition to using descriptive, personal, recognizing, and encouraging feedback, nonjudgmental responses can also communicate acceptance. By using validating, acknowledging, or appreciating responses, teachers not only refrain from evaluating and judging students, but they also communicate acceptance and respect for students. When teachers respond with acceptance, it keeps the responsibility with the student, yet maintains the teacher's involvement. Such responses help students solve their own problems.

With all of these types of responses, the student is granted the responsibility for personal behavior. Although we have been socialized to respond to others in judgmental ways, acceptant responses are preferable to judgmental ones, whether they be judgmental-positive or judgmental-negative, because they recognize that individuals are ultimately responsible for themselves.

Validating Acceptant Responses.   When teachers respond with validating responses to students, they recognize and respond to the feelings that underlie students' behavior by conveying understanding and acceptance of their feelings. In doing so, the teacher neither encourages nor discourages the feelings. Often teacher messages tell students to stop feeling, as if they can turn their feelings off on notice. Feelings are what they are; they need to be acknowledged. They should not be evaluated in terms of right or wrong, good or bad.

Validating feelings means accepting without evaluation, but it doesn't mean the teacher has to condone behavior that results from students' feelings. Validating communicates acceptance, although not necessarily agreement. Validating feelings is an important way to connect with students and can help them work through their feelings and move on. Students can have intense feelings, and often they don't know what to do with them (and sometimes teachers don't either). Validating these feelings can make a difference to students and serves to strengthen relationships between students and teachers.

It is important to attend to feelings first, because the student who is upset is not likely to be receptive to any information, directives, or corrections. When teachers validate feelings they show concern and give words to feelings by describing what they see.

> *I can see you're very involved in your discussion, but it's time to put your materials away now.*

Validating feelings doesn't mean that students are exempt from classroom responsibilities, but it does tell them the teacher understands and accepts their frustrations, anger, or hurt.

> *Oh, clean up time came too soon. I know it's hard to stop playing.*

It acknowledges students' right to have such feelings and lets them know the teacher cares about what they are feeling.

> *You seem really upset. Do you need to take a break?*

Sometimes the validation may be merely saying you're sorry for the student's feelings without retracting your position about the action you expect from the student.

> *I'm sorry about what happened in science class, but you need to calm down and start your work.*

Validating feelings helps the teacher to stay in tune with students' feelings. It also helps the teacher refrain from blaming, criticizing, or attacking. When you merely acknowledge your students' feelings, it keeps you from becoming defensive and taking on responsibility for those feelings. When you validate feelings, you are honoring your students' feelings rather than evaluating or denying them. When you become accustomed to hearing an issue with concern for the student, you don't hear it as a criticism and have a need to defend, take responsibility, or counterattack.

Appreciating Acceptant Responses.   Letting students know that you appreciate them helps students feel important. Taking notice of what students do and what's important to them communicates that they are valued members of your class. Simple statements expressed with interest and enthusiasm communicate to students that the teacher values what they do. Students interpret such acknowledgment to mean they have importance and status. Teacher comments such as the following communicate that the teacher notices what a student does.

> *I appreciate the way you worked with Angelo today.*
>
> *I know you've worked hard today.*
>
> *I like that color on you, Keisha.*

Expressing appreciation is important in several ways. It

- Communicates interest and enthusiasm
- Shows recognition
- Makes students feel valued
- Creates a sense of importance

All these lead to building positive relationships. It's hard to find time to appreciate each student, but students respond to even the slightest signs of attention. Teachers can show appreciation by seizing opportunities to build small rituals into the day that provide moments to connect with students. Some simple ways teachers can show appreciation are

- Greeting each student every morning or as they enter class
- Using students' names
- Making eye contact, nodding, smiling
- Stopping what you are doing when a student comes to you
- Shaking hands
- Showing obvious pleasure for something a student does

When teachers make an effort to show appreciation, students get the message: "You don't have to do everything perfectly to be accepted. The little things count too. Your presence counts."

Acknowledging Acceptant Responses. When teachers acknowledge, they accept and show respect for students' points of view or positions. They encourage students to express their opinions and show that they value what students have to say. The teacher acknowledges that each student has a right to a perspective and thoughtfully responds to student ideas without judgment, as the following comments illustrate.

That's an interesting position. We hadn't been thinking along those lines.

Suki, I never would have thought of that one!

Acceptant versus Judgmental Responses

Teacher responses to students' behavior can be categorized as either acceptant or judgmental. Judgmental responses can be either judgmental-positive or judgmental-negative.

- Acceptant responses: recognizing that each individual is ultimately responsible for himself or herself and responding with acceptance by using a validating, acknowledging, or appreciating response.
- Judgmental-positive: judging the behavior to be desirable, good, or right and responding with an attempt to reinforce it
- Judgmental-negative: judging the behavior to be undesirable, bad, or wrong and responding with an attempt to change it

Note the difference between acceptant and judgmental responses in this example.

Leslie slams into your room, throws down his books, and tells you how unfair Mr. James is for reprimanding him.
- Judgmental (positive): *That's OK. When you have problems with him, you can just come in here.* Leslie is likely to repeat the behavior, since he was rewarded by the teacher solving the problem for him.
- Judgmental (negative): *Well, if you acted with him the way you are acting right now, I don't blame him.* Leslie's feelings are ignored, and the relationship between him and the teacher is not enhanced. The problem remains.
- Acceptant: *I can see you're very upset because Mr. James yelled at you.* Leslie's feelings are validated. *I'd like to talk with you about it later. Right now we have to get started with math.* Leslie's feelings are recognized and the teacher communicates concern while still letting him know what's expected.

LEARNING PRACTICE TASK: PRACTICING ACCEPTANT RESPONSES

Activity Directions: Working in groups of three, take turns making acceptant responses to the following situations. Get feedback on whether your responses are accepting or judgmental.

1. An upper elementary age student refuses to work with another student, saying, "He keeps picking on me."
2. A junior high school student hands you a bedraggled looking homework assignment, sheepishly explaining that she dropped it in a puddle on the way to school.
3. A high school student tells you he's thinking of dropping out of school.

CRITICAL REFLECTION ON PRACTICE: ANALYZING YOUR RESPONSES TO STUDENTS

Activity Directions: In your classroom, use a tape recorder or have an observer (peer, aide, student, parent, volunteer) record every personal response you make to students during one lesson or class period. Then transfer the data to the worksheet provided, and classify each response as judgmental-positive, judgmental-negative, or acceptant.

QUESTIONS FOR SELF-ANALYSIS

1. In which category did most of your responses fall? _____

2. Combining the first two categories, did you make more judgmental or more acceptant responses?_____

3. Which type of response is easiest for you? What does that tell you? _____

4. Select one response you are especially pleased with. What was the probable effect of that response on the student? You might ask the student for verification. _____

5. Select the response you are least satisfied with. What was the probable effect of that response on the student? Again, you might ask the student for feedback. Write a better response. _____

REFLECTIVE QUESTION
Based on this data, what would you like to change about your responses?

SUGGESTED FOLLOW-UP
As with any activity in which you collect data concerning your classroom behavior, significant changes will occur only with a long-term commitment. Continuous analyses over time, with comparisons drawn and trends noted, are essential if you are serious about changing any aspect of your behavior. Therefore, it is recommended that you repeat this activity several times to monitor your progress.

Worksheet for Analyzing Judgmental and Acceptant Responses to Students

RESPONSE	CATEGORY TYPE		
	Judgmental-Negative	Judgmental-Positive	Acceptant

Another Nonevaluative Response: Asking Students to Make Value Judgments.
The idea of acceptance versus judgment is closely aligned with Glasser's (1986)
notion of control theory, which posits that while we may try to control others'
behavior, in actuality, we can only control our own behavior. When we evaluate
students' behavior, even with a positive evaluation, we are assuming responsibility for them and attempting to exercise control over them. If you say "That's excellent!" you are implicitly reserving the right to also say "That's awful!" In either
case, it is most likely an attempt to control the student by judging the student by
some set of standards external to the student.

Glasser (1998) offers another alternative to judgmental responses to students,
advocating that teachers call on students to make value judgments about their own
behavior. Comments such as "Is that helping the group?" or "What might you do
that would be more helpful?" call on students to take responsibility for their
behavior and recognize its effect on self as well as others. Glasser challenges teachers to teach students that freedom is tied to responsibility by attempting to motivate students from within, help students establish inner controls, and learn to
regulate their own behavior.

Constructive Comments versus Destructive Comments

Constructive comments offer specific assistance while supporting students' efforts
and building self-confidence. They communicate acceptance and allow students to
draw their own conclusions and make their own judgments about their work.
Destructive comments point out errors and are interpreted by students as evidence
of their incompetence.

Although teachers may fear that correcting students' mistakes diminishes
their self-esteem, the sense of not being competent is far more damaging. Self-
esteem is enhanced when students experience the confidence of correcting their
own mistakes through hard work.

Purposeful critique is constructive feedback that is not only descriptive, but
also offers a next step for the student to move toward self-correction and, ultimately, the sense of satisfaction of having gotten it right. Purposeful critique is
feedback that specifically shows students the way, allowing them to construct
what to do next, rather than feel helpless. The following comment illustrates purposeful critique.

> *I see why you might have thought that, but it's not the correct answer. There's one
> piece of information you overlooked. Go back and see if you can find it.*

Purposeful critique lets students know they have made a mistake while helping them to embrace feedback as an opportunity to learn and improve. By interacting with students in a nonjudgmental fashion, teachers encourage student
self-evaluation and support student development of self-management skills.
Below are some additional examples.

Give personal reactions without value judgments.

> *I really liked your story, especially the part about how the two enemies became friends.*

> *I enjoyed the humor in your presentation.*

Pose questions that expand the student's thinking:

> *Have you considered other possible interpretations of what the author meant?*

> *How are these two ideas related?*

Such constructive comments support students' efforts and build self-confidence while allowing students to evaluate their own work. Giving purposeful critique enables students to develop confidence by letting them know they can do something about their errors and allowing them to see their own improvement.

Constructive versus Destructive Written Comments on Student Papers.   Teachers can spend hours responding in writing to the written work of students. Many teachers fall victim to the red pencil syndrome, merely marking everything that's wrong with the student's work. Most of the comments that teachers put on student papers don't enhance the student's self-concept. Many teacher-made comments and corrections, however subtle, contribute to a hostile environment for students.

Students pay little or no attention to the responses so laboriously made by their teachers. But why should they? Most people try to ignore or downgrade anything that tells them they are less than worthy. No one enjoys having their weak points and mistakes paraded before them, and especially not students. When commenting on written work, teachers can avoid judgmental responses by sharing personal reactions (e.g., "I'm really excited about this idea") or posing questions which extend the student's thinking (e.g., "How has this awareness affected you?"). They can also make specific comments acknowledging progress (e.g., "You've become much clearer in organizing your points") or state a need for greater clarity (e.g., "I'm not sure what you mean here. Can you make this clearer?").

Many of the comments that teachers write on student work or deliver personally can be classified into one of ten categories (Curwin & Fuhrmann, 1975). Five are generally destructive in that they point out errors that students interpret as evidence of their inadequacies. The other five are constructive in that they support the student's efforts and offer specific assistance. While destructive comments discourage students from trying, constructive ones help them build their skills and self-confidence.

Destructive Comments

1. **Simple corrections.**
   Mistakes are indicated by a mark, usually an X or a check in red. At a glance, a student can measure inadequacy.

2. **Vague references to needed improvement with no specifications of what is needed.**
   Often a question mark or a vague reference like *unclear, poor,* or *vague* is written in a margin. The student is given no assistance in understanding the reference or how to improve.

3. **Comments that indicate the teacher's disagreement but do not provide factual data.**
   The student is told that he or she is wrong but not why, or told that his or her opinion is unacceptable. Comments like *No, your thinking is fuzzy,* and *That's not what the book said,* especially in matters of opinion, are examples.

4. **Sarcastic remarks.**
   Sure!, Oh, really?, Come on, now!, You don't say! and similar statements only serve to belittle students and tell them their ideas are unacceptable.

5. **Prescriptive corrections of spelling, punctuation, grammar, and other skills.**
   Students, especially those who are unsure of their skills to begin with, are taught only that they have failed. (Prescriptive corrections do not include judicious and meaningful suggestions or help in these skill areas. Examples include *awkward, poor sentence, rewrite, these aren't sentences, fix.*

Constructive Comments

1. **Personal reactions in which a dialogue between student and teacher is initiated.**

   This idea excites me.

   Your account of your anger here brought back vivid memories of a similar situation in my life.

   I'm not sure I understand you here. Let's talk about it.

2. **Specific suggestions for improvement in which the emphasis is not on what is wrong, but on what can be done to improve.**

   This argument will be stronger if you use specific examples.

   How did this event follow from the one preceding it? Show the relationship clearly.

3. **Questions designed to extend the student's thinking, especially on the meaning of events and information to him or her.**

   How has this value affected your life?

   How difficult is it for you to uphold this opinion?

   How has this discovery been important to you?

4. **Corrections of grammar, spelling, punctuation, and other skills that are used sparingly for the purpose of clarifying thought.**

   No more than two or three such corrections on any one paper can probably be assimilated. Unlike the prescriptive corrections indicated previously, which are used simply to show students their mistakes, the focus here is on improving the meaning through better writing, not on pointing out errors.

   These are fragments, try joining them together to make one complete sentence.

   I can't tell whether you mean . . . or . . . Can you clarify which by rewriting this sentence?

5. **Specific supportive comments that indicate progress and recognize achievement.**

   General supportive comments like *good* and *well done*, though not destructive, are not as constructive as more specific comments that provide definitive and meaningful feedback.

   You've become much clearer in organizing your presentation.

   This is an excellent use of metaphor!

LEARNING PRACTICE TASK: USING CONSTRUCTIVE COMMENTS

Activity Directions: For each of the five categories of constructive comments, write one of your own. Remember the idea is to provide purposefully constructive comments that show students the way to move toward self-correction.

Personal reactions.

_____

_____

_____

Specific suggestions for improvement.

_____

_____

_____

(continued)

LEARNING PRACTICE TASK   Continued

Questions designed to extend the student's thinking.

_____

_____

Corrections of grammar, spelling, punctuation, and other skills for the purpose of clarifying thought.

_____

_____

_____

Specific supportive comments that indicate progress and recognize achievement.

_____

_____

_____

CRITICAL REFLECTION ON PRACTICE: EVALUATING YOUR WRITTEN COMMENTS ON STUDENT PAPERS

Activity Directions: Using the ten categories of destructive and constructive comments, analyze the comments you recently wrote on at least twenty student papers. You can use your latest batch of papers or you can ask students to return old papers and choose some at random. Copy each comment you made onto the worksheet provided. Then classify each one as either destructive or constructive. You can also categorize them by type, using the numbers of the ten types in the list, if you wish.

1. Add up the number of destructive comments and the number of constructive comments. What do these numbers say to you about the comments you put on these papers? _____

   _____

2. Which kind of comment, destructive or constructive, is easier for you to make? What does that mean to you? _____

   _____

3. Pick out three comments that you classified as destructive. What do you imagine the students' reactions to these might have been? Rewrite each as a constructive comment. _____

   _____

   _____

   _____

REFLECTIVE QUESTION
What implications does this activity have for you?

SUGGESTED FOLLOW-UP
On the next set of papers that you collect, make only constructive comments. When you return the papers to your students, you might choose to tell them that you have attempted to use only constructive responses. Point out the kinds of comments you have made and explain the rationale for doing so. Observe student reactions to the comments.

Worksheet for Analyzing Written Comments on Student Papers

COMMENT	DESTRUCTIVE	CONSTRUCTIVE

INVITING VERSUS INHIBITING COMMUNICATION

Often our communication is one-way, that is, all about our personal needs and is delivered as a statement of blame, like, "I feel this way . . . and it's your fault." Instead, you want to invite your students to participate in a two-way communication, rather than defend against an attack. Inviting communication is reciprocal, with both teacher and student participating in the communication.

When the communication process is no longer reciprocal, that is, one party has taken over, it's an indication that the communication has moved from inviting to inhibiting. Inhibiting communication

- Invalidates others' feelings, thoughts, wants, and needs
- Tells others what they should want, feel, think, or do
- Advocates for your own position without acknowledging others' positions

When you inhibit, you shut down two-way communication. You

- Use the language of disrespect
- Invoke defenses
- Create an adversary

When you invite, you keep the communication channels open, or two-way. You

- Use the language of respect
- Enlist cooperation
- Create an ally

Barriers to Communication

Gordon (1974) identified twelve roadblocks to communication. He called them *the dirty dozen* because they all represent messages that inhibit the communication process. When teachers make a conscious choice to confront students with their unacceptable behavior, their confrontation messages typically not only fail to bring about the desired results, they also have a negative effect on students. The best teachers can hope for with such messages is submissive compliance, frequently accompanied by a negative attitudinal response. These roadblocks contain only information about the student, never about the teacher. Hence, students are not likely to be motivated to take the teacher's needs and feelings into consideration. On the contrary, students are usually motivated to fight back or develop other strategies to defeat the teacher's attempts to impose their solutions.

The Language of Unacceptance: Roadblocks to Communication. Gordon describes categories of messages that serve to block further communication. Such messages inhibit and sometimes completely stop the two-way process of communication necessary for helping students solve the problems that interfere with their learning. For each category the teacher's behavior and language pattern, the message it sends to students, and students' typical reactions are described.

Gordon's Roadblocks to Communication

Roadblocks 1 through 5, ordering, threatening, preaching, advising, and lecturing, in one way or another all communicate unacceptance by offering a solution to the student's problem.

ROADBLOCK	TEACHER BEHAVIOR	LANGUAGE PATTERN	MESSAGE TO STUDENT	TYPICAL REACTION
1. Ordering, Commanding, Directing	Telling the student to do something, giving an order or a command.	*You must . . .* *You will . . .*	Your feelings or needs are not important.	Fear, resentment, active resistance, testing
2. Warning, Threatening	Telling the student the consequences of action or inaction.	*If you don't, then . . .* *You'd better, or . . .*	I have no respect for your needs or wants.	Fear, submission, hostility, testing of threatened consequences
3. Moralizing, Preaching	Telling the student what should or ought to be done.	*You ought to . . .* *You shouldn't . . .* *It is your responsibility . . .*	Your judgment cannot be trusted.	Guilt feelings; resistance; defending position even more strongly
4. Advising, Giving Solutions or Suggestions	Telling the student how to solve a problem, giving advice or suggestions, providing answers or solutions.	*Why don't you . . .* *What I would do is . . .* *I suggest you . . .*	You're not capable of solving your own problems.	Dependency on others; feeling misunderstood
5. Lecturing, Teaching, Giving Logical Arguments	Trying to influence the student with facts, counter-arguments, logic, information, or personal opinions.	*Yes but . . .* *The facts are . . .* *You must learn to . . .*	You're inferior, ignorant.	Feelings of inadequacy, defensiveness, resentment; rejection of argument

Roadblocks 6 through 8, blaming, labeling, and diagnosing, all communicate judgment, evaluation, or put-downs.

ROADBLOCK	TEACHER BEHAVIOR	LANGUAGE PATTERN	MESSAGE TO STUDENT	TYPICAL REACTION
6. Judging, Criticizing, Blaming	Making a negative judgment or evaluation of the student.	*You're wrong about . . .* *You're being immature.* *You're not thinking clearly.*	You're no good.	Accepting judgment as true and feeling incompetent, or retaliating with counter-criticism
7. Name-Calling, Stereotyping, Labeling	Making the student feel foolish, categorizing, or trying to shame.	*You're just a procrastinator.* *You're acting like a baby.*	You're unworthy.	Verbal retaliation; making excuses

(continued)

Gordon's Roadblocks to Communication   Continued

Roadblocks 6 through 8 (*continued*)

ROADBLOCK	TEACHER BEHAVIOR	LANGUAGE PATTERN	MESSAGE TO STUDENT	TYPICAL REACTION
8. Analyzing, Diagnosing, Interpreting	Analyzing the student's motives.	*You don't really mean that.* *You're just trying to get out of doing it.* *You feel that way because . . .*	I have you figured out.	Feeling threatened, frustrated, exposed, embarrassed, falsely accused

Roadblocks 9 and 10, praising and reassuring, represent attempts by the teacher to make a student feel better by making a problem go away or denying that a real problem exists.

ROADBLOCK	TEACHER BEHAVIOR	LANGUAGE PATTERN	MESSAGE TO STUDENT	TYPICAL REACTION
9. Praising, Agreeing, Giving Positive Evaluations	Offering a positive evaluation or judgment, agreeing	*You're pretty smart. I'm sure you'll figure it out.* *Well, I think . . .*	You don't really have a problem. Your problem is not important.	Dependency, embarrassment; feeling patronized or manipulated to behave in desired way
10. Reassuring, Sympathizing, Consoling	Trying to make the student feel better by talking the student out of his or her feelings, trying to make the feelings go away, or denying the strength of the feelings	*You'll feel better tomorrow.* *All students feel . . .*	Stop feeling the way you do.	Feeling misunderstood; reacting with hostility

Roadblock 11, questioning, is probably the most frequently used. Teachers most often use questions when they feel they need more facts because they intend to solve the students' problems by coming up with the best solutions, rather than helping students to solve the problem themselves.

ROADBLOCK	TEACHER BEHAVIOR	LANGUAGE PATTERN	MESSAGE TO STUDENT	TYPICAL REACTION
11. Probing, Questioning, Interrogating	Trying to find reasons, motives, causes; searching for more information to help student solve the problem	*Why did you wait so long?* *What made you do that?*	I don't trust you.	Defensiveness; feeling interrogated; reacting with avoidance, nonanswers, half truths or lies

Roadblock 12, diverting, consists of messages teachers use to avoid having to deal with the student at all by trying to change the subject or divert the student.

ROADBLOCK	TEACHER BEHAVIOR	LANGUAGE PATTERN	MESSAGE TO STUDENT	TYPICAL REACTION
12. Withdrawing, Diverting, Being Sarcastic, Humoring	Trying to get the student away from the problem; withdrawing or pushing the problem aside; distracting or kidding	*Let's talk about more pleasant things.* *Come on, let's . . .* *Just forget about it.*	I'm really not interested. I'd rather not deal with this.	Hurt, put down, put off, rejected

■ ■ ■ ■ ■ ■ ■ ■

LEARNING PRACTICE TASK: PERSONAL REACTION TO ROADBLOCKS

Activity Directions: Think of a time when you shared a problem situation with another person who responded with roadblocks.

- How did you react?

  _____

  _____

  _____

Spend a few minutes discussing your situation and your response with a peer.

- Were your reactions similar?

  _____

  _____

- Were your feelings similar?

  _____

  _____

Remember, if roadblocks have these effects on you, they will have the same effects on your students.

INHIBITING COMMUNICATION: THE LANGUAGE OF DISRESPECT

Sending you-messages, moralizing with *shoulds,* and using trigger words such as *always* and *never* communicate a lack of respect for students. The following section points out some communication-inhibiting traps to avoid and inauthentic talk patterns that foster distrust.

Inhibiting Communication: Using You-Language

Meaningful communication breaks down when teachers continually tell students what's wrong with them and what they shouldn't be doing. By pointing an accusatory finger, they put students on the defensive. Such messages are usually expressed in you-language and often frame problems in the past: you'll never . . . , you always . . . , can't you ever . . .

You-language is harmful in several ways because it

- Denies students responsibility for themselves
- Fails to show understanding or empathy for students
- Implies blame
- Ignores the teacher's own feelings (which the teacher may or may not be aware of)

Making *should* statements has a similar effect. Saying to students "You should do this" or "You should have done this" makes you their voice of conscience. The typical response to such moralization or implied or expressed criticism is for the student to attempt to prove that what he or she did was right, as in the statement "I wasn't being disrespectful; I was just telling it like it is." Often the student takes it one step further by trying to justify the behavior under the circumstances. Having to defend oneself is often accompanied by a counterattack in retaliation for a character assault, either implicitly or explicitly, making the teacher just as bad, or even worse, as in the following example. "I can talk however I want to you. You never say anything nice to me, or anyone else for that matter!" The battle lines are drawn as each tries to be right and make the other wrong.

These kinds of messages serve to block further productive communication and typically move the interaction to confrontation, a battle of attack and counterattack, creating an adversarial climate rather than a spirit of cooperation. Such messages inhibit, and sometimes completely stop, the two-way process of communication that is essential for building and maintaining relationships.

Inhibiting Communication	**You-Language**
Demanding	*You will . . .*
Threatening	*You'd better or . . .*
Moralizing	*You should learn to . . .*
Name calling	*You are rude.*
Blaming	*You made me . . .*
Judging	*You are being immature.*
Interrogating	*Why did you . . . ?*
Humiliating	*You should have . . .*
Degrading	*If you had any feelings you would . . .*
Invalidating	*You'd feel better if . . .*
Manipulating	*Don't you think you should . . . ?*
Globalizing	*Why can't you ever . . . ?*

These first seven ways of inhibiting communication were described previously as part of Gordon's *dirty dozen.* Descriptions of the remaining five types of inhibiting communications follow.

- Humiliating is trying to instill guilt or shame with comments like "You ought to know better."
- Degrading comments are indirectly derogatory, as in "That wasn't too bright" implying that only someone who is stupid would do that.
- Invalidating is dismissing feelings, ideas, or opinions, as in the comment "You shouldn't feel that way."
- Manipulating comments indirectly try to get others to do what you think they should do, as in "It's none of my business, but I wouldn't do that."
- Globalizing frames behavior in global terms by using words like *always, never,* or *ever,* such as "You're never doing what you are supposed to be doing."

Habits of Language to Break

Communicating in inauthentic language is demeaning and disrespectful to students. While these language differences may seem subtle to teachers, students know exactly what the teacher means. Older students think the teacher is talking down to them. Inauthentic language also gives students an opening to mock teachers, as in the following example:

> *Don't you think we've had enough of that!* leaves the teacher wide open for a retort from the student like *No, I don't* or *Who's had enough?*

Third Party Talk: *We, Let's, It, Some People.* Using *we* and *let's* is inauthentic communication because it implies that the teacher will participate too, and that's usually not true.

> *Let's see if we can all sit up straight.*
>
> *Let's cut it out.*
>
> *We are supposed to . . .*
>
> *Some people in here . . .*

Providing Ultimatums Disguised as Choices. Telling students that they have a choice is a popular recommendation. However, when the real message is "Do what I say, or I will punish you," it is an inauthentic choice. The following example is an ultimatum.

> *You can put that away or go to the principal's office* really says, do one of the two things I tell you.

Telling Students What They Need. Need statements should be about what the teacher needs, not about desired student behavior. Rather than say "You need to put that away now" the teacher should say directly what the teacher needs or wants, as in "I need you to stop talking until I finish giving the directions" or "I want you to put that away."

Pseudodirections: Directions Disguised as Questions. When giving directions, teachers give *pseudodirections*, often in the form of questions that aren't really questions at all—they're directives. Rather than direct language, they use indirect language, hinting instead of issuing clear directives. Teachers give pseudodirections because they do not want to sound harsh or autocratic. They want to appear to be nice by making their directives more pleasing and friendly. They think they are being tactful by not using direct language, but such pseudodirections not only fail to give students clear direction, they also make teachers appear weak and phony, fostering distrust. Speaking to students directly, unambiguously, and honestly builds trust. Following are examples of pseudodirections.

Appearing to Give Students Choices. Asking if the student is able to or if the student would like to, as if there is a choice.

> *Would you like to answer the next question?* means answer the question.
>
> *Bud, could you do the next problem?* means do the problem.
>
> *Can you write your name in the upper right corner?* means write your name.

Giving Commands Disguised as Solicitations of Students' Opinion.   The real intent is to tell students what they should be doing, not soliciting an opinion.

> *Don't you think it would be better if you . . . ?*
>
> *Isn't it time to . . . ?*
>
> *Don't you think you should clean out your desk?*

Hedging with Tag-On Questions.   When you hedge saying what you want or need by adding tag-on questions, you give the impression that you need to seek approval for your requests.

> *It's time to put that away, don't you think?*
>
> *You've had enough time to work on that, haven't you?*

Sarcastic Questions.   Rather than make a direct request of a student, the teacher sarcastically asks a rhetorical question.

> *Could we now get back to work?*
>
> *Don't you think that's enough?*
>
> *Are you done yet?*

Other Communication-Inhibiting Traps to Avoid.   Teachers often think they have to prove to students that they are right. Doing so serves to inhibit communication and is likely to start a fault-finding cycle with the student.

- Trying to prove you're right (*I'm not being unfair. You . . .*)
- Having to have the last word (*But you . . . ; I did it because . . .*)
- Extracting a confession: attempting to get the student to admit wrongdoing (*Here's why you are wrong . . . ; Do you realize . . . ?; Why did you . . . ?*)
- Giving logical arguments for why the student is wrong (*Can't you see that . . . ?*)

INVITING COMMUNICATION: THE LANGUAGE OF RESPECT

The goal of any relationship is the mutual meeting of needs and desires. Expressing dissatisfaction can be done in a way that is either facilitative and respectful or in a way that is obstructive and disrespectful, making it more difficult to maintain an amicable relationship. Using I-language and making impact-statements are two approaches that are facilitative and respectful.

Using I-Language to Invite Communication

The term *I-language* represents a broader concept than the term *I-message*, which connotes a particular format. I-language serves the primary function of allowing students to maintain self-respect and responsibility for their own behavior. With I-language, teachers speak from their own perspective and clarify for students why they're concerned while respecting students' capacity to make appropriate adjustments on their own. Using I-language instead of you-language helps maintain a positive relationship by promoting consideration by others of the impact of their actions and fosters a willingness to change. Such nonblameful messages don't require justification because they don't imply a negative evaluation. When there is no accusation of wrongful behavior, there is no need to become defensive, and self-worth is not at stake.

Contrary to what is typically presented, the main purpose of using I-language is to avoid attributing blame by keeping the focus on why the behavior is a problem; expressing feelings is secondary. Teachers don't have strong feelings about everything that happens in the classroom. Frequently, in the classroom setting, clarifying the impact is more essential than expressing the feeling. The goal is to effect a change in disposition, allowing students the opportunity to correct their own behavior.

When teachers use I-language, they encourage students to choose to change the behavior that is causing a problem. They provide students with data for stopping and thinking about the ramifications of their actions, while leaving the decision in their hands.

I-language has a very different effect on students than you-language. As an example, suppose you are frustrated because one of your students is constantly interrupting you while another student is responding to a question. The behavior (interrupting) is causing you a problem—you are feeling frustrated. If your message to the student is "Jack, you're being rude," you are in effect transferring your frustration into a label of the student's character. By labeling the student's behavior, you avoid communicating your own feeling of frustration. If you send a message that accurately portrays what is going on with you, it will inevitably be in I-language, as in

> *Jack, I get frustrated when you keep interrupting, because I can't hear either of you when you're both talking.*

While using I-language communicates what the teacher is experiencing, you-language is a negative judgment about the student. From Jack's perspective, he hears an evaluation of how bad he is in the first case and a statement about the teacher in the second case. When you use I-language, you take responsibility for your own reaction and you leave the responsibility for the student's behavior with the student.

I-language has the following advantages. I-language

- Doesn't require justification from the student
- Is nonthreatening
- Provides a concrete reason for the teacher's concern
- Doesn't imply a negative judgment of the student
- Supports students' consideration of the impact of their behavior
- Fosters acceptance of responsibility for change
- Promotes a willingness to change the behavior
- Maintains a positive relationship
- Models appropriate expression of negative (or positive) emotions

Making students aware of the impact of their actions, without trying to make them feel guilty or ashamed, tends to put them in a cooperative frame of mind. Stating the impact of the actions of students is valuable for two reasons. First, it helps clarify why the student's behavior bothered (or pleased) the teacher. Pointing out why the behavior is a problem can sometimes help the teacher recognize when feelings are stemming from enforcing an expectation that may not be interfering with a productive learning climate. Secondly, telling students about the impact of their actions can help clarify for them the results of their actions.

Constructing an I-Message.   I-messages convey only the teacher's reaction and concern. Using I-messages transfers the focus from students to teacher by refocusing attention on the needs and feelings of the teacher. I-messages communicate far more than you-messages. They let students know how the teacher feels, why he or she feels that way, and what they can do. I-messages communicate the teacher's feelings to students about how their behavior affects the teacher's ability to teach and maintain a productive learning environment. When teachers send I-messages they share personal feelings by stating facts about their feelings in the situation without blaming the student for those feelings.

In contrast to expressing irritation using I-language, aggressively expressing irritation using you-language tries to make the student responsible for causing the teacher's feelings. In the following example, the first statement is a you-message, and the second statement is an I-message.

You really make me mad when you always butt in! Why do you have to do that?

When I'm constantly interrupted, I lose my train of thought and then I start to get irritated. I'd like you to wait until I've finished speaking.

Typically, an I-message has three parts. First, students need to know exactly what's causing the problem.

- Part 1 is a nonblameful description of the behavior, situation or event. For example,

  When materials are left everywhere, . . . represents a condition or situation, whereas

  When you interrupt, . . . represents a specific student behavior of concern.

- Part 2 is the feeling or emotional state associated with the behavior or situation. This component states the feelings generated as a result of the problem. For example,

  When your feet are in the aisle [description], *I'm afraid someone might fall* [feeling].

- Part 3 is the tangible or concrete effect of the behavior, or the condition it creates. This component addresses the tangible effect on the teacher by describing why the teacher has a problem. For example,

  When materials are left everywhere [description], *I get annoyed* [feeling] *because I have to stay after school to pick them up* [effect].

Using I-language also provides an opportunity to help students develop empathy for others. While students may not agree with your policies and classroom practices, they can't argue with your feelings. Likewise, you shouldn't argue with theirs. A statement like the following leaves little opportunity for students to take issue.

I'm disappointed about the way you behaved when I was out of the room.

It is important to make sure that your claimed effect is credible in the eyes of your students. Stating why the behavior is a problem causes teachers to consider whether student behaviors actually have a tangible effect. If there is no tangible effect, it will be hard to convince students they should change their behavior.

The usual format of an I-message is

When . . . [description of behavior], *I feel . . .* [feeling state] *because . . .* [concrete effect or problem the behavior creates].

When . . . I feel . . . because . . . , or *I feel . . . when . . . because . . .*

Learning to Use I-Language.   The following two questions can help guide teachers in effectively utilizing I-language.

1. Will students identify with my concern?
2. Will students be invited to make the right choice on their own?

It is not necessary to always use the specific components; you can begin to practice I-language by just beginning your communication with the word *I*, as in

I'm very tired because I only got three hours sleep last night. I just can't take all this noise right now.

I don't want you to . . . because . . .

I'd like you to . . .

I have a problem with . . .

Sometimes you may just want to make a statement describing what you are worried or concerned about, as in

I'm concerned that everyone won't get to say what they want to say.

I'm worried for you when I hear you talk like that, because I'm afraid that . . .

When commenting about something that has already happened it may only be necessary to say

I was disappointed that you missed class yesterday.

It might also be helpful to think to yourself "This is a problem for me because I have to . . ." If you can complete the sentence to yourself, then you can communicate exactly why the behavior is causing a problem.

I-language is particularly effective for helping teachers express difficult negative feelings, as in

I don't like stuff being thrown at me.

I don't want to be treated that way.

I'm really angry because . . .

I'm becoming more and more aggravated by your tone of voice.

Sometimes for the classroom setting, it is also helpful to add what you'd like the student to do, what you want to happen, or what would improve the situation, by adding a fourth component. This last component could be in addition to or in place of either the feeling or the effect, as in

When . . . I feel . . . because . . . and I'd like . . .

When you're out of your seat, it distracts the students around you. I want you to stay in your seat until this activity is over.

The *I want* part of the I-message should be used purposefully. Although excluding it gives the student maximum opportunity to offer ideas for dealing with the situation, including it gives the student specific information as to what you want to see happen.

I-messages don't always have to express a concern or negative feeling. They can be used to make a positive assertion, as in

I felt really proud when you were selected as student of the month.

I-language may at first seem artificial, but much of the awkwardness is due to unfamiliarity. As you practice and adapt the language to your own style, I-language will begin to sound more and more natural. While the I-statement format is initially presented as a formula, after you become comfortable using I-language, you can interchange the three components or omit parts so that your message matches your own natural style of speaking. For example, the *I feel* part of the statement can be omitted. While saying *I feel* does clarify precisely what you're feelings are and may reduce misunderstandings, describing your feelings may be inappropriate in some situations or you may not think stating your feelings is necessary.

Some teachers may not be comfortable expressing their feelings in the classroom or may think that a statement of feelings is inappropriate in certain situations or with particular students. The primary reason for using I-language in the classroom is to avoid blame attributing language by focusing on the impact of the behavior, not the students' shortcomings. Often clarifying the impact is more important than communicating the teacher's feeling.

Summary

The critical elements of I-language are that it (1) speaks from the teacher's perspective, (2) clarifies why the behavior is a problem, (3) gives students data about their behavior, (4) communicates respect for students' ability to make their own choices, and (5) is nonblameful. Delivering an I-message is usually just the first move. You want the I-message to begin a dialogue that leads to students solving their own problems.

Once teachers are well versed in delivering I-messages, they can teach their students to use them. With students, it's important to stress that sharing their feelings helps others understand the reasons behind their actions. Students can be coached to make statements like the following.

When you interrupt me, I get confused and forget what I was saying, [rather than] *Hey man, I'm talking.*

I feel sad when you won't let me in the game because I have no one to play with, [rather than] *You jerks, who wants to play with you anyway!*

Cautions

It is important to note that although I-messages have many advantages over you-messages, there are some potential drawbacks to consider. I-messages can

- Involve the risk of self-disclosure
- Reveal your own vulnerability
- Elicit inappropriate levels of intimacy or self-disclosure
- Go unheard by some students.

Even the best I-statement won't be effective unless it is delivered appropriately, that is, unless there is congruence between your nonverbal and verbal message. If your words are perfect but your tone of voice, facial expression, and posture all are communicating a you-message, the student is likely to hear a blaming message and respond defensively. And even if both your words and stance are sending an I-message, the student may still become defensive. Sometimes students can be so uncooperative or unreachable that even an I-message will not facilitate communication. However, I-messages certainly have a far greater potential than you-messages for keeping the communication channels open.

When you send an I-message you are exposing yourself as you really are and revealing your own vulnerability for being hurt or upset. Occasionally, I-messages can elicit inappropriate levels of intimacy or self-disclosure.

Common Mistakes When Learning to Use I-Messages.   Several mistakes are common when first learning I-messages.

1. Disguised you-message: Embedding a you-message in the I-language format. This is a masked message and is actually blameful.
2. Undershooting: Downplaying the actual feeling or emotion, resulting in an insincere message
3. Stating a secondary feeling: Sending a message that states a secondary feeling that results from a more basic, primary feeling
4. Inauthentic or incongruent message: Using a rational message in place of the real feeling. This is a bogus message that is out of touch with the actual feeling.
5. Failure to shift to active listening: After the initial I-message, failing to respond to the student's defensive response

The following examples illustrate these five potential problems when sending I-messages.

Example 1: Mr. Jackson's seventh-grade class is involved in an art project to accompany their studies of ecological problems in their local area. John is wandering from table to table talking to other students, sharpening pencils, and occasionally teasing other kids by pretending to steal materials from their desks. Two students have complained that John is bothering them. Mr. Jackson tells John, "When you wander around the room I feel you are being inconsiderate of the needs of the other students." John sits down and stares out the window.

Problem: Disguised you-message.

Mr. Jackson substitutes "I feel" for "I think" and then sends the blaming, judgmental "you are inconsiderate" message.

Example 2: When Mrs. Klein leaves her kindergarten room to join her class on the playground she sees Greg standing on his head on the platform at the top of a slide. He yells, "Look, Mrs. Klein. I'm way up here." She says, "I worry when I see you up there, Greg." Greg continues to stand on his head at the top of the slide.

Problem: Undershooting

Because Greg is in danger, Mrs. Klein's appropriate reaction isn't being worried, it's being scared to death.

Example 3: Mrs. Flores is at an interminable faculty meeting. She is expecting guests for dinner and needs to stop at the store. She is on a tight schedule to prepare dinner. Meanwhile, the principal is droning on about how to handle problems with chewing gum. Finally, Mrs. Flores says, "When we sit around here talking about chewing gum I'm bored out of my mind."

Problem: Sending a secondary feeling.

Mrs. Flores' real feelings are probably anxiety and frustration. Because of these primary feelings she may become bored with the discussion.

Example 4: Mr. Daniels has individualized the instructional program for his sixth-grade class. It is working well, students are highly motivated, and the quality of work is the best he's seen. However, at the end of the day Mr. Daniels finds that, despite a clean-up time, he has to spend 20 minutes shelving reference books, straightening up the science center, and putting away construction and art materials. He confronts his class and says, "When you leave the room messy, I'm afraid the principal is going to come in and think we are a bunch of slobs."

Problem: Inauthentic or incongruent message.

Mr. Daniels has difficulty articulating his real feelings so he makes up the plausible message about his fear of being negatively evaluated by the principal.

Example 5: Mrs. Clark and her fourth-grade class have divided up the routine duties needed to operate the class efficiently. For this week, Maria volunteers to keep the trash containers emptied. For the first 2 days she performs her task diligently, but for the past 2 she has had to be reminded repeatedly. Today Mrs. Clark says, "When I see the trash basket running over I know we can't keep our room clean and this bothers me." Maria says, "I'm the only one who has to work around here." Mrs. Clark responds, "I'm disappointed when someone volunteers for a job and then doesn't do it." Maria angrily grabs the trash container and goes out the door, slamming it behind her.

Problem: Failure to shift to active listening.

After confronting Maria, Mrs. Clark fails to hear Maria's defensive response and instead sends another I-message.

Potential Pitfalls to Avoid.   When you let others know exactly what's causing the problem with a nonblameful description of the situation and address the concrete effect on you, it communicates why the behavior is causing a problem for you. It is a factual account without editorial commentary. When evaluation creeps in, you get messages that may sound nonblameful but are actually blameful. They are in an I-language format, but are actually you-messages in disguise, as the following examples illustrate.

When I find I can't trust certain troublemakers in here . . .

When you act like a bully, I feel . . .

Often when you attempt to communicate your true feelings, you actually express not your feelings but attitudes, interpretations, or opinions. For example, if you say, "I feel you did that on purpose," you have expressed only your interpretation. If you say, "I feel like leaving," you have expressed what the behavior leads you to want to do, not a feeling. In this case, the feeling behind this statement is most likely hurt or anger.

You may disguise a feeling behind a message that's a statement of opinion by saying, "I feel you're wrong." This phrase doesn't express any feeling; it is merely your position. Another example of a disguised you-message is: "When you . . . , I feel you are being inconsiderate." "I feel" is substituted for "I think," transforming the message from a true feeling message to a blaming, judgmental, "You're inconsiderate" message.

Avoid using the words *you, that* or *like* after *I feel*.

I feel that . . . Once you use *that*, the message is an opinion and is usually a judgment, not a feeling.

I feel you should know better than to do that. . . The real message is *You're inconsiderate*.

I feel that you were acting childish . . . The real message is *You're immature*.

I feel like you don't care . . . The real message is *You're uncaring*.

The following sequence of practice activities asks you to recognize examples and nonexamples of I-messages, convert you-messages to I-messages, put parts together, and finally to construct I-messages without prompts.

LEARNING PRACTICE TASK: RECOGNIZING I-MESSAGES

Activity Directions: Classify each of the statements below as either a you-message or an I-message. Remember, if the message labels, blames, or orders, regardless of the words, it is a you-message.

TEACHER RESPONSE	YOU-MESSAGE	I-MESSAGE
1. Quit fooling around.	_____	_____
2. It's impolite to speak out of turn.	_____	_____
3. When you're late for class, I get frustrated because it's distracting.	_____	_____
4. Are you enjoying making me angry?	_____	_____
5. The hair on my arms stands on end when you shout like that.	_____	_____
6. Stop that yelling. You're driving me crazy.	_____	_____
7. I'm very tired and just can't take extra noise right now.	_____	_____
8. Mind your own business.	_____	_____
9. I really get annoyed when people get pushed around in this room.	_____	_____
10. I'm becoming more and more aggravated by your tone of voice.	_____	_____

LEARNING PRACTICE TASK: REWRITING YOU-MESSAGES

Activity Directions: For the two situations below, rewrite the you-message as an I-message.

Situation: Eddie knocks his books off the desk.
You-message: "Eddie, you pick up those books right now! I don't want to see that again."
I-message: _____

_____

Situation: Sally and Sue are talking while Thea is giving a presentation.
You-message: "Pay attention. You're being rude."
I-message: _____

_____

LEARNING PRACTICE TASK: CONSTRUCTING I-MESSAGES

Activity Directions: 1. List three student behaviors that cause a problem for you. 2. Describe the effect on you and your feeling. 3. In the next section, join these separate components and write the three I-messages the way you would actually deliver them. Use the examples provided as a guide.

BEHAVIOR: NONJUDGMENTAL DESCRIPTION OF THE PROBLEM.	EFFECT: CONCRETE EFFECT OF THE BEHAVIOR ON ME.	FEELING: MY FEELING ABOUT THE BEHAVIOR.

Example

John interrupts another student.   *I can't hear what either student is saying.*   *frustration*

1. _____   _____   _____
2. _____   _____   _____
3. _____   _____   _____

Example

John, I get frustrated when you interrupt Sue, because then I can't hear what either of you is saying.

1. _____
   _____

2. _____
   _____

3. _____
   _____

LEARNING PRACTICE TASK: WRITING I-MESSAGES

Activity Directions: Write an I-message for the three frequent classroom problems listed below.

1. Student is late.

   _____
   _____
   _____

2. Student is talking while you are giving directions.

   _____
   _____
   _____

3. Student puts down another student.

   _____
   _____
   _____

For what type of classroom situations do you think I-messages are most appropriate?
For what type of classroom situations do you think I-messages are least appropriate?

Using Impact-Statements to Invite Communication

When you think stating your feelings is inappropriate, undesirable, or unnecessary an *impact-statement* can be used rather than an I-statement. An impact-statement is similar to an I-statement, without the statement of feeling component. Both impact-statements and I-statements have three components. In an impact-statement there is a nonblameful description of the behavior and a statement of its tangible effect, as in an I-statement, but instead of stating your resulting feelings, you specify the person affected by the behavior. In the classroom setting, the person affected could be the teacher directly, the student engaging in the behavior, or other students.

Impact-statements are less personal and appeal to the student's sense of responsibility, rather than feelings for the teacher. The idea of an impact-statement is to state the actual consequence of the behavior and what direct effect it has on the classroom situation or learning environment.

Delivering an Impact-Statement.   An impact-statement includes three components.

- A nonblameful description of the behavior
- The direct impact of the behavior
- Those affected or the situation created as a result of the behavior or resulting situation.

Impact-statements could describe the impact on (1) the teacher directly, (2) the teacher's sense of responsibility for students (e.g., their learning, security, or safety), (3) the lesson or learning activity, (4) the student(s) engaging in the behavior, or (5) other students. The following example illustrates an impact-statement.

> *When you ask me a question while I'm with another group* [behavior], *I have to stop what I'm doing* [impact] *and the students in the group have to wait for me* [those affected].

The focus is on the immediate impact of the behavior rather than on the feelings the teacher has, as in an I-statement. Also, like I-statements, the direct impact as well as the resulting consequence should be believable to your students. Often in delivering the impact-statement, you would combine the impact and the effect or just state those affected (part 3) and omit the impact (part 2) because it is unnecessary or implicit.

> *When you ask me a question when I'm with another group, the students in the group have to wait for me.*

The following example illustrates various effects of the same behavior.

> *When you call out the answer . . .*

> Effect on other students: *Other students don't have a chance to think of their own answers.*

Effect on teacher: *I'm not able to call on another person and give everyone a chance to answer.*

Effect on student's own learning: *You don't have a chance to learn from other students who may have different ideas.*

LEARNING PRACTICE TASK: DEVELOPING YOUR SKILL AT DELIVERING I- AND IMPACT-STATEMENTS

Activity Directions: The following activities can help you develop your skill at delivering I-statements and impact-statements.

Activity 1: Think of a time when you have sent the following you-messages.

You really make me mad!
You are so self-centered!

Practice writing alternative messages in I- and impact-language.

_____

_____

_____

Activity 2: Write three you-messages you could send, one to a student, one to a peer, and one to an administrator in your school. Transform each of these statements into I- or impact-language and rehearse them with a peer.

_____

_____

_____

You should practice making I-statements and impact-statements in a safe setting. Try them out on people you feel comfortable with on relatively minor issues. Solicit feedback on others' reactions.

Take a few minutes twice a day during the coming week and reflect on the language you use with students. List any you-messages you can remember and practice writing them as either an I- or impact-statement.

LEARNING TO LISTEN

The basis for many communication problems lies in the inability of individuals to listen effectively. Listening is perhaps the most overlooked form of communication. Genuine listening requires much practice. Listening skills are used both proactively and reactively. When the teacher owns the problem, the teacher uses listening skills as part of the problem-solving process, to transition to a mutually acceptable solution. When teachers place themselves in a helping role in response to a student-owned problem, they are in more of a reactive mode.

Listening is probably the most essential element of any supportive relationship, and it is at the core of acknowledging and comforting students. When a teacher listens to a student with quiet attention and silent affection, the teacher supports the student in discovering what to do about problems. By listening to students, the teacher serves as the mirror of reflection, so the picture becomes clearer. By facilitating self-reflection, the teacher helps to unmuddy the waters, enabling students to tap their own resources for coping with their problems.

Developing the Art of Listening

Developing the art of listening means learning to really listen, rather than rehearsing in your mind the next thing you are going to say as you wait for the other person to finish talking. Often you get caught up in a your turn–my turn response format in which each person is only waiting for the other to stop talking and to have a turn to talk. This is the kind of nonlistening characterized by fragmented conversation in which neither person really listens to or cares what the other person has said.

Probably the most exasperating nonlistening is when the person appears to be listening but responds with a comment completely unrelated to what you said. That's when you want to scream, "You didn't hear a word I said!" Nonlistening can be extremely frustrating because the person is hearing the words but not listening to the message, often preoccupied with his or her own thoughts. These ways of interacting masquerade as listening but are poor substitutions for the real thing.

For many teachers, it's difficult to just listen. The tendency is to want to jump in with solutions to the student's problem. Hence, the first tool to develop in learning to listen is to catch yourself before you offer a solution by controlling the impulse to talk and just remaining silent. Although silence communicates some degree of caring by just being there, it doesn't necessarily communicate acceptance. So the second tool in developing the art of listening is to demonstrate acceptance. You show acceptance by letting the person know you are really present by providing nonverbal and verbal support.

Being silent and demonstrating that you are truly present communicate caring and acceptance, but they don't necessarily communicate that you are willing to take the time to help the student delve into and explore issues and concerns. So you need to move to the next tool in developing the art of listening, which is to explicitly provide an invitation to talk. This involves a more proactive role on the part of the listener to ask open-ended, nonevaluative questions that invite the student to talk more. With the final tool, active listening, you become an active participant with the student, by reflecting, paraphrasing, and clarifying what you are hearing.

Styles of Listening

Figure 4.1 shows the characteristics and the interaction of the two components of listening style, listening and responding. You can either listen or not listen (depicted in the vertical axis). Likewise, you can either respond or not respond (depicted in the horizontal axis). The interaction of these two components produces four styles of listening.

- Active nonlistening (quadrant 1)
- Passive nonlistening (quadrant 2)
- Passive listening (quadrant 3)
- Active listening (quadrant 4)

Active and passive nonlistening represent ineffective styles of listening, whereas passive and active listening represent more effective ones. In quadrant 1,

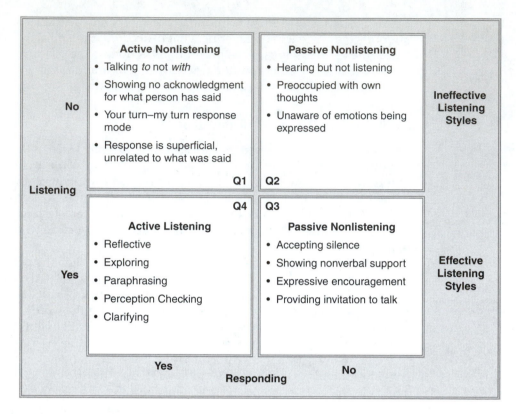

FIGURE 4.1   Styles of Listening

the individual is only waiting for the speaker to stop to have a turn to talk. By failing to capture the speaker's meaning, the quadrant 2 passive nonlistener can be extremely frustrating. The quadrant 3 passive listener communicates acceptance and empathy, thereby encouraging the speaker to continue. In quadrant 4, the active listener goes one step further by trying to comprehend the underlying emotions as well as the words.

Nine Ways to Listen

Developing the art of listening can be thought of as progressing through four levels. At each level, the listener becomes a more active participant in the process. Moving through the levels involves the nine listening skills described below.

Level 1: Passive Listening.   In passive listening, the listener just listens without any interaction with the speaker.

1. Silence. Merely listening is an effective tool because it invites the person experiencing a problem to discuss it. Remaining a silent listener allows the person to release feelings and emotions.

While silence does communicate some degree of acceptance by just being there, it does not communicate empathy or warmth. The student doesn't know if the teacher is really paying attention and understanding. Students may even think that the teacher is evaluating them while being silent.

Level 2: Acknowledgment.   These types of responses indicate that the teacher is really listening.

2. Nonverbal Support. Nonverbal messages help communicate that you are really paying attention. Cues such as nodding, smiling, or leaning forward indicate to the person that you are tuned in.

3. Encouragers. Minimal verbal responses can offer encouragement to the student to continue and serve to reassure the student that you are still attentive and interested in the student's problem.

Expressions such as "Uh-huh," "Oh," "I see," or "Really" let the student know that it is okay for him or her to continue. Although these types of responses do communicate some empathy, they do not indicate acceptance or understanding of the situation.

Level 3: Invitation to Talk. This skill is primarily used at the beginning to let students know you want to help and are willing to take time.

4. Opening. This skill involves a more active role on the part of the teacher to ask open-ended, nonevaluative questions that serve as door-openers to get the student to talk more. Some examples are

Do you want to tell me about it?

That's interesting. Want to tell me more?

Would you like to tell me what happened?

Openings are genuine invitations to students to share their feelings or concerns. They open the door but do not necessarily keep the door open because, although they do demonstrate caring, they do not demonstrate understanding.

Level 4: Active Listening. Levels 1 to 3 have limitations in that they do not provide much interaction nor do they let the student know that he or she is being understood.

Active listening is when you try to understand the feelings being expressed or what the real message means (i.e., hearing the emotions as well as the words) and then putting your understanding into your own words and sending it back to the person for consideration or verification. Active listening involves interaction with the student and it provides feedback (proof) to the student that the teacher understands. The process of active listening involves several specific skills.

5. Reflecting. When you reflect, you verbalize the feelings and attitudes that you perceive lie behind the message. The purpose of reflecting is to let the student know you are aware of the emotions involved as well as the words. Because spoken words often don't clearly articulate how one is feeling, responding in terms of the student's perspective, not your own, by feeding back the feelings perceived can help bring a troublesome emotion to the surface. In many cases, going beyond the spoken word to the often unspoken emotions can actually help the student identify his or her feelings and assume ownership for those feelings. The following are examples of reflective statements.

Cindy really irritates you when she acts like that.

You seem disappointed with your assignment.

I can see you're angry with me right now.

Sometimes reflective statements may be rejected by the student. It's important to realize you won't always be exactly on the mark. You don't have to be right every time. One of the advantages of reflection is that it conveys that you are trying to understand the feelings, and when you are off target the relationship is not hindered. The student will generally feel comfortable restating his or her feelings and you'll have another chance.

6. Exploring. This technique calls for questioning in an open-ended way to extend the student's thinking and expand the student's range of consideration. It can be used when the student is only expressing feelings, not facts or when there are missing links in the story. The following are examples.

Can you tell me more about . . . ?

What's causing you the most trouble?

I'm wondering if the plan you chose is really what you want. It seems to me that you are experiencing some doubt. Are you?

The following example illustrates a teacher response to help the student explore other options.

Student: There's nothing else I can do.

Teacher: Are you sure you've considered all your options?

7. Paraphrasing. Paraphrasing calls for translating or feeding back to the student the essence of his or her message but in a simpler, more precise way. In paraphrasing, you listen for the basic message, summarize what you heard in your own words, and restate it in fewer but similar words. The following example illustrates paraphrasing.

Student: Sometimes I think I'd just like to quit school. Then I wouldn't have to put up with all this crap from everyone, but then I start to feel like that would just be copping out.

Teacher: So you think you'd be ashamed of yourself if you gave up now.

In paraphrasing, you make sure that you are clear about what the student said. You demonstrate understanding without adding ideas, clarifying, or trying to interpret. Paraphrasing not only demonstrates understanding of what was said, but it also communicates that you care enough about what the student said to get it right. Although the simple step of restating what you thought you heard and playing it back to the student might seem unnecessary, it often helps the student take a more objective look at what he or she is saying. Sometimes you may want to follow up your paraphrase with an additional question if you think you need to clarify a certain point.

8. Perception Checking. The purpose of perception checking is to make sure you are interpreting what the student said the way it was intended. In perception checking, you verify any confusion you might be having in understanding the message. To do this, you pose a question, usually providing more than one possible interpretation, and ask for feedback. The goal of perception checking is to verify the accuracy of your interpretation, not to be right. In the following example, the teacher checks to see if the student thinks the material is too difficult versus another issue, like too much work.

Student: I'll never be able to learn all this. I don't even know what to do.

Teacher: Is it that the material seems too hard for you, or is it that it's too much work?

Perception checking reflects an attitude of respect and concern for the student, saying in effect, "I need your help to make sure I'm correctly interpreting what you're saying." The following is another example.

I'm not sure I understand. Was it that she left that really made you mad?

9. Clarifying. Sometimes there is a need to sort out something confusing. Clarifying involves restating what the student has said to clear up any confusion. Often it involves stating your own confusion and asking for help to clarify your understanding. The following are examples of clarifying.

I'm not sure how you feel. Earlier you said . . . Now you seem to be saying . . . I'm confused.

Can we stop here? I really don't understand what you mean. Can you tell me more?

Let me see now, in other words you . . .

Sample Teacher–Student Dialogue Using Active Listening

Student: I don't want to stay in school today. Can I go home?

Teacher: You do sound unhappy, Manny. [reflecting]

Student: I just hate those fifth graders. They think they're really hot stuff.

Teacher: Hmm. [encouraging]

Student: Leroy Brown is the worst one. He thinks he's a big shot, just because he has a new baseball glove.

Teacher: I see. [encouraging]

Student: They always make fun of me because I have to play with my dad's old glove.

Teacher: You get upset when they make fun of you. [reflecting]

Student: Yeah. Dad said he would get me a new glove but I have to pay for half of it. And I only have two dollars.

Teacher: It's pretty discouraging when you can't see how you're going to get the glove. [reflecting]

Student: Yeah, it sure is! I've been trying to save my allowance but it's hard to do. I'll bet Leroy Brown didn't have to buy half of his glove.

Teacher: You think it's not fair for you to have to spend your money on a glove when the other kids don't. [paraphrasing]

Student: Well, I guess it's a fair way to do it. But I just can't save money, that's all.

Teacher: Oh. You think it's an okay idea, if you could only do it. [paraphrasing]

Student: Yeah, that's right. How can I save $10 more when my allowance is only $2 a week?

Teacher: Wow! You would have to save all your allowance for five whole weeks. [paraphrasing] That's pretty frustrating, huh! [reflecting]

Student: Yeah—what I need is money quicker. Maybe my dad would give me my allowance early.

Teacher: Do you think that could be the answer? [exploring]

Student: Yeah—no. Then I'd have no allowance for anything else for a long time!

Teacher: Hmm. [encouraging]

Student: Yeah! I'll bet my mom would let me help her pull weeds from the garden. And I could clean up Mr. Smith's yard. He's already asked me about that!

Teacher: Wow! Sounds like you're pretty excited about all these new ideas you've come up with. [reflecting]

Student: Yeah. Thanks. You've really helped me out.

Teacher: I'm glad I was here to help, Manny. I want to see that new glove when you get it, okay? [appreciating]

Student: Sure! Thanks. See you later.

- - - - - - - -

LEARNING PRACTICE TASK: RECOGNIZING ACTIVE LISTENING RESPONSES

Activity Directions: For each of the following student statements, several teacher responses are given. For each one, decide which response is an active listening response, that is, a response that invites further discussion and best reflects the idea or feeling being communicated.

1. "Sometimes I think I'd like to drop out of school, but then I start to feel like a quitter."
   a. "Maybe it would be helpful to take a break. You can always come back, you know."
   b. "You're afraid that you might fail if you stay in school now, is that it?"
   c. "I can really relate to what you're saying. I feel like that myself sometimes."
   d. "So you'd feel ashamed of yourself if you quit now, even though you'd like to?"

2. "I hate David! I hate him. I hate him. I hate him."
   a. "You must never hate people, Monica."
   b. "David really makes you mad when he bothers you."
   c. "What did he do?"
   d. "Oh, you really don't feel that way, do you?"

3. "I don't get it. Why do we have to learn this stuff anyway?"
   a. "You'll need it to get into college."
   b. "Just keep at it. It'll make sense after a while."
   c. "Something isn't making sense to you?"
   d. "Would you like to come in for extra help after school?"

4. "I don't want to sit near Juan anymore."
   a. "Sorry, but seats have been assigned."
   b. "If he's bothering you, just ignore him."
   c. "You ought to be able to handle this on your own."
   d. "Would you like to tell me what happened?"

5. "Mr. Jones, can a person die from chicken pox?"
   a. "No."
   b. "Don't be silly."
   c. "Do you have chicken pox?"
   d. "Sounds like you're a little worried about somebody."

6. "Ms. Adams, look at my math paper! I got an A."
   a. "Hey, you must be pretty proud of yourself today!"
   b. "That's very nice, Angie."
   c. "See what happens when you really try."
   d. "Well, don't let it go to your head!"

- - - - - - - -

LEARNING PRACTICE TASK: CATEGORIZING ACTIVE LISTENING RESPONSES

Activity Directions: For each of the following student statements, decide which response is an active listening response. Then decide which type of active listening response it is. For each response that is not an active listening response, indicate which type of roadblock is being used. Follow the example provided.

	TYPE OF ROADBLOCK OR ACTIVE LISTENING RESPONSE
This school sucks!	
a. *Don't use that language.*	*Ordering*
b. *Come on, things aren't so bad.*	*Diverting*
c. *That attitude will get you nowhere.*	*Judging*
d. *School's getting you down these days?*	*Active listening–reflecting*

"Ms. Smith, I don't think I'll ever learn to read." _____

a. "Of course you will, Jamie. You just need to try harder." _____

b. "Well, it really doesn't matter, honey. Everyone will like you anyway." _____

c. "Why do you think that?" _____

d. "You sound pretty discouraged about this." _____

"My daughter is very upset. She says she doesn't understand anything." _____

a. "She needs to pay closer attention in class." _____

b. "Please go on. I'd like to hear more about this." _____

c. "She's very anxious, but she'll do just fine." _____

d. "Most students find my explanations quite clear." _____

■ ■ ■ ■ ■ ■ ■ ■

LEARNING PRACTICE TASK: WRITING ACTIVE LISTENING RESPONSES

Activity Directions: During this activity you will work with a partner to analyze your active listening responses. Follow the steps listed below.

Step 1: Working independently, write an active listening response for each of the following statements.

Peer: "My fifth period class is driving me up a wall."

_____

_____

Friend: "I'm so fat! Nobody can stand me!"

_____

_____

Student: "I tried to explain to Mr. Adams why my assignment was late, but he wouldn't listen to me."

_____

_____

Parent: "I've tried to get Jack to do his homework but he won't, and I just don't know what to do about it."

_____

_____

(continued)

LEARNING PRACTICE TASK   Continued

Step 2: Exchange task sheets with your partner. For each of the active listening responses, determine the following.
a. Are there any roadblocks?
b. Are there any you-messages (either direct or disguised)?
c. For responses that are active listening responses, what type of active listening response is it (e.g., clarifying, reflecting)?

Step 3: Exchange task sheets and rewrite your responses based on your partner's feedback.

_____

_____

_____

_____

_____

_____

_____

_____

_____

Paraphrasing is an especially helpful strategy when conferencing with parents. It demonstrates an understanding of what was said. In paraphrasing the teacher does not add any new ideas or try to impose the teacher's own frame of reference. Such restatement helps the parent to feel understood and encouraged to continue the dialogue.

LEARNING PRACTICE TASK: RECOGNIZING PARAPHRASING RESPONSES IN CONFERENCING WITH PARENTS

Activity Directions: For each situation below decide which response is the most complete and accurate paraphrasing of the parent's message.

1. "Maria is very upset and needs more help or she won't be able to pass. She says she doesn't understand anything."
    a. "Maria needs to pay closer attention in class."
    b. "She's very anxious, but actually she'll do just fine. She only needs to review more before tests."
    c. "Most students find my explanations to be quite clear. Perhaps she isn't listening."
    d. "You're concerned because Maria can't keep up, and you think she needs more help."

2. "I don't know what to do about my son. His whining is driving me crazy."
    a. "Even though whining is natural, it's getting to you?"
    b. "Sometimes you really get fed up with his complaining?"
    c. "You're getting angry at him?"
    d. "Even the best parents get irritated sometimes."

3. "Every day there seems to be a new crisis with Lionel. He's constantly on the go and I just can't seem to settle him down."
    a. "You're really having difficulty keeping up with Lionel."
    b. "Oh, he'll outgrow it sooner or later."
    c. "You need to set limits for Lionel."
    d. "Perhaps he needs more physical activity."

4. "I've heard kids calling the special class kids 'retarded.' I don't want Will made fun of. I definitely don't want him to be in a special class."
   a. "You really don't believe that do you?"
   b. "But we have a good program here."
   c. "You're worried about the other students' reactions to Will."
   d. "What would make the other kids say that?"

Perception Check

A perception check generally has three parts.

1. A description of the comment, behavior, or situation
2. Offering of alternative interpretations
3. A request for feedback

Example

Special Education teacher: The committee has recommended that we put Mary into the regular class. She will be given one hour a day special assistance.

Parent: I don't want Mary in a regular class for any part of the school day. I don't want her to suffer setbacks.

Perception check: When you say you don't want Mary to suffer setbacks are you worried about how she will react to the new situation or are you more concerned about the other students' reactions? Could you clarify what you're worried about?

LEARNING PRACTICE TASK: PERCEPTION CHECK EXERCISE

Activity Directions: Write a perception check response for the situations below.

Teacher: "I've had it with Donny. He doesn't seem to want to do anything right."

Perception check:

_____

_____

_____

Parent: "My child is floundering in your class."
Perception check:

_____

_____

_____

Student: "I'm not putting up with that crap from him."
Perception check:

_____

_____

Managing a Learning Community: Collaborative Participation

A democratic society is founded on the principles of equal opportunity and social justice. Preparing democratic citizens requires establishing an arena for critical conversation and respectful dialogue as the foundation for breeding tolerance and acceptance. This chapter presents classroom management practices that align with the principles of creating a democratic community.

Making the classroom a caring, democratic community adds two other dimensions. First, classrooms become more nurturing places, with teachers paying attention to making connections with students and fostering emotional bonding. And second, the classroom becomes need fulfilling, that is, structured to meet students' basic needs. Creating a need-satisfying classroom environment means providing a safe haven for students and meeting their basic needs. Ensuring a caring climate involves creating a sense of belonging, importance, and personal power. Creating such an environment involves meeting the following nine needs.

9 Needs of a Learning Community

A SENSE OF BELONGING	A SENSE OF IMPORTANCE	A SENSE OF POWER
1. Status among peers	4. Positive identity	7. Competency
2. Safety, both emotional and physical	5. Recognition	8. Control
3. Affection	6. Attention	9. Freedom

INTEGRATING THEORIES OF HUMAN DEVELOPMENT INTO CLASSROOM PRACTICE

The foundations for what has been called the humanistic education movement that began in the 1960s are the acceptance of basic human needs and the drive to satisfy those needs, coupled with the development of the person as a whole, or the complete person. This movement was an offshoot of the larger human potential movement, spearheaded by such pioneering psychologists as Abraham Maslow (1968) and Fritz Perls (1976). Maslow has been called the father of humanistic psychology; Perls is the founder of Gestalt therapy. Gestalt psychology is predicated on the notion that the whole person is greater than the sum of its parts.

Pertinent to this discussion is the notion that a student is greater than the sum of his or her behavior. Given the confines of the classroom setting, inappropriate behavior has to be managed, but at the same time the teacher needs to look beyond the student's action and consider the student's development as a whole. This is not to imply that creating an understanding of the depth of a student's need deprivation and resulting emotional turmoil means that the teacher should excuse inappropriate behavior. Quite the contrary, the position advocated here is that the teacher help the student gain competence by giving the student alternatives and helping the student learn new tools to engage in more productive behaviors.

In the past, most students arrived at school relatively well adjusted psychologically, having benefited from early nurturing and healthy family connections. In today's classroom, more and more students begin their school careers maladjusted. Many models of psychological development are based on the importance of getting basic human needs met. What the models all have in common is that the environment should be need fulfilling for developing and sustaining healthy psychological well being. The following chart compares and contrasts the viewpoints of six authors who propose theories of psychological development useful to educators.

Theories of Basic Need Fulfillment and Lack of Fulfillment

MASLOW	GLASSER	BRENDTRO, BROKENLEG, & VAN BOCKERN	DREIKURS	ERIKSON	WOOD
Hierarchy of Needs	*Basic Human Needs*	*Essential Developmental Needs*	*Mistaken Goals*	*Psychosocial Developmental Needs*	*Developmental Anxieties (When Needs Are Unmet)*
Survival	Survival				
Safety or security				Trust (lack of security)	(Anxiety of abandonment, lack of security)
Belonging and affection	Belonging and love	Belonging	Recognition, attention	Identity (lack of belonging)	(Anxiety of identity, lack of acceptance and belonging)
Esteem, recognition, and achievement		Mastery, competence	(Inadequacy, lack of mastery)	Industry (lack of self-esteem)	(Anxiety of inadequacy, lack of self-esteem)
Self-actualization					
	Power, control	Interdependence, autonomy	Power, control	Autonomy (self-doubt)	(Anxiety of conflict, lack of power and autonomy)
	Freedom, choice		(Revenge for lack of freedom)		
	Enjoyment, fun, satisfaction				
		Generosity			
				Initiative (guilt)	(Anxiety of guilt, lack of self-worth)

Note: Parentheses ( ) are used to indicate unmet need or response to unmet need.

The authors in the first three columns describe needs that, when fulfilled, lead to healthy personality adjustment and development of skills to successfully navigate life. Implicit in these models is the idea that students whose needs for attention, approval, and acceptance have not been met by primary caretakers will bring a greater range of problematic behaviors to the classroom. The authors in the next three columns specifically address what happens when these needs are not met in child-rearing and the long-term psychological consequences of need deprivation.

As can be seen in the chart, belonging is a need common to five of the six models. When a student feels "I'm worthy. There's a place for me" and "I'm needed and I can contribute," the student is well on the way to school adjustment. In the school setting, the teacher is the primary provider for students' needs and the school is the context for building a sense of belonging. If this doesn't happen, students suffer alienation and seek other avenues for need fulfillment. The need for students to develop a sense of competence, particularly related to school expectations, was also a common element in five of the models. Successful school experiences and academic accomplishments lead a student to feel "I am capable" and to want to participate in what school has to offer.

Also common to five of the models is the need for power, control, and autonomy, typically defined as personal power to influence one's environment. Feeling a sense of empowerment leads to the belief that "What I do makes a difference." This is similar to what is commonly referred to as an internal versus an external locus of control.

Maslow (1968) proposed a hierarchy of five levels of needs that motivate human behavior. In his model, the lowest level of need must be satisfied in order to seek out the next level. If students are deprived of food, shelter, and safety needs, they will be stifled in their drive to seek the fulfillment of higher needs. Glasser (1986) posits five fundamental needs, the fulfillment of which he considers critical to students' psychological welfare. He puts the onus on teachers and schools to create learning opportunities that meet these needs. Both Glasser and Maslow concur on the need for survival and belonging. Glasser's theories are discussed in greater detail in subsequent sections of this chapter.

Building on Native American child-rearing practices, Brendtro, Brokenleg, and Van Bockern (1990) propose four essential needs of developing children. Their model is based on the symbol of the medicine wheel, or Circle of Courage. They believe all children, regardless of culture, will become healthy adults if their needs for belonging, mastery, independence, and generosity are met. Characteristics of their model are described below.

- Children need to belong to the tribe by having many "mothers." Over time, children become a part of a larger community and gain a clear identity and a sense of trust regarding their cultural roots and feelings of belonging.
- Children develop mastery by observing and listening to their elders and participating in tribal games, stories, and work. This process of learning reflects the importance of mastering a skill, based on the value of cooperative achievement, personal persistence, creativity, and problem solving.
- Children are encouraged to hunt by themselves, to be accountable for their actions, and to take risks by venturing into the unknown. These expectations develop autonomy, responsibility, assertiveness, and self-discipline.
- Children are taught the importance of giving and sharing their resources instead of accumulating them for personal wealth. Personal acts of generosity are a significant way of building the importance of helping others.

Brendtro et al. advocate reclaiming troubled youth by promoting the fulfillment of these four needs. In particular, they believe that without opportunities to give to others, young people do not develop as caring persons. Some may be involved in pseudoaltruistic helping, or they may be locked in servitude to someone who uses them. Others plunge into lifestyles of hedonism and narcissism. The antidote for this malaise is to experience the joys that accrue from helping others.

Dreikurs was one of the first to address the issue of unmet needs for teachers. Like Glasser, Dreikurs believed that students will behave in ways that they think will get their needs met (Dreikurs, Grunwald, & Pepper, 1982). His position was that students misbehave because they think that's what will get them what they want (i.e., attention, power, revenge, to be left alone). Dreikurs's theories are also presented in more detail later in this chapter.

Both Erikson and Wood, like Maslow, propose a hierarchical relationship, noting that if children fail to advance successfully from one stage to the next, they will be inhibited in their capacity to develop a well-balanced personality, with diminished capacity to respond productively to life experiences. Erikson stressed the importance of the quality of early child rearing to the child's later psychological adjustment, noting that if the child is not supported in developing trust and a sense of self during infancy and the toddler years, the effects of mistrust and self-doubt will haunt the child throughout his or her adult life. Erikson's first five developmental stages are presented in the chart below.

Erikson's Stages of Psychosocial Development

PSYCHOSOCIAL STAGE	PSYCHOSOCIAL DEVELOPMENT	NEED FULFILLMENT
Trust versus mistrust (Approximate age: Birth to 18 months)	Develops varying degrees of trust and mistrust depending on the degree of support and nurturing provided by primary caretaker; quality of initial care will have a profound effect on the degree to which the maturing child expresses trust.	Need to trust that the basic needs of nourishment, caring, and safety will be met.
Autonomy versus self-doubt (Approximate age: 18 months to 3 years)	Begins to express a strong sense of self; attempts to gain a degree of independence and competence; intensely investigates environment.	Need to explore the environment for the sake of curiosity; should be encouraged to express self verbally.
Initiative versus guilt (Approximate age: 3 to 6 years)	Begins to explore sexual identity; begins to identify with male and female role models.	Need to establish a sense of self and own identity; should reinforce identity at this point.
Industry versus inferiority (Approximate age: 6 to 12 years)	Forms social alliances reflecting growing interest in other people and in things beyond the family; actively explores; tests self; works hard to achieve goals.	Need to develop confidence in ability to do things, such as schoolwork, successfully.
Identity versus role confusion (Approximate age: 12 to 18 years)	Uses logic to solve hypothetical problems; makes decisions based on objective evidence; develops capacity for empathy; develops need to improve things; acquires personal responsibility for growth.	Need to develop an identity not based on the desires of others, but based on one's own interests and desires; should be given real, self-directed experiences.

Wood (1986) proposed that unmet emotional needs at early stages result in persistent anxieties. Her theory is that all children experience five developmental anxieties throughout childhood. If an anxiety is not resolved at the appropriate age, it carries on to the next developmental level, creating more intense unmet emotional needs. Wood, like Maslow, emphasized that unresolved developmental anxieties will eventually become a primary motivation for students, interfering with all future relationships. Needs can be met or unmet at age-appropriate developmental levels. When needs are met, healthy or normal development occurs; when needs are not met, unhealthy or pathological behavior results. Early emotional deprivation in the form of abuse, abandonment, neglect, or rejection has devastating, long-term impact, potentially causing the child to suffer from feelings of insecurity, anxiety, helplessness, hopelessness, low self-esteem, anger, and rage. The following chart shows the types of anxiety, the associated unmet needs, and the resulting behavior.

Wood's Stages of Intrapsychic Anxiety

STAGE	ANXIETY DEVELOPMENT	UNMET NEED (UNRESOLVED ANXIETY)	RESULTING BEHAVIOR
Anxiety of abandonment (Birth to 2 years)	If young child bonds with significant adult, receiving care and nurturing, feelings of abandonment will be resolved and a growing sense of trust will develop.	Love, safety	Develop superficial relationships, hoard objects, have overriding desire to be accepted by others.
Anxiety of inadequacy (3 to 6 years)	Feelings of inadequacy and self-doubt are normal for children as they come to understand the expectations of the important adults in their lives. If the child experiences success rather than failure and the ability to meet adult standards, feelings of inadequacy are resolved.	Self-worth	Learn to deny or justify mistakes by blaming others, lying, projecting feelings on others.
Anxiety of guilt (6 to 9 years)	If children have not resolved anxiety of inadequacy and come to think they are unworthy, they will put themselves down for not meeting their own standards.	Self-esteem, empowerment	Actually seek out punishment; become scapegoats and willing victims of exploitation; engage in self-abusive behavior.
Anxiety of conflict (9 to 12 years)	This anxiety emerges when the need for budding independence conflicts with the will of authorities. If this is resolved, self-confidence to solve conflicts, independence, and a sense of freedom emerge. Also, one becomes personally accountable for one's decisions and behaviors.	Self-confidence, independence	Fights with authority figures; may come to believe there is status and power in being bad.

| **Anxiety of identity** (12 to 18 years) | Adolescents struggle with such questions as "Who am I" and "Can I handle this?" These questions reflect the dynamic interplay between feelings of independence and feelings of dependency. The struggle is intensified by the adolescent's maturing body to create additional concerns about sexuality, attractiveness, and group acceptance. | Acceptance, belonging | Develop false identity and seek recognition and status in inappropriate ways; reject adult values and put down adults; have no direction. |

Consequences of Failure to Develop Secure Attachments

Students who fail to develop healthy, secure attachments to significant adults are typically products of inconsistent, detached, neglected, or abused caregiving at significant developmental stages. Children whose primary caretakers oscillated between giving adequate to effusive attention and being indifferent to totally inaccessible, become insecure. The uncertainty and unpredictability they experience lead to obsessive attachments which may play out in the form of anxious obedience or overreliance on external comfort (Bowlby, 1982; Herman, 1992). Because children who fail to develop healthy attachments anticipate abandonment, they try to do whatever they can to prevent it. They can become clinging vines, hovering about and constantly requiring attention.

Students who suffer from detached caregiving fail to have their needs for touch, love, affection, and genuine interest met. When caregivers are rejecting or detached, with no affirmation or support forthcoming, children come to feel worthless. Hostility and rejection of adults may become their protection against the possibility of rejection. They may crave closeness, but fear of the pain they may endure if they fail becomes unbearable, something to avoid at all cost (Morrow, 1987). In more extreme cases, they may operate by the motto: "I'll reject you before you reject me." They come to find solace in being the rejecter instead of the rejected. The inner turmoil created by avoiding while desperately seeking connection causes anger to ferment and frequently the teacher is the object of their sting of rejection (Gootman, 2001).

Abusive parents may be kind and loving and then, in a rage, beat their children, then hug them and beg forgiveness. Neglected children suffer the pain of knowing no one cares. Disinterest in and hostility toward others is their protective shield to guard themselves against the overwhelming effect of apathy and rejection.

Children who have experienced such emotional deprivation may be less socially competent, fight more, bully others, and engage in other behaviors that cause teachers concern. Students who have such unresolved anxieties and unmet needs often behave in ways that drive teachers away, and yet these are the very students teachers have the greatest potential to influence by providing an alternative adult role model. Understanding the dynamics of insecure attachment and how it manifests can help teachers to go beyond simply trying to control or to retaliate for a student's inappropriate and abusive behavior. By finding ways to provide secure attachment, without feeling overwhelmed themselves, teachers can do much to bolster the development of feelings of worthiness.

Troubled students who have experienced such early, intense, and prolonged abuse, neglect, and rejection no longer are motivated by personal trust or the spirit of human kindness. These students come to the classroom with the intent to avoid interpersonal closeness. Teachers who reach out to these students can be the victims of "psychological biting of any hand that tries to feed them" (Long & Morse,

1996). Their well-honed negative attitudes and rejecting behaviors are difficult for teachers to accept and deal with productively. Students who are seriously troubled typically do not readily respond to teacher attempts to be supportive and nurturing. They seem to have developed psychological antibodies against the warmth of healthy relationships. They have been conditioned to consider close relationships as toxic rather than enriching. For these students, closeness holds the despair of a new cycle of rejection and abandonment, not the hope of affection, trust, and bonding. It feels much safer to try to manipulate others than to take charge of their lives.

From the perspective of how the human brain develops, secure attachment can be compared to having a very satisfying meal. Once the infant is full, it can turn its attention to other things. With infants the safety and security and love found in fully bonding with one or more significant adults can allow it to turn its attention to the world around it in order to explore, discover, and learn. These experiences and resultant brain connections all serve as a foundation for later learning.

The infant brain is directly affected by its experiences with early caregivers. An infant develops basic mental representations about the world that help it predict what others will do and what it can expect. Ultimately these representations come to act as assumptions and beliefs that underlie behavior. The ability to make sense of what is happening serves as a foundation for healthy emotional development and continuous learning. Being fed, cared for, and lovingly touched develops foundational connections in the brain. Closeness and continuity provide security (Caine & Caine, 1997; Caine, Caine, McClintic, & Klimek, 2004).

The mechanism in the brain that signals fear is developed before many of the more cognitive areas of the brain, acting as a biologically programmed alarm bell that sets off intense discomfort when fear and helplessness are experienced simultaneously. Attention is then hijacked away from other events and potential learning while the entire emotional system goes on automatic and reacts to ensure survival. One overpowering or extremely frightening event, or continuous arousal of the fear mechanism, can alter the brain so that the infant becomes emotionally more volatile (easily upset or frightened) on a more or less permanent basis. Hostile or neglectful parenting could create hormonal responses that repeatedly engage the child's biological mechanisms for fear.

Even at one month, babies have learned whether their parents tend to ignore their needs or respond to them quickly. Early separation from the mother or changes in critical routines can trigger a sense of abandonment, as can parents arguing loudly or anger expressed through physical action, and become sources of frustration and fear in the infant. Because the infant cannot understand or give itself intellectual explanations, emotions that arise because of feelings of helplessness can cause permanent changes in the infant's brain and, thereby, in their psychological health.

Teachers often encounter students who literally cling to them, relying desperately on their every word and action; students who don't seem to relate to anyone without creating conflict or ending up in a fight; students who never bother anyone and basically want to remain invisible; and children who arrive with hostilities seemingly toward all adults. Many times, students who have been moved from school to school in their young years enter each new situation with defense shields raised. Teachers need to understand the critical role that attachment plays in the lives of students and what this implies for how schools and classrooms need to be organized.

GOING BEYOND REACTING TO RESPONDING BELOW THE SURFACE

These models of psychological needs and development provide a more holistic framework for conceiving students' misbehavior. The same underlying problem (unmet need, unresolved anxiety, mistaken goal) can be expressed in a multitude of ways. The corollary of this statement is also true: different behaviors that are problematic in the classroom setting can be motivated by the same underlying cause. The message these authors have for teachers is that, in the long run, it is far more beneficial to students to try to identify the unmet needs they have and then to attempt to address those needs within the confines of the classroom setting. The unmet need might be safety, belonging, competency, attention, identity, power, status, recognition, satisfaction, or control.

Much inappropriate classroom behavior stems from unmet needs, undeveloped skills, or expectations incompatible with an individual student's personality, preferences, learning style, or cultural background. When the problems that students experience and act out are positioned within this framework, the teacher is empowered as the critical force, because it is the teacher who controls whether the classroom climate is need-satisfying, whether students are taught skills they lack, and whether the range of individual differences are accommodated.

Some students may need to learn how to make friends or to respond to frustrating life events, not only to function more effectively in the classroom but also to be successful in life. As Kohn (1996) points out, what matters is the reasons and feelings driving the behavior. Viewing student behavior from this perspective will require a very different orientation than discipline programs that merely control or attempt to change behavior temporarily.

All behavior is purposeful and, according to the beliefs of many, this author included, most behavior is an attempt, albeit misguided, to satisfy a need. Most misbehavior teachers confront is sending out a signal. When teachers learn to read these signals, they go beyond reacting to students' misbehavior to responding beneath the surface behavior. They are willing to adjust their methods, routines, and expectations and assess the teaching–learning environment they create against potentially unmet student needs. They examine classroom policies and practices to determine factors that may be contributing, even exacerbating, student anxiety or frustration. Rather than blaming the student, teachers first consider factors within their power to change, such as instructional format, grouping, testing practices, curriculum content, peer relationships, or student–teacher relationship.

The message for teachers is to channel basic drives, which are expressed disruptively, into socially acceptable expressions. The goal then becomes discovering the student's motive and attempting to rechannel the unacceptable behavior by offering the student acceptable options, as the following example illustrates.

MISBEHAVIOR	POSSIBLE COMMUNICATIVE INTENT OR UNMET NEED	ALTERNATIVE TEACHER RESPONSE
Frequent arguing with teacher	Power, independence, status	Allow student to be teacher for a specified time
		Allow student to critique teacher or a lesson

Many classroom situations warrant a need for deeper understanding of the socioemotional problems many students experience. Teachers need to uncover the reason or function of a particular misbehavior, then formulate a strategy likely to have an impact on the motive that is driving the behavior.

Long and Morse (1996) suggest that teachers might respond by *regulated permission* or providing an outlet for the student, for example, allowing the student to express anger by flattening clay or banging erasers. Similarly, they cite the example of the teacher asking a student why she always calls out answers, and the student replying " 'cause those dummies think I don't know anything." Such a retort should give the teacher a pretty clear indication that attempting to devise ways for this student to have increased competence status among her peers would be a more meaningful intervention than attempting to squelch her calling-out behavior.

Learning to Reframe Events, Situations, and Circumstances

Thoughts like the following serve to limit a teacher's range of responses to classroom problems: "If it wasn't for *him,* my class would run fine," or "If I didn't have *these kinds* of kids to contend with, maybe I could actually teach!"

Teachers can learn to reframe or reposition classroom situations and school circumstances. When faced with a problem, you basically have two choices, change the situation or change your reaction to the situation. Often you can't change the situation, but you can change how you emotionally respond to cope more effectively. Reframing means you put the experience in a new frame, one that views the situation from a different angle or one that includes parts of the picture that weren't visible from your first vantage point.

The term *reposition* connotes the idea of changing your perception by moving out of your old position and creating a new one from which to view a situation (Larrivee, 1996). It's your personal framing that shapes how you attribute meaning to your experiences. Seeing new ways of interpreting a situation enables you to move beyond a limited perspective. By challenging yourself to create a new vantage point, you can assign new meaning to the classroom situations you confront. By repositioning a seemingly negative event, the teacher seizes the opportunity to discover the potential in a situation. In repositioning, the teacher looks for openings to extend and learn in any situation.

Some helpful ways of repositioning for the classroom setting include

- Repositioning conflict as opportunity for relationship building
- Repositioning confrontation as energy to be rechanneled
- Repositioning an attack as a cry for help
- Repositioning defiance as a request for communication
- Repositioning attention seeking as a plea for recognition

Repositioning calls for a change in your perception of misbehavior, by making the shift in thinking from

This kid is a problem to *This kid poses a problem for me to solve.*

So rather than try to *teach the kid a lesson* for misbehaving with cease and desist tactics, you really do teach the kid a lesson by using the problem situation as an opportunity to teach a skill that the student lacks. By using a problem-solving approach instead of just trying to stop the behavior, you work with rather than against the student by seizing *teachable* moments to show students how to get what they want in more appropriate ways.

What Pushes Your Buttons

Teachers, like everyone else, are sensitive to, or self-conscious about, some aspect of their background, status, or image. However, in their position as role model to developing students they are often "put to the test" to examine their reasons for the way they respond. Physical attributes, appearance, lack of content knowledge, computer illiteracy, and need for acceptance are a few of the areas that may be a source of insecurity or concern.

Students are astute observers of teachers' reactions, and teachers often reveal much about themselves in how they react when their students find the right button to push.

CRITICAL REFLECTION ON PRACTICE: WHAT PUSHES YOUR BUTTONS?

Activity Directions: Working with a partner, take turns sharing the following. Think about an area that represents a source of insecurity to you.

Briefly describe what it is.

_____

_____

_____

What is your typical reaction when this button is pushed?

_____

_____

_____

How might that affect students?

_____

_____

_____

REFLECTIVE QUESTION
What message are you sending by your reaction?

AUTHORITY STRUCTURES

Teachers are placed in the role of managing student behavior in order to maintain an environment conducive to teaching and learning. When attempting to change or deal with students' inappropriate behavior, the typical teacher response is to try to control their behavior by exercising power and control, rather than consider the appropriateness of the learning context for accommodating individual student needs. Teachers can choose to manage student behavior by using their authority and exercising direct control by dispensing rewards and punishment, or they can choose not to use their power in favor of strategies that empower students to make their own choices.

Traditionally, effective classroom management has been largely viewed as tantamount to controlling student behavior, keeping students on task and maintaining lesson flow, calling for constant teacher vigilance and appropriate teacher intervention. Furthermore, student behavior is judged to be inappropriate irrespective of consideration of individual student characteristics, performance expectations, or appropriateness of the learning task. The implicit assumption is that students are unable or unwilling to exercise control or solve their problems. Hence, teachers may impose their requirements for order without relating them to student requirements for learning.

Shifting the classroom management focus from obedience to responsibility calls for the teacher to foster student autonomy. The shift from authoritarian hierarchy of authority to democratic community also redefines the concept of control from control of students to helping students develop internal control and exercising teacher self-control in conflict situations.

Sources of Power

The teacher has four power bases from which to operate. The chart below defines each of these types of power and lists corresponding key characteristics of classroom organization and management.

Characteristics of Power Bases

POWER TYPE	POWER BASE	CHARACTERISTIC CLASSROOM ORGANIZATION AND MANAGEMENT
Coercive	Authority by virtue of power to reward and punish	Dictates rules and procedures Uses system of incentives and punishments Requires careful teacher surveillance
Legitimate	Authority by virtue of appointed position	Clearly communicates delineation of teacher and student role Prescribes standards for appropriate behavior Reminds students of their position of authority
Expert	Authority by virtue of knowledge and expertise	Centers around content Focuses on keeping students on task Uses procedures that redirect students to the learning task Carefully monitors student progression through the lesson
Referent	Authority by virtue of relationship power	Establishes democratic procedures Respects students' rights Negotiates mutual solutions to problems

Coercive Power.   Teachers acting with coercive authority demand compliance, exercise rigid control, deny students a role in decision making, and set arbitrary limits on acceptable behavior. Their foremost concern is with maintaining order, and they often view order and control as ends in themselves rather than means to an end.

Coercive power is exemplified by systems of imposed rules of order and standards of acceptable behavior with contingencies attached. Often the rules are posted in large print as commandments in front of the class as constant reminders. These are the rules that the system is ready to enforce with sanctions ranging from verbal reprimands, point losses, time-outs, and referral to higher authority in the chain of command.

Legitimate Power.   Legitimate power is power granted to teachers because of their position as the teacher. Teachers who manage by this type of authority believe it is their rightful role to prescribe standards. They typically operate in a businesslike fashion, maintain distance from students as a symbol of their unequal power base, and frequently remind student who's in charge.

This management style might be thought of as the default posture. Teachers who use this type of power believe they have the right to exert authority over students because of the authority vested in them as part of their role. They feel they are sanctioned by society by virtue of their teaching certification to run the classroom the way they see fit.

At one time, teachers could depend primarily on legitimate power by virtue of their title. However, changes in our society have lessened the effectiveness of this type of authority. Whereas in the past, most students tacitly agreed to be managed by the teacher, today's students are more likely to challenge the authority of the teacher. Role models available via the media, for instance, from sports, may promote confrontation, not obedience.

In relationships such as student–teacher in which the distribution of power is unequal, coercive and legitimate power are readily available and easy to wield. Yet use of these types of power over students generally alters behavior only temporarily and largely fails to induce long-term change, growth, and learning.

Legitimate and coercive power bases exercise overt control over students and decrease student self-control. These management types encourage extrinsic motivation and afford fewer opportunities for developing self-esteem. In addition, these management strategies are more effective at the primary level. They lose their effectiveness as students get older and are relatively ineffective by the secondary level. Teachers who manage by attempting to control students are also more likely to experience high stress levels, precipitate more student confrontation and aggressive behavior, and suffer from teacher burnout.

Expert Power.   Expert power is attributed to one who has a specialized body of knowledge. Teachers are attributed expert power by students when they view them as knowledgeable, competent, and in charge. Students are usually willing to follow the teacher's direction because they feel confident that the teacher knows what he or she is doing.

Teachers who value management by expert power usually show great enthusiasm for the subject, have subject matter command, exercise academic leadership, establish orderly procedures, and actively involve students. These teachers know how to make involvement with the learning activity much more interesting than off task or disruptive behavior. They inspire and challenge students to excel.

Teachers with an expert power base orchestrate learning tasks to keep students interested, ground activities in sound rationale, give clear directions, ensure that students know what is expected, and monitor for individual and group progress. They also consider individual learning style differences in their planning and are able to gauge the appropriate level of structure for a particular lesson goal. Teachers with expert power act with authority, although their power is subliminal.

Referent Power.   Referent power is the power that comes from connecting with students in authentic and humane ways. Referent power is power teachers have based on students' admiration and respect. Teachers who have referent power elicit expected behavior from students because their students like them. The relationship with students is more personal and is characterized by nurturing, supportive, and caring behaviors. These teachers exhibit genuine concern for students and place high value in cultivating human relationships. Fostering the personal growth of their students and helping them feel good about themselves are high on their agenda. They value student opinions and trust students to make appropriate choices and to be accountable when they don't.

Teachers who manage by referent power command rather than demand respect. They do not assume that their position gives them any right to treat students differently from anyone else. They use power judiciously and involve students in setting reasonable and ethical expectations for acceptable behavior. For these teachers, their job is to be "of service" to students.

When teachers have referent power, students are willing to adjust their behavior to maintain the teacher's respect. Power is implicit and based on influence and positive identification with the teacher. Students want to maintain a positive relationship because they identify with the teacher as a role model.

Although referent power is often associated with teacher charisma, it can be developed by any teacher. The route to establishing referent power is through treating students with dignity and respect. A teacher doesn't lose power when assuming a nurturing posture, in fact he or she may gain it (Gootman, 2001). Several studies examining the effectiveness of various power bases have shown referent power to be the most effective, and coercive and legitimate power as the least effective (Golanda, 1990; McCroskey & Richmond, 1983; Stahelski & Frost, 1987).

Teachers who use referent and expert authority bases are concerned with facilitating student development, encouraging intrinsic motivation, and supporting the development of self-esteem by increasing student competence and power. These teachers are also less likely to suffer from high stress level or burnout.

Although teachers have a primary power base from which they operate, a total management plan represents a coalescence of several forms of power. Teachers who effectively manage their classrooms do so by skillfully combining forms of influence and judiciously using the power vested in them. They weave in and out of various modes of authority. Having expert or referent power doesn't preclude them from using other types of authority when they deem it necessary. Sustaining a democratic community, maintained by a mutually agreed-upon code of conduct, does not negate the teacher's right to, on occasion, exercise more direct control. There are situations that arise in which the ethical use of authority does not rule out unilateral control. A teacher who sees a student abusing another student must exercise authority. The teacher can exercise more, or less, control as the situation demands. Noblit (1993) used the term *moral authority* to refer to the type of authority whereby a teacher develops classroom procedures and routines, engages in reciprocal negotiation, yet still retains the right to steer the curriculum and interactions toward goals deemed worthwhile for students. Each teacher will need to seriously consider what constitutes ethical authority, how and when shared responsibility and negotiation serve the needs of both the teacher and students, and conversely, when they do not.

Several authors who have translated principles of human behavior into strategies for classroom teachers offer alternative models to compliance models for creating an optimal atmosphere for teaching and learning. The work of William Glasser, Rudolf Dreikurs, and Haim Ginott has been selected for inclusion here. These three authors encompass the range of orientations to addressing classroom and behavior management that align with the principles of building a caring, democratic community. The principles they espouse are most consonant with those emerging from the school-as-community literature.

Their theories provide the cornerstone for establishing the communication, interaction, and intervention strategies necessary for creating classrooms that embrace the principles of respect, authenticity, thoughtfulness, and emotional integrity (RATE) described in Chapter 3.

Although a number of other authors of approaches and programs recommend strategies that are also consistent with the basic tenets of caring communities, the work of these three theorists provides the foundation for the theories underlying these other approaches (Albert, 1996; Coloroso, 1999; Curwin, 1992; Curwin & Mendler, 1988, 1997; Freiberg, 1996, 1999; Nelson, Lott, & Glenn, 2000; Queen, Blackwelder, & Mallen, 1997; Rogers, 1969; Rogers & Freiberg, 1994). They offer combinations of approaches, strategies, and techniques that represent different renditions of similar themes.

The work of William Glasser, from the 1960s through the 1990s, emphasizes the importance of satisfying students' basic needs as a necessary condition to establishing a learning community. These basic human needs include the need to belong, the need to have power and freedom, as well as the need to experience personal satisfaction. Understanding the motivation that drives students' behavior, based on the work of Dreikurs and his colleagues (1968, 1972, 1982), offers another perspective. Dreikurs reminds us that we all need to have avenues for receiving recognition. If the classroom environment fails to offer students opportunities to get recognition, students will find ways, often inappropriate, to get the recognition they thrive on. Enhancing student self-esteem through continuous encouragement and validating and accepting both teachers' and students' feelings is the means for developing the positive socioemotional climate advocated by Haim Ginott (1972).

Dreikurs, Glasser, and Ginott all focus on meeting the psychological needs of students by calling on teachers to

- Show genuine concern for students
- Support student emotional growth and development
- Respect the rights and needs of students
- Deal honestly and openly with students
- Recognize both their own and their students' feelings

From the work of these authors several themes relative to classroom interactions emerge. These consistent themes call for minimizing blame by clearly differentiating between rejection of the student's behavior and rejection of the student, allowing and encouraging student choices, and providing continuous encouragement while at the same time calling on students to take responsibility for their own behavior.

GLASSER'S MANAGING WITHOUT COERCION: SATISFYING STUDENT NEEDS

William Glasser's early work in reality therapy represented a shift from psychoanalysis to assessing present reality. According to Glasser, individuals need to fulfill two basic needs, for belonging and to have a sense of worth to self and others. Students need to accept the reality of classroom demands. The primary vehicle for implementing reality therapy is the individual student conference.

Key Principles for Teachers: Glasser's Reality Therapy

Glasser developed reality therapy as an alternative to conventional psychotherapy. In his book *Reality Therapy: A New Approach to Psychiatry* (1965), he called for a shift in focus from uncovering conditions in one's past that contribute to inappropriate behavior (psychoanalysis) to assessing the present reality of the current situation. The underlying premise of reality therapy is that an individual must face reality and assume responsibility for his or her own actions. Reality therapy attempts to guide the individual toward competent functioning in the real world by assisting him or her to effectively deal with his or her environment to fulfill personal needs. The following principles are integral to Glasser's beliefs.

Individuals need to fulfill two essential psychological needs

1. To love and be loved
2. To feel worthwhile to self and others

The primary objective of reality therapy is to teach the ill/irresponsible person responsible behavior. Thus, therapy and the teaching–learning process are the same.

Reality therapy is the process of teaching an irresponsible person to face existing reality, to function responsibly, and as a result fulfill one's personal needs for love and self-worth.

Responsibility is the ability to meet one's own needs in a manner that does not deprive others of their ability to fulfill their personal needs.

Classroom Application.   Applied to the classroom, Glasser (1969) maintained that a student's background and socioeconomic status do not exempt him or her from responsibility to behave appropriately. The present reality of the classroom is what matters. Teachers should not excuse irresponsible behavior. Rather, they should guide a realistic assessment not of why it occurred, but of what behavior the student engaged in and its impact. Glasser's basic tenet is that students are capable of controlling their behavior. They choose to act the way they do.

The reality therapy teaching–learning process requires

1. Involvement with a person perceived by the student as caring about him or her
2. A teacher who is able to accept the student while rejecting the irresponsible behavior
3. For the student, learning responsible means of fulfilling personal needs

Reality therapy applied to the classroom is viewed as a cooperative interchange in which both the teacher and the student commit to the process. The process calls for teachers to engage in direct instructions, discussions, conferences, planning sessions, and group meetings. In essence, in reality therapy, the teacher provides emotional support while maintaining focus on deriving a resolution to the problem at hand (i.e., calling for responsible behavior on the part of the student). In order to guide the student toward more responsible behavior, the recommended vehicle is the reality therapy interview or individual conference. The following guidelines are offered for teachers during the student conference.

Student Conference Guidelines
1. Demonstrate caring.
2. Provide emotional support and security.
3. Use active or empathic listening.
4. Do not probe by asking why questions.
5. Ask what, who, and how questions.
6. Focus on present behavior, not past behavior.
7. Curtail excessive venting.
8. Refrain from judging the student's behavior.
9. Call on students to make value judgments about their behavior; offer suitable alternatives when necessary.
10. Help students make a plan to increase responsible behavior.

A New Beginning: Ten Steps to a Fresh Start with a Problem Student.   When nothing you do seems to work and you're at your wits' end, it's time for a fresh start. Glasser (1974) offers the following sequential steps for dealing with your "behind-in-his-work, disruptive, doesn't-listen, never-on-time, always-picking-fights Tom (or Susan)."

The process begins with an attitude adjustment on your part. Let's face it. You've tried everything you know and still the student is driving you crazy. Steps 1 to 3 provide a systematic way for you to change your own attitude and resolve to start fresh. The intermediary steps suggest nonpunitive, nonblameful responses to the student when he or she breaks a rule. The strategy is to keep the tone "cool and crisp," until the student makes some effort to comply, and to continue to try to "inject some warmth and recognition into the student's day." Steps 4 and 5 call for you to be warm and supportive and minimize teacher-talk. In step 6 you call for conference time and engage in structured dialogue. The remaining steps are a graduated series of "benching techniques" to be used when the student's behavior is so serious he or she has to be removed. The process is slow and you'll need to commit at least a month, since progress is not likely before then.

Ten Steps to a Fresh Start

Step 1: Commit to Changing Your Approach
If what you're doing hasn't worked by now, it probably won't. Itemize all the things you're doing now when Tom misbehaves. For the next 4 weeks try to refrain from doing anything on your list.

Step 2: Make Your Motto: *Every Day's a New Day*
When Tom misbehaves, try to act and react as if it is the first time he's ever behaved inappropriately. Avoid comments like "I've had enough of that!" When he does something right, give him verbal or even physical recognition.

> *I appreciate your staying in your seat this morning.*

Step 3: Make an Effort to Make Tomorrow a Better Day
Find something, no matter how small, that you can do to help Tom have a better day tomorrow and every day for at least 4 weeks. It could be just a simple warm gesture, 20 seconds of unexpected recognition. The next time you need to send a message to the office, you might ask Tom to deliver it. The objective here is to try to break the pattern of recognition only for misbehavior.

Step 4: Quiet Correction
This step involves confronting the student with short, simple directives.

> *Tom, put the ruler down and get back to work.*
>
> *Tom, take a seat until you've finished your work.*

When the student does not comply, the strategy is to calmly pose short questions to focus the student on the present behavior and to help him or her think rationally about the behavior. Remember to establish the mind set that this is the first time the student has misbehaved.

When a straightforward directive doesn't work, then use the *broken record* technique in which you repeatedly ask "What did you do?" until you get an answer. You relentlessly press the student to admit the behavior. As an example, let's say this time Tom cuts in line and starts a fight in the process. You say, "Tommy, stop fighting and go to your place in line." He continues. The ensuing dialogue might go something like this.

> **Teacher:** What did you do, Tom?
>
> **Tom:** What?
>
> **Teacher:** What did you do, Tom?
>
> **Tom:** Nothing.
>
> **Teacher:** Please, Tom, I just asked you what you did. Tell me.
>
> **Tom:** Well, this is my place in line, and they won't let me in.

> **Teacher:** What did you do, Tom?
> **Tom:** It's my place, so I pushed my way in.

Then, with no further discussion, you take him by the hand and walk him to his correct place and stay with him, maybe still holding his hand.

> **Teacher:** Can you walk quietly now?
> **Tom:** What are you going to do?
> **Teacher:** I just asked you if you can walk quietly now. We'd all like lunch.
> **Tom:** Okay, I'll try.

When this step doesn't work you continue with the next step. With this procedure you are attempting to establish that, although Tom needs to take responsibility for doing something wrong, if he accepts your correction, it's over, no blaming, yelling, or threatening.

Step 5: Insist on a Plan
In this step you press for a plan from the student. You will need to be very insistent and continually focus on following the rules. Your agenda is to tell the student he or she broke the rule; of course the student's agenda will be to evade this issue in every possibly way. The following prototype questions are recommended.

> *What did you do?*
>
> *Just tell me what you did.*
>
> *Please tell me what you did.*
>
> *Where are you supposed to be now?*
>
> *What are you supposed to be doing now?*
>
> *Do you think you can* [appropriate behavior] *now?*
>
> *What's the rule?*
>
> *Was it against the rules?*
>
> *Are you willing to* [appropriate behavior]*?*
>
> *Can you make a plan?*

Step 6: Conference Time
Up to this point, you have kept your talking at a minimum. If the behavior persists, a conference is in order. You tell the student you want to talk over the problem. The message you want to try to communicate to the student is

> *Yes, we have a problem.*
>
> *I want to help.*
>
> *I think you are capable of coming up with a solution.*

During the conference you should make clear that you appreciate the student's wants and needs; however, you cannot allow the student to hurt or take advantage of others. Appeal to the student's sense of fairness. The following phrases are illustrative of the suggested language.

> *I know you want to . . .*
>
> *I can't allow you to . . .*
>
> *Can you think of a way to . . . ?*

It is sometimes helpful to put the plan in writing to reinforce the commitment.

Step 7: Off to the Castle

This is isolation within the classroom. It differs from the traditional time-out in that the designated area is not meant to be unpleasant. The teacher should create a private space within the classroom, making it a comfortable retreat so that any student wouldn't mind spending time there. In fact, it should be available to any student who might on occasion want a private place.

When the student's behavior is so serious he or she has to be removed, the student is sent *off to the castle* with the simple directive, "Go sit in the castle." The teacher should pay no obvious attention to the student and should not worry about how long the student stays there. Later the teacher asks the student if he or she is ready to return and insists on some plan of action, regardless of how simple.

Step 8: Off to the Office

When steps 1 to 7 haven't worked, the student has to be removed from class. This step requires the principal's support in two ways. First, in providing a nonpunitive environment or *rest spot* and, second, in using consistent dialogue and insisting that the student make a plan for getting back into class. To enact this phase, the teacher should simply say, "Go down to the office and take a rest."

It is imperative that the student come to realize that there are only two choices, to be in class and behave appropriately, or to be out of class and sit.

Step 9: A Tolerance Day

If the student is totally out of control and can't be contained in the office rest area, then the student is sent home. The student is then put on a *tolerance day* in which he or she comes to school in the morning and stays until step 9 is reached.

Step 10: Removal from School with Hope for Reentry

If the student can't be contained in school, then he will have to stay at home and be served by some other agency. When the student seems ready, he or she can reenter at the lowest possible step. However, step 10 should be necessary only in very rare instances.

Glasser on Helping Students Develop a Plan.   Glasser recommends that the teacher develop a plan of action with the student to accomplish their mutual goals. The plan can be as simple as avoiding the other person(s) involved in the conflict or avoiding the conflict situation. Or the plan can be a more involved strategy. Explorations like the following can be used to help develop a plan of action.

1. What do you want to happen?
2. What needs to happen for you to get what you want?
3. What do you have to do to make what you want happen?
4. What specifically are you going to do to accomplish that?

Each of these exploring questions focus responsibility on the student by asking what actions he or she is going to take.

CRITICAL REFLECTION ON PRACTICE: ANALYZING YOUR CURRENT BEHAVIOR PATTERN

Activity Directions: Think of a student you are having trouble with now or have had trouble with in the past. During this activity you will be working with a partner to analyze your current behavior pattern in dealing with this student. Follow the steps listed below.

(continued)

CRITICAL REFLECTION ON PRACTICE Continued

1. List the student's most frequent inappropriate behaviors.

   _____

   _____

   _____

   _____

2. List what you currently do when this student misbehaves.

   _____

   _____

   _____

   _____

3. Compare your behaviors with those of your partner and list similarities and differences.

   SIMILARITIES   **DIFFERENCES**

   _____   _____

   _____   _____

   _____   _____

   _____   _____

   _____   _____

REFLECTIVE QUESTION
What message do you think your behavior might be giving the student?

CRITICAL REFLECTION ON PRACTICE: PLANNING AN ATTITUDE ADJUSTMENT

Activity Directions: Using your own problem student case, work with your partner to develop a self-prompting strategy to systematically change your attitude and start every day with a clean slate.

Strategy 1:   **Start fresh every day.** Develop a self-regulation strategy to prompt yourself to erase the slate and begin anew each day with your student.

   _____

   _____

   _____

   _____

Strategy 2:   **Plan for a better day tomorrow, and the next day.** Find something you can do to help your student have a better day tomorrow. List things you could do for the student and to the student to make his or her day a little brighter. It doesn't have to be much, a simple gesture can go a long way. Try to list at least ten things.

   _____

   _____

   _____

   _____

_____

_____

_____

_____

_____

_____

REFLECTIVE QUESTION
What do you need to do to sustain your attitude adjustment?

Glasser on Classroom Rules. For Glasser, classroom rules are essential. He considers rules to be especially critical for students who have not been successful in school. Permissiveness for such students is often counterproductive and fosters lack of respect for teachers and others. Rules should be jointly formulated by teachers and students, reasonable, related to efficient learning, and always enforced. Classroom rules should support a learning environment that facilitates individual and group achievement. Rules should be constantly reevaluated for utility and purpose and should lead to class and individual success.

Rules should be adapted to the age and ability of the students as well as other realities of the classroom situation. Below are some examples of appropriate rules at various grade levels.

Examples of Appropriate Classroom Rules

Primary level	1. Help others.
	2. Take turns.
	3. Walk in the classroom.
	4. Raise your hand to talk.
Upper elementary level	1. Do your best work.
	2. Be kind and help others.
	3. Settle disagreements peacefully.
	4. Listen when someone is talking.
Secondary level	1. Come to class on time.
	2. Bring the materials you need.
	3. Be considerate of others.
	4. Respect others.

Characteristics of Effective Classroom Rules. Effective rules should be

- **Jointly established.** Students should take part with the teacher in establishing class rules. Rules should address both personal behavior and work habits.
- **Reasonable.** Rules should focus on important behavior and be reasonable both in terms of duration of time and performance capabilities.
- **Clearly defined.** Rules should be clear and understandable. It should be clear to both the student and the teacher when the rule has been broken.
- **Observable.** Rules should address behaviors that can be observed. Words that are value laden should be avoided (e.g., good, nice, polite).

- **Positive.** Rules should be phrased in positive rather than negative terms, stating what students should do and emphasizing positive actions.
- **Succinct.** Rules should be brief and specific. Rules that are short and to the point are easily remembered.
- **Few in number.** There should be only enough rules to address areas of main concern. From three to six rules are adequate depending on the situation. Rules should govern general behaviors. Specific instructions for special occasions can be given when the occasion arises.
- **Enforceable.** If the teacher cannot enforce a rule consistently, he or she cannot expect students to follow it. Teachers should ensure that the established rules can be adhered to.
- **Enforced.** Rules must be enforced. Students should know the consequences of breaking a rule in advance.
- **Constantly evaluated.** Rules are established to support individual and class success. Rules should be constantly reevaluated to ensure their continued utility.

LEARNING PRACTICE TASK: EVALUATING YOUR CLASSROOM RULES

Activity Directions: Step 1: List your class rules below.
Step 2: For each rule, check the categories that are met.

EFFECTIVE RULE CRITERIA

CLASSROOM RULES	Clear	Observable	Succinct	Positive	Reasonable	Enforceable
1.						
2.						
3.						
4.						
5.						
6.						

Glasser on Classroom Meetings. For Glasser, the classroom meeting is essential for maintaining an effective system of discipline. Classroom meetings provide a forum to continually review rules, responsibilities, and problems and to explore and clarify student responsibility. It is a way of involving students and keeping the communication channels open. Glasser (1969) suggests that the class be viewed as a problem-solving group, with the teacher serving as the group leader. A description of the essential elements of the classroom meeting is provided below.

Description. The classroom meeting is a regularly scheduled time when the whole class engages in open-minded, nonjudgmental discussion of personal, social, or academic problems in an effort to find collective solutions.

Purposes
1. To foster caring and supportive relationships that help students satisfy their needs to belong, have power, feel in control, and experience satisfaction or enjoyment

2. To identify and discuss problems
3. To seek mutually agreed-upon solutions

Kinds of Meetings
1. Problem-solving meetings
   - Attempt to solve problems that arise among people living and working together in a school setting
   - Are opportunities to consider matters of discipline
   - Are usually initiated by the teacher but could be initiated by anyone
   - Are group oriented
   - Direct discussion toward arriving at a solution
   - Seek solutions that don't include punishment or fault-finding
   - Focus on the situation, rather than the individual(s)
   - Facilitate discussion through storytelling, role-playing, and pictures depicting specific situations or incidents

2. Open meetings
   - Provide an opportunity for an individual to express frustrations or feelings resulting from another member(s)
   - Focus on intellectually important subjects
   - Deal with any topic of concern to students
   - Address any current topic or experience of a class member

3. Educational decision-making meetings
   - Need not be a problem
   - Address issues such as curriculum, instructional activities, tasks, assignments
   - Can address how well students understand concepts in the curriculum
   - Include planning events, trips
   - Involve discussion of classroom procedures, such as subject or activity order, furniture arrangement, rewards, and so forth

Setting and Time Allotment. Meetings should be conducted with the teacher and all students seated in a tight circle. This seating arrangement fosters interaction, student involvement, and a sense of equal status. At the early grades (K through 2) 10 to 20 minutes should be allotted, increasing to 30 to 45 minutes at the upper grades.

Glasser on Dialogue with Students. Glasser's key principles for responding to students are, make it clear that the student has the problem, invite cooperation, offer assistance, and state consequences. In creating dialogue with students, he advocates the following types of communication.

Characteristics of Glasser Dialogue
1. Invite cooperation
2. Request a value judgment
3. Ask student to make appropriate choice
4. Ask nonthreatening questions about who, what, when, how, but not why
5. Request alternative behavior(s)
6. State behavior expectations
7. Offer help
8. Quiet correction
9. Simple directive
10. Remind student of consequences (*If . . . then . . .*)

Glasser's Newer Views

Glasser's newer views are geared primarily toward secondary schools.

- Schools need to be restructured to provide more satisfying experiences for students.
- Schools need to find ways to reduce both teacher and student frustrations.
- Less than 50 percent of students are willing to make an effort to learn.
- Only a discipline program that produces classroom satisfaction can work.
- Four fundamental needs play powerful roles in student behavior: the need to belong, the need for power, the need for freedom, and the need for fun.
- In our present organization of schools, cooperative learning offers the greatest promise for providing for these four needs.
- Although much of what teachers do is an attempt to control others' behavior, in reality we can only control our own behavior (i.e., control theory). Hence, students will control their own behavior so that what they choose to do is the most need-satisfying thing they can do.
- Integrating leadership style theory with his other notions, Glasser defines what he calls *the quality school* where
  —Students' needs are satisfied
  —Teachers don't try to coerce students
  —Teachers lead, don't boss students
  —Teachers build the link between classroom tasks and students' perceptions of quality.

Comparison of Glasser's Earlier and Current Work

In his earlier work, Glasser maintained that schools offered students the best, and sometimes their only, chance to interface with adults who genuinely cared about them. Thus schools afforded students an opportunity for belonging, success, and positive self-identity. To avail themselves of this opportunity, students were continually called on to make value judgments about their behavior, make appropriate choices, and accept the consequences of their good and bad choices.

In Glasser's more recent work, he places greater onus on the schools to meet student needs, rather than molding students, to deal more effectively with the conditions they encounter in school.

Glasser's More Recent Position

Glasser's more recent position has evolved from focusing on helping students deal with the conditions they encounter in schools (*reality*) to calling for a restructuring of schools to provide more satisfying experiences for students. He now says if schools are to enjoy good discipline, they must reduce both teacher and student frustrations by creating a more need-satisfying environment.

Glasser's views are geared primarily toward secondary schools. He takes the position shared by many that major restructuring is needed because in our current system less than one-half of the students are willing to make an effort to learn and thus cannot be taught. In fact he goes as far as stating, "I believe that we have gone as far as we can go with the traditional structure of our secondary schools" (p. 6). In *Control Theory in the Classroom* (1986), Glasser emphasizes the school's role in meeting student basic needs as a prime factor in discipline and work effort. He contends that only a discipline program that is concerned with classroom satisfaction can work. He calls for schools to be restructured to fulfill four fundamental needs that play powerful roles in student behavior. Those needs are

1. **The need to belong,** to feel accepted, to be a member of the group or class.
2. **The need for power,** not so much power over others as power to control part of one's own life and power to do things competently.
3. **The need for freedom,** to feel at least partly in control of self, self-reliant, without constant direction from others.
4. **The need for fun,** for enjoyment, for pleasure, for satisfaction.

Glasser and others advocate cooperative learning as an instructional strategy that is most likely to provide for these four needs in our present organization of schools. Cooperative learning provides a structure that allows students to meet their needs for belonging and acceptance, since all members of the group participate and have roles. Talking and working with others fulfills the need for fun and enjoyment. Shared leadership offers some freedom in making decisions and serves students' need to have some control. Most important, cooperative learning gives students power, power to influence others, power to do something well, and power to be recognized. Glasser sees the power need as central for secondary level students.

In cooperative learning, small groups of students work together to complete instructional activities. Students work collaboratively and share responsibility for task completion. Of course, not all working together in a group setting constitutes cooperative learning. Johnson and his colleagues in *Circles of Learning: Cooperation in the Classroom* (1984, p. 8) identified the following four elements as necessary for cooperative learning to be effective.

1. **Positive interdependence.** This distinction is critical. Students must be dependent on each other for the completion of the assigned activities. This dependency is generally accomplished by assigning students to different roles within the group. However, the overall task cannot be completed without the contributions of each member.
2. **Face-to-face interaction.** Students must be able to interact with one another and exchange information easily.
3. **Individual accountability**. Each member is held individually accountable for accomplishing the intended learnings. Students are assigned to groups to provide a mix of abilities, so that students comprising each group have different ability and achievement levels. This allows students to learn from each other while providing mutual assistance and support.
4. **Use of interpersonal and small group skills.** Students must use effective social skills for collaborative learning to be successful, but often such skills are lacking. Therefore, students must be taught how to use such skills as leadership, effective communication, and conflict management. In their groups they are given time and procedures for analyzing the overall effectiveness of their group work.

Control Theory.   According to Glasser (1986), the need for control is one of the basic needs we all have. Whenever people feel that they do not have control, they will do whatever they think is necessary to regain it. Attempting to control another's behavior ultimately leads to conflict as that person attempts to meet his or her own need for control.

Control theory posits that most of what we do is not a reaction or response to events around us. Glasser more recently renamed control theory to "choice theory," believing it to be a more appropriate term (Glasser & Dotson, 1998). We are not controlled by external forces outside of our control, rather we control ourselves by forces that lie within. How we feel is not controlled by others or events. It is our nature to try to satisfy, as best we can, basic needs for survival, acceptance, freedom, power, and satisfaction. We control our own behavior by choosing to do things that satisfy these basic needs. All any of us do, think, or feel is always our best attempt at satisfying one of these needs. And often, our attempt is an ineffective response.

The notion of control viewed from this perspective is an inner action rather than a response to events, people, or situations. It is not about controlling others' behavior, it is about self-control.

By contrast, in the behavioral model of reinforcement theory, behavior is controlled by external stimuli, or reactions to behavior. Adhering to this theory leads to trying to manipulate the behavior of others by dispensing rewards and delivering punishments. If, on the other hand, you believe control to be an inner action governed by an internal thought process and mediated by inner speech, or self-talk, the way to exercise control is to monitor and regulate what you think and what you tell yourself. Clearly, this is a very different way of perceiving control. So if, as the teacher, I think and say to myself "I'll show him who's boss," then I will impose a negative consequence. But if I think and say to myself "I'll remain calm," then I will respond by helping the student exercise self-control.

Calling for Students to Make Value Judgments.   When students behave inappropriately, teachers should ask questions to help them make value judgments about their behavior. Glasser (1977) suggests the following procedure when a student is misbehaving.

> **Teacher:** What are you doing? [Asked in nonthreatening tone of voice.]
>
> **Student:** [Will usually give an honest answer if not threatened.]
>
> **Teacher:** Is that helping you or the class?
>
> **Student:** No.
>
> **Teacher:** What could you do that would help?
>
> **Student:** [Names better behavior; if none is suggested, teacher suggests appropriate alternatives and lets student choose.]

Of course, the student won't always respond in an acceptable way. When that happens, Glasser offers the following protocol teacher responses.

> **Student:** [Behaving irresponsibly.]
>
> **Teacher:** What are you doing? Is it against the rules? What should you be doing?
>
> **Student:** [Responds negatively, unacceptably.]
>
> **Teacher:** I would like to talk with you privately at [specifies time].

During private conference between teacher and student.

> **Teacher:** What were you doing? Was it against the rules? What should you have been doing?
>
> **Student:** [Agrees to proper course of behavior.]

Later the student repeats the misbehavior and the teacher calls for another private conference.

> **Teacher:** We have to work this out. What kind of plan can you make so you can follow the rules?
>
> **Student:** I'll stop doing it.
>
> **Teacher:** No, we need a plan that says exactly what you will do. Let's make a simple plan you can follow. I'll help you.

Clarifying Ownership of the Problem.   Glasser suggests that teachers make it perfectly clear that the student's disruption is his or her own problem, not the teacher's, and that the teacher knows exactly what to do. The teacher should say something like the following to the disruptive student.

> *It looks like you have a problem. How could I help you solve it? If you'll just calm down, as soon as I have the time, I'll talk it over with you and I think we can work something out. As long as you're doing what you're doing now, we can't work anything out.*

Sometimes a joking remark (at the teacher's expense, not the student's) can help relieve the tension. The teacher might try saying in a mock serious tone

> *Wow, you're upset. I must be doing something really terrible. Calm down, and as soon as I can, we'll get together and maybe you can help me work things out.*

Glasser maintains that if the student will not calm down after this reasonable request, there is no good way to deal with him or her in class. The teacher should not get into an argument or even a long discussion with an angry student. Above all, the teacher should never threaten the student.

In order to solve problems that arise, teachers need the cooperation of the student. If the student refuses to cooperate, he or she must be asked to leave the room. The teacher should say something like the following.

> *Since you won't calm down, I have to ask you to leave. I hope we can get together later and work this out, but if you are not willing to settle down, it's better that you leave now.*

The disruptive student is often looking for someone to blame in order to sustain a grievance. But it's hard to stay angry at a teacher who is saying, in words, attitude, and behavior,

> *I want to help you work this out. I am not looking to punish you for what you have just done. If there is a problem, let's solve it.*

The only reasonable solutions to discipline problems are systematic and long term, and thus must be developed while the student is in control. So the first strategy should be to get the student to calm down. Then you need to find a few minutes to talk to him or her, either in class, between classes, before or after school, or at any time you can spare a few minutes. When you have the time, you should say something similar to the following.

> *What were you doing when the problem started? Was this against the rules? Can we work it out so that it doesn't happen again? If this situation comes up in the future, let's work out what you could do and what I could do so we don't have this problem again.*

The Quality School.   Glasser's more recent book, *The Quality School. Managing Students without Coercion* (1990, 1998), again emphasizes the importance of meeting students' basic needs within the learning environment. He reiterates that although much of what we do is an attempt to control others, in reality we can only control our own behavior (i.e., choice theory). It is human nature to try to satisfy as best we can our basic needs for survival, belonging, freedom, power, and enjoyment.

Translating choice theory to the classroom setting means that students will control their own behavior, so that what they choose to do is the most need-satisfying thing they can do at a given time (Glasser & Dotson, 1998). More often than not, something other than the learning task is more need satisfying at the time.

Glasser also integrates organizational theory and leadership style theory with his other notions to define what he calls the *quality school*. In the quality school the following conditions prevail.

1. Students' basic needs are satisfied.
2. Teachers recognize that they can only control their own behavior and do not try to coerce students.
3. Teachers lead rather than boss their students.
4. Teachers manage their classes so that students can easily see the connection between what they are asked to do and what they believe is quality work.

His ideas about quality work are based on the work of Dr. W. Edwards Deming, who tried after World War II to promote the power of participatory management for workers in order to achieve quality products. Applying Deming's notions to education, Glasser notes that students are both the workers and the products of schooling. The theory is that once students see that they themselves are gaining in quality they will make an effort to continue. So the role of the teacher becomes one of building the link between what students believe to be quality and what they are expected to accomplish.

Glasser draws an interesting parallel.

Just as the American auto industry in the 1970s concentrated on building low-quality, high-profit cars, schools have concentrated on getting more students to meet the low-quality standards required for graduation. Thus we produce students who, like workers, merely "lean on their shovels."

A comparison of managers who lead and those who boss is provided below.

Comparison of Boss-Management and Lead-Management.   The lead-manager

- Confers with students when deciding about the work to be done, the time needed to do it, and the quality standard
- Models the job and seeks student input about better ways to achieve quality
- Invites students to evaluate their own work for quality
- Provides the tools and setting that promote self-confidence and congeniality among students

In contrast, the boss-manager

- Does not consult students about what work needs to be done
- Tells students what to do without asking them how it might be done better
- Sets quality standards and evaluates work without involving them in the process
- Relies on coercion to get students to do what they are told, creating an adversarial climate

Quality Teaching Leads to Quality Learning.   Glasser (1998) in his recent books advises teachers to support quality teaching, quality learning, and quality student work by striving to do the following:

- Make the classroom warm and supportive. Let students know you and like you by sharing who you are and what you stand for. Show you're always willing to help. Clarify what you will expect from them as well as what you will do for them.

- Ask students to do only useful work, consisting of skills, not just information, that students and teachers view as valuable.
- Ask students to do quality work, the best work they can do.
- Discuss quality work often so students know what you mean by quality work.
- Then ask students to evaluate their own work and improve it.
- Help students to see that doing quality work makes them feel good. When they experience this feeling of pride and accomplishment they will want more.
- Help students to see that quality work is never destructive to oneself, others, or the environment.

■ ■ ■ ■ ■ ■ ■ ■

LEARNING PRACTICE TASK: CASE STUDY OF STAN

Activity Directions: Working with a partner, develop some strategies that would be consistent with Glasser's views on discipline for the problem situation below.

Stan has arrived for class in his usual nasty mood. He goes to sharpen his pencil and while in route he can't resist giving Joe a "friendly" shove. Joe responds with a complaint to the teacher. The teacher asks Stan to return to his seat at which point Stan retorts with "I'll go when I'm ready!"

How would Glasser deal with Stan?

_____

_____

_____

_____

■ ■ ■ ■ ■ ■ ■ ■

CRITICAL REFLECTION ON PRACTICE: IS YOUR CLASSROOM NEED-SATISFYING?

Activity Directions: Take a few minutes to think about the procedures and strategies used in your classroom organization that address Glasser's view of students' four basic needs. Then share your list with a peer and complete Part 2 together.

Part 1: Complete independently.

STUDENT NEEDS

WAYS I ADDRESS THIS NEED IN MY CLASS STRUCTURE

1. Need to belong and be accepted.

   1. _____
      _____
      _____

2. Need to have some power, influence others, and be recognized.

   2. _____
      _____
      _____

3. Need to have freedom and to be in control of self.

   3. _____
      _____
      _____

(continued)

CRITICAL REFLECTION ON PRACTICE   Continued

4. Need for enjoyment and satisfaction   4. _____
   from learning.   _____
                                                _____

Part 2: Work with a peer.

List other things you might do to make your classroom a more need-satisfying environment.

_____

_____

_____

_____

_____

REFLECTIVE QUESTION
What's the one thing you are willing to commit to that will make your classroom more satisfying for students?

DREIKURS'S DEMOCRATIC DISCIPLINE: IDENTIFYING STUDENTS' MISTAKEN GOALS

Rudolf Dreikurs, long associated with psychiatrist Alfred Adler, immigrated to the United States eventually to become director of the Alfred Adler Institute. Throughout his long career, he continued to focus on family–child counseling, but became well known in the area of classroom behavior through his books *Psychology in the Classroom* (1968), *Discipline without Tears* (1972), and *Maintaining Sanity in the Classroom* (1982).

Dreikurs's approach to discipline is based on understanding the motivations behind student behavior. He believed that students react to negative feelings by developing defense mechanisms to protect their self-esteem. Dreikurs called on teachers to identify students' goals and use that information to help students recognize the purpose of their inappropriate behavior. All students want recognition, and most misbehavior occurs when they attempt to get it. When unable to get the recognition they want, they turn to misbehavior to gain the recognition they are seeking.

Dreikurs's approach to classroom discipline is based on three key ideas.

1. Students are social beings and as such their actions reflect their attempts to be important and gain acceptance.
2. Students are capable of controlling their behavior and choose either to behave or to misbehave.

   Combining these two points, Dreikurs contends that

3. Students choose to misbehave because they are under the mistaken belief that it will get them the recognition they want. Dreikurs refers to such beliefs as *mistaken goals*.

   All students want to belong, so they try all sorts of behavior to see if it gets them the recognition they want. If they do not get recognition through socially acceptable means, they turn to unacceptable means. Such behavior reflects the mistaken belief that inappropriate behavior is the only way to get recognition.

Dreikurs identifies four mistaken goals: attention getting, power seeking, revenge seeking, and displaying inadequacy. These goals are usually sought in sequential order. When attention getting fails to gain recognition, the student progresses to seeking power, then to seeking revenge, and finally to displaying inadequacy. Dreikurs recommends a three-step process for teachers in dealing with students' mistaken goals.

Step 1. Identify the student's mistaken goal.
Step 2. Confront the student in a nonthreatening manner.
Step 3. Explore with the student his or her motivation (i.e., mistaken goal).

Key Principles for Teachers

The first thing teachers need to do is identify the student's mistaken goal. Two factors can help the teacher gauge which mistaken goal is operating, the teacher's own reaction to the student's behavior and the student's counterreaction to the teacher's reaction. The teacher's response is an indication of the student's expectation.

If the teacher	Then the student's goal is
Feels annoyed	Getting attention
Feels threatened	Seeking power
Feels hurt	Getting revenge
Feels helpless	Displaying inadequacy

If the student	Then the goal is
Stops the behavior but then repeats it	Getting attention
Refuses to stop	Seeking power
Becomes hostile	Getting revenge
Refuses to cooperate or participate	Displaying inadequacy

The strategy that Dreikurs recommends for teachers is threefold. First, the teacher needs to identify the student's mistaken goal. Next, the teacher should confront the student in a nonthreatening way with an explanation of the mistaken goal. Third, the teacher should discuss with the student the faulty logic involved, to get students to examine the purposes behind their behavior. The process calls for teachers to ask students specific questions, in sequential order and to look for reactions that might indicate a mistaken goal. Dreikurs advocates the following questions:

1. Could it be that you want me to pay attention to you?
2. Could it be that you want to prove that nobody can make you do anything?
3. Could it be that you want to hurt me or other students in this class?
4. Could it be that you want everyone to believe you are not capable?

Once the mistaken goals are identified, teachers can begin to take action to defeat the student's purposes and initiate more constructive behavior.

The following two charts provide elements of Dreikurs's approach both from the student's and the teacher's perspective. The first chart shows, for each mistaken goal, the student's belief and purpose as well as the student's typical behavior and reaction to teacher intervention attempts. The second chart shows the teacher's feelings, typical reactions, and ineffective and effective strategies for dealing with each mistaken goal.

Mistaken Goals: The Student's Perspective

STUDENT'S MISTAKEN GOAL	STUDENT'S BELIEF	STUDENT'S MESSAGE AND PURPOSE	STUDENT'S BEHAVIOR AND ACTION	STUDENT'S GENERAL REACTION TO TEACHER INTERVENTION
Attention	I belong only when I'm noticed or served. I'm important only when everyone is paying attention to me.	"Look at me!" Tries to keep teacher's attention on self	Pesters, is nuisance Clowns around, shows off Constantly disrupts class Asks endless questions Is bashful Uses excessive charm	Temporarily complies with teacher request to stop behavior Later resumes same behavior or seeks attention in some other way
Power	I belong only when I'm in charge or when I'm proving that no one can make me do anything. I'm important only when I'm the boss.	"You can't make me!" Tries to control teacher and dominate situation	Disobeys Argues Refuses to follow directions Has temper tantrums Tells lies Does little or no work	Defiantly continues the behavior Intensifies action if reprimanded Submits with defiant compliance
Revenge	I belong only when I'm hurting others and getting even. I'm important only when I'm fixing my hurt by hurting others.	"I'll get even with you!" Tries to compensate for own hurt by hurting others	Makes mean remarks Calls others names Destroys property Physically attacks others Is defiant Runs away	Becomes violent or hostile Intensifies the hurtful behavior Seeks further revenge, retaliation In retaliation, directs hostility toward the teacher May become sullen Initially rejects efforts made by others
Display of Inadequacy	I belong only when I convince others that I am unable and helpless. I'm important only when I'm proving I'm a failure.	"I'm no good, so leave me alone!" Feels that he or she can't do anything right so doesn't try to do anything at all	Rarely participates Gives up easily Never gets work done Keeps to him- or herself Plays dumb Is often absent	No response or half-hearted response Shows no improvement Becomes more passive, refuses to interact

Mistaken Goals: The Teacher's Perspective

Goal: Attention

TEACHER'S FEELING OR THINKING	TEACHER'S COMMON REACTIONS	SPECIFIC QUESTIONS FOR DIAGNOSIS	EFFECTIVE STRATEGIES	INEFFECTIVE STRATEGIES
Annoyed Irritated "This student occupies too much of my time." "I wish he or she would stop bothering me."	Gives service to student Frequently reminds Tries to coax Pays attention by reminding, nagging, or scolding student	"Could it be that you want me to pay attention to you?" or "Could it be that you want me to do something special for you?"	When possible, ignore the student's bid for attention. Give attention and encouragement at other times. Give attention in unexpected ways. Recognize positive behavior. Walk away when student demands attention. Make a contract (*If . . . , then . . .*). Analyze how your own behavior might be affecting the student. Identify alternatives for the student. Give permission to the student to bid for attention with parameters. When not possible to ignore, make eye contact without any comment or call student's name. Follow through by allowing natural or logical consequences to occur.	Showing annoyance Giving negative attention by nagging, scolding, or correcting Giving attention by answering excessive questions, reminding, coaxing, or talking to

Goal: Power

TEACHER'S FEELING OR THINKING	TEACHER'S COMMON REACTIONS	SPECIFIC QUESTIONS FOR DIAGNOSIS	EFFECTIVE STRATEGIES	INEFFECTIVE STRATEGIES
Threatened Angry Provoked Defeated "He or she can't get away with this." "Who's running this class?"	Fights "power with power" Engages in power struggle Defends authority Threatens Argues Punishes	"Could it be that you want to prove that nobody can make you do anything?" or "Could it be that you want to be boss?"	Refuse to engage in conflict. Withdraw as an authority figure. Help student use power constructively by enlisting his or her help. Redirect student by inviting participation in decision making. Give student position of responsibility. Put student in charge of something.	Becoming emotionally involved Arguing Threatening Punishing Raising voice Giving in

(continued)

Mistaken Goals   Continued

Goal: Power (continued)

TEACHER'S FEELING OR THINKING	TEACHER'S COMMON REACTIONS	SPECIFIC QUESTIONS FOR DIAGNOSIS	EFFECTIVE STRATEGIES	INEFFECTIVE STRATEGIES
	Tries to force student		Give responsibility for students' own work by providing options.	
	Gives in		Give sincere encouragement.	
			Stop the entire class and have them wait for student to stop behavior.	
			Make an agreement.	
			Enlist help of class.	
			Remain calm.	
			Speak softly.	
			Provide for a cooling off period.	

Goal: Revenge

TEACHER'S FEELING OR THINKING	TEACHER'S COMMON REACTIONS	SPECIFIC QUESTIONS FOR DIAGNOSIS	EFFECTIVE STRATEGIES	INEFFECTIVE STRATEGIES
Hurt	Retaliates	"Could it be that you want to hurt me or others in the class?" or "Could it be that you want to get even?"	Examine behavior that is being interpreted by student as hurtful.	Retaliation
Angry	Gets even		Try to understand the student's feelings of hurt.	Punishment
Outraged	Punishes harshly		Build a trusting relationship.	Acting hurt
Humiliated	Raises voice		Set up situations for student to exhibit talents or strengths.	Continuing the alienation
Rejected	Counter-attacks		Call on class to support and encourage the student.	
"How can I get even?"	Seeks revenge		Enlist a buddy.	
"How mean can he or she be?"				

Goal: Display of Inadequacy

TEACHER'S FEELING OR THINKING	TEACHER'S COMMON REACTIONS	SPECIFIC QUESTIONS FOR DIAGNOSIS	EFFECTIVE STRATEGIES	INEFFECTIVE STRATEGIES
Despair	Withdraws	"Could it be that you want to be left alone?" or	Stay involved with the student.	Giving up
Hopelessness	Gives up helping		Encourage and reward effort, no matter how small.	Pitying
Discouragement	Concedes defeat		Demonstrate that the student can be successful.	Doing for the student what he or she can do for self
	Criticizes			

TEACHER'S FEELING OR THINKING	TEACHER'S COMMON REACTIONS	SPECIFIC QUESTIONS FOR DIAGNOSIS	EFFECTIVE STRATEGIES	INEFFECTIVE STRATEGIES
Powerless-ness "I can't do anything with him or her." "I don't know what to do anymore."		"Could it be that you want everyone to believe you are not capable?"	Break difficult tasks into smaller segments. Demonstrate desired behavior. Make student feel worthwhile. Assign student helpers. Trust the student with responsibilities.	Giving outward signals of frustration Criticizing Expecting immediate results

Examples of Appropriate Teacher Reactions to Mistaken Goals.

1. For attention-getting behavior. Sometimes it is not feasible for teachers to ignore behavior that is disrupting the class. In such cases teachers need to give attention in ways that are not rewarding to the student. The teacher may call the student's name and make eye contact without any comments. Or the teacher may describe the behavior without any trace of annoyance by saying

I see that you are not finishing your assignment.

One technique that is sometimes effective is to privately confront the student with his or her goal and ask, "How many times do you think you will need my attention in the next hour?" The student will usually not know what to say. The teacher might then say "If I give you attention fifteen times, will that be enough?" This will sound like an exaggeration to the student. Then when the student misbehaves the teacher responds by saying, "Joel, number one," "Joel, number two," and so forth. The teacher does not comment on the behavior or scold, which would give Joel the attention he seeks, but simply lets him know his behavior is being noted.

2. For power-seeking behavior. Teachers can also redirect students' ambitions to be in charge by inviting them to participate in making decisions or by giving them positions of responsibility. A teacher might take a student aside and say, "The language during physical education is very unsportsmanlike. The others look up to you. Do you think you could help out by setting an example?" Or in the same situation the teacher might say, "I have a problem. It concerns the language I am hearing. What do you think I should do?" In this way, the teacher gives the student power while avoiding a power struggle.

Teachers may also confront the behavior openly. When a disruption begins, the teacher could say, "I cannot continue to teach when you are doing that. Can you think of a way you could do what you want and I could still teach?" If students cannot think of any ways, the teacher should be prepared to suggest some alternatives.

By withdrawing as a power figure, teachers take fuel from a student's fire. Students cannot be involved in a power struggle with themselves. They will not receive status or recognition if they cannot get the best of the teacher. Teachers who withdraw thwart the purpose of power-seeking behavior.

3. For verbal or physical fighting between students. The probable goals are attention, power, or revenge directed at the teacher, attention directed at the rest of the group, or power or revenge directed at an antagonist.

The problem owners are the students involved or you, if the fight is disruptive or dangerous, although the actual disagreement belongs to students. Avoid reinforcing mistaken goals by taking away students' responsibility for solving their own problems. Whenever possible, let students settle their own disputes.

Some Other Alternatives

1. If verbal, and for attention, power or revenge. Let students who complain about each other settle their own disputes. Tell them to do this only once. Ignore future complaints.

2. If physical, and for attention, power, or revenge. On the playground, if the fighters aren't attracting a crowd, ignore them and deprive them of an audience. Or establish a no fighting rule: students who fight are demonstrating their decision to sit on the sidelines until they are ready to stop fighting.

If students fight in the building, establish a place for them to talk over their conflicts. With young students, designate two chairs the *talk-it-over chairs*. Let students work out their problems independently. Stay silent and uninvolved. Your only concern is that they stay away from the group until they're ready to stop fighting. Accept any solution except fighting, including complete silence while they're supposedly talking it over. If they return too soon, say "I see you've still not decided how to get along. Please leave the group and decide how you'll get along. I'll come over in a few minutes to see if you've solved your problem and are ready to return." Keep returning students to the negotiation area if fighting continues, gradually increasing the time away.

Separate students who are too angry to negotiate. Say "I can see that you two need to cool off. Christine, you go _____ and Geraldine, you go _____. I'll check with you in a while to see if you're ready to talk it over or return to the classroom."

Dreikurs's Guidelines for Teachers. Dreikurs advocates teachers developing an ongoing relationship that promotes a spirit of cooperation and team effort. Teachers should provide consistent guidance that will facilitate students developing their own inner controls. Discipline is far more than imposing limits at times of stress and conflict. Accordingly, Dreikurs offers the following strategies for teachers.

DOs and DON'Ts for Teachers

DOs   Give students clear-cut directions for expected behavior.

Apply logical consequences rather than arbitrary punishment.

Allow students a say in establishing rules and consequences.

Let students assume responsibility for their own behavior and learning.

Be firm. Let students know that you are a friend, but that you will not accept certain behavior.

Set limits from the beginning, but work toward developing a sense of responsibility.

Teach students to impose limits on themselves.

Close an incident quickly and revive positive feelings.

Forgive and forget.

Mean what you say, but make simple demands.

Always distinguish between the deed and the doer.

Treat students as social equals.

Encourage students' efforts.

DON'Ts   Act in ways that reinforce mistaken goals.

Nag and scold.

Find fault with students.

Threaten students.

Ask students to make promises.

Praise students' work and character.

Point out how much better the student could do.

Encourage comparison with others.

Have double standards—one for you and another for your students.

Dreikurs's Distinction between Praise and Encouragement

As mentioned earlier, Dreikurs makes a clear distinction between praise and encouragement. He takes the position that continuous encouragement is a crucial element in the prevention of problem behavior. Through encouragement teachers exhibit trust in students' abilities to manage themselves constructively while facilitating the development of a positive self-image.

Dreikurs's Distinction between Logical Consequences and Punishment

Dreikurs recognizes that at times these approaches will be ineffective in redirecting misbehavior, and then students will have to pay the consequences of their misbehavior. At such times, he advises teachers to act democratically, not autocratically, and to use logical, not arbitrary, consequences. He equates arbitrary consequences with punishment.

A democratic teaching style calls for teachers to learn to distinguish logical and natural consequences from punishment. According to Dreikurs, although it is quite permissible for the democratic teacher to employ logical consequences, or to permit natural consequences following misbehavior, it is not permissible to use punishment. Dreikurs defines punishment as any hurtful action taken by a *superior authority* as a means of coercing an *inferior being* to do the bidding of the authority. Natural and logical consequences replace punishment in the democratic classroom. Natural consequences take place automatically without teacher intervention, while logical consequences are specifically designed to have a logical relationship with the misbehavior.

For Dreikurs, distinguishing between logical consequences and punishment represents a critical distinction. When applying consequences, teachers should

1. Pose alternatives that fit the situation and let students decide either verbally or through their behavior.

   Terry, I'm sorry but throwing the blocks is not permitted. You can play with them correctly or stop playing with them for a while. You decide.

   If you go to the library, you go to work on your report.

2. Offer choices firmly but respectfully.

   Either help us out on this project or leave the group.

   When the books are put away, we can go to lunch.

Summary of Dreikurs's Views

When Dreikurs's principles are implemented effectively, they have the potential to bring about genuine attitudinal change among students, so that they eventually behave more appropriately because they choose to do what they think is the right thing. Dreikurs refers to his approach as democratic in that teachers and students decide together on rules and consequences and take joint responsibility for maintaining a classroom climate conducive to learning.

Dreikurs's approach requires a commitment over time for its results to become apparent. It also requires that teachers spend considerable time talking to students about their actions. With its emphasis on mutual respect, acceptance, encouragement, student effort, and general responsibility, this approach represents a powerful technique for students' personal growth enhancement.

Dreikurs's greatest contribution to classroom discipline lies not in how to suppress undesirable behavior in the short run, but rather in how to build over time an inner sense of responsibility and respect for others.

Albert's Cooperative Discipline: The Three Cs, Capable, Connected, and Contributing

Building on the work of Dreikurs, Albert (1996) and Dinkmeyer, McKay, and Dinkmeyer (1980) point out that intervening to redirect students' disruptive classroom behavior prompted by mistaken goals is only part of the overall democratic management of classroom problems. The need to belong in the classroom is interpreted as a desire to feel significant and important and to find a satisfying place within the classroom or group. Before students can choose more positive forms of classroom behavior as means of belonging in the classroom setting, they must feel capable, connected, and confident in their ability to contribute to the classroom. Albert called these the three Cs. When these are satisfied, students achieve a strong sense of belonging. To belong, students must feel capable of completing academic and other tasks, believe that they can connect successfully on a personal level with teachers and classmates, and think they can contribute in a significant way to the group or class.

Three factors affect students' abilities to satisfy the three Cs: the quality of the student–teacher relationship; the classroom climate, especially regarding opportunities for cooperation and success; and the classroom structure for encouraging contributions from all.

Examples of strategies that help students feel more capable include the following.

1. Communicate to students that it is all right to make mistakes. Teachers can talk about mistakes as being a vital part of learning. They can equate mistakes and effort and generally attempt to minimize any negative effects that might be associated with making mistakes.
2. Build student confidence by focusing on improvements, noticing contributions, acknowledging strengths, and generally showing faith in students. Teachers also can ensure that students are not left to fail at tasks for long periods of time.
3. Assist students in recognizing past successes students have experienced. This can be done by keeping checklists of skills or flowcharts of concepts that track students' progress by recording and displaying what they have learned. Another vehicle is accomplishment albums in which students keep examples of past work that has been done successfully.
4. Recognize success by providing opportunities for students to acknowledge their own and others' accomplishments. This might be accomplished by occasionally assisting students in running their own award assemblies or providing positive time-outs that give students opportunities for self-congratulation and selection of self-rewarding activities.

Here are examples of strategies that help students connect with the teacher and their classmates.

1. Accept students by showing a willingness to accept differences in students' personal styles, such as personal idiosyncrasies in dress, habits, or mannerisms.
2. Attend to students by greeting them warmly, listening to them, and helping them seek attention in appropriate ways when they desire it.
3. Appreciate students' efforts to contribute positively in the classroom, and to their own and others' learning. Explicit oral or written statements of appreciation can acknowledge a student's actions, the teacher's own positive feelings about these actions, and the benefits accrued when students act in helpful and supportive ways.
4. Show appropriate affection to students, especially when such affection is not contingent on any accomplishment, per se, and when students are upset or troubled by events in their lives, both inside and outside the classroom.

These are examples of strategies that might help students think they can contribute.

1. Invite students' help with daily tasks.
2. Ask students to make choices and give input about classroom practices and curriculum.
3. Encourage students to help each other through peer tutoring, peer counseling, and peer recognition.

By helping students feel capable of connecting and contributing, teachers can help build students' self-esteem so that they will be more likely to pursue their goals of belonging in positive ways that will benefit themselves as well as their classmates.

LEARNING PRACTICE TASK: CASE STUDY OF DARRYL

Activity Directions: Read the case study below. Then, working with a partner, respond to the questions based on Dreikurs's concept of mistaken goals.

Case Study. *Darryl entered the classroom and smiled at Ms. Dunn. She smiled back and told Darryl his assignment was at his desk. Darryl then responded, "I ain't got no book." Ms. Dunn gave him a book. "I ain't got no paper" was his next response. Ms. Dunn handed Darryl a piece of paper. Darryl followed with "I ain't got no pencil." Ms. Dunn asked Cindy to lend Darryl a pencil. Finally, Darryl slammed his books on his desk and yelled, "Shit!" He immediately glanced at Ms. Dunn fully expecting an angry response. Ms. Dunn frowned and went on with what she was doing. Realizing his attempt to provoke Ms. Dunn wasn't working, Darryl settled down to work.*

What was Darryl's agenda?

_____
_____
_____
_____

(continued)

LEARNING PRACTICE TASK   Continued

What was Ms. Dunn attempting?

_____

_____

_____

_____

Do you think Ms. Dunn's behavior was appropriate? _____

What would you have done?

_____

_____

_____

_____

LEARNING PRACTICE TASK: IDENTIFYING EFFECTIVE STRATEGIES

Activity Directions: For each of the cases below
- Identify the student's mistaken goal.
- List two strategies Dreikurs would consider effective.
- List two strategies Dreikurs would consider ineffective.

1. Sarah habitually comes to class late, making sure her arrival is noticed. When Ms. Banner asks her to explain why she is late, she retorts with, "You're always on my case."

    Mistaken goal: _____

    Effective strategies: _____

    _____

    Ineffective strategies: _____

    _____

2. Mario can often be found staring into space. He avoids both the teacher and his classmates. His teacher has made many attempts to get him to work. He rarely does any work at all.

    Mistaken goal: _____

    Effective strategies: _____

    _____

    Ineffective strategies: _____

    _____

3. Mike is always taunting his classmates. Today he pulled Jessica's hair when she refused to give him a pencil.

    Mistaken goal: _____

    Effective strategies: _____

    _____

    Ineffective strategies: _____

    _____

GINOTT'S CONGRUENT COMMUNICATION: SANE TEACHERS–SANE MESSAGES

Haim Ginott is the author of three books that address the relationship between adults and children. In his first two books he presented specific strategies for dealing with parent–child conflict, urging parents to communicate to their children that, although they may disapprove of their behavior at times, they still accept and love them (Ginott, 1965, 1969). In his final book, Ginott (1972) extends his notions of acceptance to the classroom, advocating styles of communication that humanize rather than dehumanize students. He emphasizes the socioemotional climate of the classroom and calls on teachers to demonstrate concern for students' feelings. Ginott recognizes that the messages teachers communicate to students have a significant impact on their self-esteem.

The following quote illuminates Ginott's position on interacting with children.

> I've come to a frightening conclusion that I am the decisive element in the classroom. It's my personal approach that creates the climate. It's my daily mood that makes the weather. As a teacher, I possess a tremendous power to make a child's life miserable or joyous. I can be a tool of torture or an instrument of inspiration. I can humiliate or humor, hurt or heal. In all situations, it is my response that decides whether a crisis will be escalated or de-escalated and a child humanized or de-humanized. (Ginott, 1972, p. 13)

Ginott was the first to emphasize the importance of how teachers talk to students and how teachers' talk is linked to students' behavior. Adult messages are a direct line to a child's self-esteem. Teachers have the power to help construct or to erode a student's self concept, and that power is wielded largely through their style of talk with students. For Ginott, the two most important factors are the teacher's self-discipline and the communication style the teacher uses. Before teachers can work effectively with students, they must learn to accept, understand, and express their own perspectives and feelings in ways that respect, help, and empower students. Teachers must model what they want to foster in students. Their own behavior should extend empathy, warmth, and genuineness. Student alienation and class disruptions result from a communication style that is characterized by indifference, disrespect, ridicule, sarcasm, stereotyping, and inappropriate displays of personal frustration.

Implicit in Ginott's recommendations for adults dealing with children is the underlying belief that all human beings need to feel respected, understood, and cared for to reach their greatest potential.

Key Principles for Teachers

This section describes the main themes of Ginott's message for teachers.

The Danger of Equating Work with Worth.   Most children are socialized beginning with storybook tales, TV programs, and adult talk to accept that the degree to which a person is loved, appreciated, and valued by others depends on how well he or she performs, accomplishes commendable deeds, and achieves desirable goals. Parents often attempt to motivate their children to achieve by displaying greater signs of love and appreciation for their children after they succeed in an endeavor than they display after their children fail. Consequently, many students enter school believing that their personal worth depends on how well they perform in school.

Just as parents need to communicate their love for their children even when they fail, teachers need to communicate that they still accept their students even when they perform poorly. Ginott warns of the danger of continual association between achievement levels and character judgments. For Ginott, it is imperative that teachers distinguish between a student's accomplishments and the value of that student. Rather than view a student's display of off-task or inappropriate behavior as a reflection of a character flaw, the teacher takes responsibility for teaching each student to be on task to achieve learning goals.

Although the promise of approval and respect as a positive reinforcer for on-task and productive behaviors can be effective in the short run, it produces undesirable side effects over time. Thus, rewards for achievement or on-task behaviors that communicate "You are a better, more worthwhile person because you have succeeded or behaved as someone else wants you to behave" are destructive reinforcers. Likewise, withholding affection and displaying personal disappointment after off-task behaviors are destructive punishments.

When students are led to believe that the most successful among them will be accepted and respected more than those who are less successful, their ego defense mechanisms discourage their participation in what can seem like a game with excessively high stakes and few winners. When students believe they are worth less in the eyes of others if they are less successful in school-related activities, they become defensive about participating in such activities. A defensive attitude undermines a cooperative stance (Cangelosi, 1999).

Students Are People Too.   For Ginott, an important aspect of the learning environment is the socioemotional climate in the classroom. His position is that discipline problems will be markedly reduced if teachers create an atmosphere of concern for students' feelings. His main thrust for teachers is that they should deal positively with students' emotions and recognize that their communication pattern will strongly influence students' feelings and, ultimately, their self-esteem.

Ginott also advocates that teachers deal openly with their own feelings. He reminds teachers that *students are people* and should be treated with respect. When conflict arises, teachers often resort to attacking students by putting them down rather than dealing with their feelings.

Guidance via effective communication is practiced over an extended period and takes time to take hold. Ginott described this process as "a series of little victories." When teachers influence behavior through compassion, understanding, support, and respect, they can turn volatile situations into victories and, over time, develop student self-direction, responsibility, and concern for others. He emphasizes the importance of teachers modeling the behavior they expect of their students by exercising self-discipline. Students observe how teachers handle conflict situations and tend to imitate them.

Teacher Self-Discipline.   The importance of teachers' self-discipline and maturity is a fundamental premise of Ginott's approach to classroom discipline. These qualities are reflected in their ability to listen sensitively to students' communications and respond to students in positive ways. Teachers should accept the validity of students feelings, assist students to take appropriate responsibility for their actions, and help students engage in styles of conflict resolution and problem-solving that do not lead to power struggles.

Communicating in Sane Messages.   Ginott's main message for teachers is to distinguish between the *deed* and the *doer* at all times. He refers to messages that address the problem situation without attacking the student personally as *sane messages*. Sane messages address the situation that is creating the difficulty, express anger appropriately, acknowledge students' feelings, and invite cooperation. *Insane messages* go beyond the problem at hand to attack students personally. These types of messages tell students to deny their feelings about themselves and to base their sense of self-worth on others' judgments. *Congruent messages* are communications that allow students to trust their own perceptions and feelings.

Ginott warns teachers of the disabling effect of labeling students and of using sarcasm. Such character assassinations as labeling, diagnosing, and offering analyses of students' character contribute to negative self-images that often turn into self-fulfilling prophecies. Comments such as "You're always so irresponsible" only serve to limit students' visions of what they can do and be.

Similarly, Ginott warns of the danger of sarcasm. Although teachers may only be intending to be clever, this form of wit is often at the student's expense. Students often do not understand the intended wit and end up with hurt feelings because they feel they are being put down. It is better to avoid sarcasm than to run the risk of hurting students' feelings.

Furthermore, a sane and congruent communication never denies feelings, whether students' or teachers'. Ginott not only believes teachers have a right to their anger, he also recommends that they express their anger directly. He thinks that given the demands put on teachers, it's natural to get frustrated and angry occasionally.

The Perils of Praise. Like many others (Dreikurs, Brophy, Gordon, Kohn), Ginott takes issue with teacher praise. As with negative comments, praise can have detrimental effects on forming a positive self-image. Ginott warns of the drawbacks of using praise, especially when it is evaluative.

Evaluative praise evaluates students; the teacher becomes a source of approval deciding a student's worth. Appreciative praise shows recognition for what a student has done, acknowledges the student's effort, and shares the teacher's personal reaction. Rather than evaluative praise, teachers should describe their own feelings, provide honest recognitions, and comment on student efforts, as in "The words you chose really painted a picture for me."

Ginott's points about praise are also discussed along with other authors' positions on praise in Chapter 4.

Why to Avoid the Why-Question. Rather than promoting a helping relationship and building trust, asking *why* hints at criticism. The implicit assumption with the why-question is that the student should have acted differently. This gives the message that you are judging, not accepting the student.

For many, the word establishes a mindset of disapproval, for instance, "Why didn't you . . . ?"; "Why can't you . . . ?"; "Why are you . . . ?"; "Why do you have to . . . ?" Thus, feelings of being threatened or judged are often evoked, leading to either withdrawing or the need to rationalize or defend, distracting from the communication process.

As Ginott sees it, why-questions are character assassinations in disguise, just another form of criticism. They tell students they have a problem. These questions don't prompt inquiry, and they don't really call for answers. Such questions as the following are merely hostile inquiries, used primarily to make students feel guilty.

Why can't you get along with anyone?

Why are you always the last one finished?

Why can't you ever find your work?

Ginott's Guidelines for Teachers
Teachers should
- Model the behavior they want to see from their students
- Handle conflict reasonably and respectfully by exercising self-discipline

- When correcting students, send sane messages that address the situation, not the student
- Express anger, but in sane (appropriate) ways
- Describe the student's behavior and offer acceptable alternatives
- Use encouragement rather than praise

Teachers should not
- Equate work with worth
- Label students or diagnose their character
- Use sarcasm
- Get into arguments with students
- Preach, moralize, or try to impose guilt
- Give evaluative praise

Classroom Strategies and Interventions

Ginott has some important recommendations for teachers. Regarding punishment, he believes punishment only produces hostility and a desire for revenge. It never makes students want to improve. Hence, he suggests teachers find alternatives to punishments. Below are some specific examples of classroom strategies.

Eliminate Labeling.   Ginott coined the phrase *labeling is disabling,* believing that it limits students' vision of themselves. Repeated messages over time become self-fulfilling prophecies. Instead, he suggests that teachers make statements that encourage students to set goals for themselves by expressing their belief in students.

I think you can solve this on your own, but if you need help let me know.

Invite Cooperation.   Teachers invite cooperation by describing the situation and indicating what needs to be done. By avoiding direct commands, teachers allow students to decide what they should do.

This is time to work silently now.

Ginott also suggests another way to invite cooperation. Teachers can decide with the class before an activity what kinds of personal behavior will be needed during the activity.

Express Anger in Sane Ways.   When teachers lose control, they tend to communicate with students in ways that blame students for whatever is happening. Their comments focus on students' personality flaws, rather than genuine expression of the feeling they are experiencing. What is called for is a clear distinction between what the teacher is experiencing and what students are doing. Not

You're always talking when you're supposed to be working. Can't you keep your mouth shut or *I can't believe you are that irresponsible,*

but rather,

I'm so angry right now I want to scream! or *I'm disgusted by that comment you made to Jackie.*

Teachers also can encourage students to communicate their own messages in nonblameful language by facilitating the communication process and asking students to relate their own experiences and reactions, rather than blame the other person. So the teacher might say

Instead of telling us why Manny did what he did, tell us about your own feelings and reasons for doing what you did.

The teacher can provide further guidance by offering the student a way to start, as in

Try starting by saying, "I got angry when . . ." and then go on from there.

Stay in the Present.   For Ginott, staying in the present means teachers don't prejudge or hold grudges. Like Glasser, he thinks teachers' motto should be "Every day is a new beginning."

Let's start with a clean slate today, Latisha.

Use Self-Discipline.   Teachers should refrain from using behaviors they are trying to eliminate in their students, such as raising their voice to stop loud talking, using force to break up a fight, or being rude to students who are showing disrespect.

Accept and Acknowledge Students' Feelings.   When students are upset or afraid, telling them not to feel that way, explaining that no one else feels that way, or telling them that they shouldn't feel that way sends the message that their feelings are not real. It doesn't dispel their emotions; it causes them to doubt their own inner feelings. The message they get is that the teacher doesn't understand and, therefore, may not be helpful in times of trouble. Ginott cautions teachers to treat children's fears carefully. A better response is to acknowledge what they feel and offer assistance.

I see you're upset. How can I help?

With older students, invalidating feelings tells them they are not accepted. Such dismissal implies that students are not entitled to their feelings, and that the teacher knows how they ought to feel.

Use Laconic Language.   Laconic language is short and to the point. All too often, teachers give long, drawn-out directions. Rather than pontificate, teachers should talk sparingly. He suggests they talk the way reporters write—in headlines and soundbites. Ginott thinks unnecessarily detailed talk about what to do is disrespectful to students. Furthermore, it slows down learning activities, conditions students to tune out, and provokes annoyance.

Direction Rather Than Correction.   Misbehavior requires that students be redirected, not reprimanded. Ginott recommends that teachers issue simple requests, just the facts with no editorial commentary. The teacher simply states the facts and lets students decide whether their behavior is in keeping with what they expect of themselves.
For example, the teacher might say

I would like you to stop talking, so you can hear the directions.

Ginott recommends that teachers redirect, not reprimand, with simple requests. In general, directives are more effective when you tell students what you want them to do, rather than what you don't want them to do. Following are some examples.

Direction	Correction
Return to your seat and continue working on the assignment.	*Stop wandering around the room.*
Close the door quietly.	*Don't slam the door.*
Try to work these out on your own, without help.	*Don't copy your neighbor's work.*
Quiet down—you're getting too loud.	*Don't make so much noise.*
Raise your hand if you think you know the answer.	*Don't yell out the answer.*
When you're done, put the scissors back and throw bits of paper in the wastebasket.	*Don't leave a mess.*

A Word of Caution

Developing the kinds of communication and dialogue advocated here will require a considerable amount of commitment, practice, and effort. Teachers' efforts to communicate understanding and empathy for students will not always be reciprocated by trust and cooperation. The multifaceted nature of the student–teacher relationship make it impossible to predict connections between what and how the teacher communicates and how students will react. A whole host of social and cultural as well as individual differences affect perceptions and interpretations of, and reactions to, any communication.

Although using effective communication, displaying empathy, and valuing students' feelings are necessary tools for today's classroom, they may not be sufficient as a total classroom management plan. These strategies will need to be supplemented for dealing with students who display defiant, hostile, or verbally abusive behavior, at least initially.

Interacting with students in the manner prescribed here involves more than skill. It must be accompanied by a genuine desire to make the classroom a learning community. It is also important to realize that in order for these strategies to work optimally, teachers need to make them their own by integrating them into their own personal style. Direct experience with particular students, groups, and classes will allow teachers to determine what works, in what setting, and in what context.

LEARNING PRACTICE TASK: DISTINGUISHING BETWEEN THE DEED AND THE DOER

Activity Directions: For each of the following student behaviors, write an alternative statement that rejects the student's behavior, but not the student.

STUDENT BEHAVIOR	STATEMENT REJECTING STUDENT	STATEMENT REJECTING BEHAVIOR ONLY
Paul won't let Tommy have a turn.	*Nice boys let others have their turn.*	_____ _____ _____
Sally has left the reading center a mess.	*Don't you know any better?*	_____ _____ _____

Jimmy is talking while Sue is giving her answer.

Don't be so impolite.

_____
_____
_____

Becky doesn't complete her part of a group assignment.

You haven't been much help to your group.

_____
_____
_____

Francisco teases Carla about being fat.

Other people have feelings, too, you know.

_____
_____
_____

LEARNING PRACTICE TASK: CASE STUDY OF KATE

Activity Directions: Read the case study below. Then working with a partner, develop some strategies that are consistent with Ginott's ideas about dealing with students.

Kate, a student in Ms. Bee's class, does little socializing with other students and never disrupts class. But Ms. Bee cannot get her to do her work. She hardly ever completes an assignment. She puts forth very little effort on work she does do.

Ginott would advise teachers to use a number of gentle tactics to encourage Kate to do her work. Give an appropriate example for each of the following.

Sending a sane message. _____

_____

_____

Inviting cooperation. _____

_____

_____

Acknowledging feelings. _____

_____

_____

Correcting by directing. _____

_____

_____

CHAPTER SIX

Managing by Rewards and Consequences

For some students, especially younger students still in the early stages of moral development and older students who are testing the waters, teachers will need to apply appropriate consequences. Extrinsic reinforcers are sometimes the only way to get some students to begin to behave appropriately, in particular, those who have a history of unsuccessful school experiences and very limited success with classroom learning tasks. Even for these students, however, once more adaptive behavior is demonstrated, other strategies that help them develop their own self-control should be introduced.

USING REWARDS AND CONSEQUENCES: SOME ISSUES AND CONCERNS

Traditional wisdom for managing individual student behavior and maintaining order in the classroom has relied on the use of extrinsic rewards and punishment, praise, modeling, and teacher evaluation of appropriate behavior and acceptable work. When teachers use consequences to manage students' behavior, they are using their authority position to convince students to control their behavior.

Although it also may be necessary to use consequences to suppress, control, and redirect behavior that is aggressive, abusive, or disruptive to learning, teachers should view getting students to behave in a desired way for the moment with extrinsic motivation only as a short-term goal. Motivating students to want to behave appropriately is the ultimate long-range goal and involves systematically supporting students' independence and self-management. Teachers who are most successful in dealing with students who pose behavior challenges use long-term, solution-oriented approaches rather than short-term desist and control responses (Brophy & McCaslin, 1992). In so doing, they typically enlist students to become active participants in developing a resolution to the problem.

For the most part, the behavioral approach does get students to comply with the teacher's demands, but it perpetuates student reliance on the teacher rather than enhancing student autonomy. Several issues that question the use of rewards and punishment to modify student behavior have been raised by researchers.

Although the behavioral approach has several benefits, it is not without its potential drawbacks. There are some research findings, especially relative to the effects of contingent use of rewards on classroom behavior, indicating that the relationship between rewards and punishment and subsequent individual student behavior is more complex than had been assumed by those advocating primary use of the behavioral approach. Several issues have been raised by researchers that serve to question the use of rewards and punishment to modify student behavior.

Extrinsic positive reinforcement doesn't always increase desired behavior. Under certain conditions, positive reinforcement can have detrimental effects. For example, giving expected tangible rewards simply for doing a task, without regard to standard of performance, has a negative effect (Cameron & Pierce, 1994).

Extrinsically motivated actions are characterized by pressure and tension and can result in low self-esteem and anxiety (Deci & Ryan, 1985). Using rewards for desired behavior and academic performance can erode intrinsic motivation (Dickinson, 1989; Doyle, 1986; Lepper, 1983; Richmond & McCroskey, 1984; Schwartz, 1990; Sutherland, 1993). Students who are already motivated to learn can lose their intrinsic motivation to do so if they become too interested in earning extrinsic rewards (Condry & Chambers, 1978; DeCharms, 1976; Deci, 1976, 1978; Deci & Ryan, 1987; Lepper & Greene, 1978; Pittman, Boggiano, & Ruble, 1982; Ross, 1976).

Another issue relates to the alignment of teacher intention with actual student effect. Students don't always experience consequences congruent with the teacher's intention. For example, praising certain students in front of their peers can be counterproductive. For some students, teacher attention in the form of recognition or praise is embarrassing or threatening rather than rewarding.

Furthermore, the behavioral change brought about by positive and negative reinforcements in one situation has not been shown to generalize to others (e.g., classes, teachers, environments) or to be maintained when the extrinsic reinforcers are dropped (Brophy & Putnam, 1978; Emery & Marholin, 1977). In addition, the effectiveness of positive and negative reinforcements as classroom management tools varies according to the student's age and developmental level, with the pattern being that it is most effective with younger students, somewhat less effective with upper elementary and middle school students, and least effective with secondary school students (Brophy & Putnam, 1978; Forness, 1973; Stallings, 1975).

Another important issue is that positive reinforcement can increase students' learned helplessness and dependency if they come to rely excessively on teacher approval in lieu of their own motivation (Ginott, 1972; Weiner, 1979). Similarly, positive reinforcement can discourage creativity if students become more concerned about pleasing their teachers or conforming to their teachers' expectations than on finding their own solutions to problems (Johnson & Johnson, 1987; Soar & Soar, 1975).

Inhibiting behavior should not be confused with instilling attitudes. Student obedience cannot be equated with student motivation. Conditions that foster quick obedience do not foster internalization of self-control, and internalized self-control, or self-regulation, is necessary to function adaptively both in classrooms and in society (Kohn, 1993; Lepper, 1983; McCaslin & Good, 1992). As long as conceptions of classroom management remain rooted in the behavioral model, the responsibility for student motivation and effort will fall largely on teachers, and outside of students themselves.

Another potential danger with the use of consequences to control students not often considered is that it can serve to insulate teachers from important feedback on their classroom practices. For example, students might disguise the fact that they are bored, frustrated, or even angry because of feared negative consequences. Hence, teachers fail to realize the need to use other strategies that might enhance learning and student–teacher relationships. Such lack of feedback can also serve to sustain inferior or less effective teaching practices (Grossman, 1990; Ryan, 1979).

Perhaps the most important limitation of management by consequences is that focusing on the obvious and overt behavior can keep the teacher from addressing the underlying motivation for the inappropriate behavior, accommodating basic unmet needs, or discovering the real message being communicated by the inappropriate behavior.

In relying primarily on a behavioral approach for classroom management, teachers will need to consider the following potential drawbacks and structure their use to create more awareness of these limitations.

- What the teacher may think is reinforcing may have the opposite effect for some students.
- Becoming too interested in extrinsic rewards can lessen students' intrinsic motivation.
- Students may become dependent on teacher approval, working only toward that goal.
- Creativity can be discouraged.
- Teachers may be deprived of important feedback if students are silenced and fear negative consequences.
- Behavior change in one situation does not generalize to other situations.
- Its effectiveness lessens as students get older.

These principles as applied to the classroom have been given a variety of labels by educators. It has been referred to as contingency management, precision teaching, positive feedback, reinforcement theory, operant conditioning, applied behavior analysis, and, most commonly, behavior modification. Regardless of the label, the essence of the approach is that you deal with the student's here-and-now behaviors that are readily observable, rather than look at the student's past history to try to determine the cause of the behavior.

Managing students' behavior by applying consequences has three major benefits.

1. It offers teachers alternatives in working with students that emphasize positive reinforcers, helping them move away from primarily using reprimands and punishment to control student behavior.
2. By emphasizing rewarding appropriate behavior, the behavioral approach helps teachers focus on identifying potentially meaningful reinforcers for students and, thus, is more likely to produce positive interactions with students.
3. Its focus on actual behaviors helps teachers to be more objective and keep from labeling a student's character (e.g., lazy, inconsiderate, manipulative).

Getting students to behave in a desired way for the moment with extrinsic motivation is only a short-term goal. Motivating students to want to behave appropriately is the ultimate long-term goal and involves systematically supporting students in developing internal controls. Nonetheless, teachers will sometimes need to use consequences to ensure a safe and productive learning environment for all students.

PRINCIPLES OF BEHAVIOR MODIFICATION

The basic principle of reinforcement theory is that voluntary behavior is largely determined by the events or consequences that immediately follow it. That is, behavior is learned, and an individual learns whether a behavior is acceptable or not acceptable based on how others or the environment responds. Hence, what is important is the consequence that the behavior produces because that is what will over time strengthen, maintain, or weaken the occurrence of the behavior in the future.

Here is an overview of reinforcement theory.

- The basic premise for using consequences to effect behavior change is that behavior is influenced by the consequences that follow it.

- Behavior can be developed, maintained, strengthened, or weakened by the consequences that follow the behavior.
- Reinforcement theory, or behavior modification, is based on the notion that behavior that is rewarded will tend to be repeated while behavior that is not rewarded (i.e., ignored or punished) will tend to be weakened or eliminated.
- Research supports that positive reinforcement is a much more powerful behavior modification tool than punishment, hence management strategies advocated for the classroom emphasize using positive reinforcement or rewards to modify student behavior.

The following chart presents a brief overview of behavior modification principles.

Behavior Modification Principles Simplified: Adding and Taking Away Reinforcers

Options for Increasing Desired Behavior

Add (+)	Take Away (−)
Positive Reinforcement: Add reward or incentive	**Negative Reinforcement:** Take away something negative
Shaping: Reward improvement until desired behavior is reached	
Premack Principle: Contingent pairing of a reward with something negative	

Options for Decreasing Undesired Behavior

Add (+)	Take Away (−)
Punishment (Type I): Add negative consequence	**Punishment (Type II):** Take away positive reinforcer
Reinforcing Incompatible Behavior: Add reinforcement for opposite (incompatible) behavior while ignoring undesirable behavior	**Response Cost:** Contingent withdrawal of a specified amount of reinforcement while maintaining the potential to earn a reward
	Time Out: Take away from reinforcing environment
	Extinction: Take away any reinforcement (ignore)

Some Classroom Applications of Reinforcement Principles to Increase Desirable Behavior

Using contingency relationships, or pairing, allows teachers to refocus on providing incentives rather than disincentives as the following examples illustrate.

The Premack principle makes students' preferred behavior dependent on the occurrence of a less preferred behavior in order to increase the preferred behavior. Teachers are using this principle when they make the following *deals* with students.

If all of you get your books and materials put away, you can leave for recess early.

If you work quietly for 20 minutes, you can have free time to talk to anyone you like for 5 minutes.

Reinforcement of incompatible behavior attempts to eliminate a problem behavior by refocusing on its incompatible opposite. This allows the teacher to use a reward for the incompatible behavior rather than punish the behavior that is causing a problem.

The following are examples of inappropriate behaviors and corresponding incompatible behaviors.

Inappropriate Behaviors	Incompatible Behavior
Students being late	Students arriving on time
Talking without permission	Raising hand and being called on
Requiring teacher attention to complete work	Working independently

Here are three specific examples of teacher interventions to decrease problem behaviors that are reward based.

Example 1
Problem Behavior Students arriving several minutes late for class

Intervention Strategy
The teacher read a short segment of an exciting mystery story for the first few minutes after lunch one day, then announced that it would be continued during the first ten minutes of class each morning. Those present would have a chance to hear what happened next.

Reinforcer Hearing a mystery story

Reinforcement Principle Reinforcing incompatible behavior

Example 2
Problem Behavior Juan frequently talking without permission

Intervention Strategy
Juan was given five poker chips when he entered the classroom. Each time he talked without permission he "paid" the teacher one chip. At the end of the day, each chip he had left was worth an allotted period of time to be spent working on the computer.

Reinforcer Using the computer

Reinforcement Principle Response cost

Example 3
Problem Behavior Students talking out excessively

Intervention Strategy
The teacher informed students that she would allow them a special privilege the last 5 minutes of class each day if they decreased their talking out to less than 5 times during a class period. The students suggested games, snacks, and free time as special privileges. Instances of talking out were recorded with a check mark on the board.

Reinforcer Special privilege for the last 5 minutes of class

Reinforcement Principle Premack principle

■ ■ ■ ■ ■ ■ ■ ■ ■

LEARNING PRACTICE TASK: IDENTIFYING CLASSROOM EXAMPLES

Activity Directions: List examples of your use of any of the reinforcement principles in your classroom.

Strategies to increase desired behavior: Positive and negative reinforcement, shaping, and the Premack principle.

_____

_____

_____

_____

_____

_____

Strategies to decrease inappropriate behavior: Punishment, time-out, response cost, planned ignoring, and reinforcement of incompatible behavior.

_____

_____

_____

_____

_____

_____

Using Time-Out.   The time-out strategy can be an effective one for calming down a rowdy or misbehaving elementary school child. Basically, the student is sent to a stimulation-free area or time-out room for 2, 5, or perhaps 10 to 15 minutes. The time-out area should be free of high-interest stimulation—no windows; no secretaries to watch; no lunch bags to plunder; no equipment to fiddle with; and no appealing magazines, posters, or calendars. The purpose of time-out is for the student to calm down and think about his or her behavior, not earn a refreshing change of scenery.

Many junior and senior high schools have created in-school monitored suspension rooms that are used for short periods during the day, as well as for all-day detentions. The suspension rooms operate in basically the same way as time-out areas, except that teachers or supervisors monitor the room on a rotating basis. The suspended students are expected to continue working as if they were attending their normal classes (Davis & Thomas, 1989).

An important consideration is that if time out is being used as a routine response to student inappropriate behavior, then it should indicate to the teacher the need to try additional strategies.

Guidelines for Effective Use of Time-Out.   The following guidelines are important to follow when using time-out (Alberto & Troutman, 2002).

A teacher should work through the following sequence of steps in using a time-out room or any of the forms of this procedure.

1. Before beginning to use time-out as a management procedure, identify the behavior(s) that will result in use of a time-out. Be sure the students understand the behavior. Explain the behavior expected of students while they are in time out. Tell them how long the time-out period will last.
2. When the misbehavior occurs, reidentify it. Tell the student in a calm manner, "That is fighting. Go to time-out for ___ minutes." No other conversation should ensue. Ignore any statements the student may make as an excuse for misbehavior or relating to feelings about time-out. If necessary, lead the

student to the time-out area. If the student resists, Hall and Hall (1980) suggest that the teacher do the following.

    a. Gently but firmly lead the student to time-out.

    b. Be prepared to add time to time-out if the student refuses to go or yells, screams, kicks, or turns over furniture.

    c. Require the student to clean up any mess resulting from resistance to time-out before the student may return to classroom activities.

    d. Be prepared to use a backup consequence for students who refuse time-out.

3. Once a student enters the time-out area, the time begins. Check your watch or set a timer. Gast and Nelson (1977a) review three formats for contingent release from time-out rooms.

    a. Release contingent on a specified period (for example, 2 minutes) of appropriate behavior

    b. Release contingent on a minimum duration of time-out, with an extension until all inappropriate behavior has terminated

    c. Release contingent on a minimum duration of time-out, with an extension (such as 15 seconds) during which no inappropriate responses are exhibited

4. Once the time interval has ended, return the student to the previous appropriate activity. Do not comment on how well the student behaved while in time-out. A student should be returned to the activity he or she was engaged in before time-out to avoid negatively reinforcing an escape from that activity.

Monitoring the Use of Time-Out. To monitor the effects of time-out and to substantiate proper and ethical use of the procedure, records should be kept of each time-out occasion, especially when a time-out room is used.

Records should include at least the following information (Gast & Nelson, 1977b).

1. The student's name
2. The episode resulting in the student's placement in time-out (behavior, activity, other students involved, staff person, and so on)
3. The time of day the student was placed in time-out
4. The time of day the student was released from time-out
5. The total time in time-out
6. The type of time-out (contingent, exclusion, or seclusion)
7. The student's behavior in time-out

Reflective Questions to Ask Yourself. Prior to selecting a time-out procedure, the teacher should consider the following questions concerning its use.

- Have more positive procedures, for example, reinforcement strategies, been considered?
- Have both nonseclusionary and seclusionary time-out procedures been considered?
- Can time-out be implemented with minimal student resistance? Can you handle the possible resistance?
- Have the rules of appropriate behavior and the results for misbehavior been clearly explained and understood?
- Have the rules of behavior while in time-out been clearly explained and understood?

Types of Reinforcers: The Reinforcement Hierarchy

There are a variety of reinforcers that can be effective for promoting desired behaviors. Effectiveness of a reinforcer will depend on individual student characteristics and preferences as well as the particular setting and the task demands. Factors such as age, social class, learning aptitude, task difficulty, and skill acquisition level will influence reinforcer effectiveness.

Reinforcers can be thought of on a continuum beginning with more tangible rewards and ultimately ending with personal satisfaction. The following continuum represents eight levels of reinforcers.

LEVEL	1	2	3	4	5	6	7	8
Reinforcer	Consumable	Tangible	Token	Activity	Privilege	Peer Recognition	Adult Approval	Self-Satisfaction

The continuum is hierarchical, moving from lower-order consumable reinforcers toward higher-order reinforcers that occur naturally in the classroom environment, like special privileges, teacher praise, and eventually, self-satisfaction with accomplishments.

There are two principles that apply to this hierarchy of reinforcers.

Principle 1: You should not use lower levels of reinforcement than are actually necessary to initiate or maintain behavior.

Principle 2: You should continually move along the continuum toward higher-order reinforcers that occur naturally in the environment.

Material Reinforcers.   Consumable, tangible, and token reinforcers are all material rewards. Consumable reinforcers are edible rewards such as M&Ms, jelly beans, Lifesavers, peanuts, raisins, or chips. Tangible rewards are items such as toys, badges, certificates, stars, or stickers. Although material reinforcers can be quite effective, higher-order types of reinforcers can be just as effective.

Token reinforcers are tangible place holders that can be exchanged at a later time for other reinforcers. They work like money in that they can be accumulated and spent for something desired sometime in the future. Frequently poker chips, stars, check marks, happy faces, or points are used in classrooms as tokens. Token systems are often used in special education classes either for the whole class or for individuals who have not responded to praise, activities, or other reinforcers common to the classroom setting. In general education classrooms, teachers who use points or checks that accumulate toward earning other rewards are using token systems. Token systems are successful partly because they allow the reinforcement to be broken down into small segments, thereby providing immediate and frequent reinforcement.

Token reinforcement systems, when properly implemented, can be effective for managing a wide range of behaviors. Token systems usually work best if the class or individual students involved participate in setting up the system and defining the types and costs of the reinforcers to be earned. Token systems should be kept simple so that the record system and the exchange policy are manageable for the classroom teacher.

Sometimes token systems can be used to condition other naturally occurring reinforcers. Students who have not responded to typical classroom reinforcers will work for tokens that allow them to have things they want or to do things they want to do. Pairing adult approval with giving tokens can eventually lead to the withdrawal of the token reinforcer.

Activity or Privilege Reinforcers.   Activity or privilege reinforcers are things students like to do, such as playing a game, helping the teacher, having lunch with the principal, taking roll call, or collecting materials. Because classroom teachers could find it prohibitively expensive to use tangible reinforcers, activity reinforcers offer an alternative. Among those research has shown to be effective in a school setting are jobs that carry responsibility, such as helping the principal, being a hall monitor or messenger, running audiovisual equipment, or correcting papers.

Social Reinforcers.   Social reinforcers include both adult and peer approval and include various forms of attention, praise, and recognition. Using social reinforcers in conjunction with other reinforcers being used will over time lead to being able to give social reinforcement only.

Structured Contingency Systems.   Although it is usually easier and more natural to arrange contingencies and consequences on an informal basis, sometimes it may be necessary to establish a very structured contingency system in order to increase the likelihood that the behaviors you want to change are clearly defined and the reinforcement contingencies are explicitly specified. Two formalized and systematic ways of linking reinforcement with behavior are contingency contracts and token systems.

Contingency Contracts.   A structured written contract might be necessary when working with more than one student or when the behavior being worked on is an agreement that either the student or the teacher wishes to keep between themselves. The basic contract is in the form *If . . . , then . . .*

To ensure the effectiveness of a contract it is useful to

- Meet privately with the student and explain the rationale and procedures for developing the contract
- Agree on the responsibilities of others (teachers, parents) in helping the student achieve the goals of the contract
- Agree on a more long-term goal to encourage the learner to sustain his or her progress over an extended period of time

Token Systems.   A token is used much like money in that it can be exchanged for a desired object or activity at some future time. A token system is typically used in special education classes and in other special environments.

Ms. Archer's system, described below, is an example of a classwide token system. Note that her approach also incorporates other principles (i.e., self-evaluation, reflection, and goal setting).

Ms. Archer's Classwide Token System

Ms. Archer used a classwide token system for encouraging appropriate behavior in her third-grade class. Throughout the year she used a system in which the class as a whole earned blue chips for desirable behavior and red chips for undesirable behavior. When a monthly goal for the number of blue chips was reached, the class was rewarded with a special treat or privilege.

Goals and rewards escalated during the course of the year, beginning with a class party at the end of the first month and culminating in a class-selected field trip. During each day blue chips were dropped into a container for various appropriate behaviors—two for transitioning from one activity to the next in a timely fashion, five for each satisfactory room cleanup, one for each student who at the end of the day had completed all his or her work, and so on. Red chips were dropped into the container for fighting or arguing, excessive noise, throwing trash on the floor, returning late from lunch or recess, or other transgressions.

Shaking the container of chips was often used to signal that there was too much talking or misbehaving and that failure to get quiet would result in another red chip. At the end of the day the blue and red chips were counted and a daily tally was kept.

Ms. Archer often used the results of the tally to discuss with the class the kind of day it had been. She would ask students what they thought might have contributed to an especially pleasant or disruptive day. Sometimes during these discussions the class would set goals for the next day (or week). Occasionally she would ask particular students to commit to "a better day tomorrow. "

Setting Up a Contingency Contract.   The following steps should be included in setting up a contingency contract.

- The student should participate in the development of the contract.
- The task or behavior to be accomplished should be stated in positive terms.
- The performance criteria should be stated in specific terms.
- The contract should extend for a brief but specified time period.
- The contract should be designed to ensure success. The student should be capable of accomplishing the specified task.
- The reinforcement should be mutually determined.
- Reinforcement should be frequent and immediate in the beginning.
- The contract should be signed by all persons concerned with its success.

Setting Up a Token System.   In setting up a token system, the following items will need to be determined ahead of time to ensure that the system is manageable.

- The specific behavior(s) that can earn tokens
- A convenient token
- How often the tokens will be given
- When tokens will be given
- Who will administer token distribution (i.e., teacher, peer, or self-monitored)
- The back-up reinforcer(s) the tokens will earn
- A reinforcement *menu* for cashing in the tokens
- When the exchange times will be

Sample Contract Formats

Social Behavior

A simple contract to change a social behavior could follow this format.

(Student's name) and (Teacher's name) agree to the following.

If (Student's name) performs the positive behavior(s) listed below, (Teacher's name) will provide the reinforcement listed below.

Positive behavior(s): (List in specific terms the behavior to be performed. Specify the time, place, and frequency of performance required. State how and when observations and evaluations are to be made.)

Reward: (State the reinforcement in precise terms. Specify the time, place, frequency, and quantity in which the reinforcement will be provided for satisfactory performance.)

(Student's signature)   (Teacher's signature)

(date)   (date)

Academic Behavior

A simple contract for academic behavior could follow the following format.

I, (Student's name), agree to complete the following learning activities, according to the (stated performance criteria) to obtain the (reinforcement listed below).

Learning activities: (List the activity or sequence of activities to be performed.)

Requirements: (List the performance criteria to be used, for example, percent correct. Also state the time period allowed.)

Reward: (State the grade or other reinforcer provided upon satisfactory performance.)

(Student's signature)   (Teacher's signature)

(date)   (date)

Determining Effective Reinforcers

The best way to determine whether a consequence is rewarding is to observe its effect on the behavior it follows. Consequences that are rewarding for some students may not be effective reinforcement for others. The teacher may find that Mary will beam and work harder when told, "I'm so proud of you!" However, the same statement will cause Tim to wince and result in decreased effort.

Choosing Reinforcers.   The following specific strategies can be used to help choose reinforcers.

1. Observe the student. Watching what the student likes to do will often indicate what reinforcers will be most powerful.
2. Ask the student. Reward questionnaires and surveys, both open-ended and structured, can be administered to provide information when necessary.
3. Use novel reinforcers. The surprise element can sometimes be effective.
4. Allow reinforcer sampling. This technique can give students experience with rewards they have not experienced. It also can prevent satiation, or tiring of a reinforcer.

The following chart lists potential activities, privileges, and tokens that can be used in the classroom for reinforcers.

Potential Classroom Reinforcers

Activities

Using the computer	Visiting another class	Independent study
Reading a story	Running errands	After-school activity
Assisting the teacher with teaching	Reading chosen book	Helping in the principal's office
Caring for class pets, plants, etc.	Erasing boards	Working in the cafeteria
Collecting materials	Planning daily schedule	Presenting hobby to class
Doing a craft activity	Collecting lunch tickets	Decorating classroom or bulletin board
Helping other students	Helping custodian, librarian	Going to library
Presenting a skit		

Privileges

Taking a short break	Time to work on special project	Listening to music
Choice of seat for specified period	Classroom supervision	No homework on chosen night
Free time	Omitting specific assignments	Team captain
Playing a game with a friend	Talking period	Early dismissal

Extra or longer recess or gym

Being first in line

Displaying student's work

Picking a partner to work with

Individual conference time

"Citizen of the Day or Week"

Removing lowest grade

Leading a class activity

Room manager

Hall monitor

Individual conference time

Lunch with teacher or principal

Earning privilege for entire class

Using media equipment

Using teacher's materials

Keeping score for class game

Tokens

Badges to be worn for day

Special certificate of completed work

Points or chips

Puzzle piece or model piece

Happy face on paper

Check marks

Cards

Stars or stickers

Noting progress on chart

Reward certificates

Play money

Reinforcer Surveys. Reinforcer surveys can be either open-ended or more structured surveys in which alternatives are provided. They can either be completed by the student independently or can be administered in an interview format where the teacher records the student's responses. Students could also interview each other. Examples of an open-ended format and a choice format are provided.

The *Student Reinforcement Choice Survey* was adapted from Raschke (1981). The following are provided only as suggested formats. Teachers should tailor specific questions and reinforcement menus to their own students.

Student Reward Questionnaire

1. The best thing that could happen to me in school is _____

2. What motivates me the most to do well is _____

3. The most fun I have in school is when I _____

4. If I could do anything in school I wanted, I would _____

5. If I could change a class rule, it would be _____

6. What I like best about school is _____

7. Something I really enjoy doing at school is _____

8. I feel good at school when I'm _____

9. My favorite activity in class is _____

10. What I like least about school is _____

11. The school subject or period I like best is _____

12. The thing I need most in school is _____

13. I would work hard in school for _____

14. When I do well at school, I would like my teacher to _____

15. The person at school I would like most to praise me is _____

16. If I did a good job, the person I would like someone to tell is _____

17. My favorite adult in school is _____

18. The best thing my teacher can do for me is _____

Student Reinforcement Choice Survey

1. The way I best like to learn about something new in this class is
   a. Lecture and discussion
   b. Guest speakers
   c. Books
   d. Films, tapes, videos, CDs
   e. Completing projects
   f. Conducting experiments
   g. Small-group work

2. My favorite seating arrangement in this class is
   a. Desks in rows
   b. Chairs at small tables
   c. Desks randomly scattered
   d. Study carrels
   e. Desks in a circle

3. The special job I like to help the teacher with the most in this class is
   a. Handing out or collecting papers
   b. Running errands
   c. Decorating a bulletin board
   d. Running the media equipment
   e. Writing the assignment on the chalkboard
   f. Helping other students

4. The privilege I would like to earn in this class for doing my best work is to
   a. Sit anywhere I want in the class
   b. Help the teacher grade papers
   c. Individual conference time
   d. Give the class assignments
   e. Pick a partner to work with

5. When I do well in this class, I like it most when the teacher
   a. Tells me privately
   b. Tells the class about my good work
   c. Writes a note on my paper
   d. Puts my work on the bulletin board
   e. Puts a sticker on my paper

6. When I work hard in this class I would most like to earn
   a. Free time
   b. Lunch with the teacher
   c. A favorite activity with a friend
   d. Time with my favorite adult at school
   e. My work displayed on a bulletin board

7. My favorite free-time activity in this class is
   a. Using the computer
   b. Listening to music
   c. Doing a puzzle or a craft activity
   d. Visiting with a friend
   e. Reading a book

8. What I would like most for doing my best work in this class is
   a. Receiving an award in front of the class
   b. Receiving an A+
   c. A phone call or note to my parent(s)
   d. Having my work displayed in the hallway
   e. Earning free time for the whole class

■ ■ ■ ■ ■ ■ ■ ■ ■

LEARNING PRACTICE TASK: BEHAVIOR MODIFICATION SAMPLE PROBLEMS

Activity Directions: Below are some sample cases that require intervention strategies. Try your hand at designing behavior modification programs for these four students. Ask yourself, "What behavior could take the place of the undesirable behavior? What might be reinforcing for the student? What factors might be sustaining the behavior?"

1. Carlos bullies and frightens other students. Three of his classmates are reluctant to go to recess because he picks on them. How would you go about reducing his aggressive behavior? How would you strengthen his cooperative and socially desirable behavior?

   _____

   _____

   _____

2. Keisha is bright and very verbal. Her relationship with the teacher is excellent, but her relationship with the other students is posing a problem. During recess she prefers talking to her teacher to playing with other students. What can you suggest to increase her approaches toward and involvement with other students?

3. Ronnie swears excessively. Not only are these comments disruptive, they are contagious. A few of the other students are beginning to see if they can get away with swearing. As the teacher, what would you do about his swearing?

_____

_____

_____

4. Joanne is an eight-year-old of average intelligence who has just been transferred from a self-contained learning disabilities class to a general education third-grade classroom. However, she seems overwhelmed by the larger class size and the lack of structure in her new learning environment. Joanne is constantly out of her seat, walking around the room and talking to her classmates. How would you decrease Joanne's out-of-seat behavior? How would you improve her ability to remain on task?

_____

_____

_____

Student Self-Managed Behavior Intervention Plans

When systematic reinforcement programs are necessary to help students learn to control their behavior, teachers can support students in managing their own intervention programs to a great extent. With student-managed rather than teacher-managed intervention programs, students are in charge of the consequences and apply positive and negative reinforcements to their own behavior. Initially, students will have to be taught how to get started, will require monitoring to make sure they know what to do, and are following through and doing it correctly. Helping students use self-management effectively will take a collaborative effort between the teacher and the student.

Effectively implementing self-management approaches begins with motivating students to want to modify their behavior through active listening, reasoning with them, and other respectful, interactive behaviors, so they will cooperate voluntarily. Together the teacher and the student identify the inappropriate behavior that is interfering with the student's learning and more productive behavior.

To the degree feasible, students can self-manage all or some of the following aspects of their intervention plans.

1. Decide which behavior(s) to target.
2. Establish a baseline of how often, and in which situations, the student behaves unproductively.
3. Identify a more appropriate behavior that the student can substitute for the problem behavior, if possible.
4. Set realistic goals for behavior change.
5. Establish consequences that are significant to the student and are positive if possible, negative if necessary.
6. Develop a manageable and unobtrusive system for self-observation and recordkeeping.
7. Record the student's observations on charts or graphs so behavior can be monitored.

8. Evaluate behavior to determine the kinds and amounts of positive or negative consequences the student earned during each observation period.
9. Have the student administer his or her own reinforcement.
10. Evaluate progress periodically.
11. Modify a program when necessary (goals, consequences, observation, and reinforcement schedules).
12. Generalize improved behavior to other situations and in relationships with other people.
13. Have the student self-reinforce the behavior with internal satisfaction such as thinking about how much better they feel, how much better they get along with others, and how they are staying out of trouble.
14. Eliminate the extrinsic reinforcements.
15. Determine whether the student's behavioral improvement is maintained in the absence of extrinsic consequences.

PUNISHMENT

If and when to punish students has been the subject of wide debate. In general, the effects of punishment are limited and specific. Although punishment can control misbehavior, it does not teach desirable behavior or reduce the desire to misbehave. And punishment has retaliatory side effects that can either be active (spite, revenge, vandalism, assault) or passive (tardiness, truancy, inattention, theft, restlessness). In addition, punishment over time can induce resistance to teacher influence.

Problems Associated with the Use of Punishment
- When punished, children learn to escape and avoid the punisher.
- Whatever removes the punishment will be strengthened (e.g., pleading, false promises, lying).
- Punishment generates negative emotional feelings.
- Punishment can cause counter-aggressive behavior (i.e., desire for revenge or retaliation).
- Punishment does not teach the desired behavior.
- Punishment suppresses the undesirable behavior temporarily but does not weaken it long term.
- Punishment can actually be reinforcing in that it requires the attention of significant adults.

Using Punishment Effectively

Punishment is never a solution by itself; at best it is only part of a solution. To be effective punishment should be

- Used discriminately rather than routinely
- Combined with positive procedures
- Used only when students are not responsive to reward-based interventions
- Used in response to repeated misbehavior
- Considered a treatment of last resort for students who persist in the same kinds of misbehavior
- Employed consciously and deliberately, as part of a planned response to repeated misbehavior

Characteristics of Effective Punishment
- Is given immediately
- Makes it clear that it is the behavior that is being rejected, not the person

- Relies on taking away reinforcers while providing a clear-cut method for earning them back
- Makes use of a single warning (either a signal or verbal)
- Is delivered in a calm, matter-of-fact manner
- Is given along with reinforcement for behavior incompatible with the punished behavior
- Is consistent in that the undesired behavior does not receive reinforcement
- Is logically related to the type of misbehavior

The type of discipline received as a child, both at home and at school, leaves a lasting imprint. These early models of discipline can be a helpful guide for teachers in managing problems of varying severity in the classroom setting. They can also serve to limit the range of potential responses to situations.

Teachers' reactions to problem behaviors are influenced by the adult models they experienced. Many of our ways of disciplining stem from our own experiences as children. The way we respond to particular types of behavior in the classroom, likewise, says much about how we were brought up and what our early school experiences were like. In addition, our current school norms and expectations provide further enculturation. There is some evidence that teachers' childhood disciplinary experiences in their family of origin affect their disciplinary styles. Teachers who use more punitive consequences experienced more punishment as children, experienced more harsh physical punishment as children and as teenagers, were less likely to have been told the reasons behind their parents' rules, and were more likely to have been prohibited from questioning parental authority (Hyman, 1990; Kaplan, 1992).

■ ■ ■ ■ ■ ■ ■ ■

CRITICAL REFLECTION ON PRACTICE: EXAMINING YOUR PAST EXPERIENCES

Activity Directions: Working with a partner, take turns sharing the following.

1. How were you disciplined as a child?
2. Did your mother and father discipline in different ways? How were they different? Did you learn to use this difference to your advantage? How?
3. In general, what was your parents' demeanor during discipline situations? Angry? Calm? Disappointed? Patient? Conciliatory?
4. Did you feel good about some of the ways you were disciplined?
5. Think of a situation where an adult in your life handled a discipline situation badly. From your perspective, what was wrong with the way that person handled the situation? Why do you think you remember this incident?
6. Think of a situation where an adult in your life handled a discipline situation effectively. Why was it memorable?
7. Can you recall a time when you were disciplined and you felt you really learned a lesson? What was the lesson you learned? How has this lesson served you in your life?

REFLECTIVE QUESTIONS

Would the strategies that were effective for you be equally appropriate or effective for the various types of students you may teach?

What aspect of your approach might you need to challenge to better align with today's classroom?

What aspect of your approach might you need to challenge to better align with your core beliefs?

■ ■ ■ ■ ■ ■ ■ ■ ■

CRITICAL REFLECTION ON PRACTICE: ROLE MODELS FOR DISCIPLINE

Activity Directions: Working with a partner, take turns sharing the following.

1. What aspects of parental discipline that you experienced are you carrying over to your classroom?
2. Have you made a conscious choice to use these disciplinary procedures, or is it merely habit?
3. Conversely, what aspects of parental discipline are you deliberately choosing not to use in your classroom? Why?

INSTEAD OF PUNISHMENT

As Heider (1985) has aptly stated, "The instrument of justice cuts both ways. Punishing others is punishing work." For this and a multitude of other reasons, alternatives to punishment abound in the literature. Rosenberg (1999) recognized a critical point when he commented, "You can't make them behave, you can only make them wish they had." The following section discusses alternatives to punishment.

Differentiating between Protective and Punitive Uses of Force

According to Rosenberg (1999), the *protective* use of force is to prevent injury or injustice, while the *punitive* use of force is to cause individuals to suffer for their perceived misdeeds. Grabbing a child who is running into the street is applying protective force; inflicting a physical or psychological attack, such as spanking or reprimands like "How could you be so stupid! You should be ashamed of yourself!" is the punitive use of force.

Exercising the protective use of force focuses on the life or rights we want to protect without passing judgment on either the person or the behavior. The assumption behind the protective use of force is that people behave in ways injurious to themselves and others due to some form of ignorance. This being the case, Rosenberg advocates that the corrective process should be one of education, not punishment. Ignorance can include a lack of awareness of the consequences of our actions, an inability to see how our needs may be met without injury to others, or the belief that we have the right to punish or hurt others because they deserve it.

Punitive action, on the other hand, is based on the assumption that people commit offenses because they are bad or evil. Relying on this assumption, the corrective measure would be that they need to be made to repent. Their correction is undertaken through punitive action designed to make them suffer enough to see the error of their ways, repent, and change. In practice, however, punitive action, rather than evoking repentance and learning, is more likely to generate resentment and hostility and to reinforce resistance to the very behavior we are seeking.

Distinguishing between Discipline and Punishment

Coloroso (1999) advocates that teachers differentiate between discipline and punishment. Discipline helps children become responsible, resourceful, and resilient. Punishment causes children to become adept at making excuses, blaming, and denying, while feeling powerless, manipulated, and not in control.

Discipline helps children learn how to handle problems they will encounter throughout life. It does so by providing four things.

1. It helps make students fully aware of what they have done.
2. It gives students as much ownership of the problem as they are able to handle.
3. It provides options for solving problems that involve students.
4. It leaves student dignity intact.

Coloroso's Inner Discipline and Reconciliatory Justice. Coloroso distinguishes between discipline and punishment, defining three types of student misbehavior, mistakes, mischief, and mayhem, that can be handled with either punishment or discipline. Mistakes are simply errors in behavior, made without intent to break rules. They provide opportunity to learn how to behave more acceptably. Mischief goes beyond mistakes in that it is intentional misbehavior and presents an opportunity for teaching students that all actions have consequences, sometimes pleasant and sometimes not. Mischief also provides an opportunity for showing students ways to solve their problem. Mayhem usually involves intentional misbehavior, and when it does, it calls for application of the Three Rs of reconciliatory justice—restitution, resolution, and reconciliation. *Restitution* means repairing the damage done; *resolution* involves identifying and correcting whatever caused the misbehavior; and *reconciliation* is the process of bringing about healing with those hurt by one's actions. Application of the Three Rs involves a genuine commitment to make restitution and live up to resolutions. It also involves trying to regain the trust of those who were hurt.

Alternatives to Punishment from *How to Talk So Kids Will Listen* and *Listen So Kids Will Talk*

Faber & Mazlish (2002), students of Ginott and authors of *How to Talk So Kids Will Listen* and *Listen So Kids Will Talk,* offer the following alternatives to punishment.

1. Express your feelings strongly, but without attacking character.
2. State your expectations.
3. Show the student how to make amends.
4. Give the student a choice.
5. Take action when the student fails to.
6. Seek a mutually agreeable resolution.

Distinguishing between Logical Consequences and Punishment

Typically, authors differentiate among three types of negative consequences: natural, logical, and arbitrary. Natural consequences occur automatically as the result of a particular behavior. They are the unavoidable consequences or inevitable reactions brought about by a student's actions when no one interferes to prevent these consequences from occurring. Natural consequences are based on the natural flow of events, taking place without teacher interference. On the other hand, logical consequences involve teacher intervention. Logical consequences are arranged by the teacher, but are related to the behavior in question. Although they are structured by the teacher, they must be experienced by the student as logical. Arbitrary consequences are also arranged by the teacher and are *not* clearly related to the behavior being punished. Following are characteristics of logical consequences and punishment.

Logical Consequence
- Logically related to the behavior
- Deliberately planned and delivered
- Emotionally neutral
- Rational and depersonalized
- Develop self-control
- Protect self-esteem

Punishment
- Arbitrary or contrived
- Reactionary
- Emotionally charged
- Personalized
- Produce avoidance behavior
- Erode self-esteem

The following examples compare natural, logical, and arbitrary consequences.

BEHAVIOR	NATURAL	CONSEQUENCE LOGICAL	ARBITRARY
Student teases peers.	Student isn't chosen to be included in game students are playing during recess.	Student is required to play alone during recess.	Student loses points.
Student is late for class.	Student misses information needed for test.	Student is responsible for making up any work missed.	Student is sent to principal's office for rest of class period and then has to make up all work.
Student hits another student during recess.	Student is hit back.	Student misses recess the next day.	Student is kept after school.

Several authors define differing categories for types of consequences and also offer different definitions for similar types of consequences. They criticize the use of punishment in favor of more respectful and humane responses to student misbehavior, focusing instead on solution-oriented and skill-building alternatives.

Democratic Discipline and Reasonable Consequences

Hoover and Kindsvatter (1997) suggest that in democratically conducted classrooms, remediation be applied in accordance with the concept of *reasonable consequences*. They define a reasonable consequence as a measure with a developmental focus that targets a personal learning outcome for the student. Ideally, when a reasonable consequence is applied, the student will recognize a connection between the misbehavior and the consequence that goes beyond a simple chronological one. For example, two students who persist in having a private conversation instead of doing their classwork may be separated, but it should be clear that the consequence is being applied because a previous reminder was ignored. A reasonable consequence implies taking action *for* the student or in the student's interest, rather than *against* the student. A teacher should be the student's advocate in a proactive way. In using a reasonable consequence, the teacher takes into account the overall impact of the disciplinary measure to minimize negative emotional overlay.

A reasonable consequence is based on the assumption that the student can ultimately be persuaded by principles of reason, justice, mutual consideration, fair play, and social responsibility. The idea is to apply a judicious resolution without having a winner and a loser. The principle of restitution may also be included as part of the response. The overall intent is to help the student learn acceptable behavior from the experience. Even though the teacher's intent may be instructional rather than punitive, students may perceive it differently. However, any unintended side effects can be mitigated by determining a reasonable consequence that involves participation, reflection, and understanding on the part of the student. Although the outcomes of reasonable and logical consequences are clearly more desirable than the outcomes of punishment, attaining such desirable outcomes is to a large extent dependent on the teacher's manner of delivery.

Although, in practice, a punishment and a reasonable or logical consequence may be hard to distinguish, the critical difference is in the spirit and purpose with which each addresses the misbehavior and the underlying message that is communicated to the student.

UNDERLYING MESSAGE WITH PUNISHMENT	UNDERLYING MESSAGE WITH LOGICAL (REASONABLE) CONSEQUENCES
I'll show you who's in charge.	I trust you to make a choice.
You deserve to be punished.	You are worthwhile and responsible.
You can't get away with doing this to me.	You can learn from your experience.
You can't be trusted to make the right decision.	You can act responsibly.

Though this line of reasoning has merit, as Grossman (2003) points out, in some cases the logical consequences of misbehaving may not be enough to counter the intrinsic rewards of students' actions. Telling students who lie that one does not believe them, making a student wash graffiti off the wall, sending a student to the end of the line for cutting when that student would have been at the end of the line anyway, and requiring a student who teases others to remain isolated may not affect the student as particularly unpleasant. In such cases, applying logical consequences can be ineffective, and the teacher may have to resort to other kinds of consequences.

Cooperative Discipline's Four Rs of Consequences.   According to Albert (1996), when students repeatedly violate the classroom rules, consequences are invoked in keeping with previous agreements. She refers to the Four Rs of consequences— related, reasonable, respectful, and reliably enforced. *Related* means that the consequence should involve an act that has something to do with the misbehavior; *reasonable* means that the consequence is proportional to the misbehavior; *respectful* means that the consequence is invoked in a friendly but firm manner, with no blaming, shaming, or preaching; and *reliably enforced* means that teachers consistently follow through and invoke consequences.

***Discipline with Dignity*'s Four Categories of Consequences.**   Curwin and Mendler (1988), authors of *Discipline with Dignity,* differentiate among four types of consequences: logical, conventional, generic, and instructional. *Logical consequences* require students to make right what they have done wrong and are logically related to the behavior. When students make a mess, they clean it up. When they speak hurtfully to others, they must then speak in a way that is not hurtful. *Conventional consequences* are those that are commonly in practice, such as loss of recess or being sent to the office. *Generic consequences* include reminders and warnings, as well as choosing and planning. Choosing allows students to select from three or four options a plan for improving their behavior. Planning, which Curwin (1992) believes is the most effective consequence, requires that students plan their own solution to a recurring behavior problem. Planning conveys that the teacher has faith in the student's competence, engendering a commitment. *Instructional consequences* teach students how to behave properly. Some behaviors, such as speaking respectfully, are learned more readily when directly taught and practiced.

Moving beyond Consequences: Focusing on Solutions

A number of authors make the important point that teachers should think beyond consequences to solutions.

Positive Discipline's **Three Rs of Solutions.**   Nelsen, Lott, and Glenn (2000), in their book *Positive Discipline*, refer to the *Three Rs of Solutions: related* to what they have done wrong, *respectful* of them as people, and *reasonable*. While consequences focus on the past and making kids "pay" for their mistakes, solutions help students do better in the future, focusing on seeing problems as opportunities for learning. They urge teachers to think in terms of solutions rather than consequences.

The authors also suggest making connections between opportunity, responsibility, and consequence. Students need to learn that every new opportunity brings with it a related responsibility. To instill a sense of responsibility the teacher might say "You decide how much time you need to calm down. Let me know when you are ready to speak respectfully." Nelsen, Lott, and Glenn believe that consequences are effective only if they are enforced respectfully and students are given another opportunity as soon as they are ready.

They point out that it is easy to misuse logical consequences, perpetuating the use of punishment despite labeling it logical consequences. Gordon (1989) likewise refers to the concept of logical consequences as "nothing less than a euphemism for external control." Kohn (1996) also questions whether the idea of imposing logical consequences is a real alternative to punishment in the eyes of students and the degree to which logical consequences are actually related, reasonable, and respectful, as is often claimed by its proponents. He notes that even those espousing the ostensible benefits of logical consequences over punishment acknowledge that what they are proposing can be difficult to distinguish from old-fashioned punishment (Albert, 1996; Canter & Canter, 1992; Curwin & Mendler, 1988; Dinkmeyer & McKay, 1989; Dreikurs & Grey, 1968). Kohn aptly labels logical consequences as *Punishment Lite*. Despite these concerns, when carefully construed and consciously administered, the differentiation is valuable.

Restitution: Restructuring School Discipline.   According to Gossen (1996) restitution creates conditions for students to both fix their mistakes and be strengthened in the process. She defines *restitution* as a strategy for helping students become self-directed, self-disciplined, and self-healed. The approach is based on Glasser's work, incorporating reality therapy and choice theory principles. Restitution is built on the following three assumptions.

1. We are doing the best we can.
2. We are internally motivated.
3. All behavior is purposeful.

The Restitution Program has the following features.

Makes things better
Is tied to common beliefs developed collectively
Enables the person to reclaim self-esteem through personal effort
Benefits the person wronged
Benefits the person who has done wrong
Avoids punishment, placing blame, or giving criticism

LEARNING PRACTICE TASK: THINKING ABOUT PUNISHMENT

Activity Directions: For this activity, you will be working with three to five peers.

1. Discuss the following.
   - Remember a time you were punished by your parent(s).
     —What was your initial response? Long-term response?
     —What did you learn, or learn to do?
     —Was it the intended lesson?
   - In your experience, does punishment work?
   - How are you still carrying the effects of punishment with you now?

2. As a group, try to get consensus on some beliefs and attitudes about punishment.

   Our consensus beliefs and attitudes about punishment:

   _____

   _____

   _____

   _____

   _____

   _____

Reasons for Growing Dissatisfaction with Behavioral Interventions

Two main reasons for the current questioning of traditional behavior modification techniques are their emphasis on external control by teachers rather than trying to foster internal control by the child and their focus on systematically manipulating consequences of behavior, which keep teachers from examining both their classroom structure as well as their own responses to students' difficult behavior as possible contributors to that behavior.

In the traditional behavior management approach, baseline data are collected and an intervention is selected, often utilizing punishment procedures such as overcorrection, time-out, or response cost. Ellis and Magee (1999) point out several problems with this approach. They raise the following concerns with the traditional behavior management approach.

- It does not examine the relationship between challenging behavior and either the environmental conditions or the learning context.
- It often utilizes time-intensive interventions without consideration of the function of the behavior.
- It may misuse behavior management procedures, such as using time-out when a student's disruptive behavior is maintained by escape from classroom activities, inadvertently perpetuating the continuation of the challenging behavior.
- It may employ punitive interventions that are unnecessary and do not address alternative appropriate behaviors that could serve the same function as the challenging behavior.
- It fails to provide a framework for teachers to understand factors that produce and contribute to the challenging behavior.

Typically, interventions used by educators to deal with challenging student behaviors have tended to be unsystematic, negative, or both (Gunter, Denny, Jack, Shores, & Nelson, 1993; Lipsey & Wilson, 1993; Shores, Jack, Gunter, Ellis, DeBriere, & Wehby, 1994). Strategies based on punishment (e.g., time-out, detention, suspension) are used most frequently, no doubt because the outcome (i.e., exclusion of the student from the setting) is particularly reinforcing to practitioners (Center & McKittrick, 1987; Walker, Colvin, & Ramsey, 1996).

BEHAVIORAL SUPPORT, NOT BEHAVIOR MANAGEMENT

The 1997 amendments to the Individuals with Disabilities Education Act (IDEA) require that schools recognize the relationship between student behavior and classroom learning. Implementing the intent of the law requires movement away from *behavior management* grounded in behavioral principles of reinforcement theory, toward *behavioral support* grounded in functional assessment based on a belief system that sees most challenging behaviors as logical responses to get important needs met.

Functional assessment is a systematic method of assessing the function or purpose of a student's behavior relative to its environmental context in order to design appropriate interventions to meet the unique needs of the student (Scott & Nelson, 1999b). Fully including students with a wider range of learning, emotional, and behavior problems means that classroom teachers, in addition to specialists, now need to be able to implement more long-term intervention procedures in addition to group management techniques. Increasingly, more students are requiring individual and systematic interventions. For these students, systematic behavior change programs are necessary, at least initially, to bring about desired classroom behavior.

The functional assessment and intervention model is built on a core set of assumptions concerning the development and maintenance of both appropriate and challenging behaviors (Chandler & Dahlquist, 2002; Repp, 1999). These assumptions guide the identification of the supports for challenging behavior and the interventions that are developed to address it. These assumptions are as follows.

- Challenging behavior and appropriate behavior are supported by the current environment.
- Behavior serves a function.
- Challenging behavior can be changed using positive interventions that address the function of the behavior.
- Functional assessment should be a team-based process.

There are also more fundamental assumptions and beliefs about human behavior that form the basis for the functional assessment process.

Underlying Assumptions about Behavior Related to Functional Assessment
1. Behavior serves a function for the individual who exhibits it. In other words, the behavior is purposeful. It meets a need for the student.
2. The function is valid for the student. The student is engaging in problematic behavior to meet a need or serve a function that is meaningful and important to the student.
3. The behavior is learned; thus, it can be unlearned. A student can learn to refrain from engaging in an inappropriate behavior, and he or she can also

learn new behaviors that serve the same function or purpose as that of the challenging behavior.

4. Challenging behavior is viewed as a form of communication. Students use challenging behavior to communicate what they want or do not want. This is often seen with students who have severe disabilities and lack a formal method of communication that allows them to meet their needs.

5. Challenging behavior often results from a lack of basic social skills. Many students have reasonably good basic communication skills; however, they may lack the social skills needed to interact effectively with peers and adults.

6. Challenging behavior may be a source of internal pleasure for the individual. Behaviors in this category would include such sensory behaviors as finger flicking, rocking, and overeating. Such behaviors provide sensory gratification to the person engaging in them.

7. Challenging behavior can be something a student does when he or she does not know what else to do. Students sometimes engage in what appears to be a pointless activity because they lack an alternative. In such cases these behaviors occur as an alternative to doing nothing. Once students are engaged, however, such behaviors sometimes evolve into other forms of reinforcement.

For many years, functional assessment has been advocated as an effective approach to behavioral assessment by professionals who work in the area of low-incidence disabilities and with students who exhibit serious behavior problems (Day, Horner, & O'Neill, 1994; Foster-Johnson & Dunlap, 1993). The amendments to IDEA now mandate functional behavioral assessment for those students with disabilities who exhibit behaviors that lead to a change in school placement or that constitute a pattern of misbehavior.

The provisions of the IDEA amendments clearly intend that functional assessment be used as an intervention planning tool for student behaviors that threaten the safety and security of the school environment. The intent of the legal requirement is to encourage proactive problem solving rather than reactive punishment of misbehavior (Nelson, Roberts, Mather, & Rutherford, 1999; Sasso, Conroy, Stichter, & Fox, 2001). The following chart contrasts past and current thinking.

Contrasting Past and Current Beliefs and Practices for Addressing Students' Challenging Behavior

CHARACTERISTIC	PAST PRACTICE	CURRENT PRACTICE
Student's Need	Behavior Management	Behavioral Support
Management Plan Focus	Behavior Management Plans focus on specifying the negative consequences for misbehavior and the positive consequences for acceptable behavior.	Behavioral Support Plans focus on understanding the purpose the behavior serves for the student and then on teaching or eliciting an alternative behavior that meets the student's needs in other, more acceptable ways. This includes teaching strategies and classroom restructuring as well as student self-management to support new skills.

(continued)

Contrasting Past and Current Beliefs and Practices   Continued

CHARACTERISTIC	PAST PRACTICE	CURRENT PRACTICE
Changing Behavior	Consequences are delivered to students in an effort to get them to stop misbehavior, either aversive, so that the student avoids the misbehavior, or positive, so that the student behaves in order to receive a reward.	Antecedents, often the triggers for misbehavior, as well as the teacher's response, are identified and viewed as critical to changing behavior. The emphasis is on determining what is available or lacking in the environment or instructional delivery that can be changed.
Underlying Belief	Problem behavior needs to be controlled or eliminated. Positive behaviors are to be expected without considering the purpose the problem behavior serves or the student's unmet needs.	More appropriate replacement behavior needs to be taught through modeling, guided practice, and cueing within a supportive environment.

It is important that functional assessment not be seen as a practice exclusively tied to special education or dangerous behaviors, or as a precursor to change in placement or school exclusion. Rather, functional behavioral assessment should be used within a system of effective behavioral support that includes a systematic approach to identifying students at risk for behavioral difficulties and providing proactive interventions (Broussard & Northrop, 1995; Colvin, Kameenui, & Sugai, 1993; Vera, Wilson, & Panacek, 1996).

The IDEA amendments reaffirm a commitment to educating students with disabilities in inclusive settings. Although inclusion in general education classrooms continues to be problematic for students with challenging behavior, the emphasis on collaborative practices has opened the door for a team approach to intervention planning (Scott & Nelson, 1999a). Because team-based intervention planning relies on collective brainstorming and input rather than an individual, "expert" functional assessment and subsequent interventions are best implemented by teams. Ideally, functional assessment should be viewed as a schoolwide practice that is implemented by teams of educators as a proactive rather than a reactive strategy.

Within the team approach, it is typically recommended that the process be facilitated by personnel who understand functional assessment. O'Rourke, Knoster, and Llewellyn (1999) recommend that the facilitator prompt team members by posing pointed questions to guide the process.

Guiding Questions for Developing an Effective Behavioral Support Plan

Regarding Consequences

How does teacher (or aide) respond to the challenging behavior?

How do peers respond to the behavior?

What happens to the task or activity at hand?

What happens immediately after the challenging behavior?

Regarding Environmental Context

What effect does the student's specific disability have?

Does the student have an effective communication system?

Have there been significant changes in the family system?

Are there any health-related issues that increase the likelihood of the challenging behavior?

Regarding Learning Context

What types of activities increase the likelihood of the challenging behavior?

What school settings increase the likelihood of the challenging behavior?

What else is going on when the challenging behavior occurs?

In what settings or situations does the challenging behavior not occur?

Regarding Function

What does the student get by behaving this way?

What might the student be avoiding or getting out of?

Does the behavior help the student gain a sense of control over others, the situation, or both?

Does the behavior help the student reduce frustration experienced with the task at hand?

What is so important for the student that he or she risks the consequences of the challenging behavior?

Following such a process helps team members understand that most challenging behavior represents the best that the student can do in situations where the student does not have or cannot use more appropriate alternatives. This perceptual shift leads to multicomponent Behavioral Support Plans with various components working in tandem to produce durable change.

The most effective use of functional assessments is as a proactive and school-wide policy in which the responsibility for conducting these assessments is not placed on any one person (O'Rourke, Knoster, & Llewellyn, 1999; Scott & Nelson, 1999a). A classroom teacher should have ready access to assistance in completing a functional assessment. Ideally, the procedure would be a normal part of the prereferral intervention process followed by all teachers.

Irrespective of the mandate of the IDEA reauthorization, teachers have not only the capacity but also the responsibility to teach behaviors that are predictive of success in life. When teachers teach *functionally equivalent* behaviors and arrange environments to maximize the probability of success they facilitate positive interactions with students.

Unfortunately, current public attitudes and school discipline policies (e.g., zero tolerance) threaten to effectively negate the proactive benefits of functional assessment. It is imperative that schools embrace the concept of functional assessment as a common routine whose procedures are adopted, supported, and shared among school personnel. These procedures will work optimally when applied consistently by all school personnel as a component of a planned system of support.

Educators who believe that children should be taught prosocial behaviors in lieu of punishment need to learn how to effectively implement functional assessments. However, mere awareness of such procedures will be insufficient to have a positive impact on altering students' challenging behavior. Because problem behavior can have multiple sources and multiple pathways, a single assumption regarding the determinants of a challenging behavior is likely to result in ineffective intervention formulation. As is the case with more traditional behavioral assessment procedures, for example, applied behavior analysis (ABA) or antecedent-behavior-consequence (ABC) analysis, direct observation is integral to generating plausible explanations regarding the function of a student's challenging behavior.

The premise for functional assessments is that behavior occurs predictably and that the ability to identify the specific predictors of challenging behavior allows for the development of maximally effective intervention plans (Johnson, 1996; Watson, Ray, Sterling-Turner, & Logan, 1999). Thus, the success of such plans depends on the proactive use of functional assessments to facilitate and predict desired behavior rather than merely react to undesired behavior. In addition, success rests on the practitioner's ability to continually assess student behavior, monitor student progress, and continue, alter, or abandon interventions according to their relative success.

DESIGNING EFFECTIVE BEHAVIORAL SUPPORT PLANS BASED ON FUNCTIONAL ASSESSMENTS

Behavioral support plans are formulated based on information collected from functional assessments. They are designed to address the "here and now" of a classroom setting, the match of learner to environment. As such, they focus on the immediate and alterable influences on behavior rather than on immutable or historical reasons for behavior. They apply contextually, socially, and culturally appropriate interventions to make the problem behavior less effective, efficient, and relevant, and to make desired behavior more functional.

A well-designed behavioral support plan specifies not just what the student will do, but what educators will do to alter environments or teach new behaviors that may be necessary for the student's success. It is essentially a *teaching plan*, not just a list of goals and objectives for the student to achieve.

O'Neill and colleagues (1997) recommend that behavioral support plans

- **Be built from functional assessment results.** This information enables teachers and others to identify specific changes in the classroom that will influence patterns of behavior.
- **Describe behavior.** Define in detail the changes expected in the behavior of teachers, paraeducators, and other school personnel (as well as family members, when applicable).
- **Make problem behaviors irrelevant.** Identify those situations (antecedents) that give rise to problem behaviors and organize the environment to reduce the likelihood that these conditions are encountered.
- **Make problem behaviors ineffective.** Provide alternative ways of obtaining reinforcement, rendering the current behavior ineffective.
- **Include a replacement behavior.** This involves identifying replacement behaviors, describing how they will be taught, and developing an intervention to reinforce students when they perform them.

Phases in the Functional Assessment Process

Phase 1: Define the Challenging Behavior.   Here the behavior is described in specific, observable terms.

Phase 2: Collect Functional Assessment Data. This phase may include both informal and structured interviews, questionnaires, and behavioral checklists, as well as behavior observation.

>**Conduct Functional Assessment Interviews.** Initial assessment involves informal conversations as well as more structured interviews with key persons who have contact with the individual student (e.g., teachers, parents) and can offer insights into the behavior. This step may also include completing more formal questionnaires and behavioral checklists.

>**Conduct Functional Assessment Observations.** Here a recording format is developed or selected that includes relevant contextual variables. Data are collected on several occasions, varying the environmental context to zero in on specific components. Included are setting and antecedent events, which may be categorized as follows.

Setting Events:	Physiological, biological (e.g., hunger, fatigue, under- or overstimulation)
	Physical, environmental (e.g., open space versus confined, noise level, distractions)
	Social, situational (family–home factors, critical incidents, time of day)
Antecedents:	Activity, task variables (e.g., content, lesson format, difficulty level, level of active participation)
	Staff, peer behavior (e.g., proximity, attention, group composition)
	Structure, pace (e.g., sequence of activities, grouping arrangement, change in routine)

Phase 3: Summarize Observational Data to Identify Predictable Patterns. Observational data are summarized to identify probable relationships between the behavior and the environmental context. All possible factors gleaned from the assessment data are considered to answer these two questions.

>Under what conditions does the behavior occur, increase, or get worse?
>Under what conditions does the behavior not occur, decrease, or get better?

Phase 4: Develop Plausible Hypotheses or Explanations for the Behavior. Plausible hypotheses define the relationship between observable antecedents and consequences that predictably occur in the presence of the behavior. Recognizing repetitive patterns of antecedents and consequences provides clues that may predict or explain the behavior. A functional hypothesis states the events or circumstances associated with the behavior and the perceived function or purpose of the behavior.

Phase 5: Conduct a Functional Analysis. Here the validity of the hypothesis is assessed either by systematic manipulation of setting events, antecedents, or consequences, or by simple direct observation. Then, if necessary, an alternative hypothesis is reformulated and retested in an ongoing process ending with the eventual validation of a hypothesis that verifies the function or purpose of the behavior.

Although the most powerful manner of validating a hypothesis is to systematically manipulate antecedent and consequent variables, in the scope of a complex placement such as a classroom, systematic manipulations may not be feasible. In such instances, simple direct observations may suffice. Simply assessing the correspondence between behavior and specific environmental contexts provides an informed best guess that certain setting and antecedent events predict behavior. Although not as robust as manipulations, systematic observations of consistent patterns of predictable behavior can confirm a hypothesis and be used to create effective behavior intervention plans.

Phase 6: Design an Intervention Plan (Behavioral Support Plan).   Knowing what factors predict an undesirable behavior provides information necessary to develop an intervention plan. Once the function of a problem behavior has been identified, the teacher asks, "How can I arrange the classroom context so that the student can achieve his or her desired outcome by engaging in acceptable behavior?" The basic rule of thumb is to replace the undesirable behavior with a desirable behavior that can serve the same function for the student.

Although the student can receive the same functional outcome via the identified replacement behavior, the student likely will not engage in replacement behaviors without instruction, because his or her undesirable behaviors have served that function over a period of time and are not easily abandoned. The replacement behavior will need to be taught using effective strategies likely to maximize potential for success, such as modeling the replacement behavior for the student, allowing opportunities for guided practice, and gradually fading out supports until the student can demonstrate self-management.

A comprehensive plan should include the following

1. Modifying the events or circumstances (i.e., setting events, antecedents, consequences) associated with the problem behavior
2. Teaching an alternative (replacement) behavior(s) that serves the same function
3. Teaching self-management and social skills
4. Specifying a Response Plan for when the problem behavior occurs

Although the hope is always to have a plan that works, a backup system, or Plan B, needs to be in place and ready, in case the student reverts to a previous behavior or has a crisis. A Response Plan involves a planned intervention sequence (or escalation) to be used to encourage or invite the student to return to more prosocial behavior.

Phase 7: Implement and Evaluate the Intervention.   In this phase, the intervention is implemented and ongoing data are collected on the effectiveness of the intervention. Based on the data, the intervention will be continued or modified to increase the likelihood of success.

Behavior Observation and Data Recording

Recording observational data allows the teacher to see under what circumstances the behavior occurs or does not occur, increases or decreases. It is important to collect data in relation to various settings, learning tasks, peers, adults, times of day, and other circumstances, and to consider factors such as activity sequence, task demands, and proximity of the teacher, aide, or peers. The data will begin to clarify the impact of contextual factors on the behavior. Contextual information is critical in pinpointing the circumstances associated with the problematic behavior. It also helps determine timing and location for further, more specific observations.

The focus of a functional assessment is to determine what environmental events predict and currently maintain the student's problem behavior. Structured assessment procedures reliably capture not only those events related to the challenging behaviors, but also those events occurring prior to and after occasions when the problem behavior is absent. In the absence of recording observational data, these subtleties often are beyond the discrimination of the teacher within the normal flow of the classroom.

It is usually not possible to identify all the subtle pieces of this puzzle from a simple and limited number of observations. The relationship between behavior and antecedent or consequent variables is one that requires repeated measures over time. Whether in the form of an antecedent-behavior-consequence (ABC) analysis, another behavior observation format, anecdotal notes, or simple repeated observations with mental notes, direct observation is crucial to providing information necessary for determining the function a behavior serves for the student. In general, the more detailed and descriptive the functional assessment data, the more efficient the process of determining the function of the behavior.

A Word of Caution

Although most conceptualizations of behavioral function are in terms of positive reinforcements (getting something desired) and negative reinforcements (avoiding something undesirable), some believe that human behavior is far too complex to be reduced to these limited interpretations. The concept needs to be broadened to take into account underlying needs, or communicative intent, that go beneath the surface, such as the needs for power, control, recognition, acceptance, and belonging. Taking into consideration these needs would lead to development of interventions that also include creating a sense of significance or personal potency.

Finally, it is important that behavioral support plans not be construed as meeting all of a student's needs. Some students will require mental health services and interventions to address longer-range issues, such as emotional disturbances and other home and life stressors. Some students need only Behavioral Support Plans, some need only mental health services and interventions, and some need both.

CHAPTER SEVEN

Helping Students Develop as Self-Regulated Learners

Because students have typically been socialized to a classroom environment in which the teacher directs activities, manages student behavior, and evaluates student performance, asking students to be responsible for their own behavior requires a shift in student-acquired expectations and ways of behaving. Teachers can initially facilitate this shift by asking students to engage in self-diagnosis of the appropriateness of their behavior. This changes the student–teacher interaction pattern from one in which the teacher evaluates students' behavior to one in which students provide their own assessment of their actions. The notion of self-assessment is a key concept for establishing shared responsibility for maintaining a supportive learning community.

Often students fail to act in appropriate ways not because of lack of motivation, conscious choice, or unwillingness, but because they have not learned what constitutes acceptable ways of behaving or under what circumstances a behavior would be appropriate or inappropriate. Specific strategy instruction and structured learning experiences can enable students to learn social and self-management skills that will help them develop positive peer relationships, work cooperatively in learning groups, and participate productively in classroom activities. Crucial to this learning is the modeling provided by the teacher.

DEVELOPING COLLABORATIVE PROBLEM SOLVING

If teachers want to move away from a teacher-controlled environment and call on students to be active participants in making choices and solving problems, they may have to (at least initially) engage in strategy building to teach students the strategies they may be lacking in areas such as decision making, problem solving, self-control, and conflict resolution. If students are lacking the necessary repertoire to make appropriate choices, then it is incumbent on teachers to teach students strategies so that they will eventually become more capable of making better choices in the future. Thus the teacher may need to provide sequenced lessons and structured experiences to teach students strategies, so that in time, the teacher can turn over responsibility to students and function in a more facilitative role. Students could then be expected to make choices and find solutions, having a response repertoire for making appropriate choices.

Using Classroom Meetings to Develop Decision-Making Skills

To encourage ongoing communication between teachers and students, many believe that regularly scheduled class meetings offer the best forum (*Child Develop-*

ment Project, 1996; Glasser, 1969; Gordon, 1974, 1989; Kohn, 1996; Nelsen, Lott, & Glenn, 2000). Like any community, a class has goals to achieve, problems to resolve, opportunities to assess, interpersonal conflicts to work out, and decisions to make. All of these issues can be handled in class meetings.

Topics for class meetings can range from individual concerns that the whole group can help solve to whole-group concerns. Topics can be brief and informational or may require lengthy discussion. In addition to *class meeting,* terms such as *circle time, weekly meeting, problem solving, shared decision making,* or any suitable name can be used. Teachers who have made the class meeting an integral part of their program most typically hold class meetings weekly.

Some teachers like to chair meetings; others prefer a rotating chair in which students take turns running the meeting and have the opportunity to practice leadership skills. Some teachers have students submit ideas beforehand, whereas others encourage students to raise issues at the meeting. Another option is to post a folder marked *Next Class Meeting,* which allows students to participate who might not otherwise initiate a topic for consideration.

Sometimes the teacher may want to call everyone together again and ask, "Are you still satisfied with our solution?" It's important to communicate the message that decisions are not chiseled in stone and that they can be discarded in search of a better solution. Also, this reinforces the value of students' solutions. By beginning each meeting with a discussion of the solutions developed at the previous meeting, students feel their solutions are useful and important. Class meetings are designed for the purpose of teaching problem solving, so reinforcing students' successful efforts, analyzing failures, and helping them develop increasingly more effective solutions is integral to the process.

Glasser's Suggestions.   Glasser suggests the classroom meeting as an effective vehicle for attending to matters such as class rules, behavior, and discipline. He recommends two ground rules to set the stage for students and teachers to interact without finding fault, placing blame, or seeking to punish or retaliate. The ground rules should be established in the first meeting, kept to a minimum (two or three), and stated in positive terms. Glasser's two major ground rules are

1. Class members deal with each other with mutual respect.
2. Meetings are established for class members to help each other.

He also recommends the following general procedures.

General Procedures
1. Meetings should be held at a consistently scheduled time or times each week.
2. Once established, meetings should never be canceled as a punishment.
3. Topics for the meeting may be placed on the agenda and introduced by the teacher or by class members.
4. All topics relative to the class as a group or to any individual class member can be discussed in the class meeting forum.
5. Brief minutes should be kept including only lists of options generated and final decisions. This provides a record that can be referred to should the class decide to reconsider their decision at some time in the future.

Guidelines
1. Don't expect the effectiveness of the classroom meeting to be immediate. Social problem solving is a complex process and will require practice to be successful.
2. The role of the teacher is to serve as a facilitator to keep students focused on the topic, ensure a democratic atmosphere in which everyone is listened to, and reflect student comments back to the group.

3. Teacher input as a facilitator may need to be extensive at initial class meetings; however, the teacher should diminish his or her role and remain in the background as soon as the students have learned the problem-solving process.

The Process

Conducting class meetings involves the following systematic problem-solving process.

Step 1: Establishing a climate of warmth and trust
Step 2: Exposing and clarifying the problem
Step 3: Making personal value judgments
Step 4: Identifying alternate ways to act
Step 5: Determining an appropriate consequence
Step 6: Making a commitment
Step 7: Following up with an evaluation of effectiveness

According to Glasser, classroom meetings should do the following.

- Provide a stable way to bridge the gap between school and life
- Help students believe that they can control their own destinies and that they themselves are vital parts of the world they live in
- Keep a class together because the more and less capable can interact
- Promote involvement because students can always succeed in a meeting—no one can fail
- Help motivate students to do some of the less exciting fact finding that may evolve from the meetings
- Reduce isolation and failure so that a spirit of cooperation can exist
- Help students gain confidence when they state opinions before a group, thus helping them prepare for the many opportunities in life to speak for themselves
- Increase responsibility for learning and for the kind of learning that is fostered by and shared with the entire class
- Provide for the kind of involvement, value judgments, plans, and commitments that produce changes in behavior

Increasing Students' Involvement in Class Meetings.   A major goal in implementing class meetings is teaching students the skills involved in functioning effectively in a problem-solving group. With this goal in mind, teachers need to consider gradually increasing student responsibility for facilitating class meetings. Jones and Jones (2001) note that this is difficult to do with primary grade children, but third-grade students can be taught to run their own class meetings successfully. They offer the following four steps for having students take over the class meeting.

1. After leading approximately ten class meetings, present students with a handout describing the major functions a leader serves when facilitating a group meeting (see chart, Class Meeting Jobs). Discuss each function and behavior with the class and inform them that they will soon be asked to lead their own meetings by having students serve these important functions.
2. Introduce an agenda item or classroom problem. While the class discusses this situation, point out and define each intervention you make. Because you continue to do these three things, the discussion will be interrupted on numerous occasions. Students are usually excited about learning these new skills, however, and enjoy your instructional interventions.
3. After running three or four actual class meetings in which you consistently point out the function of each intervention, meet with and teach one student

the role of discussion leader. At the next meeting, this student serves as the discussion leader while you maintain the other roles. Prior to the next meeting, you meet with another student who learns the role of task observer. At the following meeting, the student serves this function. After this meeting, you instruct a third student in the role of behavior and feeling observer, and at the following meeting you become a group member who abides by the group responsibilities, while the students run the meeting.

4. Each student should function in a role for five or six meetings, so that he or she can master the skills associated with the role and effectively model it for other students. If a student has difficulty with a role, take time between meetings to instruct the student in the skills associated with the role. Providing students with this type of experience requires a small amount of time and considerable restraint and patience, but students respond to their new responsibilities by becoming more positive, productive class members. Indeed, problem students often respond especially well, because they gain self-esteem and peer acceptance serving as productive participants in class meetings.

Class Meeting Jobs

Discussion Leader
   1. Makes sure everyone is comfortable and all distracting things are out of the way
   2. Makes sure everyone can see all others in the circle
   3. Gives the speaker time to get his or her point across
   4. Gives the speaker a nod or a smile
   5. Asks clarifying questions

   Are you saying that . . . ?

   Do you think that . . . ?

   6. Summarizes

   Is there anything else you would like to say?

   Would someone briefly summarize what has been said?

Task Observer
   1. Makes sure the task gets finished on time
   2. Watches the time
   3. Suggests alternatives to solve the problem
   4. Points out behaviors that are not helpful in solving a problem
   5. Listens carefully and understands what the discussion leader is doing
   6. Knows the agenda and introduces each agenda item

Behavior and Feeling Observer
Asks questions such as:

   How did this discussion make you feel?

   What could we do now? What might help us?

   _____ (person's name), was anything asked that caused you to be concerned? Can you tell us what it was and how you felt about it?

   _____ (person's name), you usually help us out. Do you have any ideas for this problem?

Has anyone thought of new ideas for improving our discussions?

How many of you think that the discussion was of value to you? Why?

Topics for Class Meetings.   Many different kinds of issues can be raised at class meetings. Here are some examples to suggest the wide variety of topics possible (adapted from Kirschenbaum, 1995).

- The teacher is concerned about students frequently interrupting each other.
- Several students have complained that things have disappeared from their desks.
- A student wants to suggest to the class that they raise money for famine relief in Africa.
- Some students are concerned about the cliques in the classroom.
- The teacher is concerned that white and African American students always sit separately in the classroom.
- The class needs to decide what service project it is going to do.
- The teacher would like some ideas for the next unit he or she is planning.
- A student thinks the teacher is being unfair in applying one of the class rules.
- A student has an idea for a class trip.
- Several students think a new rule is needed to solve a problem they are having.
- The teacher wants the class's feedback on the unit they just completed.
- The solution from a previous class meeting is not working. It needs to be reexamined.

Purposes for Class Meetings.   Lickona (1991) has identified purposes the class meeting can fulfill.

- Deepening students' sense of shared ownership of the classroom
- Improving students' moral reasoning, including their ability to take the perspective of others
- Developing their listening skills and abilities to express themselves in a group
- Developing their self-worth by providing a forum in which their thoughts are valued
- Teaching the skills and attitudes needed to participate effectively in democratic decision making.

As Kohn (1996) describes it, the classroom meeting can be a forum for sharing (e.g., talking about interesting things that happen), deciding (e.g., how best to arrange the classroom), planning (e.g., figuring out all the logistics for making a field trip happen), or reflecting (e.g., thinking about what kind of place a classroom should be).

Inviting Participation and Consensus Building.   For classroom meetings to work effectively teachers need to do more than merely allow students to make decisions. They need to actively support student autonomy by inviting participation while teaching the necessary skills. There are good ways to invite participating and there are better ways. Although it is desirable to give students a chance to pick their favorite option from a teacher-derived list, it is better to have them generate the list themselves. It is good when students get to vote rather than being told, but it is better when they are encouraged to hash out a consensus together or reach a compromise (Kohn, 1996). Voting produces losers who often have no commitment to what the majority wants; the hard work of listening, considering others' perspectives, and creating new solutions is lost when matters are simply put to a vote (*Child Development Project*, 1996).

Perhaps the most difficult aspect of class meetings is reaching consensus on decisions or solutions. And many class meetings won't end neatly with a final decision or plan of action. Sometimes it is enough just to bring up and discuss an issue, raising everyone's awareness about it.

But when the class does need to make a decision or resolve a problem, it is important that all concerned, that is, teacher and students share a desire to reach consensus. When thirty-odd students are struggling with an issue, it can be tempting—for everyone involved—to seek the will of the majority by simply having students vote. The problem with voting is that it can be a divisive experience, creating winners and losers and diminishing a sense of community. The process of how a class arrives at a decision is as important as what the final decision is. The consensus-building process not only reaffirms students' sense that their individual participation is meaningful and worthwhile, but it also is invaluable in helping build their lifelong abilities of perspective taking, negotiation, and seeing compromise as a winning solution rather than a sign of weakness or failure.

The Child Development Project (1996) defines consensus as "Everyone can live with the decision, even if it's no one's first choice."

The Project offers the following five steps to consensus building.

Five Steps to Consensus Building

Step 1: Define the problem or issue in concrete terms.
> Explain why the problem concerns everyone or will benefit from everyone's help.

Step 2: Brainstorm solutions.
> Ensure a climate in which everyone is invited to offer ideas, all ideas are accepted, and no ideas are critiqued.

Step 3: Discuss solutions.
> Reduce the number of ideas and narrow the choices.

Step 4: Reach consensus.
> Facilitate consensus building through combining, developing, or compromising on ideas.
>
> Determine whether consensus has been reached by asking students whether they "can live with a solution." If any answer no, then consensus hasn't been reached yet.
>
> Discuss the experience with the class to identify what the group has learned that they can use the next time to try to reach consensus.

Step 5: Evaluate the decision.
> Later, discuss how well the decision worked or is working.

Strategies for Narrowing Choices.   The Project also recommends the strategies described below to help students reduce their options to a manageable number.

Benefits and Burdens
Students explain what they think are the advantages and disadvantages of each idea.

- Ask students to explain what they see as the benefits and burdens for each option.
- Ask whether these ideas help students eliminate or combine any of the options.
- One way to do this is to move into one of the following strategies.

Unlivable Only
Students name the choices they can't live with, and explain why.

- Have each student state or write down the ideas he or she can't live with and why (some might feel safer writing down their thoughts than stating them).
- Eliminate the unlivable ideas.
- Work with students to reach a consensus on the remaining ideas. If all the ideas have been rejected, have students brainstorm new options or amend previous options. If some ideas have been rejected by only a very few students, those ideas might be modified so that everyone can live with them.

Livable Only
Students name all the choices they can live with.

- For each option, ask students to raise their hands if they can live with it, count the number of raised hands, and record that number beside the idea.
- Work with students to build consensus around the ideas that have the highest *livability scores.*

One Why
Students each choose one idea and explain why they chose it.

- Ask students to identify the one idea they prefer and to explain why.
- Record each student's choice and reasoning, and eliminate any options that received no support.

Three Straws
Students cast three straws.

- Give each student three straw votes and explain to students that they can distribute in any way they choose.
- Tally students' votes. For the few clear preferences that emerge, help students reach a consensus.

Apply Criteria
Students assess objective criteria that can be applied to the decision.

- Help students identify objective criteria that affect the issue.
- Use a simple matrix to assess the impact of these considerations, listing options vertically and criteria horizontally. Then, as a group, mark where the options meet the listed criteria.

Strategies for Reaching Agreement.   Once the number of options is reduced, the teacher helps students focus on their areas of agreement and build on alternatives so that these become more widely acceptable. Can an option be modified so that everyone can live with it? Can two ideas be combined to satisfy the whole class? This stage of the consensus-building effort is the most challenging to the teacher as facilitator because most students have little or no experience with this process. If the process becomes frustrating, the teacher can model and explain how the skills of negotiation, perspective taking, and creative accommodation are valuable for many situations in life.

If the class gets bogged down and seems at an impasse, the teacher may have to return to the brainstorming, discussion, and list-reduction process. Challenge the students to examine and extend their thinking: "Did we generate enough alternatives during the brainstorming? Are there other areas to explore? Did we overlook some criteria?" Perspectives are often broader once students have wrestled with a problem, and they may find new ideas while covering old ground. Sometimes, however, it is best to end the meeting and return to the topic at another time.

Reflective Questions to Ask Yourself. Here are some key questions to consider in planning, executing, and evaluating classroom meetings.

- Am I remaining open about the issue or do I have a predetermined solution?
- Am I willing to let students act on their ideas?
- Do I allow students an opportunity to reflect on and revise previous decisions and plans they want to bring up?
- Have I taught students different processes for coming up with a resolution?
- Do I model effective listening behavior?
- Do I ask open-ended questions?
- Do I model how to clarify information from a student?
- Do I model ways to make connections between ideas?
- Am I able to wait in silence for students to think about their answers before jumping in?
- Do students feel safe expressing their own ideas, rather than ideas they think I want to hear? If not, what can I do to encourage creative thinking?
- Do students understand why we try to reach a consensus rather than just vote?
- Am I comfortable when things "heat up?"
- Do I encourage students to reflect on the process and to suggest thoughtful revisions?

The Define, Personalize, and Challenge Procedure. Class meetings, like other group participation formats, require judicious planning to achieve the desired results. Even though class meetings are more open ended, they should be structured while remaining open and sufficiently flexible to entertain unexpected events. One way to prepare for class meetings is to formulate questions that can steer the meeting. One specific questioning format provides a progressive procedure to advance to more thoughtful and insightful development of a topic. A description of specific elements of the define, personalize, and challenge procedure follows (Froyen & Iverson, 1999).

Defining Questions. These questions explore the meaning of an idea or issue. The emphasis is on gathering information. Using this format invites all students to contribute something without the fear of evaluation.

> *Why do we have rules?*
>
> *What is an important rule?*
>
> *What does it mean to say, "Those are the rules of the game" or "You have to play by the rules to get ahead in life."*

Personalizing. Questions in this stage ask students to personalize what has been contributed in Stage 1. Students are asked to make personal connections so that they can experience the topic as less abstract and impersonal. Here they associate feelings with the topic or issue. This stage also calls for examining the topic in light of experiences common to others. The intent is for students to begin to see that common experiences are interpreted in different ways and have different effects on each individual's beliefs and behavior.

> *How do rules affect your life?*
>
> *When do you want to make rules?*
>
> *How do you feel when you break a rule?*

Have you ever tried to get someone to break a rule?

What are the rules at your dinner table?

Challenging.   In this last stage, students are asked to do something about the problem or with the ideas that have emerged. Students are asked to exercise judgment and arrive at conclusions. The questions are designed to engage students in analysis and evaluative thought processes.

What would happen if we didn't have rules?

If you could make just one rule, what would it be?

Are there times when rules should be broken?

Community Meetings

Community meetings serve the same purpose as classroom meetings, only for a larger cohesive group. The community meeting can serve as a forum for teaching students critical skills and attitudes for democratic citizenship. In this format, entire grades or the school as a whole come together to discuss issues, solve problems, and make decisions as a community.

Modeled on the traditional town meeting, community meetings give everyone the opportunity to speak. There is no single method that works best in all types of communities; each school will need to find its own best approach to community meetings. It will be important to clarify what problems and issues students are willing to allow community decisions on.

Initially, the principal or a teacher leads the meeting in order to model practices that facilitate broad-based participation, encourage and respect divergent viewpoints, and achieve fair decisions. At one school, the principal helped students establish the following four criteria for considering decisions (Kirschenbaum, 1995).

- Is it fair?
- Is it consistent?
- Is it safe?
- Is it necessary?

A community meeting by definition includes the whole community. This means janitors, nurses, cafeteria workers, bus drivers, and anyone else who is a part of the school. Everyone has a voice, and teachers can have an influential voice at the meeting while also being conscious of their status. Participating judiciously is a fine line teachers will need to walk.

Development of Moral Judgment and Problem Solving

Most students between the ages of 7 and 11 realize the need to work collaboratively in the classroom, according to Kohlberg (1975). Kohlberg's six stages of moral judgment offer a model for understanding the types of moral thinking students are capable of at various developmental stages. Teachers can play important roles in guiding their students toward functioning at higher levels of moral judgment if they consider students' moral development as well as their conceptual and affective development in their choice of potential solutions to classroom and group functioning management issues. The chart detailing Kohlberg's Stages of Moral Development identifies stages that typify moral development.

Kohlberg's Stages of Moral Development

MORAL STAGE	MORAL DEVELOPMENT	CHARACTERISTIC BEHAVIOR
Preconventional Orientation		
Stage 1 Punishment and obedience	Measures right and wrong based on physical consequences; avoids pain; fears getting caught; sees the world from personal perspective only.	Obeys those with power to avoid punishment; acts according to pleasure pain principle–doesn't see that others have rights too.
Stage 2 Instrumental– relativist	Satisfying personal needs and desires determines rightness of an act; aware of needs of others; begins to understand concepts of sharing and fairness.	Does things for others if it will fulfill personal needs.
Conventional Orientation		
Stage 3 Good boy– nice girl	Bases what is right on the approval of others; begins to understand importance of intention; thinks in terms of distinct stereotypes; develops empathy and affection and appreciates such from others; assesses right and wrong clearly.	Pleases others; seeks others' approval; conforms to what dominant group defines as acceptable; applies the Golden Rule; identifies with significant others.
Stage 4 Law and order	Underlying ethic is to act within legal guidelines to protect the group–society; laws and legal sanctions are the basis for legitimate action; laws are rigid and have to be followed to maintain society; develops sense of shared responsibility and loyalty to community.	Respects authority; does one's duty; acts to protect and guarantee rights of others; acts for common good; acts on allegiance to more than one group; can step into others' shoes and see how one's own actions affect others.
Postconventional Orientation		
Stage 5 Social contract	What is right is determined by society, such as laws made in a democracy; moral dilemmas necessitate an ability to reason abstractly and to consider arguments and consequences in relation to democratic principles.	Acts in accordance with standards, requirements, and rights of the individual; considers various positions; considers situational context.
Stage 6 Universal ethical principle	Decides what is right by making conscious choices based on a set of self-chosen ethical principles; ethical principles must be logically consistent and broadly applicable; principles are not dependent on written formulas.	Acts according to principles of justice, reciprocity, and equality of human rights.

Although moral development follows a path similar to that of cognitive and psychosocial development, progression from birth through adolescence is not as certain or as rapid. Although Kohlberg (1975) originally proposed an invariable and universal sequence for developing moral judgment, more current thinking recognizes the influence of environmental and cultural factors. Many factors affect the pace and culminating level of moral judgment achieved by an individual. The age level at which a child passes through the various stages will vary with individual differences and life experiences as well as opportunity to test out and contemplate moral dilemmas.

Piaget (1965) put the onset of moral development at the age of 6; Kohlberg posited three levels with typical ranges. The preconventional level is usually operating up until the age of 7 or 8, progressing to the conventional level typically between the ages of 7 and 11, and reaching the potential for the postconventional level somewhere in the early teen years, though not everyone will reach the highest level.

According to George (1980), the development of a child's moral code reflects progressive changes in judgment and vantage point from which the child looks at moral predicaments. The sequence is described in the following chart.

Moral judgment	Decision-Making Criteria
Ethical absolutism (self-interest)	Moves from succumbing to outside authority in Stage 1 to personal gratification in Stage 2
Ethical relativism (other's acceptance)	Moves from approval of significant others in Stage 3 to maintaining group solidarity in Stage 4
Ethical reciprocity (personal values)	Moves from democratically agreed-upon rights in Stage 5 to equality of all in Stage 6

Teachers can make use of Kohlberg's moral development sequence both to design disciplinary measures and develop problem-solving strategies in alignment with students' logical abilities. Teachers can use their influence to maximize the development of moral judgment. Throughout the lower primary grades, students begin to understand the concept of fairness and to appreciate the natural consequences that follow from sharing and cooperating. Relative to classroom management, this means that teachers need to explain why certain rules and procedures are necessary to assure fair treatment of all students, and to give their rationale in ways the students can understand and appreciate.

During the primary elementary grades, most students internalize the need to work collaboratively toward common goals in the classroom setting. They also come to understand relationships and how their behavior affects others. At the same time they see that some rules are necessary for order and smooth functioning of the group, they recognize that other rules are arbitrary and don't serve a meaningful purpose. They are less willing to do things just because the teacher says so and may question why they are expected to behave in certain ways. They reason that chewing gum or wearing a hat doesn't infringe on anyone's rights, and therefore shouldn't be prohibited. Because they can distinguish between necessary and arbitrary rules, see others' points of view, and empathize with the feelings of others, teachers are able to expand moral consciousness at this level by involving students in setting class rules and consequences.

As all teachers know, not all students within this age range have reached this level of moral functioning for a multitude of reasons, which might include poor modeling, not having the benefit of an explanation for behavior expectations from primary caretakers (i.e., they learn to obey but not reason), failure to identify with their class, or immaturity. Teachers can help counteract lack of opportunity to learn by modeling; explaining the reasons behind expected behavior; using role playing to help students see the effects of their behavior on others; engaging students in cooperative learning experiences; and finding ways to foster group identification (Grossman, 2003).

At the primary level, children learn by example, so teachers will need to show them, in concrete ways, how to act. Children learn situation-specific rules before they are able to grasp universal principles of justice. When students consistently see the teacher listening respectfully to everyone's point of view, they are more likely to adopt this practice than if they are constantly reminded to listen.

Teachers can also help students develop moral reasoning by asking them to think about the implications of their actions for the group by responding to "What would happen if . . . ?" questions such as

What would happen if everyone called out whenever they wanted.

What would happen if no one picked up after themselves and put things back where others could find them.

To learn the principle of reciprocity in relationships, teachers can explain to students the kinds of reactions their behavior evokes in others, and ask students to consider how they would feel, what they would think, and how they would react if someone behaved the same way toward them. For example, the teacher might ask "If you had been waiting for a long time and someone cut in line ahead of you, how would you react (feel)?"

Students functioning at the conventional level behave responsibly because they're involved with people who matter to them. As long as class and teacher relationships are positive and rewarding, students act according to class norms. However, if the relationship between teacher and student or between student and other students deteriorates, a student may revert to thinking he or she has only him or herself, and logically act in self-interest only. If the communication channels break down, the teacher loses the opportunity to impact the life of the student. As a reaction to the student's self-serving behavior, the teacher may revert to using power over the student, causing a conflict between the developmental level of the student and the use of teacher control through punishment.

At higher stages, students have moved from being concerned about what the teacher might do to them, or what other students might think of them, to basing their decisions on their own values. They behave appropriately because it's the right thing to do and they can feel good about themselves. Using higher-order principles of justice involves cognitive, affective, and behavioral components, and hence most educators believe that all three areas need to be incorporated for bringing about change. Typically, the recommendation at this level is to present moral dilemmas for students to solve and to engage students in values clarification exercises. However, such cognitive approaches alone will likely be insufficient; what is needed to enhance moral judgment is to motivate students to want to behave for the good of all. One approach is for you as the teacher to tell students how and why you live by the principles you do or, if such self-disclosure seems inappropriate, to use other public figures as examples. Another approach in the affective arena is to give students the chance to help others so they can learn from experience how helping can make them feel good about themselves.

Teachers can influence the moral judgment of students at this level by pointing out lack of congruence between values and actions, although some adolescents may resist and assume a defensive posture. Teachers can also engage in rational discussions about students' behavior, appeal to social responsibility, and orchestrate class discussions about moral issues. Teachers also might engage students in school and community projects that right injustices and inequity. After all, a democratic society is predicated on its citizens reaching this highest stage of moral justice.

Engaging Students in Self-Reflective Questioning

Teachers also can engage students in self-reflective questioning to facilitate their thinking about decision-making criteria. Following are some appropriate questions at each of the six stages for influencing a student's moral reasoning regarding respecting others' property offered by Froyen and Iverson (1999).

Stage 1: What do you think I should do when I see someone taking another student's backpack?

Stage 2: When you are tempted to help yourself to something that belongs to someone else, what can you ask yourself to reconsider that decision?

Stage 3: What can you do so that your classmates will think you are someone who respects their right to decide who can use their stuff?

Stage 4: What can you do if you see a classmate being forced to relinquish a personal possession to someone else?

Stage 5: What would life be like if people disregarded others' property rights?

Stage 6: How would your view of yourself as a responsible person be affected if you were told that you behaved in ways that others saw as inconsiderate of their property?

The reference points that one applies in decision making for determining what represents justice do not remain stable. The degree of complexity of a situation may constrain a child from applying the cognitive reasoning he or she has developed in intellectual functioning in a given moral dilemma. On the other hand, children often select a solution when presented with a moral dilemma that represents one stage higher than their current level of thinking, indicating that they are able to recognize a better solution than they might generate on their own (Froyen & Iverson, 1999).

Under one set of conditions a student may use Stage 1 criteria and in another set of circumstances adopt a Stage 3 perspective. Likewise, a teacher may choose to reinforce Stage 2 conceptions of justice or challenge students to function at Stage 6 by questioning the congruence between their values and their actions. Unless, or until, students have opportunities to test ideas, it is unlikely that moral reasoning will match cognitive capacity at the upper stages of moral development. In adolescence, the student has the cognitive capacity for reflectively viewing values and society, although not many students actually reach the highest stage of moral development during their school years where they base decisions on equity of human rights.

The Cultural Assimilator: Enhancing Cultural Awareness and Tolerance.   The Cultural Assimilator is an intercultural training strategy intended to help students understand the perspectives of persons from other cultures and to teach them about those cultures (Albert, 1983). Teachers can devise a variety of their own ways to use appropriate cultural assimilators in their classrooms to enhance moral judgment, cultural awareness, and acceptance of differences.

The Cultural Assimilator consists of a number of situations, episodes, or critical incidents depicting interactions between persons from two cultures, followed by alternate attributions or explanations of their behavior. Each incident presents typical interaction situations in which misunderstandings are likely to occur. The four alternate attributions presented are all plausible interpretations of the situation, three of them fitting best the assumptions of the learner's culture, the fourth being a typical attribution of the other (target) culture. Learners read the incident and the alternative attributions and select the one attribution they believe members of the other culture typically choose. After each choice, learners receive culturally relevant, misperception-correcting feedback.

The example, *The Rock Concert*, illustrates this approach, giving culture assimilator critical incidents, alternative attributions, and corrective feedback.

CULTURAL ASSIMILATOR: THE ROCK CONCERT

Judy is a 15-year-old U.S. high school student spending a month in Mexico as part of an international living program. She lives with a middle-class Mexican family and has become a good friend of the 14-year-old daughter, Rosa, and her circle of girlfriends. Judy finds life in Mexico interesting because of the novelty of the situation but feels a little frustrated at the restricted range of activities she is permitted to indulge in compared with her life back home. Whenever she suggests they do something a little different or daring, the others seem very uncomfortable and refuse to discuss it.

Thus, she is excited to learn that a popular American rock group is to play in the city next week and suggests to Rosa and her friends that they all go. Although they admit they would like to go, the others look very apprehensive and say they could never get permission to attend such an event. Judy then proposes that they pretend to visit someone else and sneak off to the concert. The group refuses even to consider the idea, and Judy concludes exasperatedly that they are a very unadventurous lot.

What is the source of the Mexican girls' reluctance to consider Judy's proposal?

1. They are much more conscious of conforming to social norms than Judy.
2. They resent Judy (a foreigner) trying to tell them what to do.
3. They do not really want to go to the rock concert and are just making excuses so as not to offend Judy.
4. They are scared of what might happen at the concert but do not wish to admit their fears.

Here are rationales for the alternative explanations.

1. This is the most probable explanation. In Latin cultures the socialization of children is strictly controlled (especially for girls), and they learn early the value and necessity of conforming to social norms. Behavior that may be viewed in more individualistic (and less conforming) societies as simply adventurous or explorative is regarded in conformist societies with apprehension and as potentially disruptive of the close, interdependent social network. Thus, there is a lower rate of rebelliousness or delinquency among the young in such societies. The Mexican girls are much more conscious than Judy of the need to strictly adhere to social norms and expected behavior, and they fear the consequences and shame they may experience if they do not. Sojourners should be aware of the social pressures to conform in such cultures and should not place hosts in situations in which they are asked to go against social norms.
2. There is little indication that this is the case. They seem to accept Judy as part of their group and although they may not be willing to take up her suggestions, they do not resent them. There is a more probable explanation.

(continued)

CULTURAL ASSIMILATOR   Continued

3. This seems unlikely. They are probably as interested in rock music as Judy, and probably would not see the need to fabricate excuses to Judy if they were not. There is a better explanation.
4. They are not so much afraid of what may happen at the concert as of the consequences if it is found out that they did attend.

From R. W. Brislin, K. Cushner, C. Cherrie, and M. Yong. *Intercultural interactions: A practical guide.* Newbury Park, CA: Sage Publications, 1986, pp. 82, 105, 106. Reprinted by permission.

STRATEGIES FOR ENHANCING SELF-MANAGEMENT

Often students will need to increase their repertoire of skills in order to make more appropriate choices to control and manage their own behavior. Most students need to be taught strategies for dealing more effectively in trying situations that evoke such feelings as hurt, anger, disappointment, frustration, and so forth. This section offers specific strategies that teach students alternative behavior and decision-making strategies.

Social skills training is an umbrella that includes a variety of skills. Generally, it refers to teaching students coping skills for dealing with situations that pose problems for many students. Social skills strategies include helping students learn to manage their own impulses, control anger, and cope with disappointment and frustration. Also included is helping students build positive relationships, deal with the unreasonable behavior of others, and use problem-solving strategies.

Traditionally, the terms *social skills* or *coping skills* have been used for any skills or strategies that help students manage their behavior in ways that are productive to learning and adaptive to the demands of the classroom setting. Attempts to modify behaviors, cognitions (beliefs and attitudes), and emotions are all included here. Specific intervention strategies can be behavioral, physiological, or cognitive or strategies that use a combination of these approaches. Labels such as problem solving, self-instructional training, self-control, cognitive and metacognitive strategies, aggression replacement training, anger and stress management, coping skills, and life skills have all been used to describe types of social skills training.

Different approaches to social skills training involve variations in levels and intensity of training. Alternatives available range from traditional lessons, which create an awareness and offer specific strategies, to structured learning that involves teaching a series of steps or subskills to master, to long-term processes, which involve modifying basic beliefs and self-talk (cognitive–metacognitive strategies).

Teaching social skills is not different from teaching other skills in that effective instruction involves using direct instruction, including explaining, demonstrating, modeling, guided practice, and providing opportunities for performance feedback. Modeling is especially important in teaching social skills, as is engaging in role playing. As with other complex skills, teaching social skills may involve breaking down the desired skill into components that may need to be taught separately.

Because many of today's students lack desired social and self-management skills, many now believe that these skills should be taught not only in special settings such as special education classes or counseling sessions but also as part of the mainstream curriculum.

Teaching Emotional Literacy

Currently the goal of raising students' levels of social and emotional competence applies not only to those identified for special programming (e.g., emotionally disturbed, troubled, at risk) but also for every child as part of a set of necessary skills. This position is based on the ground-breaking work of Goleman (1995) set forth in his best-selling book *Emotional Intelligence.*

Teaching emotional literacy has its roots in affective education that began in the 1960s. The difference between eras according to Goleman is that the current movement turns the term inside out—instead of using affect to educate, it teaches affect itself. More recently the momentum has come from the documented success of many school-based prevention programs, targeting specific problems such as school dropouts, drug use, teen pregnancy, and violence. Research shows that such programs are more successful when they directly teach coping skills such as managing anger, handling frustration, being assertive, and resolving conflicts constructively.

The current emphasis is on taking the lessons learned from highly focused programs for targeted youth and generalizing them as a preventive measure for all students, with skills being taught by general classroom teachers or school personnel. This departure brings emotional literacy into schools by making aspects of students' emotional and social lives viable topics in themselves. Embedded in the general curriculum, delivered regularly and imparted over a sustained period of time, emotional lessons become ingrained. As experiences are repeated over time, the brain reflects them as strengthened pathways, neuron connections to be accessed in times of trouble (Caine & Caine, 1997).

Recognizing it as much more complex than had been considered, the notion of intelligence has been drastically reconceived. The work of many experts has contributed to this growth in understanding: This work includes Goleman (1995) on emotional intelligence, Gardner (1993) on multiple intelligences, Sternberg (1988) on executive intelligence, and Perkins (1995) on reflective intelligence.

Researchers have begun to redefine what it means to be intelligent, and out of that research, a much more powerful predictor of future success has emerged called emotional literacy. Even more important is the evidence that many types of intelligence are learnable. Many attribute this discovery, at least in part, to brain research that provides a much deeper understanding of the link between thinking and emotions (Bocchino, 1999; Caine & Caine, 1997; Combs, 1991; Goleman, 1999; Perkins, 1995). The term *emotional literacy* is a purposeful distinction from the term emotional intelligence. Emotional intelligence is the characteristic, or potential, that can be nurtured and developed in a person. Emotional literacy is the constellation of understandings, skills, and strategies that a person can develop and nurture throughout a lifetime (Bocchino, 1999). The intended outcome of teaching emotional literacy is emotional competence as a learned capacity to better deal with everyday life situations.

Models for Teaching Emotional Literacy.   The three models outlined in the following section are being used as the basis of a number of educational programs currently being used in the schools to teach emotional literacy.

The Life Skills Model is based on combined systems of psychotherapy, preventative health curriculums, and discipline–parenting programs (Peele & Brodsky, 1991; Larzarus 1997; Seligman 1995).

The Life Skills Model

1. Emotional Management. The ability to label one's emotional state, see the relationship between thinking and emotional consequences, and develop an internal locus of control.

2. Self-Regulation or Soothing. The ability to reduce tension or stress through self-talk such as "Ease up and let it go," thereby relaxing without resorting to inappropriate behaviors such as having a temper tantrum.
3. Goal Formation. The ability to develop a goal or a set of goals based on the individual's long-term self-interest.
4. Problem Solving. The ability to develop a step-by-step plan to deal with either an interpersonal conflict or practical problem.
5. Communication Skills. The ability to use language in a socially acceptable manner and have one's message clearly understood by others.
6. Behavioral Skills. The ability to act in an assertive versus aggressive manner in conflict situations.
7. Literacy and Academic Skills. The ability to develop sufficient mastery in reading, writing, math, etc., in order to survive occupationally in one's life.

The Significant Seven model is based on the work of Glenn and Nelson (2000).

The Significant Seven

Life Resources

Types of Outcomes

1. Perceptions of Personal Capabilities
   Capable of facing problems and challenges and learning through experiences.
2. Perceptions of Personal Significance
   Capable of contributing in significant ways and believing that life has meaning and purpose.

   Three pillars of healthy self-concept and healthy self-esteem
3. Perceptions of Personal Influence
   Capacity to understand that one's actions and choices influence one's life and to hold oneself accountable.
4. Intrapersonal Skills
   Capacity to manage emotions through self-assessment, self-control, and self-discipline.
5. Interpersonal Skills
   Capacities to communicate, cooperate, negotiate, share, empathize, resolve conflicts, and listen effectively when dealing with people.

   Twin pillars of emotional intelligence, self-discipline, and effective relationships
6. Strategic Skills
   Capacity to respond to the limits and consequences imposed by everyday life with responsibility, adaptability, flexibility, and integrity.

   Social and personal responsibility
7. Judgment Skills
   Capacities for planning and identifying choices and making decisions based on wisdom and moral and ethical principles such as honesty, respect, fairness, equality, and compassion.

   Decision making, moral and ethical development

The Emotional Competence Framework is based on Goleman's (1995, 1998) work.

The Emotional Competence Framework
Personal Competence.   These competencies determine how we manage ourselves.

Self-Awareness.   Knowing one's internal states, preferences, resources, and intuitions

- Emotional awareness. Recognizing one's emotions and their effects
- Accurate self-assessment. Knowing one's inner resources, abilities, and limits
- Self-confidence. A strong sense of one's self-worth and capabilities

Self-Regulation.   Managing one's internal states, impulses, and resources

- Self-Control. Keeping disruptive emotions and impulses in check
- Trustworthiness. Maintaining honesty and integrity
- Conscientiousness. Taking responsibility for personal performance
- Adaptability. Flexibility in handling and responding to change
- Innovation. Being open to novel ideas, approaches, and new information

Motivation.   Emotional tendencies that guide or facilitate reaching goals

- Achievement drive. Striving to improve or meet a standard of excellence
- Commitment. Aligning with the goals of the group or organization
- Initiative. Readiness to act on opportunities
- Optimism. Persistence in pursuing goals despite obstacles and setbacks

Social Competence.   These competencies determine how we handle relationships.

Empathy.   Awareness of others' feelings, needs, and concerns

- Understanding others. Sensing others' feelings and perspectives, and taking an active interest in their concerns
- Developing others. Sensing others' development needs and bolstering their abilities
- Service orientation. Anticipating, recognizing, and meeting others' needs
- Leveraging diversity. Seeing diversity as opportunity and respecting people with diverse backgrounds
- Political awareness. Reading social and emotional currents and power relationships

Social Skills.   Adeptness at inducing desirable responses in others

- Influence. Wielding effective tactics for persuasion
- Communication. Listening openly and sending convincing messages
- Conflict management. Negotiating and resolving disagreements
- Leadership. Inspiring and guiding individuals and groups
- Change catalyst. Initiating or managing change
- Building bonds. Cultivating and nurturing instrumental relationships
- Collaboration and cooperation. Working with others toward shared goals
- Team capabilities. Creating group synergy in pursuing collective goals

Strategies for Social Skill Enhancement

Specific skill instruction and structured learning experiences can enable students to learn social and coping skills that will help them develop positive peer relationships, work cooperatively in learning groups, and participate productively in classroom activities. Many strategies advocated for effectively teaching social skills are the same as those for teaching academic skills. These strategies emphasize teacher modeling of self-questioning and providing examples from the teacher's own life experiences (i.e., metacognitive strategies). Students are prompted to think ahead. Specifically, students can be taught and prompted to

- Think of a number of different alternatives to solve particular problems
- Determine what is likely to happen when a particular strategy is chosen
- Predict short-term versus long-term consequences
- Compare results of similar strategies
- Contrast results of different strategies
- Analyze best and worst that could happen
- List pros and cons, payoffs and costs, or benefits and burdens of alternative choices

Structured Learning for Teaching Social Skills

Goldstein and his colleagues (1983) have advocated structured learning as a method for teaching social skills. Characterized by regular and systematic direct instruction, structured learning incorporates four methodological elements: modeling, role playing, performance feedback, and transfer of training. Structured learning is best conducted in groups of five to eight students. The approach has been adapted for use in the general classroom setting as well as the special class and is generally recommended for students in the upper elementary grades through senior high. In structured learning a single skill is taught by following a sequential order of presentation that involves moving from a modeling phase to a transfer phase.

Modeling.   The teacher exposes the group to examples of the skill by presenting several different examples of the skill being used in different settings with different people. The teacher breaks down the skill into specific behavioral steps that are demonstrated in the modeling displays, then elicits group discussion. The focus of the discussion is on the personal impact of the modeling on each member of the group.

Role Plays.   Role plays are developed from the examples generated by students in the discussion. Each student is given an opportunity to role play (or practice) the skill following the behavioral steps that comprise the skill. The teacher's role is to provide support in the form of suggestions and coaching throughout the role play.

Performance Feedback.   Following the role play, the teacher asks for performance feedback such as praise, constructive criticism, or approval from the main actor and the other group members. The goal is to provide the main actor with support, as well as suggestions on how to become more effective in using the given skill.

Transfer of Training.   The final phase of structured learning is generalization of the skill beyond the classroom setting to enhance the probability that the skill will transfer into the student's real-life behavior repertoire. To facilitate transfer of learning, overlearning and real-life reinforcement are used. Overlearning occurs when the student is given the opportunity to practice the skill in different situations and over a long period of time. Real-life reinforcement occurs when teachers give students feedback and recognition whenever they see the skill being applied. They might also make suggestions on when the student can use a given strategy.

The following strategies enhance the transfer and maintenance of social skills in the structured learning approach (McGinnis & Goldstein, 1984).

1. Providing instruction in natural environments in which the skill is actually needed or in a setting that is similar to those environments in which the skill is to be used

2. Teaching the skill in the context of a variety of situations and settings through multiple role plays with different persons

3. Ensuring overlearning of the skill by practicing several times in different sets of circumstances

4. Planning withdrawal of instruction with periodic review and reteaching of the skills as needed

5. Teaching students to use the skill when conditions indicate the skill would be applicable

6. Planning for opportunities in which students can practice the skills they learned in the teaching session

Structured learning can be integrated into the teacher's behavior management system such that when problems arise in the classroom, the teacher elicits a prosocial response from the student by suggesting that the steps to a particular skill be used. This provides a positive alternative to reprimanding the student for having the problem, as well as a means for teaching the student when to use a given skill. In so doing, the teacher is reminding the student what to do rather than what not to do. Such an approach turns naturally occurring problem situations into learning opportunities and provides an environment in which a positive emphasis is placed on learning how to deal with interpersonal problems.

Role Reversal

Role reversal can be a useful technique in structured learning, especially with older students. It can be especially helpful when a student's performance anxiety creates difficulty in role playing his or her own role. The teacher or even a peer can act out the main actor role, while the main actor takes on the role of the person with whom he or she has the problem. In this case, role reversal assists the student by having another person model the behaviors the student him or herself needs for dealing with the specific problem. Role reversal may also contribute to the student's empathy or understanding of the other person's position.

Using the Role Play Effectively

Role playing is a creative series of enactments and reenactments in which students have the opportunity to analyze a problem, explore their feelings about it, and then consider many different alternatives and the consequences of those alternatives. In role playing, students experience situations in an environment that is safer than that of real life. Role playing can be used to enact a wide variety of school situations for the group's input and to provide opportunities for class members to give feedback and discuss their perceptions of the situation.

Role playing is especially useful in solving relationship problems among students. It is a valuable intervention for helping students stand back and look at their problems through the eyes of others. It can help students understand the situation of another who might be feeling rejected, unwanted, or unable to handle frustration in an acceptable manner.

Morgan and Reinhart (1991) describe three uses for role playing as an effective intervention strategy.

Clarifying a Problem. This intervention is used to enact an incident that needs clarification, such as a fight. It brings out not only the details of the incident but also the emotions that precipitated the event. The incident (the fight) is acted out only up to the point of contact.

This type of role playing serves several purposes for both the teacher and the students. The teacher does not have to try to figure out who did what to whom first and does not have to serve as the judge and jury. The teacher will not have to lecture, reprimand, or pass judgment. Instead, the students observe the role play, discuss it, and then they decide. To begin the role play, the teacher insists that the students show, not tell, what happened.

Role playing is helpful for students because they gain insight into their own behavior. In time, they learn to recognize what starts conflicts, how they become involved, and how they often create their own problems.

When the role play is finished, the teacher recounts the details observed and turns it over to the group. The following types of questions can be asked.

Now, what did you all notice?

How did that make _____ feel?

What about _____'s feelings?

What really happened here?

What could be done?

Finding Solutions.   This type of role play is used to demonstrate to and impress upon the students that many problems have more than one solution. It is important for the students to see how others feel in certain situations and to discover for themselves that certain behaviors do not solve some problems. In this type of role play, the event or problem is acted out more than once.

For the first enactment, the involved students make a report of what happened. Then actors are assigned (*not* the students involved), and they act out the incident exactly as it was described. A group meeting follows where the teacher asks several questions to get everybody involved in finding optional solutions to the problem. The teacher might start by saying "Let's discuss what you liked about the way this problem was handled. Were there any mistakes made? Was there a solution? How many think they could handle this situation in a better way?"

For the second enactment, the teacher designates a new set of actors who act out the same situation, but this time they must come up with a different solution. This is followed with another group discussion asking the same questions. Also, the group is asked to compare the two solutions and determine which one was most helpful.

Getting in Touch and Developing Empathy.   This type of role play is used to help students become aware of their feelings and to recognize the impact that their emotions have on their bodies and how their behavior is affected. Empathy for others does not come about until students are in touch with their own feelings first. There are a number of situations and problems experienced by almost all students that can be used to help students get in touch with their own feelings and begin developing empathy for others. Following is a list of situations that can be used.

- Someone told a lie about you.
- Someone tore up your paper.
- Someone shoved your books off the desk.
- Someone called you a name.
- Someone told you to shut up.
- You have just failed a test.
- You stole something and now you have to face up to it.

The teacher begins by inventing situations that cause emotional reactions. Then the students are asked to "freeze" their facial expressions. For younger students, a mirror can be passed around so that they can see how they are affected by their emotions. The teacher points out all of the outward signs of emotion such as frowning, rolling their eyes, and twisting their mouths.

This is followed by having them freeze their whole bodies and describe where they feel tension. Next they should improvise a dialogue with another person and act out the situation. As in the other types of role play, the group observes and provides other alternatives to the actors' solutions.

In designing a role play experience, teachers need to prepare students to participate; engage students in warm-up activities; structure the actual role playing; and provide for adequate closure to help students integrate the experience. The following guidelines will help teachers develop role plays that are meaningful to students and promote personal reflection and growth.

Setting the Stage.   It is important that the teacher convey to the students that there are many problems that are not easily solved. The teacher should emphasize that there are many solutions to most problems and that everyone has difficulty from time to time.

In setting the stage for the role play, the teacher presents the problem the students are going to act out and gives them time to think about it beforehand. To set the tone for the role play, students should be warmed up to the characters by teacher questioning such as

- What is _____ like?
- How does _____ feel?
- What do you think _____ is thinking about?

The teacher should be careful not to typecast a particular student who frequently engages in aggressive behavior, fighting, swearing, yelling, crying, and so forth.

Warm-Up.   Because role playing may be a new experience for many students, they may be uncomfortable at first. Initial warm-up activities for younger students might include asking them to pretend that they have just won a ball game and then that they have just lost. They might also be asked to act as if they were walking home on a cold day.

With primary children, teachers can give them practice in a nonthreatening atmosphere by starting out with games and warm-ups that have the whole class participating, building in students a feeling of confidence in role playing.

Here are some warm-ups to get started.

Picking Cherries.   Have children stretch up high, to the sides, behind them. This gets the blood flowing.

Statues.   Give children a statue to become, such as the world's strongest person or a person catching a huge fish.

Rubber band.   Tell students that their bodies are rubber bands, and that they stretch them by spreading their hands.

The Role Play.   The teacher decides when to stop the role play. If the role play gets off focus, the teacher stops the role play and asks questions such as

- Are you really playing the character?
- What kind of person is _____?

- Are we working on the problem?
- Does this seem like something _____ would really do?

It should be noted that this is not a time to reprimand or allow other members of the group to tell one of the actors what to do. The student should be allowed to work out his or her own idea of the role.

The teacher should instruct the audience to watch how the different characters act in the situation and be prepared to make suggestions for alternate solutions.

One type of situation in which it is preferable for a teacher to play a part is when inappropriate behaviors must be enacted as part of the role-play situation. A student should not be placed in the position of exhibiting inappropriate behaviors even when the goal is to create a realistic role-play situation. Often the students enjoy the part of tormentors, and this is easily carried too far, with the main point of the role play being lost. In addition, you do not want students acting in the role-play setting in ways you do not want them to act in real-life settings. It is also beneficial to have the teacher participate in a role-play when it is crucial to have an adult role realistically portrayed.

Discussion and Closure.   The class should evaluate how well each part was portrayed and how each could have been more effective. The teacher can structure the discussion by asking probing questions such as

- What was the solution?
- Was the problem solved?
- How do you suppose _____ felt?
- What would you have done?
- Where could you use what you have learned today?

The teacher should try to bring about an awareness that each individual performed the part differently and encourage discussion of individual differences in student styles, background, and experiences. It is important to bring closure to the experience to help students process the role play and make personal connections.

■ ■ ■ ■ ■ ■ ■ ■ ■

LEARNING PRACTICE TASK: DESIGNING A ROLE PLAY

Activity Directions: Working with a small group, design a role-play experience to address a class, group, or individual problem area (e.g., excessive peer criticism, group exclusion, lack of consideration for others' feelings). First define the problem, then create a structured role-play scenario.

Problem to be addressed

_____

_____

_____

Role play experience

(Include a warm-up activity, guidelines for the role play, a selection procedure for the actors and audience, and a closure activity.)

_____

_____

Red Light, Green Light: A Strategy for Developing Empathy

Red Light, Green Light is a strategy used to help students learn to develop empathy for others (Bocchino, 1999). In this technique, a red-light behavior is something someone else does that makes you see red. The student first recognizes his or her feelings and then identifies the behavior that is upsetting. Once the behavior and emotion (the red light) are identified, the student moves on to the yellow-light question, "Under what circumstances or conditions would I behave like that?" Here, the student is encouraged to brainstorm many options. It is important to help the student realize that although the first response might be to say that he or she would never respond that way, there must be some circumstances that would lead him or her to such behaviors. It is his or her responsibility as an emotionally literate person to imagine what they might be. Using this strategy, students begin to recognize that sometimes it is lack of knowledge, skill, or information that contributes to inappropriate behaviors or decisions. After answering the yellow-light question, the student decides how to "go." In the green-light step, the student chooses a specific behavior, a way to go forward. Armed with his or her understanding of possible contributing factors that have led to the other student's inappropriate behavior, the student can make better choices regarding his or her own response. This is the "green-light" choice. By this time, the student is much more likely to be able to make a clearer, wiser decision.

TEACHING COGNITIVE BEHAVIOR MANAGEMENT (CBM) STRATEGIES

Recent strategies for modifying student behavior focus more on internalized behaviors such as thoughts and feelings as powerful mediators for behavior. Such intervention strategies are generally referred to as cognitive or metacognitive strategies. Attempts to modify behavior are directed toward the covert behaviors of thinking and feeling as the primary vehicles for appraising and interpreting events.

Our beliefs (cognitive structures) strongly influence both the way we think about something (cognitive processes) and our self-talk (inner speech or covert self-instruction). Our thinking process, which materializes in our inner speech, forms the basis for our behavior. This position is represented in a category of interventions typically labeled *cognitive behavior modification (CBM)* as distinguished from conventional behavior modification, which focuses primarily on externally directed environmental changes.

Meichenbaum is often considered the founder of cognitive behavior modification (CBM), a self-management strategy emphasizing helping students think before acting. His work has shown that students are quite capable of managing their own behavior with teacher-mediated instruction, guidance, and practice. He has developed self-management techniques that students can use to gain control over their actions as well as effective procedures for teaching students to employ these techniques consistently in the school setting.

Some children in the classroom seem to know what to do and just do it. These children have a series of adaptive routines and procedural scripts for performing both academic and social tasks that allow them to be self-directed. In contrast, some children, especially those with attentional problems and hyperactivity, tend to have difficulty in following rules and procedures, especially when they are designed to sustain their behavior over a period of time and when they don't receive continual feedback.

Cognitive behavior management intervention strategies are: self-administered; emphasize self-control; involve self-talk; and use modeling. The characteristics that distinguish cognitive behavior management from other forms of behavior management used to modify student behavior are

1. Students themselves rather than the teacher serve as the primary change agents (if not initially, at least by the end).
2. The focus is on helping students gain self-control.
3. Verbalization is a primary component. The student talks to him- or herself, first out loud, then on a covert level (silently).
4. Modeling is an essential element.

Three cognitive behavior management strategies have been used successfully for promoting positive behavior change in school settings: cognitive restructuring, self-instructional training, and stress inoculation.

Cognitive Restructuring: Changing Irrational Beliefs That Lead to Problem Behavior

Cognitive restructuring simply means modifying one's beliefs. The basic theory underlying cognitive restructuring training is that

Behavior is a manifestation of the feelings produced by what we are thinking. The way to change problem behavior is to modify the irrational thinking that leads to the behavior problem.

Cognitive restructuring is a strategy applied to modify irrational beliefs. Rational beliefs are distinguished from irrational beliefs by the following characteristics.

Rational Beliefs	**Irrational Beliefs**
Follow from reality	Do not follow from reality
Are supported by evidence	Are not supported by evidence
Help you get what you want	Do not help you get what you want
Lead to appropriate feelings (irritation, regret, concern, sadness)	Lead to inappropriate feelings (anger, guilt, anxiety, depression)

| Are realistic assessments of a situation (inconvenient, frustrating) | Are extreme exaggerations of a situation (awful, terrible) |
| Are preferences or desires | Are demands placed on oneself, others, or the universe (shoulds, musts, oughts) |

Examples of common irrational beliefs many children and youth hold include

- I must be stupid if I make mistakes.
- Everything must go my way all the time.
- I never have any control over what happens to me.
- I must be good at everything I do.
- If people do things I don't like, they must be bad and need to be punished.
- Everyone should treat me fairly all the time.
- I should not have to wait for what I want.
- I should not have to do anything I don't want to.

Belief systems develop through modeling and reinforcement. This is why many children use only aggressive behaviors when they are frustrated or want something—these are the only behaviors they have experienced.

Because beliefs are learned, they can also be unlearned through the process of restructuring. Many of the basic beliefs we learned in childhood are actually irrational beliefs (Ellis & Harper, 1975). As a child grows, the child begins to incorporate a sublanguage that serves to attribute meaning to the events occurring in his or her life. This sublanguage eventually becomes the child's belief system, which develops as does language, primarily through modeling.

The belief system of the significant person(s) in the child's life will largely determine whether the child thinks rationally or irrationally about the events in his or her life. If, for example, the child misbehaves and the parent(s) says, "You know better than to do that!" the child will most likely come to believe, "It's bad to make a mistake, I am bad because I make mistakes and because I'm bad I should be punished." The more rational belief is that mistakes are a normal part of learning and that making a mistake doesn't make me bad. If I didn't learn this as a child, I will probably continue to interpret my mistakes as intolerable unless I am able to dispute and change my belief. If I hold onto this belief, I am likely to set unrealistic expectations for myself and others.

Ellis (1974) takes the position that much of our behavior is influenced by the way we feel and that our feelings are a product of our beliefs. When individuals hold an irrational belief, they are likely to behave inappropriately because the irrational thinking produces a negative emotional state (e.g., anger, anxiety). An event triggers a counterproductive belief, often at an unconscious level, and strong emotions surface, generally manifesting in a maladaptive behavior.

Ellis developed an intervention program originally called rational-emotive therapy (RET) based on the premise that it is not life events that cause a person distress, rather it is the way a person views the events that causes the emotional reaction (Ellis & Bernard, 1984).

More recent terminology applied to these strategies is rational-emotive behavior therapy (REBT), specific interventions for addressing problematic behavior, and rational-emotive behavior education (REBE), preventive educational strategies. Rational-emotive behavior therapy (REBT) is based on the belief that most emotional problems and behaviors stem from irrational self-statements people make when events in their lives do not turn out as they want them to. The focus of intervention is on identifying irrational beliefs and replacing them with more logical, reality-based ways of interpreting events.

Fundamentally, REBT attempts to show individuals how they behave in self-defeating ways and how they can change these ways. Teachers and others in helping roles serve as clarifiers, helping students to see more clearly that they have a range of alternative reactions for any given situation.

According to Ellis and Harper (1975), these irrational ideas are developed early in life from a variety of sources. These include our inability to accurately distinguish real from imagined dangers; our dependence as children on the thinking of others; the biases and prejudices inculcated by our parents; and the indoctrinations by the mass media of our culture.

Although there are literally hundreds of irrational beliefs that cause emotional distress, Ellis and his colleagues identified twelve fundamental irrational beliefs, of which three account for most of our irrational thinking (Bernard & DiGiuseppe, 1994; Ellis & Harper, 1975). These three basic irrational beliefs are learned in childhood and they typically plague us and cause us to function ineffectively throughout our lives. These beliefs are related to how we perceive personal rejection, personal competence, and fairness. These beliefs are (1) you *must* have love and approval *all* of the time from *all* of the people you consider significant; (2) you must prove yourself thoroughly competent, adequate, and achieving; and (3) you must view life as awful or catastrophic when things do not go the way you would like them to go. There are also several other second-order irrational beliefs that typically arise after one of the three basic beliefs is operating.

The main intervention strategy used with students is *disputing irrational beliefs* (Bernard & Joyce, 1984; DiGiuseppe, 1999; Ellis & Dryden, 1997; Vernon, 2002). Here the student either goes through a structured process with the help of the teacher or alone. Disputing irrational beliefs has students go through the following process.

Describe the event eliciting a behavior
Identify their thoughts and feelings
Describe their response
Provide support for their thoughts
Dispute their thoughts by providing counter evidence
Replace their irrational thoughts with more productive thoughts

The process involves the following seven steps.

Step 1: Describe the event associated with the inappropriate behavior.

Step 2: Identify the thinking triggered by the event. What does the student usually think or say to him- or herself? This is difficult for students because they don't actually "speak to themselves." If students get stuck here they may need some prompting, such as providing a list for the student to choose from. Or, the teacher may provide a scenario to illustrate the irrational thinking.

Step 3: Describe the feeling the student has when he or she thinks about the belief and the event. Here the teacher may need to use role playing or guided imagery to help the student identify the feeling.

Step 4: Describe the behavior. The teacher may need to ask leading questions such as "What did you do when . . . ?"

Step 5: Provide evidence (facts) to support the student's belief.

Step 6: Give evidence that his or her belief might not be true. The teacher needs to be prepared to cite such evidence even if the student denies the validity of any evidence. If the student persists in denial, the teacher may ask the student to collect evidence that his or her belief is true while the teacher collects evidence that it is false. Then the teacher sits down with the student to compare data.

Step 7: Think of a rational belief or thought to take the place of the irrational belief. The teacher should prompt the student to practice saying the new belief to him- or herself or tape it and play it frequently. Alternatively, the student may read the statement from a card he or she carries around. Since changing a student's thinking is a long-term process, the teacher should periodically have the student review with the teacher ahead of time what he or she plans to do if an event likely to trigger the old thinking occurs.

This strategy can be used in a group or with an individual student, either verbally or in writing, with the teacher's facilitation. Roush (1984) offers an alternative approach that is more appropriate for use with younger students. He recommends that students become familiar with the following six types of irrational thinking so that they recognize them in others and in themselves.

1. Robot thinking ("It's not my fault.")
2. I Stink thinking ("It's all my fault.")
3. You Stink! thinking ("It's all your fault.")
4. Fairy Tale thinking ("That's not fair!")
5. Namby Pamby thinking ("I can't stand it!")
6. Doomsday thinking ("Woe is me!")

He uses the following five questions for challenging beliefs, and teaches the acronym *A FROG* to help students remember them.

A   Does it help keep me alive?
F   Does it make me feel better?
R   Is it based on reality?
O   Does it help me get along with others?
G   Does it help me reach my goals?

In Roush's approach to cognitive restructuring, the teacher cues students with comments like "It sounds like you're doing some 'You stink!' thinking. Are you?" If the student agrees, the teacher directs the student to consider each of the five questions.

Obviously, the task of cognitive restructuring is a difficult one. Teachers can help students learn to use the following progression.

■ Use a logical argument.
■ If necessary, move to an empirical argument where the student looks for physical evidence of the validity or fallacy of his or her belief.
■ If this fails, move to a functional argument in which the student is asked to examine whether the thinking makes him or her feel better or worse.

The following two illustrations provide examples of the three argument types for "You stink!" and "Doomsday" irrational thinking (Kaplan, 1995).

"You Stink!"

Logical: Do you do bad things (or things others don't like) sometimes? Are you a bad person? Should you always be punished for doing something that others don't like? Have the student try to give you an example of doing something to someone that he or she didn't like or thought was bad (e.g., calling someone a name or taking something away from someone, or disappointing another person). The point you want to get across is that people are fallible and often do things that hurt or disappoint others; if we do such things and we don't consider ourselves bad or deserving of punishment, why should we consider others bad and deserving of punishment?

Empirical: Have the student collect data to support (or disprove) his or her argument. For example, if the student believes that all teachers are always picking on him or her, have the student collect data for a few days on positive and negative comments teachers direct at him or her. Hopefully, these data will show that not all (but some) of the student's teachers pick on him or her some (not all) of the time.

Functional: Simply ask the student if his or her thinking makes him or her feel better or worse: *How do you feel when you think that all of your teachers always pick on you? Does that make you feel good or bad? Do you like feeling bad? Maybe if you changed your thinking you might start feeling better—wouldn't you like to feel better?*

"Doomsday"

Logical: Bad things are always happening. If you worry that bad things will happen all the time, you will never feel happy. It's not worth worrying about things over which you have little control.

Empirical: Have the student collect data about good or positive things that happened to him or her over a one-week period.

Functional: How do you feel when you think that only bad things happen to you?

Cognitive restructuring involves developing an awareness in students of those events and thoughts associated with negative feelings and resulting in inappropriate behaviors. Students need to first be in touch with their feelings, then reflect on the event or action that led to the feeling, before they can identify the thinking that mediated between the event and the feeling. For some students, this awareness will need to be developed at length prior to the use of other higher-order skills.

Teachers interested in implementing cognitive restructuring strategies can combine aspects of both of the approaches described, develop their own lessons and procedures to match their students' developmental levels, or use the approaches suggested in the commercial materials available.

Two more recent book series deal with a wide range of self-management and social skills areas, utilizing cognitive restructuring strategies. These are *The Passport Series: A Journey through Emotional, Social, Cognitive, and Self-development* (Vernon, 1998a, b, c) and *Program Achieve: A Curriculum of Lessons for Teaching Students how to Achieve and Develop Social-emotional-behavioral Well-being* (Bernard, 2001).

The following Angry Thinking–Positive Thinking Worksheet is an application of Ellis's disputing irrational beliefs. It simplifies his seven-step process into five steps. Teachers can find ways to infuse this or similar worksheets into ongoing classroom practices.

ANGRY THINKING–POSITIVE THINKING WORKSHEET

Directions: Describe the situation and your thoughts and feelings about the situation. Then write a different, more positive thought and the different feeling you would have.

What happened

_____

_____

_____

What I was thinking

_____

_____

_____

How I felt

_____

_____

_____

A different, more positive thought

_____

_____

_____

The new feeling

_____

_____

_____

Rough Spot Training: A REBE Program for Primary Students

According to its authors London and Monjes (1999), _rough spot_ training is a concrete strategy to help children develop more consistent emotional-behavior control that can easily be integrated into any system of supportive classroom discipline. The rough spot strategy combines components of the life skills model and rational-emotive behavior education (REBE). The life skills model is based on a merging of systems of psychotherapy, preventative health curriculums, and discipline–parenting systems. It is composed of seven skills: emotional management, self-regulation or soothing, goal formation, problem solving, communication skills, behavioral skills, and literacy and academic skills. Rough spot training helps young children develop the first three skills through cognitive mediation and restructuring. These three primary life skills mainly are developed when a child develops cognitive proficiency as described in the following (Kendall & Braswell, 1985):

1. **Rational evaluations (cool self-talk)** that lead to the arousal of healthy emotional responses to life situations. ("I don't like this but I can deal with it!")
2. **Self-regulating self-talk** that leads to physical relaxation. ("Stop. Take a deep breath and relax.")
3. **Self-reinforcement self-talk** that leads to internal reinforcement for emotional or behavioral choices. ("Good for me! I'm staying cool and in control.")
4. **Goal formation self-talk** that leads to self-cueing about what the child wants to emotionally experience about a life situation. ("I don't like feeling this way. What would be a good 'cool thought' to think now?")

The specific goals of rough spot training are these.

1. Teach the relationship between self-talk and emotional arousal and behavioral choices.
2. Help develop a more internal locus of control.

3. Develop a set of rational beliefs (cool self-talks) to replace irrational beliefs (hot self-talks).
4. Decrease the frequency, intensity, and duration of unhealthy anger, low-frustration tolerance, worry, and hurt feelings.
5. Build proficiency with the first three life skills and generalize these abilities to ongoing and new life situations.

The program consists of five lessons, each taking about 25 minutes. Thereafter, the teacher only spends a few minutes daily going over a child's rough spot as it occurs. The first lesson concretely defines what a rough spot is and helps students identify their rough spots. It is defined for students as

> *A rough spot is anything I find*
> - *unpleasant*
> - *uncomfortable*
> - *hard*
> - *unfair*

Next they learn "how to shrink a rough spot" by using "cool self-talks." They are presented with the following rule.

> **The Self-Talk Rule:** *The way I make myself think*
> *is the way I will make myself feel.*
> *And the way I make myself feel is the way I will*
> *make myself think.*
> *Because how I make myself think and feel*
> *is the way I am going to behave or act!*

Then students are taught to distinguish between the two types of self-talk utilizing a poster depicting hot self-talks and their corresponding cool self-talks.

Hot Self-Talks
- I can't stand it!

- I just can't be happy at all if it is this way. This is too hard!

- I am no good because people do not like me!

- Poor me! I can't deal with this at all!

- It, he, she, makes me mad/angry!

- It just can't be this way!

- I am no good because I can't do it!

Cool Self-Talks
- I don't have to like it to do it! I can still handle doing this!

- This is hard, but I can deal with it!

- Too bad! Not everyone has to like me! I can deal with that!

- It is only too bad but not the end of the world!

- No one or nothing can make me feel mad or hurt! I can choose not to make myself upset over it!

- It does not have to be the way I want all the time!

- Just because I did not get it, doesn't mean I won't if I keep trying!

Students learn that *hot self-talks* make a rough spot bigger and harder to deal with and *cool self-talks* you say to yourself shrink a rough spot and make it smaller, smoother, and much easier to deal with.

The fourth lesson uses guided practice through story telling and real-life illustrations. As a final component of the program, students learn to use self-help recording sheets on an ongoing basis when they have a rough spot. The following is an example.

Helping Myself

Name _____ Date _____

My rough spot is _____

_____

My hot self-talks are

1. _____
2. _____
3. _____

I can change the way I make myself think by telling myself these cool self-talks

1. _____

_____

2. _____

_____

3. _____

_____

SELF-INSTRUCTIONAL TRAINING (SIT) STRATEGIES

Self-instructional training is based on the work of Luria (1961) and Vygotsky (1962), whose research on socialization and language development suggests that young children go through three stages where others' speech initially controls their behavior, then their own overt speech, and eventually their own inner speech governs their behavior. The basic theory that underlies self-instructional training is that language and socialization skill development is based on children moving from an overt speech stage to an inner-speech stage. Self-instructional training involves recreating this progression. Meichenbaum (1977) developed a practical program based on this theory to self-instruct children to control their behavior. His strategy has the following five steps.

1. **Cognitive modeling.** The teacher performs the task while talking out loud and the student observes.
2. **Overt external guidance.** The student and teacher perform the task while talking out loud together.
3. **Overt self-guidance.** The student performs the task while instructing him- or herself aloud, using the same verbalizations as the teacher.
4. **Faded overt self-guidance.** The student whispers the instructions (often in an abbreviated form) while going through the task.
5. **Covert self-instruction.** The student performs the task guided by inner speech, or self-talk.

The following example illustrates Meichenbaum's self-instructional strategy for self-control (Kaplan, 1995).

Self-Instructional Strategy for Self-Control Example

Step 1: Teacher models and talks out loud while student watches and listens.

    a. Teacher imitates student doing work and starting to get upset. Teacher says out loud, "My muscles are getting tense and my face feels hot. I must be starting to get upset. What am I supposed to do when I get upset about my work?"

    b. Teacher says out loud, "First, I'm supposed to take a few deep breaths."

    c. Teacher models diaphragmatic breathing.

    d. Teacher says out loud, "That feels better. What should I do next?"

    e. Teacher says out loud, "I'll raise my hand and ask for help."

    f. Teacher models hand raising and waiting-for-attention behavior.

    g. Teacher says out loud, "Good! I controlled my behavior. I can do it!"

Step 2: Student performs tasks while teacher gives instructions out loud.

    a. Student role plays self doing work and starting to get upset. Teacher says out loud, "My muscles are getting tense and my face feels hot. I must be starting to get upset. What am I supposed to do when I start to get upset about my work?"

    b. Teacher says out loud, "First, I'm supposed to take a few deep breaths."

    c. Student does diaphragmatic breathing.

    d. Teacher says out loud, "That feels better. What should I do next?"

    e. Teacher says out loud, "I'll raise my hand and ask for help."

    f. Student models hand raising and waiting-for-attention behavior.

    g. Teacher says, "Good! I controlled my behavior. I can do it!"

(Steps a through e are repeated in each step.)

Step 3: Student performs tasks while repeating steps out loud.

Step 4: Student performs tasks while whispering steps.

Step 5: Student performs tasks while thinking them.

Self-instructional strategies can be used to help students work on a variety of academic behaviors (paying attention, writing a report), social behaviors (reducing aggressive behavior, building tolerance for frustration, working cooperatively with others), and self-control (dealing with anger, provocation). The idea is that the student will eventually be able to talk him- or herself through the situation by going through the steps without teacher assistance. Sometimes cue cards are used to act as a reminder. Other helpful strategies include using peer modeling, cueing and prompting, rehearsing meaningful self-talk translated by the student into his or her own words, and encouraging and reinforcing use outside of the classroom.

The Sample Cue Card: Keeping Out of Fights illustrates a self-control strategy tailored to a particular student. It includes a self-evaluation component, so the student can evaluate his or her own performance. If these cards are completed on a regular basis, they can also provide assessment data for the teacher regarding the usefulness of the strategy.

SAMPLE CUE CARD: KEEPING OUT OF FIGHTS

1. Stop and count to ten.
2. Think about what is making you want to fight.

3. Decide what you want to happen.
4. Think about other choices besides fighting.
   a. Walk away from the situation (for now).
   b. Talk to the person in a calm voice.
   c. Ask the person for what you want.
   d. Ask someone for help solving the problem.
5. Do what you think is your best choice.

How did you do? Great _____ OK _____ Not so good _____

Following are some descriptions and examples of specific strategies. Examples of self-statements for dealing with anger and stress are included. Using self-talk strategies is also very useful for teachers. These strategies help to manage teachers' own behavior when dealing with difficult situations and serve as illustrations for students.

Self-Statements for Dealing with Anger and Stress

Stage 1: Preparing for an Anger-Provoking Situation
- *I won't let this get me mad.*
- *I'm ready. I know how to deal with this.*
- *I can follow my plan.*
- *I know what to do.*
- *I can do this.*
- *I know it's all up to me.*
- *I can handle my anger.*
- *I will not argue.*
- *I can control my thoughts.*
- *It won't be easy, but I'm confident.*
- *Don't take yourself too seriously.*

Stage 2: Reacting during the Encounter
- *Nothing can discourage me.*
- *Stay cool.*
- *No one else can control me.*
- *I don't have to prove myself.*
- *I'm not going to let this get to me.*

Accentuating the Positive
- *Keep things in perspective.*
- *Don't blow this out of proportion.*
- *It's not that important.*
- *I've got a handle on this situation and I can control it.*
- *Keep smiling. Hang in there.*
- *Keep a sense of humor.*

Stage 3: Coping with Anger Symptoms
- *I'm determined to handle this.*
- *I can feel my muscles starting to get tight.*

- *It won't get me anywhere to get angry.*
- *Getting upset won't do any good.*
- *I'm going to hold my ground, but I'm not going to get crazy.*
- *Be respectful—don't accuse.*
- *Be constructive, not destructive.*
- *Remember, I'm in control.*
- *I'm upset, but I'm handling myself pretty well.*
- *Take it easy, don't counterattack.*
- *I can't expect others to act the way I would.*
- *Try to relax. Take a few deep breaths.*

Stage 4: Reflecting on the Encounter Unresolved Conflict
- *I did not argue—that's progress.*
- *Don't take it to heart.*
- *Forget about it.*
- *This will take time to work out.*
- *Remember to relax.*
- *I'm not going to worry about it.*
- *I won't take it personally.*
- *I'll think positive thoughts.*
- *It's not that serious.*
- *I'm not going to let this get me down.*

Resolved Conflict, Successful Coping
- *I did it!*
- *I'm proud of myself.*
- *I really handled that well.*
- *It wasn't as bad as I thought.*
- *I kept myself from getting angry.*
- *I can control myself.*
- *I'm getting better at this all the time.*

Skill Alternatives to Aggression: Using Self-Control is an example of a structured sequential program which is more general. It incorporates stress inoculation by paying attention to body signals and connects the event with the feeling, a cognitive restructuring strategy.

■ ■ ■ ■ ■ ■ ■ ■

SKILL ALTERNATIVES TO AGGRESSION: USING SELF-CONTROL

STEPS	TRAINER NOTES
1. Tune in to what is going on in your body that helps you know that you are about to lose control of yourself.	Are you getting tense, angry, hot, fidgety?
2. Decide what happened to make you feel this way.	Consider outside events or internal events (thoughts).
3. Think about ways in which you might control yourself.	Slow down; count to 10; assert yourself; leave; do something else.
4. Choose the best way to control yourself and do it.	

SUGGESTED CONTENT FOR MODELING DISPLAYS

A. School or neighborhood: Main actor controls yelling at teacher when teacher criticizes harshly.

B. Home: Main actor controls self when parent forbids desired activity.

C. Peer group: Main actor controls self when friend takes something without asking permission.

COMMENTS

It is often helpful to discuss various ways of controlling oneself before role playing the skill. The list of self-control techniques can be written on the board and used to generate alternative tactics youngsters can use in a variety of situations.

From A. P. Goldstein. *The prepare curriculum: Teaching prosocial competencies.* Champaign, IL: Research Press, 1988, p. 118. Reprinted by permission.

The Cognitive Model for Self-Management

In the cognitive model, there are three steps in self-managment: (1) self-monitoring, (2) self-evaluation, and (3) self-reinforcement. Self-monitoring involves having students become aware of their behavior (self-observation), often keeping track of it (self-recording). Self-monitoring leads to self-evaluation, comparing their performance to some standard.

For students who are not able to accurately judge their behavior, having them place self-monitored data on a graph and set a performance goal helps promote self-evaluation. Self-reinforcement occurs after students meet or exceed their performance standard. In a review of research on self-monitoring, Reid (1996) concluded that it is an intervention repeatedly proven to be effective and can easily be incorporated into existing classroom structures and activities.

Self-reinforcement provides students with ways to reinforce themselves. It can be either external, receiving reinforcement after meeting or exceeding a goal, or internal, where students tell themselves something positive about their performance. The key to getting students to use self-reinforcement, and to maintaining its effectiveness, is to ensure that they set goals for appropriate behavior. Once students have set realistic goals, they can decide whether to use external or internal self-reinforcement. External self-reinforcement means students deliver their own reinforcer. A prerequisite step is for students to generate a list of potential reinforcers. According to Bandura (1997), there are three necessary conditions for students to engage in external self-reinforcement: the student determines the evaluative criteria, controls access to the reinforcement, and administers it.

Teaching children self-control strategies (under the headings of cognitive behavior modification, self-instructional training, problem-solving training, metacognitive training, and cognitive strategy instruction), is designed to help students become more self-regulated. The following chart illustrates the six components of cognitive strategy instruction (CSI) with the corresponding self-questions students learn to ask themselves.

Cognitive Strategy Instruction (CSI) Components with Self-Questions

Problem defining	*What is it I have to do here?*
	What am I supposed to do?
Attention focusing	*How can I do it?*
	I have to concentrate and think only about my work.
Strategy generating	*To do this right I have to make a plan.*
	First I will write as many ideas as I can.
	I will make an outline before I write my paper.
Self-guiding	*I need to be careful, look at one at a time.*
	I'll turn back and see if I can get some help from the directions.
	I'll isolate myself from anything that distracts me.
	I'm not sure here, I better review my notes.
Self-coping	*I need to go slow—take my time.*
	It's okay. Even if I make a mistake, I can back up.
Self-reinforcing	*I think I'm getting it.*
	I did it by myself. No one had to help me.
	If I do well on a test, I treat myself to a movie.

Problem-Solving Training

Problem-solving training is a CBM intervention used to resolve conflicts requiring either initiation of action or reaction to the responses of others. It generally involves teaching students: to practice the skills of self-interrogation and self-checking; to analyze tasks by breaking problems into manageable steps; and to proceed through these steps.

Some type of problem-solving training is generally incorporated into all CBM interventions. This training covers a variety of skills that can be used to resolve conflicts. Hughes (1988) describes the following four problem-solving thinking skills.

1. **Problem identification.** Component skills involve problem sensitivity or the ability to sense the presence of a problem by identifying uncomfortable feelings. Also included are skills for identifying major problem issues and maintaining a general problem-solving orientation or *set*. These skills counteract a tendency to deny, avoid, or act impulsively in dealing with the problem.
2. **Alternative thinking.** This is the ability to generate multiple alternative solutions to a given interpersonal problem situation.
3. **Consequential thinking.** This skill involves the ability to foresee the immediate and more long-range consequences of a particular alternative and to use this information in the decision-making process.

4. **Means–ends thinking.** This is the ability to elaborate or plan a series of specific actions (a means) to attain a given goal, to recognize and devise ways around potential obstacles, and to use a realistic time framework in implementing steps toward the goal.

Gesten, Weissberg, Amish, and Smith (1987) have described several factors to guide the selection of problem-solving curricula relative to a students' age.

1. The ability to generate multiple solutions, regardless of quality, is most effective for preschool and primary grade students.
2. The quality of solutions (i.e., their assertiveness and effectiveness), rather than their quantity, and emphasis on the consequences associated with each solution choice is most effective for middle school students.
3. Secondary students require less training in solution generation or consequential thinking than in the means–ends thinking necessary for overcoming obstacles and successfully implementing the chosen solutions.

An early problem-solving intervention known as the *turtle technique* helps students control aggressive or impulsive responses and develop alternative ones (Robin, Schneider, & Dolnick, 1976). This is a CBM intervention, combining elements of problem-solving training, self-instruction, and relaxation training. The turtle technique consists of three phases: (1) turtle response, (2) relaxation, and (3) problem solving. In Phase 1, the teacher introduces the turtle response by telling students the following story.

Little Turtle was a handsome young turtle very upset about going to school. He always got in trouble at school because he got into fights. Other kids would tease, bump, or hit him; he would get very angry and start big fights. The teacher would have to punish him. Then one day he met the big old tortoise, who told him that his shell was the secret answer to all his problems. The tortoise told Little Turtle to withdraw into his shell when he felt angry and rest until he was no longer angry. So he tried it the next day and it worked. The teacher now smiled at him and he no longer got into big fights. (Robin, Schneider, & Dolnick, 1976, p. 450)

The teacher explains the four situations appropriate for students to display the turtle response: a student believes that an aggressive interaction with a peer is about to occur; a student becomes frustrated or angry and is about to "lose it"; the teacher calls out "turtle"; and a peer calls out "turtle."

During Phase 2, students are taught muscle relaxation exercises to further diffuse negative emotional reactions resulting from the situation. Specifically, they are taught to alternately tense and relax various muscle groups independently and then while doing the turtle response. The goal is to pair the turtle response and relaxation.

In Phase 3, problem solving is introduced through the use of role playing and discussion. Students are taught to generate alternative strategies for coping with the problem situations that initially resulted in their displaying the turtle response and examining the consequences of their choices. Specifically, the teacher presents incomplete stories of typical problem situations and requires students to role play alternative endings. The teacher reminds students of their choices whenever they display a turtle response during normal class activities.

Problem-solving training often incorporates some type of "think sheet" as a typical mode for analyzing problem situations. The following Incident Think Sheet is an example.

Incident Think Sheet

Name _____

Date _____

What happened? _____
_____

Why do you think it happened? _____
_____

What is the problem? _____
_____

What did you do? _____
_____

What were you feeling when you did this? _____
_____

What were you trying to do? _____
_____

What result did you get? _____
_____

Are you satisfied with the way(s) you handled the problem? _____

What could you have done instead that would probably have been a better solution to the problem? _____
_____

What negative result could you have avoided if you had made a better choice?
_____

Publishers of Materials to Teach Emotional Literacy

The following list provides the addresses and websites for many publishers of materials that teach life skills and enhance students' levels of social and emotional competence.

Albert Ellis Institute
45 East 65th Street
New York, NY 10021-6593
(800) 323-4738
www.rebt.org

American Guidance Service
PO Box 99
4201 Woodland Road
Circle Pines, MN 55014
(800) 328-2560
www.ags.com

Aspen Publishing, Inc
7201 McKinney Circle
Frederick, MD 21701
(800) 638-8437
www.aspenpublishers.com

Children's Creative Response to Conflict
PO Box 271
Nyack, NY 10960
(914) 353-1796
www.planet-rockland.org/conflict

Comprehensive Health Education Foundation
1420 Fifth Avenue, Suite 3600
Seattle, WA 98101
(800) 323-2433
www.chef.org

Education Development Center
55 Chapel Street
Newton, MA 02158-1060
(800) 223-4276
www.edc.org

Educators for Social Responsibility
23 Garden Street
Cambridge, MA 02138
(800) 370-2515
www.esrnational.org

Free Spirit Publishing
400 First Avenue North, Suite 616
Minneapolis, MN 55401
(800) 735-7323
www.freespirit.com

Love Publishing Company
9101 East Kenyon Avenue, Suite 2200
Denver, CO 80237
(303) 221-7333
www.lovepublishing.com

National Crisis Prevention Institute
3315-K North 124th Street
Brookfield, WI 53005
(800) 558-8976
www.crisisprevention.com

National Educational Services
1252 Loesch Road
Bloomington, IN 47404
(800) 733-6786
www.wnesonline.com

New Society Publishers
PO Box 189
Gabriola Island, BC V0R 1X0
Canada
(800) 567-6772
www.newsociety.com

Peace Education Foundation
PO Box 191153
1900 Biscayne Blvd.
Miami, FL 33132
(800) 749-8838
www.peace-ed.org

Prima Publishing
3000 Lava Ridge Court
Roseville, CA 95661
(800) 632-8676
www.primalifestyles.com

PRO-ED
8700 Shoal Creek Blvd.
Austin, TX 78787
(800) 897-3202
www.proedinc.com

Research Press
2612 Mattis Avenue
Champaign, IL 61820
(800) 519-2707
www.researchpress.com

Sopris West
1140 Boston Avenue
Longmont, CO 80501
(800) 547-6747
www.sopriswest.com

Sunburst Communications
101 Castleton Street
Pleasantville, NY 10570
(800) 431-1934
www.sunburst.com

Teaching Tolerance
400 Washington Avenue
Montgomery, AL 36104
(334) 264-3121
www.teachingtolerance.org

Timberline Press
PO Box 1056
Gig Harbor, WA 98335
(253) 858-6227
www.pumsy.com

LEARNING PRACTICE TASK: DEVELOPING AN INDIVIDUALIZED CUE CARD

Activity Directions: Working with a small group, follow the steps below to develop a cue card for a specific student's problem behavior.

Step 1: Decide on a problem behavior.

Step 2: Review the strategies discussed in this chapter to determine which ones you want to incorporate in planning your cue card.

Step 3: Decide which strategies to include.

Step 4: Develop your cue card.

Step 5: Incorporate an evaluation component.

CHAPTER EIGHT

Conflict and Stress Management Strategies

In conflict situations, students often use strategies that have negative consequences and are aggressive, passive, or passive-aggressive. Students frequently resort to verbal or physical abuse, retreat from the situation, tattle, or attempt to enlist others to solve problems for them.

Most students need help in building a repertoire of effective strategies for managing conflict. In order to learn new strategies, students will need to experience the results of using positive approaches and discover workable strategies through structured learning experiences that give them opportunities to practice more effective strategies for resolving conflicts.

TEACHING STUDENTS CONFLICT MANAGEMENT STRATEGIES

The following section describes some strategies that students can be taught to use. They will also need to be taught decision rules for determining when a procedure is likely to result in a positive outcome. Though each is listed separately, they often will be used in combination. Some strategies involve individual decisions and self-control, whereas some require the cooperation of others. Some strategies are for immediate problem resolution; some offer defusing or delaying tactics.

Strategies 1 to 5 require cooperation from all of the parties involved. Strategies 6 to 11 are strategies that provide immediate defusing of a situation in which conflict resolution is delayed for the time being. Strategies 12 to 15 involve structured language and implementation of effective communication techniques. Strategies 16 and 17 are assertion strategies. They involve making direct statements expressing the person's position. Strategies 18 and 19 are self-control strategies and involve impulse control. Strategy 20 involves seeking assistance.

Twenty Conflict Management Strategies

Strategy 1: Negotiating. In negotiating, students express their individual positions in the conflict and try to decide what can be done. Negotiating can be a simple discussion or a more structured step-by-step approach. The idea is to break down the points of the conflict and examine each aspect. In negotiation a period of discussion occurs for the purpose of bringing about a resolution that is mutually agreed to. Other, less involved strategies that immediately diffuse the situation may need to be taught first to pave the way for the process of negotiation.

Strategy 2: Compromising. Compromise not only requires mutual cooperation but also a period of negotiation to establish that compromise will be used to resolve the problem. In a compromise, everyone agrees to give up a little. It allows both students to save face while each gets some of what he or she originally wanted. The concept of giving up something to get something back is often a difficult concept for children to grasp.

Strategy 3: Sharing.   In sharing, individuals decide to share for mutual benefit. Inherent in the sharing process are the notions of reciprocity and equality. These are both difficult concepts for children to understand because their world is the here and now.

Strategy 4: Taking Turns.   Taking turns is one of the simplest strategies. The key to teaching turn taking is getting students to recognize that whoever goes second needs some kind of face saving for giving up the first turn. Although a student could act alone by relinquishing his or her turn, the strategy is more effectively used when students decide who will have the first and second turn.

Strategy 5: Chance.   Using chance generally moves the conflict toward resolution and offers face saving for everyone. In using chance, those involved need to agree on its use and on the consequences of the outcome. Any method that leaves the resolution to chance such as flipping a coin, drawing straws, or picking a number can be used.

Strategy 6: Distracting.   This strategy offers a way to defuse a potentially volatile situation by diverting attention. It allows a cooling off period and can also be a face-saving tactic. When used appropriately it is not avoidance but a temporary move that leaves the door open for conflict resolution at a later time.

Strategy 7: Postponing.   Postponing conflict resolution to a more appropriate time often allows the problem to be handled more successfully. Postponement strategies are useful when one or both persons are not up to handling the conflict situation at the time.

Strategy 8: Exaggerating.   In this strategy, the involved parties engage in an exaggerated interpretation of the issue. Exaggeration often helps students put their issues in perspective.

Strategy 9: Humor.   Humor is used to defuse the angry feelings associated with conflict. Quick wit, the saving remark, laughing at oneself, or poking fun at one's own expense take the pressure off a situation. If the other person can begin to look at things from a different perspective, he or she can be more objective. There is risk involved in using this strategy because students sometimes misinterpret humor as making fun of them, hence humor works best when it is self-directed. It can seize the moment by helping students recognize the awkwardness of the moment. It can also serve to mask real feelings, make someone a scapegoat, or cause hurt and should be used with these cautions in mind.

Strategy 10: Abandoning.   This strategy involves moving away from a situation and is appropriate when the person cannot handle it. When the student comes to the realization that nothing but harm is likely to result, or that he or she needs to exercise self-control, this strategy is appropriate.

Strategy 11: Apologizing.   Apologizing can mean admitting responsibility when the student recognizes that his or her behavior was wrong. It can also be a simple way of saying you are sorry that the other person feels hurt without accepting responsibility for why the person feels hurt. Such recognition of the other person's feelings can often serve as a tension defuser.

Strategy 12: Blame-Free Explanation. Expressing anger by attacking or blaming others elicits angry retaliation. Expressing your position or feelings in a way that does not blame the other person will elicit a more positive reaction.

Strategy 13: Sending an I-Message. In this strategy you refrain from blaming the other person or evaluating the person's behavior and simply state the concrete effect of the behavior and your feelings about the behavior.

Strategy 14: Making an Impact-Statement. Here you state the effect of the behavior and why it is causing a problem for you. This is similar to the previous two strategies, however here you limit your comments to the consequences of the behavior.

Strategy 15: Active Listening. This is the most difficult of the structured language strategies and is a strategy that necessitates highly developed skill. Active listening involves listening to what the other person is saying, trying to grasp the feelings the other person is having, and sending back a message that communicates to the person that you understand what they are feeling. The process involves learning to listen not only to what the person is saying in words but also what message is being communicated by other signals such as voice intonation or nonverbal signs. Conflicts are often the result of not listening or misinterpreting what is being said. Even young children can be taught to listen by using such phrases as "Go ahead, I'm listening to you," "You talk first, then it will be my turn," and "You said . . . , is that what you meant?"

Strategy 16: Stating Your Intention. This strategy is an assertion strategy and involves stating exactly what you intend to do either right now or the next time the behavior occurs.

Strategy 17: Making a Request. This is another assertion strategy and involves making a direct request for the other person to change his or her behavior. It could also be a request for the other person to take a specific action.

Strategy 18: Passive Listening. This strategy is an impulse-control strategy in that the person remains silent for a time. It may involve a self-instructional strategy such as counting to ten to keep from interrupting the other person, arguing, or becoming defensive.

Strategy 19: Self-Talk. This strategy is a self-control strategy that involves the use of positive self-talk in an attempt to reduce stress and keep oneself under control by engaging in rehearsed self-dialogue.

Strategy 20: Seeking Assistance. This strategy should be reserved for situations that cannot be handled without outside help. It should be used when additional information or knowledge is necessary or the situation is too complex, involved, or volatile.

PROCESSES FOR RESOLVING CONFLICT

Sources of Conflict in the Classroom

Because the classroom is a very complex place, there are many sources of conflict. Gordon (1989) suggests three common conditions that create conflict between teacher and students: when there are no clear-cut rules or policies; when rules and policies are difficult to understand or interpret; and when rules appear unfair or unreasonable to students. Two inherent features of the classroom that encourage conflict are the structure of power differences between teacher and students and a focus on evaluation and grading. Still other causes of conflict include student competition, the demand for individual attention, differences in perception, and even teacher misbehavior. Delivering boring or confusing lectures, setting unreasonable expectations, employing unfair testing procedures, and showing favoritism may invoke conflicts with students.

Although conflict is normally viewed as negative, it can be positive in the classroom when it prompts the teacher and students to alter behavior so that the learning environment is enhanced. The goals of any productive conflict are twofold: to solve the immediate problem and to enhance the interpersonal relationship to the extent that allows the parties to continue working together. If the problem is solved but the relationship worsens, the conflict is not really settled.

Processes for Conflict Resolution: Arbitration, Mediation, and Negotiation

The following chart summarizes the features of arbitration, mediation, and negotiation.

Conflict Resolution Process	Feature
Arbitration	■ Parties relinquish responsibility for resolving the conflict themselves ■ Impartial third party considers all the positions, needs and wants of the parties involved and decides how the conflict will be resolved ■ Judgment is final and binding; involved parties must abide by the decision
Mediation	■ A participatory process in which a neutral third party facilitates by actively assisting the involved parties to work out a resolution that both or all parties can agree to ■ Mediator typically acts as the gate keeper to monitor the use of effective communication skills (i.e., listening, paraphrasing, clarifying, and assertion skills)
Peer mediation	■ Select students receive training in the communication skills involved for the mediation model used ■ Disputing students agree to the mediation process ■ Some programs have peer mediators write down the agreement and ask students to sign it
Teacher mediation	■ A process that keeps teachers out of student battles ■ Teacher does not become the enforcer ■ Role of the teacher is to use active listening to feed back the message and feelings of each or all of the students involved ■ Allows students to come up with their own solution

Negotiation	■ No third party
	■ Involved parties work through their differences and try to come to a mutually acceptable resolution
	■ Requires the cooperation of both or all individuals involved
Win–Win Negotiation	■ Negotiations in which no one loses
	■ Both persons commit to the process and avoid trying to win at the other's expense
	■ Persons involved discuss specific alternatives in order to arrive at a mutually acceptable agreement
	■ Many students simply can't perceive any alternatives to aggressive behavior in a conflict situation. Teaching students a problem-solving process can help students think of their own solutions to solve their problems effectively.

Third-Party Facilitation: Arbitration and Mediation

There are two processes for third-party dispute resolution. One involves relinquishing responsibility for the resolution process, the other is a participatory process. In arbitration, a dispute is turned over to an impartial third party who considers all the positions, along with needs and wants of the parties involved, and makes a final and binding judgment as to how the conflict will be resolved. In agreeing to use the arbitration process, the involved parties have decided to abide by the decision of the arbitrator rather than resolve the conflict themselves.

In mediation, a neutral third party facilitates the process by actively assisting the involved parties to work out a resolution that both or all parties can agree to. In this process, the mediator typically acts as the gate keeper to monitor the use of effective communication skills. Effective mediation involves listening, paraphrasing, clarifying, and assertion skills.

Many schools are now using peer mediation as a way to resolve conflicts. In most programs, select students receive training in the communication skills involved and disputing students agree to the mediation process. Examples of teacher and peer mediation processes are described in the next section.

Teacher Mediation.   Teachers spend a lot of their energy handling hassles students have with one another. They often get "sucked into" their students' battles. Teachers often act as arbitrators and offer solutions or attempt to determine who is at fault. As soon as the teacher becomes involved, he or she has taken on the ownership of the problem that really belongs to the students.

Teacher mediation is a process that keeps teachers out of student battles and helps students take responsibility for working out their problems. In teacher mediation, the role of the teacher is to use active listening to feed back the message and feelings of each of the students so that each feels that his or her position has been heard. This process lets the students take responsibility for working out the problem.

Teacher Mediation Process.   In teacher mediation, the teacher

- Has students talk directly to one another, not through the teacher
- Uses door openers ("What seems to be the problem?") rather than probing questions ("Why did you do that?")

- Uses active listening to help students clarify feelings and uncover their needs
- Does not buy into the students' problem
- Stays nonjudgmental rather than attributes blame
- Refuses to sanction either student's position
- Does not become the enforcer
- Refrains from "rescuing" the students; allows them to come up with their own solution instead

Peer Mediation.   The following is an example of a peer mediation process taught to students (Sunburst Communications, 1996). In this program students receive training in active listening skills as part of learning to be a mediator.

The Mediation Process
Step 1: Introductions and Ground Rules
- Make introductions.
- Explain the mediation.
  a. Mediators don't take sides, blame, or judge.
  b. Mediators assure confidentiality, except when weapons, drugs, or abuse are involved.
  c. Mediators help disputants reach their own agreement.
- Ask disputants to agree to the ground rules.
  a. To work to try to solve the problem
  b. To listen without interrupting
  c. To treat each other with respect

Step 2: Getting the Story
- As each disputant tells his or her story, use active listening.
  a. Concentrate on the words, feelings, and body language.
  b. Ask questions.
  c. Paraphrase what you hear.
- Try to identify each disputant's needs.
- Clearly state the problem.

Step 3: Brainstorming for Solutions
- Ask disputants
  a. What each is willing to do to resolve the problem
  b. To state any idea that comes to mind
  c. To come up with as many ideas as possible
- Ask questions to encourage ideas.
- Do not criticize or judge ideas.
- Keep track of all ideas.

Step 4: Choosing Solutions
- Ask disputants to select the solutions that best meet the needs of both parties.
- Ask disputants if they agree to accept the solution.

Step 5: Closing the Session
- Summarize the agreement.
- Write the agreement.
- Ask disputants to sign the agreement. Then sign it yourself.
- Congratulate everyone for a successful mediation and shake hands.

████████

LEARNING PRACTICE TASK: PRACTICING TEACHER MEDIATION

Activity Directions: This activity provides an opportunity to practice mediation, using participant-generated student problems. Follow the sequence of steps listed.

Step 1: Divide into groups of four for this activity. As a group, decide on a student–student problem situation to work on.

Step 2: Use role playing to portray the situation, with each person taking a turn in the role of mediator, student, and observer. Before beginning the role play, review the Teacher Mediator Feedback Checklist and clarify any behaviors you may have questions about. During the role play, when you are playing the mediator, you will be trying to engage in the behaviors listed. The observer will be completing the checklist in order to give you specific feedback. Decide who will play the mediator first and begin your first round of role playing.

Step 3: Get feedback on your performance as mediator. The focus of the feedback should be the items on the checklist. Discuss any discrepancies between your perceptions of your behavior and the observer's feedback. Also discuss any problems you experienced while trying to be a mediator.

Continue role playing until each person has had a chance to play each role.

Teacher Mediator Feedback Checklist

Behavior	PRESENCE OF BEHAVIOR		
	Yes	Somewhat	No
Teacher refrains from sanctioning either student's position	_____	_____	_____
Teacher refrains from using probing questions	_____	_____	_____
Teacher keeps students talking directly to one another	_____	_____	_____
Teacher is nonjudgmental	_____	_____	_____
Teacher uses opening questions to invite students to discuss the issues	_____	_____	_____
Teacher uses active listening	_____	_____	_____
Reflection (empathic listening)	_____	_____	_____
Paraphrasing (restating)	_____	_____	_____
Perception checking (paraphrasing, requesting feedback)	_____	_____	_____
Clarifying (restating, clarifying confusion)	_____	_____	_____
Teacher facilitates students coming up with their own potential solutions	_____	_____	_____

Negotiation

Negotiation is an alternative to arbitration and mediation. In negotiation, there is no third party; the involved parties try to come to a mutually acceptable resolution to the conflict. The process is based on the premise that the parties want to be fair and equitable and consider the needs and wishes of everyone involved.

Conflicts are usually emotional affairs and those involved often react defensively by acting aggressively and counterattacking when they perceive an attack. In order to negotiate a resolution, the cooperation of both individuals is required. You can't negotiate with someone whose agenda is to win by defeating you.

Win–Win Negotiation.   Negotiations in which no one loses are referred to as win–win negotiations. When two individuals work through their differences and end up with a solution that meets the needs of both, resentment is minimized and the relationship is usually strengthened. Negotiation is a method of resolving conflicts in which the persons involved discuss specific alternatives in order to arrive at a mutually acceptable agreement. Successful negotiating can bring about solutions that improve the situation for both parties.

Basically, win–win negotiation is a cooperative process in which two or more individuals work through their differences and come up with a resolution that meets the needs of everyone involved. Many students simply can't perceive any alternatives other than aggressive behavior in a conflict situation. Teaching students a problem-solving process can help them think of their own solutions to effectively solve their problems.

The win–win negotiation process can be used to resolve an individual teacher–student conflict or a teacher–class conflict, or it can be used as a decision-making process to ensure that the needs of all involved parties are met. It also can be taught to students as a strategy for student-managed problem resolution.

The win–win negotiation technique is a highly structured six-step process for resolving conflicts in which all involved parties participate in the generation of possible solutions. The process can be used in an obvious conflict situation or in a situation in which one person owns the problem and is proactive in confronting the other person. The process is initially presented as a step-by-step approach to be implemented in the sequence presented until the approach becomes familiar; thereafter individuals can fit the approach to their own natural style.

Steps in Win–Win Negotiation
1. Make a date acceptable to both parties.
2. Describe the problem and your needs.
3. Solicit the other person's perspective and needs.
4. Generate alternative solutions that meet both sets of needs.
5. Evaluate the solutions and select one that both parties can support.
6. Follow up the solution to make sure it is working.

In negotiation, both persons commit to the process and cooperate in mutual problem solving to end up with a solution that satisfies the needs of each. Individuals avoid trying to win at the other's expense and seek a solution that takes into consideration each person's wants and needs. The win–win approach to negotiation doesn't call for compromises in which individuals give up something they really want or need.

The process calls for both parties to agree to a time to discuss the problem, commit to the negotiation process, try to resolve the problem by considering the other person's needs as well as one's own, and arrive at a solution that meets both sets of needs.

Win–Win Six-Step Plan Application.   Teachers may want to introduce the six-step process on specific problems such as where to go on a field trip or how to study the next science unit. As they become more comfortable with the process, more student participation can be included in more complex class problems. All issues that are within the teacher's prerogative, or area of freedom, are eligible for win–win problem solving—what to study, how to study, how to evaluate classroom tasks and give teacher feedback, as well as matters of classroom behavior.

The rule-setting class meeting is a special use of the win–win problem-solving process that involves the class and teacher working together in setting the rules needed by the class (Burch & Miller, 1979).

Win–Win Six-Step Problem-Solving Process:
Setting Class Rules Lesson Plan
Step 0: Setting the Stage

1. Tell the class the purpose of the meeting.

   The purpose of this meeting is for us to develop mutually agreed-on rules for how we will work and be together in here.

2. Describe Methods I, II, and III.

   One way for us to set rules is for me to tell you what they will be and punish you if you violate them. In this way I might get my needs met and feel like a winner, but you would probably feel like you lost. (Method I)

   Another way would be for me to say nothing when your behavior became a problem to me. You might feel like a winner, but I sure wouldn't. (Method II)

   A third way would be for us to search together for rules that we mutually agree we need. That way we could all win. (Method III)

3. Ask the students if they would be willing to try Method III.

   Allow for discussion and answer their questions. After obtaining consensus to try Method III, write the six steps (see the following section) on the blackboard or, if appropriate, hand out copies. Say that you would like to begin with Step 1, defining needs.

   Explain the concept of area of freedom and give examples of issues that lie outside the freedom of the group (e.g., smoking in class) and those within (e.g., how to study the unit on the American Revolution).

Step 1: Defining Needs or Problems

1. Hand out worksheets with the heading *What Makes an Effective Class?*
2. On the blackboard, write the word *effective* and the definition, *to have a positive influence on others.*
3. Instruct students individually to think of and list for 3 minutes what they have personally found to be the ingredients of a good class—characteristics that made the class effective for them.

   (Note. Use language appropriate to the age of the students. Also, it is very important that student discussions not evolve into negative evaluations of you or your colleagues. If this should begin, send a clear I-message, such as "I'm not comfortable with that. I want to talk about rules and policies, not personalities.")
4. Next, ask the students to pair off and share their lists with each other. Allow 3 to 5 minutes for this discussion.
5. Ask the students to tell you their characteristics and record them on the board or chart pad. Use active listening to clarify; avoid listing the same characteristics more than once. Make certain your needs as a teacher are appropriately included.

Step 2: Generating Possible Solutions
1. Tell the class you now want to do Step 2 of the process. Ask them to turn to the back side of their worksheet and write the heading *Rules I Want*.
2. Tell the students to take a few moments to individually list rules that they think could best achieve the characteristics of an effective class.
3. Next, have them pair and discuss their rules with a partner for a few minutes.
4. Ask the class to tell you the rules they would like. List them on the board.

Step 3: Evaluating the Solutions
1. Ask the class to look at the list of effective characteristics and the list of suggested rules. "Which rules (solutions) do you think would have the best chance of meeting these characteristics (needs)?"

Step 4: Decision Making
1. Work with the students to facilitate consensus about the final classroom rules.
2. Point out that if anyone discovers that a solution hasn't worked well, it could be changed at a later meeting.

Step 5: Implementing the Decision
1. Obtain clarity about who will do what, and when, for each of the rules.
2. Write the agreed upon rules on the Rules Poster and post it in the room.
3. Ask each student to sign her or his name on the Rules Poster indicating agreement about those rules. Actively listen to resistance. Encourage but don't coerce them to sign.

Step 6: Following-Up on the Success of the Solution
1. Decide on a future time to have a class meeting for the purpose of evaluating how well the Rules for Class are working.
2. Make the time appropriate (i.e., one week after initiating the rules) or when it is obvious one or more rules are not working.

A Process for Evaluating Solutions

If students are having difficulty evaluating solutions, the teacher may need to provide some structure. Once students are able to generate a number of alternative solutions to a problem, the process calls for evaluating each solution. Students can be taught to use the criteria of efficacy and feasibility to provide a systematic procedure for evaluation (Kaplan, 1995).

- The efficacy criterion asks: Will this solution help me get what I want without creating new problems for myself?
- The feasibility criterion asks: Is it likely that I will be able to actually do it?

Teachers can help students apply the criteria to each alternative generated by prompting students with questions such as "Would this work?" "Would you get what you want?" and "Would you create new problems?" Teachers should help students follow the process only, not evaluate solutions. Students should arrive at their own evaluations. Teachers can initially go through each alternative with students, applying the criteria to identify solutions that are both effective and feasible. Teachers then can help students generate more alternatives if those generated do not meet the criteria. Eventually, students will be able to go through this process on their own.

ASSERTION: STANDING UP
FOR YOUR RIGHTS AND NEEDS

Assertion is the ability to stand up for your rights in ways that help ensure that others won't ignore or circumvent them. Responding assertively means stating your needs and wants without deriding, attacking, or making another person responsible for your reaction or feelings. Being assertive means letting others know what you want, need, like, don't like, and how their behavior affects you.

Unassertive people have trouble initiating conversations, often readily accommodate others' requests, accede to inappropriate demands, and are unable to ask others to respect their rights and needs. For those who are unassertive, before they can respond assertively they will have to first confront the negative thought patterns and beliefs that interfere with asserting their rights and impede assertive responses. Those who fail to act assertively typically hold nonassertive beliefs about their rights and those of others (Jakubowski, 1977). Four of those beliefs are discussed here.

1. *I do not have the right to place my needs above those of others.*
    Rebuttal: Healthy people have needs and strive to fulfill those needs. Your needs are as valid as others' needs. It's not your needs *or* my needs, it's your needs *and* my needs. The way to handle conflict over need satisfaction is through negotiation and compromise. One of the negative consequences associated with not validating your own needs is often passive-aggressive behavior. Inability or unwillingness to express your feelings of resentment or anger directly can lead to dealing with your anger in subtle and indirect ways. In the long run, if you frequently deny or ignore your own needs, you may come to feel a growing loss of self-esteem and an increasing sense of hurt and anger. It can be a double-edged sword in that you not only fail to get your needs met, but you also feel bad about yourself.

2. *I do not have the right to feel angry or to express my anger.*
    Rebuttal: Life is made up of trivial incidents, and it is normal to be irritated occasionally by seemingly insignificant events. You have a right to feel angry and to express your anger in ways that don't infringe on others' rights.

3. *I do not have the right to make requests of others.*
    Rebuttal: You have a right to ask others to change their behavior if their behavior has an adverse effect on you. A request is not the same as a demand. However, if your rights are being violated and your requests for a change are being ignored, you have a right to make demands.

4. *I do not have the right to do anything that might hurt someone's feelings.*
    Rebuttal: Deliberately trying to hurt others is undesirable. However, it is impossible as well as undesirable to try to govern your actions so that you never hurt anyone. You have a right to express your thoughts and feelings, even if someone else's feelings occasionally get hurt. To do otherwise would be inauthentic and deny others an opportunity to learn how to handle their own feelings. Some people get hurt because they're unreasonably sensitive and others use their hurt to manipulate others.

Comparing Nonassertive, Aggressive, and Assertive Behavior

In responding to a given situation, you have three behavior choices. You can respond nonassertively, aggressively, or assertively. The following sections describe each of these three types of behavior. The following chart compares these three options on several dimensions.

Comparison of Behavior Patterns

	NONASSERTIVE	AGGRESSIVE	ASSERTIVE
Approach to others	"I'm not okay, you're okay."	"I'm okay, you're not okay."	"I'm okay, you're okay."
Decision making	Lets others choose	Chooses for others	Chooses for self
Self-sufficiency	Low	High or low	Usually high
Behavior in problem situations	Avoidance, submission	Outright or concealed attack	Direct confrontation
Response of others	Disrespect, guilt, anger, frustration	Hurt, defensiveness, humiliation, frustration	Respect
Success pattern	Succeeds by luck or charity of others	Dominates others	Attempts win–win solutions

Nonassertion.   Nonassertion is the failure to assert your rights or express your thoughts or feelings when necessary. This type of behavior exemplifies lack of respect for your own right to express your ideas and opinions, needs and wants, and feelings.

Behavior in Conflict or Problem Situations
When a conflict arises behavior takes the form of two different types of denial.

- Denying your own needs
- Ignoring your needs

In both cases your response is to do nothing. In the first case, you choose to forget about your own needs and satisfy the other person's needs. In the second case, you pretend nothing is wrong, that is, you claim no problem exists. In either case, you allow others to behave in ways that show no regard for your needs.

Typical Behavior Is To
- Deny
- Forget
- Ignore
- Overlook
- Flee
- Surrender

Advantage
The advantage this type of behavior offers is that it avoids conflict. However, there are several disadvantages associated with nonassertive behavior.

Disadvantages
- You won't get what you want or need.
- You may experience feelings of inadequacy.
- You may get angry at others for taking advantage of you.
- You encourage others to take advantage of you, treat you with disrespect, or pity you.

Aggression.   Aggression is expressing your thoughts or feelings in a way that disregards others' rights to be respected. Aggressive behavior is self-enhancing at the expense of others.

Behavior in Conflict or Problem Situations
The aggressive person tends to do the following when dealing with a problem.

- Attack
- Put down
- Threaten
- Hurt

Advantage
While you generally get what you want, there are other costs.

Disadvantages
- Causes others to feel hurt or humiliated
- Causes others to feel angry or defensive
- Produces negative consequences, such as counteraggressive behavior or desire for revenge
- Closes off communication channels

Assertion.   Assertion is expressing your needs, thoughts, or feelings clearly and directly without judging, dictating, or threatening. You honestly state your feelings without either denying your own right to express yourself (nonassertion) or denying the rights of others to be treated with respect (aggression).

Behavior in Conflict or Problem Situations
When a conflict situation occurs, the assertive response is to confront the situation by

- Stating your needs
- Making your own intentions clear
- Expressing your feelings
- Describing the impact of the person's behavior
- Making your position clear (taking a stand)
- Asking for a behavior change

Advantages
- Generates positive feelings for both the sender and the receiver
- Maintains the self-respect of both parties
- Usually resolves the conflict or problem
- Leads to compromise when necessary
- Is honest
- Avoids feelings of resentment, anger, or guilt

Disadvantages
- Doesn't guarantee you'll get what you want
- The other person may feel hurt.

Responding assertively will not guarantee that you will always get what you want. However, behaving assertively offers the best chance of getting your needs met. Also, although aggressive behavior is far more likely to cause hurt feelings, behaving assertively will not ensure that the other person will not feel hurt. Some people actually use their hurt to manipulate others.

Here are examples of the kinds of responses that are typical of nonassertive, aggressive, and assertive approaches to dealing with students (Silberman & Whee-lan, 1980).

Nonassertive	Aggressive	Assertive
Plead	Blow up in anger	Persist, insist
Worry about upsetting students	Get into power struggles	Give brief reasons
Evade problems and issues	Endlessly argue	Make clear, direct requests

Example: *Angie, an extremely disorganized student in your class, can seldom find her books or work when needed. She comes to you with a look of frustration and reports that she can't locate a book report due that day.*

Response Options	**Category**
Say nothing and look exasperated.	Nonassertive
Sternly lecture Angie about the importance of keeping track of her things.	Aggressive
Empathize with her frustration and insist on an agreement as to how this might be avoided in the future.	Assertive

In the following chart, these options are differentiated in terms of who "wins" and who "loses."

Whose Rights and Needs Are Met?

	⌐Rights and Needs¬		
Response	**Teachers**	**Students**	**Win–Lose Outcome**
Aggressive	✔	✘	Teacher wins Student loses
Nonassertive	✘	✔	Teacher loses Student wins
Assertive	✔	✔	Teacher wins Student wins

Assertive Responses

Teachers need to recognize that asserting their right to maintain a classroom atmosphere conducive to teaching and learning should not interfere with respecting the rights and needs of their students. Advocating for assertive behavior is not synonymous with promoting an authoritarian stance. Developing assertion skills enables teachers to directly and honestly express themselves without attributing blame to students or denying students' rights and needs.

The key characteristics of assertive responses are

- Nonjudgmental
- Take a clear stand
- State personal needs

Assertive responses express your needs and desires directly and nonjudgmentally. Teachers sometimes need to be proactive in approaching students rather than always being reactive, or responding after a misbehavior occurs. For example, it is important to confront (approach) a student who is doing minimal or poor-quality work. Appropriate responses could take any of the following forms.

Assertive Response	**Assertive Language**
Request a behavior change	I'd like you to put that away now. I'd like you to tell me when I do something you don't like.

Express a need	I need to leave by 3:00.
	I need everyone in their seats now.
State an intention	When this happens I will . . .
Make your position clear	This is really important to me.
	I want you to know how much this worries me.
Take a stand	I'm not willing to do that, but I would . . .
	You're not allowed to do that here.
Describe the impact	I can't give everyone a chance to answer when you are calling out the answer.
Express a feeling	I'm feeling sad.
	I get pretty angry when I see that.

Although developing assertion skills is important for efficiently managing the learning environment and dealing with student inappropriate behavior, it is also a valuable skill for effectively communicating in a variety of school situations. Assertion skills can support collaboration efforts among general education teachers and other special service support staff in that they provide a means for clearly communicating your needs in a manner that does not deny the needs of other involved parties. These skills can be helpful in the following situations.

- Parent conferences and confrontations
- Letting administrators and supervisors know where you stand
- Working with peer teachers and support staff

Personal Entitlements. The personal entitlements in the following list are some of our basic human rights. As such, they are rights of both teachers and students. Teachers should assert these rights for themselves while simultaneously honoring, supporting, and helping students assert their rights.

1. I am entitled to be treated with respect.
2. I am entitled to say no and not feel guilty.
3. I am entitled to make mistakes.
4. I am entitled to experience and express my feelings.
5. I am entitled to fulfill my needs.
6. I am entitled to take time and think.
7. I am entitled to change my mind.
8. I am entitled to do less than I am humanly capable of doing.
9. I am entitled to ask for what I want.
10. I am entitled to feel good about myself.

■ ■ ■ ■ ■ ■ ■ ■

LEARNING PRACTICE TASK: RECOGNIZING ASSERTIVE, AGGRESSIVE, AND NONASSERTIVE RESPONSES

Activity Directions: Here are some situations you are likely to encounter. Read each situation and response and decide whether the response is assertive, aggressive, or nonassertive. When you have finished, find a partner and share your answers. If you have different answers for any of the items, discuss how you categorized the response and try to reach consensus.

Situation 1: You are at a faculty meeting and are making a point about the new school discipline policy. Before you have a chance to finish your comment, Steve, who has a habit of interrupting, begins to make his point. You respond with,

Response: "You make me mad when you always butt in."

Response Category: _____

Situation 2: Your principal is walking down the corridor, your classroom door is open, and he steps in and says, "Your class is making too much noise." Your response,

Response: "Sorry sir. I really am awfully sorry."

Response Category: _____

Situation 3: You are team teaching but you're doing all the planning, teaching, interacting, and evaluating of students. You say,

Response: "We're supposed to be team teaching, and yet I see that I am doing all the work. I'd like to talk about changing this."

Response Category: _____

LEARNING PRACTICE TASK: PRACTICING ASSERTIVE BEHAVIOR

Activity Directions: You will be working in groups of three. Each person will take a turn playing the role of the teacher in responding assertively to a specific situation. You will also play the role of student and the role of observer. When you are serving in the role of observer, you will give structured, constructive feedback to the person playing the role of teacher, and you will complete a feedback checklist to help you give feedback relevant to use of assertive behaviors. Use the situation provided for this activity. Follow the sequence of steps listed.

Case Study: *During your lesson, a student gives a note to another student and then starts to chuckle. Other students are watching for your reaction.*

GUIDELINES FOR THE ROLE PLAY
A. It is not necessary to continue the role play to complete resolution of the situation. The purpose is only to provide experience in enacting assertive behaviors.
B. The person playing the student role should respond as naturally as possible.
C. The observer should keep the feedback focus on the use of assertive behavior.

Step 1: Divide into groups of three for this activity. Then, individually write out a statement that describes the problem clearly or that insists that your rights be respected. When each person has finished, compare and contrast your statements. After discussion, if you think it is necessary, make appropriate revisions to your original statement.

Step 2: Use role playing to portray the situation, with each person taking a turn in the roles of teacher, student, and observer. Before you begin role playing, review the *Peer Task Sheet: Assertion Feedback Checklist* and clarify any behaviors you may have questions about. During the role play, when you are playing the teacher you will be trying to use the assertive verbal and nonverbal behaviors listed. The person acting as observer will be watching you and completing the checklist in order to give you specific feedback on your performance. Decide who will play the teacher first and begin your first round of role playing.

Step 3: Get feedback on your use of assertive behaviors. The observer should follow the procedures outlined in Peer Task Sheet: Guidelines for Structured Feedback during the feedback session. Discuss any discrepancies between your perceptions of your behavior and the observer's feedback. Also discuss any problems you experienced when attempting to take an assertive stance.

Continue Steps 2 and 3 until each person has had a chance to play each role.

Peer Task Sheet: Assertion Feedback Checklist

	PRESENCE OF BEHAVIOR		
Verbal Behavior	Yes	Somewhat	No
Statements were direct and to the point	_____	_____	_____
Statements accurately reflected the teacher's goals	_____	_____	_____
Statements were firm but not hostile	_____	_____	_____
Statements showed some consideration, respect, or recognition of the student	_____	_____	_____
Statements left room for escalation	_____	_____	_____
Statements included sarcasm, name calling, or threatening	_____	_____	_____
Statements included preaching or lecturing	_____	_____	_____
Statements included pleading	_____	_____	_____
Statements blamed the student for the teacher's feelings	_____	_____	_____

Nonverbal Behavior	Assertive	Nonassertive	Aggressive
Eye contact	____ Maintained eye contact	____ Avoided eye contact	____ Glared, stared down
Voice volume	____ Appropriate loudness	____ Too soft	____ Too loud
Voice tone	____ Natural sounding	____ Whiny, tremulous	____ Shouting, yelling
Voice fluency	____ Fluent, even speed	____ Hesitant, pauses, filler words	____ Fast speed, "jackhammer"
Facial features	____ Confident, engaged look	____ Nervous twitches, inappropriate smiling	____ Impassive, stony look; contorted, disgusted expression
Body language	____ Alert, confident posture	____ Nervous gestures, trembling, fidgeting, shifting body	____ Rigid posture, pointing, shaking fists
Touch	____ Comforting, encouraging touch	____ None or erratic touching	____ Poking, grabbing, pushing

Peer Task Sheet: Guidelines for Structured Feedback

Stage 1: Begin with the strengths of the assertion (see chart). State exactly which behaviors were appropriate.

Stage 2: After you have exhausted all positive feedback, offer feedback in the areas where improvement could be made.

Guidelines for Constructive Feedback

Step 1: Describe the specific behavior without labeling it.
          Give objective rather than judgmental feedback.
          Avoid blaming, name calling, preaching, or lecturing.

Step 2: Offer possible ways to improve.
Alternate ways of behaving should be expressed in a tentative rather than an absolute manner. Do not impose a suggestion.
Step 3: Ask the person for a reaction to the suggestions.
Allow the person to accept, refuse, or modify the suggestion.

During the feedback session, keep the focus on assertion issues. Do not get involved with lengthy descriptions of the problem or anticipated negative reactions.

Teaching Students Assertion Skills

Morganett (1990) provides a series of activities to use with students to teach the concepts of aggression, nonassertion, and assertion. Specifically, the goals of these activities present the idea that everyone has certain rights, and that rights form the basis for choosing whether to be assertive. Students learn appropriate ways to make their rights known and integrate these concepts through active role play. For each of the student activities included, detailed lesson plans are provided with suggestions for conducting the activity and for establishing closure. Teachers are encouraged, however, to adapt the lessons to match their own teaching style and to address the specific needs of their students. Morganett recommends that teachers use a *Communicate Straight Chart* similar to the following to introduce the three ways of behaving.

COMMUNICATE STRAIGHT CHART

Being *nonassertive* means not saying what you think or believe, what you feel, or what you need or want.

You might do this because

- You are afraid of what the other person may do or how that person will react
- You don't know how to speak up for yourself
- You don't believe in your own rights
- You think another person's rights are more important than yours

When you behave nonassertively, you let others take advantage of you.

Being *aggressive* means saying what you think, feel, or want in a way that disregards another person's feelings and right to be treated with respect.

When you talk or act aggressively, you

- Attack others
- Threaten others
- Use put-downs
- Try to hurt or spite others

Being *assertive* means stating what you think, feel, or want clearly and honestly without blaming or threatening.

When you are behaving assertively you

- State what you want or need
- Say what you intend to do
- Express your feelings
- Tell the other person how his or her behavior affects you

She suggests that teachers make the following points with students.

- When you are nonassertive, you can usually avoid a conflict in the short term, but you probably won't get what you want or need. You might also feel like no one respects you or get angry at others for taking advantage of you.
- When you are aggressive, you may get what you want, but you may feel guilty afterwards for acting that way. Also you cause others to feel hurt and get angry at you. Sometimes others will not want to be around you or will want to seek revenge.
- When you are assertive, you have a good chance of getting what you want and need. Also, you avoid negative feelings such as anger, guilt, or resentment. Being assertive usually solves the problem or leads to a compromise when necessary. However, asserting your rights doesn't work in every situation or with all types of people. Sometimes you won't get what you want and sometimes the other person will feel hurt even though you tried to treat him or her with respect.

The lessons use many examples like the following.

Situation
Girl to friend: "Would you get my notebook from my locker for me after math?"

Response Options
Assertive: "Sorry. I can't do it today."

Nonassertive: "I'll be late for English, but if you want me to, okay."

Aggressive: "What's the matter with you? Are your arms broken?"

DEVELOPING ASSERTION SKILLS TO DIRECTLY CONFRONT STUDENTS

Teachers are faced with many situations in which they need to be proactive and confront students, peers, and even supervisors. The goal for this section is to extend the application of basic assertion skills to more difficult situations such as confrontation and giving effective criticism.

There are a variety of ways to assert yourself. Assertion involves direct, honest, and appropriate expressions of your thoughts and feelings. These kinds of responses represent assertive approaches to dealing with students (Silberman & Wheelan, 1980).

- Persist in asking for the behavior you expect
- Listen to students' points of view
- Reveal honest feelings
- Give brief reasons
- Politely refuse to do something
- Empathize
- Carry out reasonable consequences
- Make clear, direct requests

Three specific strategies are presented for approaching others when their behavior is causing a problem for you. There are also examples of how and when to use each.

Three Types of Assertion

Simple Assertion. A simple assertion is a direct statement in which you stand up for your rights by stating your needs, wants, and intentions. In a simple assertion you express personal rights, beliefs, feelings, or opinions. These are examples of simple assertions.

When telling a student you don't like his or her behavior

I don't want to see that again.

When being interrupted

I'd like to finish what I'm saying.

When being asked a question for which you are unprepared

I need a few minutes to think that over.

Validating Assertion. The validating assertion involves making a statement that conveys recognition of the other person's situation or feelings, followed by another statement that stands up for your rights. Examples of validating assertions are

When a student's display of anger is delaying the lesson

I know you're angry at James, but I want you to stop yelling so I can get the lesson started.

When two people are chatting loudly while a meeting is going on

You may not realize it but your talking is making it hard for me to hear what's going on in the meeting. Please keep it down.

Often other people more readily respond to assertion when they feel that they have been recognized. However, the validating assertion should not be used as a manipulation used merely to gain your own ends without genuine respect for the other person. Habitually saying, "I understand how you feel but . . ." can be just mouthing understanding and conning others into believing that their feelings are really being taken into account, when in fact their feelings are actually being discounted.

One advantage of a validating assertion is that it allows you a moment to try to empathize with the other person's feelings before reacting. This can help you keep perspective on the situation and reduce the chance of aggressively overreacting when you are irritated.

Escalating Assertion. An escalating assertion involves an increase in intensity or forcefulness of the assertion, moving from request to demand or from preference to refusal.

It starts with a minimal assertive response that can usually accomplish your goal with a minimum of effort and negative emotion. When the other person fails to respond to the minimal assertion and continues to behave inappropriately, you gradually escalate the assertion, becoming increasingly firm. Usually it's not necessary to go beyond the initial minimal assertion, but when it is, the idea is to be increasingly firm without becoming aggressive. The escalating assertion can move from a request to a demand, from a preference to an outright refusal, or from a validating assertion to a firm simple assertion. The following example illustrates an escalating assertive response.

A student continues to read a magazine during class.

I know that's really interesting, but it's time for math.

This is not the time for that.

Put that away now.

When using an escalating assertion, it is often effective just prior to making the final escalated assertion to offer a *contract option*. Here the student is informed of what the final assertion will be and is given a chance to change behavior before it occurs. For example, the teacher might say, "I have no alternative other than to send you to the office if you don't calm down. I'd prefer not to do that, but I will if you continue."

Whether the contract option is simply a threat depends on how it is delivered. If it is said in a threatening tone of voice that relies on emotion to carry the argument, it is a threat. When the contract option is carried out assertively, it is said in a matter-of-fact tone, simply giving information about the consequences that will occur if the situation is not resolved.

Learning to appropriately apply these types of assertions to initiate criticism and respond to persistence will take substantial time and effort, as well as considerable behavioral rehearsal in structured settings to enable teachers to become proficient.

Following are suggestions for enhancing skill in using these strategies.

- Try using each strategy to identify those strategies for which you are reasonably comfortable.
- Devise your own series of steps, or personal escalation.
- Practice with peers in role-play situations of both potential and actual situations.
- Develop written dialogues and then engage in behavioral rehearsals.
- Establish an ongoing support group to provide a forum for sharing experiences while trying to master these techniques.

Reflective Questions to Ask Yourself.   The following questions are helpful to consider when confronting students.

- Did I avoid a direct or implied message of blame?
- Did I describe rather than label the behavior?
- Did I clarify the impact the behavior had on me?
- Did I take responsibility for my own feeling?
- Did I express how I was feeling?

Guidelines for Authentic Confrontation.   When confronting students with problem behavior it is important to be honest and not demeaning, so that the student will take the problem seriously, but not become discouraged or antagonistic. Following are some guidelines for acting authentically in situations that warrant confrontation.

Get immediately to the point. Don't beat around the bush. Such behavior will make the student suspicious of your ulterior motives and will arouse defensiveness. Resist the temptation to ask a stream of incriminating questions. The student will quickly surmise that your questions are intended to bring out a confession. This approach will cause the student to feel under personal attack, and he or she is likely to counterattack or grow increasingly rigid in denying the blame. Come quickly to the point and let the student know the behavior that is a problem. Do not overwhelm the student with a flow of criticism.

Be specific. Do not use labels in describing the student's undesirable behavior (e.g., careless, lazy, irresponsible). Clearly describe the problem behavior and show how it has a concrete effect on you, the student him- or herself, and others. Send an impact message—for example, "I've noticed that you've been late three days this week. When you're late, others have to take over for you, and I have to stop and make out a tardy slip and that wastes everyone's time."

Create a positive climate. Communicate to the student that you're providing constructive feedback rather than personal attack. This can be accomplished by giving a brief rationale so that the student can see it's to his or her advantage to change the behavior. However, such rationales should be sincere—for example, "I know you're trying hard to pass this class, and when you're late it makes it harder."

Get a reaction to your criticism. When you ask for a reaction, the student is less likely to feel that he or she has been dumped on and that you're being judgmental. You might simply say, "What's your reaction to what I've said?" When you ask for a response, you need to be open to the possibility of countercriticism—for example, "All you ever do is criticize." Often there is some truth to countercriticism, and it's important to acknowledge valid criticism.

Ask for the student's suggestions and determine whether there's an obstacle preventing the student from changing his or her behavior. Asking for suggestions enhances the possibility of mutual problem solving. Any obstacles will need to be dealt with.

Get a commitment to change. Ask for a verbal commitment to change. You might also ask for suggestions on what you should do if the student fails to change the behavior.

Ten Steps for Effective Confrontation

1. Get immediately to the point. Do not ask a series of intimidating questions. Stick with a single problem behavior.
2. Clearly and specifically describe the problem.
3. State how the problem tangibly affects you, the student, or others.
4. Provide a brief and sincere rationale so the student can see that it's to his or her advantage to change the behavior.
5. Ask for a reaction from the student.
6. Acknowledge any objection from the student that seems valid.
7. Ask for suggestions on how to deal with the problem.
8. Determine whether there is a realistic obstacle preventing the student from changing his or her behavior. If so, deal with it.
9. Ask for a verbal commitment to change.
10. Ask for suggestions on what you should do if the student fails to change the behavior.

Sending Decisive Messages: The Interpretation-Impact-Instead (III) Format

One method for effective confrontation is the decisive message format, or Interpretation-Impact-Instead (III). It provides a way to express yourself clearly and directly, while ensuring that others understand exactly why you have a problem. Sending decisive messages lets the other person know you want to do more than describe the problem; you want to solve the problem. Also, decisive messages are less likely to cause a defensive reaction and shut down communication altogether. A decisive message has four components: a clear description of the problem, your interpretation, the impact, and what you would like instead. Each is described here.

Clear Description.   A clear description of an action, event, or situation that is causing a problem for you. A clear description is objective and doesn't include any value-laden or emotionally charged words, such as *always, never* or *ever*.

Example: *When you start to talk before I've finished . . .* rather than *When you always butt in . . .*

Your Interpretation.   This is the personal meaning you attach to something. Interpretations are subjective, thus there is more than one interpretation of an action, event, or situation.

Example: *When you come late, I think you don't care about this class.*

The Impact.   This describes what happens as a result of the behavior, or the situation created by the behavior. An impact statement might also include how you're acting or feeling because of the behavior or situation.

Impact statements serve the important function of helping you understand more clearly why you were affected by another's behavior and what impact it is having on you. Although you may think the other person should be aware of the impact of his or her behavior without being told, this often is not the case. It's important to explicitly state the impact of the behavior, so that the other person knows exactly why you are concerned.

What You'd Like Instead.   This is what you would like the other person to do or know. This would include stating where you stand on an issue or how important something is to you, as well as what you'd like to happen next. Telling others what you'd like to happen lets them know what they might do about the problem and helps move toward resolution, rather than letting the situation fester.

Example: *When you got in my face,* [description] *I thought you were trying to intimidate me.* [interpretation] *Now, I find I'm just waiting for you to do something wrong.* [impact] *I'd like to talk with you to see if we can get back on the right track.* [instead]

■ ■ ■ ■ ■ ■ ■ ■ ■

LEARNING PRACTICE TASK: IDENTIFYING COMPONENTS OF THE III DECISIVE MESSAGE FORMAT

Activity Directions: Identify which part of a decisive message is being used in each statement listed here. Use the following key: INT = interpretation, IMP = impact, and INS = what you'd like instead.

_____ I'm avoiding you because I'm angry.

_____ When you were late, I missed an important meeting.

_____ I'd like to talk to you about what happened.

_____ I guess you're anxious to get started.

_____ You don't value my opinion.

_____ I feel like you're not listening.

_____ I think you don't care about this class.

_____ I see you're not ready.

_____ I think you were trying to embarrass me.

_____ Ever since then I've been avoiding you.

_____ After our talk last week you seemed to withdraw.

_____ I feel you're wrong.

_____ From now on I would like you to speak respectfully to me.

_____ The next time this happens, I want you to come to me first.

_____ You must have forgotten our agreement.

_____ You're acting like something is bothering you.

The RRRR Process for Openly Confronting Students

Small irritations can accumulate, building into resentments and becoming potential sources of hostility. To prevent a stockpiling of resentments, it is helpful to deal with an annoying incident as it occurs by sharing your feelings with the student who is causing a problem for you.

In actual classroom situations, it can be difficult to deal with problems openly and positively. The pressure of the situation and the presence of other students sometimes mitigate against dealing spontaneously with your feelings. Thus, it is easy either to ignore situations and let resentments slowly build into potential hostility or to attack students by putting them down in some way. Either of these responses may alleviate the situation for a time, but they usually do little to solve the problem in the long run. Positively confronting students can lead to open communication between you and your students so that negotiation and compromise can be used to solve conflicts.

Strategies such as the RRRR Confrontation described in this section offer a process for both teachers and students to express their feelings. RRRR provides a vehicle for open communication so that negotiation and compromise can be used for mutual problem solving. Using the RRRR process to confront students with teacher concerns allows both teachers and students to express their feelings openly and honestly. The following are benefits of this confrontation process.

- Neither the teacher nor the student attacks the other.
- Both teacher and student respond honestly.
- Each considers the other's request as a viable option.
- A compromise is reached that resolves the problem for both the teacher and the student.

The RRRR Student Confrontation Process
Step 1: Relate

The teacher relates what he or she is concerned about to the student by stating only the behavior or situation of concern and the reason for concern. Next, the student responds similarly by relating to the teacher how he or she felt about the teacher's behavior and the reason for the reaction.

Step 2: Restate

To assure understanding, the student restates the teacher's concern to the satisfaction of the teacher. The teacher then restates the student's concern to the satisfaction of the student.

Note: This step may take several rounds to ensure that both are clear about each other's perception of the problem.

Step 3: Request
The teacher makes a request of the student and then the student responds with a request for the teacher.

Step 4: Resolve
Once the requests are clearly stated and restated, the teacher and student negotiate until both have decided to do something that each is comfortable with and that addresses the concern. They then negotiate and compromise, if necessary, until they reach a mutually agreeable resolution.

The following example of the RRRR Confrontation will help clarify the specific steps.

Related Concerns
Teacher: I was annoyed when you were reading another book while I was lecturing because I thought you didn't consider what I was saying important.

Student: I got mad when you kept asking me to put the book away and pay attention because it embarrassed me.

Restated Concerns
Student: You were annoyed when I was reading another book while you were lecturing because you thought that I didn't consider what you were saying important.

Teacher: You didn't like it when I kept asking you to pay attention because it embarrassed you.

Requests
Teacher: I would like you to pay attention when I am lecturing.

Student: I would like you to let me read when I am bored with your lecture.

Resolve
Teacher: I can't let you do something else during my lecture because it sets an example for others. Besides, the information might be important to the unit.

Student: I can see your concern, but why should I have to pay attention if I already know the material? I'd like you to let me work on something else if I do it so that no one sees when I know the material. That way no one will notice.

Teacher: I think that would be hard to do, but I can see that you will be bored if you are already familiar with the material. I can let you know just before class what the lecture will be about. If you feel you are familiar enough with it, you can go to the library. You can keep this privilege as long as you maintain your present academic level.

Student: That sounds good. And if I do decide to stay in class, I won't do other work during your lecture.

Restated Resolution
Student: You said that I may go to the library if I feel that I would be bored during the lesson because I'm familiar with the material already.

Teacher: You said that you'd like that arrangement and that if you decide to stay in the class, you won't do other work.

In this example, both the teacher's and the student's issues are stated clearly so that teacher and student understood exactly what each other's concern is. Neither the student nor the teacher attacks the other. Both maintain a high level of honesty and openness. Each considers the other's request and reacts to it as a real possibility. In the end, they reach a mutually agreeable solution that is reasonable for each of them, a solution that may never have been considered without the confrontation.

LEARNING PRACTICE TASK: PRACTICING THE RRRR CONFRONTATION

Confronting students openly and allowing students the reciprocal right to confront the teacher with their issues will take some practice because it is an unfamiliar format. The following activity is intended to provide practice in developing the necessary skills before transferring them to the classroom.

Activity Directions: To practice this confrontation process you need a group of six or more people, preferably about ten. One person volunteers to be teacher, one person volunteers to be coach, and the rest are students. Each member of the group should have a chance to be teacher, coach, and student in successive rounds. The teacher separates from the students and prepares a 10-minute lesson in any subject for an appropriate age group. The students, meanwhile, plan to role play different student types. The types can include a student who is bored, argumentative, arrogant, obsequious, or any type that might be found in a classroom. In role-playing students, it is helpful not to get so locked into the role that you do not react normally to responses from the teacher or other students. The quiet student, for example, should speak if he or she has something to say. The argumentative students should behave if the teacher effectively does something to cause them to settle down. The coach at this time reviews the RRRR process to become familiar with the steps.

1. When everyone is ready, the teacher begins the lesson with the students role-playing at the age level suggested by the teacher and the coach who are observing the process.
2. After about 10 minutes of the lesson, the teacher chooses the student who makes him or her the most uncomfortable to engage in the student confrontation. The two, teacher and student, sit face to face and engage in the RRRR confrontation process following the prescribed steps. Now the coach plays the important role of keeping the confrontation positive by not allowing destructive statements (personal attacks), by making sure each step is followed, and by ensuring that each person has an equal opportunity to speak.

REFLECTIVE QUESTIONS
What would keep you from using this process?

What do you know about yourself that might make it difficult to implement this procedure?

What difficulties would you anticipate in using this type of encounter?

For what type of situation do you think this procedure would likely be most effective?

How can you best use confrontation with your students?

What is the most efficient way for you to become familiar with this procedure?

TEACHER-FACILITATED PROBLEM RESOLUTION

The following presents effective procedures for teachers to use to facilitate conflict resolution with individual students or between students. A communication model is presented that invites students to engage in mutual problem solving. Inviting student participation in problem solving involves the teacher using listening skills to engage students and check for understanding, demonstrating acknowledgment of the student's perspective, focusing on the issues rather than the people, and directly confronting problems. The series of skills take the process from listening, to connecting, to problem solving.

This problem-solving process moves through the following sequence.

Step 1: Validating the student's feelings
Step 2: Connecting with the student
Step 3: Expressing your feelings and asserting your needs
Step 4: Transitioning to problem solving
Step 5: Facilitating the problem-solving process so that the solution satisfies everyone involved
Step 6: Restoring the relationship (if necessary)

COMMUNICATION SKILLS FOR INVITING COMMUNICATION AND PROBLEM SOLVING

Inviting student participation in problem solving involves moving through three stages. First, the teacher uses listening skills to engage students and check for understanding. Stage 2 involves both self-disclosing and demonstrating acknowledgement of the student's perspective. The final stage incorporates inviting cooperation, focusing on the issues, and directly confronting problem areas.

Three-Stage Model of Communication Skills for Problem Solving

Stage 1: Listening	Level 1: Engaging	Level 2: Checking	
	Opening	Paraphrasing	
	Exploring	Clarifying	
	Reflecting	Perception Checking	
Stage 2: Connecting	Level 1: Accepting Self	Level 2: Accepting Others	
	Being Authentic	Acknowledging	
	Accepting Ownership	Encouraging	
	Verifying Assumptions	Validating	
		Appreciating	
Stage 3: Resolving	Level 1: Inviting	Level 2: Focusing	Level 3: Confronting
	Inviting Cooperation	Inquiring	Challenging
	Requesting	Summarizing	Asserting
	Enlisting	Sharing Information	Restoring
	Soliciting	Suggesting	Stating Concern

Here each of the twenty-five communication skills in this model is described with examples. Some of these skills are presented in greater detail in earlier sections of this book.

Stage 1: Listening

Level 1: Engaging
These active listening skills attempt to engage the speaker.

Skill	Description	Example
Opening	Opening the door by inviting the person to talk (sometimes referred to as *door openers*)	*Do you want to talk about it?* *Do you want to tell me what happened?*
Exploring	Questioning in an open-ended way to try to extend the person's thinking about the issues	*Have you thought about . . . ?* *How is this related to . . . ?*

	Helping the person to consider alternative perceptions	
Reflecting	Responding to the emotions expressed or implied	*You sound disappointed.* *You want me to know that you are very frustrated with this situation.*

Level 2: Checking
These active listening skills check for understanding.

Skill	**Description**	**Example**
Paraphrasing	Repeating what the person has said in your own words	*I think I got the message. You said you are feeling anxious about this class and you think I'm moving through the material too quickly.*
		His behavior is causing you to doubt your effectiveness as a teacher.
Clarifying	Requesting restatement to ensure understanding	*I'm confused about this. I'll try to state what I think you have said. First, . . .*
	Used when one aspect of the story doesn't seem to follow from the previous one or when facts and feeling don't seem to match	*Let me see if I got what you said. You said . . .*
Perception Checking	Offering more than one interpretation and asking for help or clarification	*I'm having a hard time getting clear about what you're saying. When you said . . . did you mean . . . or . . . ?*
	Acknowledging the possibility of an interpretation other than the one you are making	*I'm not sure what you mean when you said . . . To me it means . . . Is that what you meant?*

Stage 2: Connecting

Level 1: Accepting Self
These three skills are all proactive and represent a person's ability to be reflective and recognize that one's own way of seeing things is influenced by one's own identity and beliefs.

Skill	**Description**	**Example**
Being Authentic	Being "upfront," honest, and self-disclosing	*I'm so angry about this I can't talk to you right now.*
		This is a difficult time for me.
Accepting Ownership	Owning your own interpretations and not projecting intentions	*I'm concerned about the way I've been acting toward you.*
	Not expecting others to do or think the way you do	*Using that tone of voice really aggravates me.*
Verifying Assumptions	Rather than projecting intentions or attributing motives without verifying, explicitly stating your assumptions	*Taylor, I assume that means . . . When you do that, I think you don't care.*

Level 2: Accepting Others
Acknowledging, encouraging, validating, and appreciating—all communicate respect for, and acceptance of, the other person(s). Also, these skills all are nonjudgmental and communicate understanding and caring. In acknowledging, the acceptance is of rights, needs, and viewpoints; in appreciating, it is actions and interests; in validating, it is feelings and mood; and in encouraging, it is efforts and individual valuing.

These skills attempt to join the needs and wants of both parties and represent an effort on the part of the person initiating the communication to connect to the other person. They are sometimes referred to as *blending skills,* in that they represent joining the other person's world and seeing things from that person's perspective.

Skill	Description	Example
Acknowledging	Accepting and showing respect for others' point of view, position, or opinion	*I can appreciate why you think that. That's an interesting perspective.*
	Accepting without judgment others' rights and needs	
Encouraging	Valuing effort, accepting individual worth, and respecting others' competence	*Okay, you know what to do. I see you found your own way to do that.*
Validating	Communicating acceptance of feelings	*I can see you are angry now.*
	Can go further to communicate concern and understanding	*I understand that you are upset because of what he did.*
	Acknowledging others' right to have and experience whatever emotion they are experiencing	
Appreciating	Showing appreciation for actions and interests	*I appreciate your willingness to work this out.*
	Recognizing what others do	*I'm pleased to see you are enjoying yourself.*

Stage 3: Resolving

Level 1: Inviting

Inviting skills attempt to ensure mutual participation.

Skill	Description	Example
Inviting Cooperation	Communicating that you need or desire the other person's help and cooperation	*I'd like you with me on this, Frieda. I need your help on this.*
Requesting	Communicating that you need or desire the other person's input or advice	*I see it this way . . . ; how do you see it?* *I would like your input about how we might resolve this.*
Enlisting	Asking what the other person wants, needs, or feels, as well as what the person may want from you	*What could I do that would make things better?* *What would you like to see happen? How can I help?*
Soliciting	Asking what the person would like to do	*Would you like to leave the room?*
	Asking what the person wants you to do	*What do you think I should do about this?*

Level 2: Focusing

Focusing skills involve trying to help move the issue toward resolution.

Skill	Description	Example
Inquiring	Asking questions to move the issue toward problem solving	*I'm wondering . . .* *What do you think would happen if . . . ?*

	Inquiry rather than advocacy—remaining open, not advocating for your own needs and position	
	Asking open-ended questions	
	Asking questions for reflection	
Summarizing	Pulling together ideas, themes	*Here's what we have so far . . . Did I miss anything?*
	Reviewing the issues covered	*Let's take a look at all the issues we've discussed so far.*
	Summarizing where you are	*So, you're proposing that . . .*
Sharing Information	Sharing ideas and information	*I think I know a strategy that may be helpful here.*
	Including statements about personal experience	*My experience is . . .*
Suggesting	Making suggestions	*What do you think about using . . . ?*
		I have an idea that might work. How about . . . ?

Level 3: Confronting

Confronting skills take a proactive stance for addressing issues and concerns.

Skill	Description	Example
Challenging	Confronting others when they attempt to get their own needs met without considering others' needs	*That sounded like an accusation to me.*
	Challenging others to reflect on, or consider, their own actions and weigh their appropriateness	*How would you feel if it were you?*
Asserting	Expressing your rights, feelings, needs, or wants	*I don't like that idea because . . .* *I'd like . . .*
Restoring	Monitoring the communication process, and intervening to keep it on track	*You're getting off track. We're talking about possible solutions now.*
		We haven't heard from everyone.
		Is there anyone else who wants to add something?
Stating Concern	Expressing a concern about the other person's behavior, the process, or a particular idea or potential solution	*I'm concerned that we don't have enough information.* *I'm worried that if we do that . . .*

The following student–teacher dialogue is an example of problem solving in which the teacher respectfully confronts the student and invites the student's participation in arriving at a mutually agreeable solution.

Teacher: Mark, when we talked on Tuesday, you said you were going to take your small-group project seriously. I don't think you are and I'm concerned. [asserting]

Mark: Yeah, I know.

Teacher: Since then, I've been impressed with how you've worked—that is, up to today. Today, I think you slipped back to old behaviors. [stating concern]

Mark: I guess I did.

Teacher: What happened? [requesting]

Mark: I don't know. I just couldn't get into it today.

Teacher: What do you think was different today? [inquiring]

Mark: I just think I didn't push myself today.

Teacher: What do you think I should do about that? [soliciting]

Mark: Give me another chance.

Teacher: If I gave you another chance, what can I expect from you? [enlisting]

Mark: I'll be serious. I won't fool around.

Teacher: That sounds good. What should I do if you slip again? [soliciting]

Mark: I won't. But if I do, then call my parents. They'll probably ground me.

Teacher: Okay. I'll give you a chance. If you stick to our agreement, I won't do anything. If you don't, I'll call your parents. Agreed? [summarizing]

Mark: Agreed. By the way, thanks.

Teacher: You're welcome.

Individual Problem-Solving Conference

In this example, the teacher moves through a six-step process with the student beginning by describing the problem, moving to brainstorming solutions, to both the teacher and student evaluating the potential solutions, then to selecting, trying out, and deciding on the solution (adapted from Gootman, 2001).

Example. Andy uses profanity when he gets frustrated with school work.

1. **Describe the problem.** The teacher uses a pattern of asserting and soliciting to get the student to accept ownership of the problem. Whether or not the student sees it as a problem, the teacher lets him know firmly that it is a problem for others. Living in a community means making compromises for the good of everyone.

   Teacher: Those words are offensive to me and to others in the classroom. [*asserting*] I've reminded you several times not to use them and it doesn't seem to help. [*accepting ownership*] We can't allow them in the classroom. [*asserting*] I notice that when things don't go right with your work, you use cuss words to express your anger. [*sharing information*] How can you help yourself not use those words in school when you're frustrated? [*soliciting*]

   Andy: But I don't think anything's wrong with them. That's how I feel. Besides, my dad uses those same words when he's driving.

   Teacher: You must decide for yourself what you do out of school but in school, it's against the rules. Besides, it's offensive to others and me. [*asserting*] The next time you feel frustrated, what could you do that would not offend other people? [*soliciting*]

2. **Brainstorm solutions with student.** Both the teacher and student offer solutions.

   Andy: You could ignore me and pretend you don't hear it.

   Teacher: What else?

   Andy: I could say a different word instead.

Andy: You could wash my mouth out with soap; that's what my friend's mom does.

Andy: I could whisper it to myself.

Teacher: You could miss recess every time you say a cuss word.

3. **Evaluate solutions with student.** Both teacher and student assert needs and wants.

- Ignore

  Teacher: I can't live with that. The words are offensive and I can't ignore them.

- Different word

  Andy: Maybe that would work if I found a word that really made me feel good getting it out.

- Wash with soap

  Teacher: I won't do that to you. That's not healthy.

- Whisper

  Andy: That might work, but I might forget and say it out loud. I'm not sure I can remember to keep it down.

- Miss recess

  Teacher: I don't want you to miss recess. It's important for you to get exercise and associate with other kids.

  Andy: I sure don't want to miss it.

4. **Select a solution.** The student chooses a solution that both the teacher and student agree on.

   Andy decides to try out a different word. He and his teacher toss around several suggestions, and he finally chooses a word to say when he is tempted to say the cuss word.

5. **Try out the solution.**

   Andy is successful in using the new word.

6. **Evaluate and decide.**

   Andy has just about quit using the cuss words, so he and his teacher decide that the problem is almost solved. If he had still been swearing frequently, then they would have had to go back to either Step 2 or 3 and settle on another solution. Perhaps the next time they may try the whispering technique.

The following section provides some examples of using these skills when dealing with students in conflict situations.

Example. Two students are arguing angrily. These students are not likely to develop a relationship, and the goal is for mutual tolerance or agreeing to disagree.

Teacher: You're both very angry.

Student 1: That's for sure!

Student 2: You'd be mad too if you had to put up with him all day.

Teacher: Rather than continue yelling at each other, I'd like you to talk about what each of you did that makes the other mad. After you do that, we'll try to see how we can come up with a solution that will satisfy both of you.

Example. In this middle school situation, the teacher mediates the conflict between two students who belong to two competing cliques.

Kayla: If you had a brain in your head, you would not act so dumb.

Christina: You and your friends would not have a brain even if you put your heads together. How can you call me dumb? You've got to be halfway intelligent to know whether I have a brain and you're not even a half-wit.

Teacher: Whoa! You two are about to erupt. I want to know what set each of you off. Kayla, tell me what upset you first. Then Christina, tell me what upset you. I want you both to close your eyes while I listen to what each of you has to say.

Kayla/Christina: Why do we have to close our eyes?

Teacher: It will be easier for me to hear what each of you has to say if I can focus on your words rather than how you treat each other. Okay, Kayla, what did Christina say or do to upset you and when did she do it? . . . Okay, Christina, what did Kayla say or do to upset you and when did she do it? . . . I can see that you both are upset and both of you believe that you have a legitimate reason for feeling the way you do. So, what do we do about your conflict? Since you can't shout one another down and we don't allow fighting in school, what do you want to have happen?

Christina: I'd feel a lot better if I could tell Kayla off and never see or hear her again.

Kayla: Me, too.

Teacher: Is one of you going to transfer to another school tomorrow? Because you both are shaking your heads no, I guess that won't be happening. Since you are going to see and hear each other and I won't let you yell or fight, what else can you do?

At this point, the teacher has identified the trigger event, calmed the situation, established boundaries for interaction (i.e., no shouting and no fighting), and has started working toward solution generation. The plan that results may be no more than a truce in which students agree to avoid each other or "turn the other cheek" rather than attack at the mere sight of one another. In this situation, the teacher probably would not attempt to have the students become friends. Rather, she would attempt to resolve the open conflict and have the students behave in an acceptable manner.

The case below illustrates the teacher's proactive use of a problem-solving conference.

Teacher: Mack, I have asked you to stay to talk with me because of a problem during class discussions. Often when I ask a question you call out the answer without waiting to be called on. Do you agree this is happening?

Mack: Yuh.

Teacher: That is a problem because it doesn't give others a chance. I need to be able to find out whether other students understand what we are discussing.

Mack: But what if they don't know?

Teacher: You mean, if nobody raises a hand or tries to answer?

Mack: Yeah, then can I answer?

Teacher: Do you suppose that some people might need more time to think about what they are going to say?

Mack: I guess so. But it's boring to just sit and wait for someone to think if I already know it.

Teacher: It is hard to wait and be patient. But I need to be able to teach the whole class and to conduct the discussions for everybody. Can you think of any way that we could handle this so I can call on others when I want to and you can still have your fair turn?

Mack: I suppose I could raise my hand and not call out my answer.

Teacher: That would be a big help. I would really appreciate that. I think you have some good ideas and should still have plenty of chances to answer.

Questioning

This is a particularly difficult skill for teachers to master because so much of their questioning is typically of a fact-finding nature and the major purpose is to get specific data or answers they are looking for. When questioning is used as part of an inviting communication, it is not a fault-finding mission. When questions are for the purpose of finding out who's wrong and doling out a fitting punishment, the teacher is acting as both jury and judge, rendering his or her decision one of authority.

Questioning as part of inviting communication assumes both or all parties are active participants and have input in the problem-solving process for the purpose of arriving at a mutually agreeable resolution. Here the goal of questioning is to explore and clarify.

In the communication model proposed here, questioning occurs at both Stage 1 and 3. In the initial stage, the idea is to: open up a potentially limiting perspective of the problem or possible solutions (exploring); clear up confusion or get more information if there seem to be missing pieces in the story or the accounting of an incident (clarifying); or clarify meaning or potential misperceptions (perception checking). In Stage 3, questioning is used to invite participation at Level 1, to get more information at Level 2, and to challenge attempts to get personal needs met at the expense of others at Level 3.

Using Listening and Connecting Skills to Transition to Problem Solving

Teachers who invite communication see issues from students' points of view and can communicate understanding of what their students are experiencing. Though they may not always agree with the actions students take to deal with their feelings, they do accept that students have a right to feelings. However, they clearly differentiate between the right to have strong feelings and the right to act aggressively. Teachers show appreciation for how and why students feel and think the way they do; but they still assert their position that students don't have the right to harm others, disrupt the class, or destroy property. They use listening and connecting skills to transition to problem solving. They do this by speaking respectfully and showing faith in the students' abilities to find a solution.

This problem-solving process moves through three phases.

- Phase 1: Accept, validate, respect
- Phase 2: Connect with the student
- Phase 3: Transition to problem solving

The following examples illustrate transition to problem solving.

I can see you're furious about what he said about your mother. I don't blame you for being angry. I'd be angry, too. But I'm responsible for everyone's safety here, so you'll have to find another way to deal with your anger.

In this example, after validating the student's feeling and acknowledging the student's right to feel angry, the teacher expresses appreciation for the feeling, but then moves to asserting her need for a reasonable solution.

I know you feel bad about knocking over Thinh's project and that it really wasn't your fault, but for Thinh, all his hard work was wasted. What do you think you should do now?

In this example, the teacher moves from validating the student's feeling to connecting, and then to resolution.

■ ■ ■ ■ ■ ■ ■ ■ ■

LEARNING PRACTICE TASK: USING INVITING COMMUNICATION FOR PROBLEM SOLVING

Activity Directions: Pair up with another person. Follow the sequence of steps listed.

1. Review all of the skills in the communication chart.

2. Select one of the following common classroom problems to work with.
   ■ Student is usually late for class
   ■ Student is abusive to other students
   ■ Student does very little classwork

3. Write an initial response for each of the categories below by selecting those types of responses from the twenty-five skills presented that seem appropriate for the situation.

a. Showing respect

_____

_____

_____

b. Connecting personally

_____

_____

_____

c. Confronting the issues

_____

_____

_____

d. Asserting the teacher's needs

_____

_____

_____

e. Problem-solving negotiation

_____

_____

_____

f. Resolution

_____

_____

_____

STRESS MANAGEMENT STRATEGIES

Although there is much information and training available for adults on how to cope with and manage stress, children and youth generally get little help in dealing with the stress in their lives. School-age children face increased emotional strain with the demise of the family support structure, putting many families in upheaval as they try to cope with the effects of poverty, transience, and divorce. Students have the additional pressure to be accepted, to succeed in school, and to belong among their peers.

Students have fewer support systems and coping skills and thus are more likely to respond in inappropriate ways to stress, such as using drugs or alcohol, committing crimes, withdrawing, or engaging in self-destructive behavior. In the classroom setting, stress reactions can include irritability, low frustration levels, underachievement, bullying, and hostility.

Some actions teachers can take to enhance the probability that students will actually use cognitive behavior management strategies include the following.

- Be a model for your students. Use cognitive behavior management strategies yourself and share with your students how you are using and have used these strategies to help you cope with stress.
- Be authentic and disclose your thinking process. Use problem-solving skills to *think ahead* for your students, even enlist their help.
- Keep in mind that you are a coping model not a mastery model. Mistakes are valuable learning tools and these, too, should be shared with your students.

Techniques available to help students manage stress include some that have previously been discussed. These include self-control strategies and social skills training, as well as strategies to help students deal with the physical reactions to stress. Coping strategies for stress management attempt to minimize the effects of stressful situations, so that students can cope more adequately with stressors. Available techniques can be categorized as follows.

Physiological	Cognitive	Behavioral
Diaphragmatic breathing	Self-instruction training	Behavioral self-control
Progressive relaxation training	Cognitive restructuring	Assertiveness training
Exercise		Social skills training

Teaching social skills in general should serve to reduce stress; some simple physiological techniques also are effective. Physiological stress coping skills produce a direct effect on the body. They are the easiest for students to learn and produce the fastest results. In this section, techniques that can help students cope with stress are described.

Diaphragmatic Breathing

This technique is easy to learn and requires the least amount of discipline to master. It also is referred to as *deep* or *relaxed breathing*. For younger students, you can call it *belly breathing*. Simply put, the abdomen pushes out when you inhale and pulls in when you exhale. Students should practice this regularly, if possible, while lying on the floor. The following is just one example of a deep breathing exercise you can teach and practice with students to help them release tension and relax. The teacher guides students through the exercise by reading the directions in a quiet, calming voice.

Beginning Breathing Exercise: Inhaling-through-Nose Breathing.
As you breathe in, imagine you are sniffing a very delicate flower. Let the flow of breath into your nose be as smooth and gentle as possible, so you barely rustle a petal.

Take a full breath.

PAUSE

Relax, letting yourself breathe out naturally, without effort.

PAUSE 5 SECONDS

Continue breathing this way, breathing in and out quietly and evenly at your own pace.

PAUSE 5 SECONDS

Notice the relaxing and refreshing rush of air as it quietly moves in and out of your lungs.

PAUSE 5 SECONDS

See how far you can follow the inward flow of air.

PAUSE 5 SECONDS

Can you feel it move past your nostrils?

PAUSE 5 SECONDS

Can you feel the air in the passages of your nose?

PAUSE 5 SECONDS

Can you feel the air flowing into your body?

PAUSE 10 SECONDS

Take your time. Breathe easily and fully.

PAUSE 10 SECONDS

Let yourself become more and more quiet, more and more relaxed.

PAUSE 10 SECONDS

Progressive Relaxation Training (PRT)

PRT is more difficult to learn, but it produces a deeper and longer-lasting state of relaxation. It involves alternately tensing and relaxing your muscles. The idea is to learn the difference between these two states so that you can more easily recognize tension in your body and use PRT to achieve relaxation. This technique generally follows a script which takes 15 to 20 minutes. Daily practice for several weeks will be required to achieve results. PRT has been demonstrated effective in helping youths reduce and control nonattending behaviors (Redfering & Bowman, 1981); decreasing test anxiety in middle school students (Smead, 1981); and calming anxious youths with mild disabilities (Morganett & Bauer, 1987). The following section provides an example with specific directions for the teacher as well as directions to guide students through the exercise.

Instructions for Learning the Tension-Release or Progressive Relaxation Method.   The general idea is to first tense a set of muscles and then relax them, so that students can relax more deeply than before they were tensed. Initially, the exercises take about 20 minutes. As students become more proficient, less and less time will be needed. The teacher can either tape the directions presented here or lead students through the exercise by reading them aloud. The setting should be quiet and free of interruptions and distractions. Have students sit comfortably, well supported by their chairs, so that they don't have to use their muscles to support themselves. Usually these exercises are done with closed eyes.

The tension-release exercises are for each group of muscles. The ultimate goal is to relax all muscle groups simultaneously to achieve total body relaxation. Each muscle group can be relaxed separately. Because relaxation cannot be achieved all at once, a gradual process is recommended for learning it. This process involves: first learning to relax your arms; then your facial area, neck, shoulders, and upper back; then your chest, stomach, and lower back; then your hips, thighs, and calves; and finally your whole body.

The basic procedure for each muscle group is the same: Tense the muscle, release the tension, and feel the relaxation. It is recommended that each muscle group be tensed and held for 5 seconds, noticing the tension, then releasing it, noticing the pleasant warmth of relaxation. The sequence is repeated three times for each group of muscles, each time taking a deep breath, saying "relax" softly or silently while breathing out slowly. The idea is to master this practice so that in the stressful situations of daily life, students learn to notice their body's tension, identify the tense muscle groups, and relax them.

Muscle Group	Tension Exercise
1. The dominant hand	Make a tight fist.
2. The other hand	Make a tight fist.
3. The dominant arm	Curl your arm up; tighten the bicep.
4. The other arm	Curl your arm up; tighten the bicep.
5. Upper face and scalp	Raise your eyebrows as high as possible.
6. Center face	Squint your eyes and wrinkle your nose.
7. Lower face	Smile in a false, exaggerated way; clench your teeth.
8. Neck	a. Pull your head slightly forward, then relax.
	b. Pull your head slightly back, then relax.
9. Chest and shoulders	a. Pull your shoulders back until the blades almost touch, then relax.
	b. Pull your shoulders forward all the way, then relax.
10. Abdomen	Make your abdomen tight and hard.
11. Buttocks	Tighten them together.
12. Upper right leg	Stretch your leg out from you, tensing both upper and lower muscles.
13. Upper left leg	Stretch your leg out from you, tensing both upper and lower muscles.
14. Lower right leg	Pull your toes up toward you.
15. Lower left leg	Pull your toes up toward you
16. Right foot	Curl your toes down and away from you.
17. Left foot	Curl your toes down and away from you.

Exercise

There is evidence that aerobic exercise has a tranquilizing effect that reduces stress and can lead to reduction in maladaptive behavior (Allen, 1980; Shipman, 1984).

Jogging, roller skating, cycling, or fast walking can readily be done at school and can be incorporated as part of the physical education program.

Some Relaxation Exercises to Use with Students

The following specific relaxation training exercises described by Morgan and Reinhart (1991) are exercises that will help get students in a relaxed state. It is important to realize that all of these techniques require practice, as with anything you do that is new to you and new to your students. Students may frustrate you in the beginning by acting silly or being uncooperative. It may seem like chaos at first and you may experience the feeling of not having control of your class. But be persistent and keep working on these interventions until they become as natural as teaching any other lesson.

Tense and Relax

To know what relaxation feels like, students must first be able to recognize their tensions. Although many are already tense, they must experience (in a conscious way) extreme tension so they can feel truly relaxed. Following are a few exercises you can use in the classroom.

Begin by having the students sit up straight at their desks, feet flat on the floor, arms to their sides, and chin resting on their chests. Now, have them curl the toes under and squeeze tight; then let go. Next, have them squeeze the muscles in the calves, then let go. Follow through with the thighs, buttocks, and abdomen, each time having them let go. Next, have them pull the shoulders up tight around their necks, then let go. Have them make tight fists, then let go. Have them tense the arms, then let go. Finally, the face muscles: Have them squeeze the eyes tightly shut, purse the lips together tightly, clench the teeth, then let go.

Follow this with stretching exercises. Have them stretch out the muscles of the feet, legs, arms, and face as far as possible. Have them hold the eyes open very wide, stretch open the jaw, stick out the tongue and stretch, then relax everything. When this exercise is finished, students should know what real tension feels like and how it feels to relax.

Breathing

Have the students practice breathing exercises for 2 or 3 minutes. This is simple and involves taking in a deep breath until the stomach is extended, then holding it for 3 or 4 seconds. Next, have them let all the air go rushing out while telling them to blow out all the bad feelings: angry feelings, scary feelings, sad feelings, nervous feelings. (They will probably act silly the first few times you do this; remind them what they are supposed to do. Keep bringing them back to the task. Once this has become a daily routine, the silliness will stop.) Now, practice rhythmic, steady, even, deep breathing. Tell your students to close their eyes and begin concentrating on breathing. Do it with them to show what you mean.

The Rag Doll

This is a short, simple exercise that can be used after the students have practiced and incorporated the basic skills of relaxation, such as tension–release and breathing. For a few minutes have them begin with tension–release and steady, deep breathing. Then tell them they are going to let each part of the body imitate a rag doll bit by bit. Give the following directions: "First, sit up and let your legs go loose and limp. Now, the body and the arms. Let them go loose and limp; let your head droop down, or back, or to the side, loose and limp just like a rag doll. Keep up your steady, deep breathing. Do this for about 10 minutes."

Using Clay
Give the students a lump of clay and have them hold it for awhile and enjoy its feel. Tell them to rub it around in their hands, kneading, pressing, folding, and squeezing it so that it oozes between their fingers. Ask them to close their eyes and imagine all of the things that they could mold out of the clay. Give them about a minute to imagine these things. Then tell them to select one of those figures and mold what they want. This is a very relaxing exercise for young children.

Behavioral and Cognitive Stress Coping Strategies

Behavioral strategies include verbal and other overt behaviors required by students to manage stress through the manipulation of their environment. They can include some social skills such as responding appropriately to criticism, name calling, or peer pressure, or time management techniques involving setting long-term and short-term goals, monitoring time spent, and prioritizing activities.

Cognitive stress coping strategies are the most difficult to learn. In cognitive restructuring, students learn how their beliefs and inner speech can cause anxiety and how to use disputing irrational beliefs and positive self-talk to change their behavior patterns. Meichenbaum (1985) has proposed an integrative strategy combining several skills and involving five stages. His integrative strategy for stress inoculation combines a number of techniques including relaxation, cognitive restructuring, and behavioral rehearsal.

1. In the *conceptual framework stage,* the student is taught basic concepts regarding stress and stress management.
2. In the *relaxation training stage,* the student learns to master some form of relaxation training, usually PRT.
3. In the *cognitive restructuring stage,* the student disputes any irrational beliefs that might be contributing to his or her high levels of anxiety or anger.
4. In the *stress script stage,* the student writes down everything he or she needs to say or do to manage stress before, during, and after being exposed to the stressor.
5. In the *inoculation stage,* the student uses his or her stress script as he or she is gradually exposed to larger and larger "doses" of the stressor.

The stress script consists of everything the student says and does before, during, and after encountering the anger-provoking stressor. The following is an example of a stress script a student might use to cope with anger provoked by peer teasing (Kaplan, 1995).

Before Confrontation	*What do I have to do? Take a few belly breaths to get ready. This is going to be hard but I can do it. I just have to remember to take deep breaths and keep repeating the magic words, "saying it doesn't make it so." Here they come. I'm ready for them.*
During Confrontation	*Stay cool. Saying it doesn't make it so. Take some deep breaths. Saying it doesn't make it so. Just ignore them. Look away. Saying it doesn't make it so. Saying it doesn't make it so.*
After Confrontation	*I did it! I kept myself from getting angry. It worked. I can control myself. They didn't tease me as much as they usually do. Pretty soon they won't tease me at all. Now let's see . . . was there anything I could improve on for next time?*

EXAMPLES OF SELF-STATEMENTS FOR COPING WITH STRESS

PREPARING FOR A STRESSOR
- What is it you have to do?
- You can develop a plan to deal with it.
- Just think about what you can do about it. That's better than getting anxious.
- No negative self-statements; just think rationally.
- Don't worry; worry won't help anything.
- Maybe what you think is anxiety is eagerness to confront the stressor.

REACTING DURING THE STRESS-PRODUCING SITUATION
- Just "psych" yourself up—you can meet this challenge.
- You can convince yourself to do it. You can reason your fear away.
- One step at a time; you can handle the situation.
- Don't think about fear; just think about what you have to do. Stay relevant.
- This anxiety you feel is a reminder to use your coping exercises.
- This tenseness can be an ally; a cue to cope.
- Relax; you're in control. Take a slow, deep breath.
- Ah, good.

COPING WITH THE FEELING OF BEING OVERWHELMED
- When fear comes, just pause.
- Keep the focus on the present; what is it you have to do? Label your fear from 0 to 10 and watch it change.
- You should expect your fear to rise.
- Don't try to eliminate fear totally; just keep it manageable.

REFLECTING ON THE EXPERIENCE
- It worked!
- It wasn't as bad as you expected.
- You made more out of your fear than it was worth.
- Your damn ideas—that's the problem. When you control them, you control your fear.
- It's getting better each time you use the procedures.
- You can be pleased with the progress you're making.
- You did it!
- You're doing better all the time.

From D. Meichenbaum. Self-instructional methods: How to do it. In A. Goldstein and F. Kanfer (Eds.), *Helping people change: Methods and materials.* Elmsford, NY: Pergamon Press, 1975. Reprinted by permission.

CRITICAL REFLECTION ON PRACTICE: HELPING STUDENTS DEAL WITH STRESS

Activity Directions: Follow these steps to begin planning to implement stress-reducing strategies for your students.

1. Devise a way to identify the sources of stress your students encounter.
2. How might you go about matching causes of stress with strategies for dealing with them?
3. What factors do you want to consider in devising your program for stress reduction?
4. What are the major concerns you want to keep in mind?

5. What preventative measures and what coping strategies fit with your teaching and interaction style?
6. What strategies could be readily integrated into your existing program without much additional time commitment?
7. How will you determine the effectiveness of your stress-reducing activities?
8. What will you consider as evidence of positive effects?

REFLECTIVE QUESTION
What can you do to model proactive stress-reducing strategies for your students?

CHAPTER NINE

Managing Students Who Exhibit More Challenging and Troubling Behavior

Much of the psychological literature addresses only the negative behaviors (i.e., violence, aggression, crime, pathology) of students who are conveniently labeled *at-risk* and how these behaviors can be ameliorated and these students remediated (Goldstein, 1991). Such a fixation with controlling deviance translates into *curriculum of control, crisis intervention,* and *obedience training* as the major vehicles for addressing the management of more challenging behavior.

By targeting what is wrong and focusing on a philosophy of *lacking,* we are likely to overlook students' strengths and resources. Rarely is the focus on the facilitation and expansion of the strengths the student who is at-risk may bring to a situation, such as resiliency, risk taking, a spirit of adventure, fortitude, coping, and survival skills. Much of the terminology used to describe such students is pejorative and demeaning. We label students as difficult, disruptive, disobedient, defiant, disordered, disturbed, deviant, disabled, deprived, and disadvantaged. We also label parents and families as dysfunctional, when that label more aptly may describe schools, bureaucratic organizations, and society in general.

Traditional ways of thinking about students who experience problems in school embrace either a deficit mentality, viewing students as deficient and rendering them disabled, or take a compensatory position in which the target of the intervention encompasses not only the deficit functioning of students but the deficient nature of their environment, rendering students disadvantaged. Both orientations require bringing students up to snuff with little regard for the social context within which learning occurs or the quality of instruction delivered. While the latter orientation still focuses interventions at the child level, it does advocate teaching coping skills, appropriate social skills, and learning strategies.

The prevailing focus is on identifying and delineating the source of disability or deficit, with little regard to the classroom context in which a student is considered deficient. We need to refocus our emphasis to pay greater attention to dimensions of the teaching–learning process rather than learner characteristics which may inhibit learning, such as class organization, task structures, and performance expectations. The contextual makeup of the classroom environment, which has been referred to as the *classroom ecology,* needs to be examined to assess aspects of instructional programming, curriculum content, social organization, and classroom demands that may cause student alienation and student–teacher conflict.

The Stigma of Labels

The stigma of educational and psychological labels can have a significant impact on self-concept and often fosters negative self-fulfilling prophecies. Richardson (2001) offers this lesson learned from his work with challenging youth: "When kids feel they have only two choices, they will choose smart ass over dumb ass any day." He provides the example of Carlos, an athletic, intelligent, and popular 15-year-old boy who a year earlier could not read. In seventh grade, Carlos was diagnosed as dyslexic and sent to a residential school. He had managed to hide his reading difficulties from all his teachers until seventh grade. After a year of individualized instruction, Carlos was reading on a sixth-grade level. Here, Carlos describes how he managed to make it so long without anyone knowing he could not read.

> Most of the teachers had us read in order so I could tell when my time was coming. Right before I was supposed to read, I would create a ruckus. I got so good at it that the teacher often blamed somebody else. Plus, I was good most of the time so the teacher never paid me no mind. I couldn't hardly read one word, but I could write all the letters and I was a master cheater. I would copy off a few friends so nobody would know. I was more funny than mean—everybody just thought I was sort of a class clown. Even the teachers would laugh. Inside, I felt like totally bogus, like the biggest idiot ever. I didn't want nobody to know. And very few of um did. They just thought I was a big time smart ass. *I'll choose smart ass over dumb ass any day.* A few times, my best friend would help me memorize what I was supposed to read, and I'd fake it. Well, one day, the teacher changed up and here I am pretending to read one page and what I'm reading is like three pages away. I was so humiliated I left school. Turns out, I may never have gotten help if I hadn't screwed up. (Richardson, 2001, pp. 132–3)

Carlos' story depicts the common sentiment that a student would rather be a smart ass than a dumb ass. Often behavior problems are merely symptoms of undiagnosed or untreated learning disabilities. Students devise a host of creative strategies to mask the feeling of being stupid. Smith (1989) identified eighteen common masks, including the mask of not caring, the mask of boredom, the mask of contempt, and the mask of being bad.

Although many teachers and other helping professionals are aware that the majority of students with learning disabilities have at least average intelligence, and in fact are often quite bright, many of these students question their own capabilities. In many ways, because he was a popular athlete, Carlos was lucky. Peer ridicule can often be relentless and vicious, but this ridicule is nothing compared to the internal dialogue that takes place every day (i.e., "I'm so dumb," "I can't do anything"). Although it can be difficult at times, it is important to continue to try to look beyond the symptoms of behavior to identify the unmet needs or the underlying problem that causes the behavior.

While working as a school counselor, Richardson (2001) encountered a student who was consistently tardy for her third-period learning resource class. He discovered that she did not want her friends and peers to see her going into the library for classes. The student pretended to be waiting outside another class down the hall, and when the bell rang, she would sneak into the library. Discussing the incident, the student commented, "I feel like everyone who walks down the hall is looking to see what the zoo animals are doing."

A Call for Restructuring

Schools must be restructured to address critical issues related to learning and schooling for youth at risk. In our current educational structure, an individual teacher cannot adequately address the complex array of risk factors. To be successful in meeting the needs of youth at risk, dramatic changes will have to be realized, including restructuring school curriculum, reconceiving the school calendar and daily schedule, better integrating school and community services, providing teachers with adequate planning and problem-solving time, and enhancing the climate of schools to provide for equitable inclusion and learning opportunities for every child (Kennedy & Morton, 1999).

CURRENT PERSPECTIVES ON EDUCATING STUDENTS WITH BEHAVIORAL AND EMOTIONAL PROBLEMS

Historically, advocated practices for working with students with behavioral or emotional problems have offered competing theories and methodologies. More recently, the field has moved away from simplistic, one-size-fits-all mind-sets.

When facing a furious student, a single theory offers a slim shield. The term *psychoeducational* is often used to describe approaches that blend multiple perspectives for intervention. Psychoeducational approaches intentionally combine a variety of methods to meet the diverse needs of troubled children (Brendtro & Von Bockern, 1994). Four principal approaches have shaped practice and ways of defining emotional and behavioral problems, leading to different intervention strategies in programs of reeducation.

1. **Psychodynamic:** Children are viewed as "disturbed" because of underlying emotional problems and unmet needs.
2. **Behavioral:** Children are viewed as "disordered" because of maladaptive patterns of learned behavior.
3. **Sociological:** Children are viewed as "maladjusted" because of association with peers who embrace negative values and behavior.
4. **Ecological:** Various ecosystems in the child's environment are seen as creating conflict and "dis-ease" in children.

Cross-fertilization has increased among all of these theories, as practitioners intuitively tinker with models once considered pure. Currently, one can find behaviorists advocating relationship building, psychodynamic programs using reinforcement concepts, and nearly universal recognition of the importance of group and ecological dynamics. With this common intermingling of theories, traditional concepts such as *behavioral* and *psychodynamic* no longer convey a clear meaning at the level of practice. Although each model has continued to develop with a separate tradition, these approaches all have become more eclectic and comprehensive overtime, warranting the label *psychoeducational.*

Psychodynamic psychoeducational approaches place major emphasis on resolving inner conflict of troubled children, blending mental health concepts with education. Exemplary of this tradition is the early work of Redl (1966), Redl & Wineman (1957), Morse (1985), and Long, Morse, and Newman (1976). Redl saw emotional disturbances as an exaggeration of feelings common to all individuals; what distinguished the troubled child was the inability to manage those feelings. Redl designed the *life space interview,* a counseling strategy used by front line staff (e.g., teachers, youth workers) to transform naturally occurring problems into opportunities for correcting distorted thoughts, feelings, and behaviors.

Behavioral psychoeducational methods use learning principles to modify the disordered behavior of children, espousing the belief that disordered behavior has complex causes and thus is treated best with comprehensive interventions that are multimodal combining cognitive, affective, and behavioral interventions (Goldstein, 1988; Goldstein & Conoley, 1997).

The eclectic behavioral approach known as the Boys Town Teaching Family Model (Coughlin & Shanahan, 1991; Tierney, Dowd, & O'Kane, 1993) systematically integrates methods including social skills training, relationship building, nonaversive crisis intervention, and structured verbal interventions called *teaching interactions.*

Sociological psychoeducational approaches consider peer groups as primary agents of change in the values and behavior of troubled youth. Unlike traditional group therapy, which tracts individuals within a group, peer groups utilize *guided group intervention* (GGI) to win over the entire group to prosocial values and behavior, thereby encouraging change in individuals. Vorrath developed this model into a program called *positive peer culture* (PPC), a comprehensive system for reeducation (Brendtro & Wasmund, 1989; Carducci & Carducci, 1984; Duke & Meckel, 1984; Garner, 1982; Vorrath & Brendtro, 1985). Positive peer culture groups identify problems and develop strategies to solve them. The goal is to create a prosocial ethos by making caring fashionable, demanding greatness instead of obedience, and challenging youth to assume responsibility for their lives (Brendtro & Ness, 1983).

The ecological psychoeducational approach has been the most actively eclectic, borrowing freely from the more traditional models. The leading author of this approach was Hobbs who created the Re-ED model (Reeducation for Emotionally Disturbed Children), and was a powerful advocate of focusing on strength, health, and joy, rather than deviance and pathology. Hobbs (1982) argued that most emotional disturbance is not a symptom of individual pathology, but a sign of malfunctioning human ecosystems. Re-ED professionals strive to develop competence in restorative relationships, working in close liaison with families and communities (Cantrell, 1992; Lewis & Lewis, 1989). Rhodes (1992), a cofounder of the Re-Ed model, has developed a life-impact curriculum that empowers children's thinking so they can "reconstruct their own reality."

As is the case with all attempts to modify others' behavior, there are no formulas for determining which approaches are likely to work for an individual student; this is even more pertinent for students labeled as behaviorally disordered or emotionally disturbed, troubled, or at risk. Given the gravity of their experiences and the complex array of problems these students have, it is best to have a whole host of alternatives at your disposal to increase the likelihood of ultimately finding an approach that is successful. Toward that end, the following sections will describe models, programs, and individual strategies that have been used successfully to address the more challenging behaviors students exhibit.

Supplemental Programs for Youth at Risk

Concern for youth at-risk during young adolescence has intensified as schools struggle to seek solutions for the problems confronting these students. Recently, a number of programs have emerged with the goal of reducing dropouts and assisting youth at-risk make the transition to college. Each of the following programs has demonstrated success and is currently in operation throughout the United States.

Coca-Cola Valued Youth Dropout Prevention Program (Grades 7–12)
A cross-age tutoring program with the goal of increasing self-esteem and school success for middle school and high school students at risk for school failure. The program attempts to reduce school dropout rates by improving self-esteem and academic achievement.

Achievement for Latinos (ALAS, Grades 7–12)
Designed for Hispanic middle and high school students from high poverty areas considered to be at high risk. The program focuses on

students with learning disabilities and behavioral problems and works with the home, school, and community to improve student behavior and performance.

Advancement via Individual Determination (AVID, Grades 6–12)

The AVID program, developed in 1981, is designed to assist students who are low-achieving with good academic potential to succeed in an ongoing college preparatory curriculum. Based on years of success, AVID is widely recognized as a program that teaches these students to excel academically. AVID is designed for students in grades 6–12 and is currently available in 900 middle and high schools in twenty-six states.

Upward Bound (Grades 9–12)

Upward Bound assists talented high school students who are poor or minority to make a successful transition to college. The program is part of the larger TRIO Program, which includes a middle school support program, Talent Search, and the College/University Assistance Support Program (CAMP). Linked together, these three programs have demonstrated remarkable success in serving and maintaining talented students from middle school through college. Upward Bound has been thoroughly and favorably evaluated for the past decade.

TEACHING ANGER MANAGEMENT

The purpose of teaching anger management is to help students understand that anger is not "going crazy," and that they can seek help and negotiate differences, instead of striking out and harming others and themselves. They can also learn strategies for avoiding situations that trigger their anger. The general objectives of anger management are to help students

- Realize that angry feelings are a normal part of living and that almost everyone has difficulty dealing with them
- Identify the kinds of situations that trigger their anger, so they can avoid them or handle them better
- Learn how to avoid giving others the power to make them angry
- Learn strategies for increasing inner control of angry feelings

Young adolescents are often overwhelmed by unfamiliar, sometimes contradictory, feelings. The desire to belong clashes with the need for autonomy, new freedoms conflict with new responsibilities, and budding empowerment can be shadowed by worries about being treated unfairly or victimized. Unsure of their middle status, their pride easily hurt, it's little wonder they often "lose it."

Strategies to Reduce Anger
Responses for Younger Students

Anger feeds on itself and if left unchecked often snowballs, so it's important to help students deescalate. Rather than tell students to calm down, teachers can guide them to specific strategies that they can use to collect themselves (Gootman, 2001). Designate a cooling-off place where children can go to collect their thoughts, take a break from a tense situation, and calm themselves down.

- Teachers should make it clear to students that any strategy is designed as an aid in anger management and not as a punishment.
- Listening to music or drawing can prevent anger from snowballing.

- The gentle back and forth of a rocking chair can sometimes extinguish the flames of anger.
- Twisting and turning something solid like clay can release negative energy. These materials can be kept in the cooling-off area. It's best to avoid punching pillows, spitting out angry thoughts, or screaming as techniques for calming down. Current brain research advises against techniques that pump up the emotional brain's arousal trigger because they can leave the person even angrier (Caine & Caine, 1997).
- The goal is to get the student calm enough to be able to verbalize his or her anger in a rational way. Once the student has cooled down, the teacher helps the student put his or her feelings into words, such as "I was afraid that I might do it wrong," or "I was embarrassed when they made fun of me." Through reflective listening the teacher draws out the feelings and guides students to label the primary feeling that lies below the surface of anger. It might be loneliness, disappointment, embarrassment, fear, worry, humiliation, or sadness.

Even young children can be taught to think before acting and solve their own problems. In one program used with kindergartners (Robb, 2003), when a problem arises, the teacher asks "What can you do about it?" Then the teacher reads a list of possible solutions for the child to choose one or two. The list is written on chart paper and posted in a prominent place. A possible list might include some of the following suggestions.

Having a Small Problem? Try one or two of these ideas.

- Take a deep breath and try to cool off.
- Take a time out to think about ways to solve the problem.
- Move away from the person.
- Talk it out with the person.
- Walk away and find another activity.
- Ask the person politely to stop.
- Tell how you are feeling.
- Try to make a deal.
- Ask your teacher for help.
- Count to 10.

By offering ideas that can help young children resolve differences, the teacher is there, but the children make the decisions and carry them out, thereby teaching children to own and solve their own problems.

Adolescent Anger Control Strategies

Feindler and Ecton (1986) recommend the following general strategies to help adolescents control their anger.

1. Identify direct anger triggers (provocations by another person) and indirect triggers (thinking someone is being unfair or lying).
2. Identify physiological states related to anger (getting hot, sweating, hand clenching, facial muscles tightening).
3. Use relaxation techniques (backward counting, deep breaths, tense–release muscles).
4. Use cognitive behavioral methods (reminders such as *chill out, take it easy, relax, I am in control of myself, just stay calm*).
5. Use think ahead methods (stopping and thinking of the consequences: *If I lose control, get in trouble, suspended*).

6. Use self-evaluation: How did I do? (*I did good, I kept in control; I did okay; I can do even better next time; I lost it; Next time this happens, I'll need to remind myself to calm down*).

Some of these strategies are described in greater detail in other sections of this text. (see Chapters 7 and 8).

ANGER MANAGEMENT FOR CHILDREN AND YOUTH WHO EXHIBIT AGGRESSIVE BEHAVIOR

Aggression Replacement Training (ART)

Aggression Replacement Training (ART) is a multimodal intervention designed to alter the behavior of youth who are chronically aggressive. It consists of skill-streaming, designed to teach a broad curriculum of prosocial behavior; anger control training, a method for empowering youth to modify their own anger responsiveness; and moral reasoning training, to help motivate youth to employ the skills learned via the other components. Aggression replacement training is made up of the following three components (Goldstein & Glick, 1994).

Skillstreaming.   Skillstreaming is an intervention in which a fifty-skill curriculum of prosocial behaviors is systematically taught to both adolescents who are aggressive (Goldstein, Sprafkin, Gershaw, & Klein, 1980) and younger children (McGinnis & Goldstein, 1984, 1990). The skillstreaming curriculum is implemented with small groups (preferably ages 6 to 8) by (1) *modeling*, that is, showing several examples of expert use of behaviors constituting the skills in which they are weak or lacking; (2) *role playing*, or providing several guided opportunities to practice and rehearse these competent interpersonal behaviors; (3) *performance feedback*, or providing praise, reinstruction, and related feedback on how well the student's role playing of the skill matches the expert model's portrayal of it; and (4) *transfer training*, or encouraging students to engage in a series of activities designed to increase the chances that the skills learned in the training setting will endure and be available for use when needed in real-life situations. The six areas that compose the entire curriculum include

1. Beginning social skills (starting a conversation, introducing yourself, giving a compliment)
2. Advanced social skills (asking for help, apologizing, giving instructions)
3. Skills for dealing with feelings (dealing with someone's anger, expressing affection, dealing with fear)
4. Alternatives to aggression (responding to teasing, negotiation, helping others)
5. Skills for dealing with stress (dealing with being left out, dealing with an accusation, preparing for a stressful conversation)
6. Planning skills (goal setting, decision making, setting priorities for solving problems)

Anger Control Training.   Anger control training (ACT), first developed by Feindler, Marriott, and Iwata (1984), is partially based on the earlier anger control and stress inoculation research of Novaco (1975) and Meichenbaum (1977). Its goal is teaching students self-control of anger. In ACT, each person is required to bring to each session a description of a recent anger-arousing experience (a hassle), which they record in a binder (hassle log). For 10 weeks students are trained to respond to their hassles with a chain of behaviors that include

1. Identifying triggers (i.e., those external events and internal self-statements that provoke an anger response)
2. Identifying cues (i.e., those individual physical events, such as tightened muscles, flushed faces, and clenched fists, that let the person know that the emotion he or she is experiencing is anger)
3. Using reminders (i.e., self-statements, such as "stay calm," "chill out," and "cool down," or nonhostile explanations of others' behavior)
4. Using reducers (i.e., a series of techniques that, like the use of reminders, is designed expressly to lower the individual's level of anger, such as deep breathing, counting backward, imagining a peaceful scene, or imagining the long-term consequences of one's behavior)
5. Using self-evaluation (i.e., reflecting on how well the hassle was responded to by identifying triggers, identifying cues, using reminders, and using reducers, and then praising or rewarding oneself for effective performance)

Moral Education. Moral education is a set of procedures designed to raise students' senses of fairness, justice, and concern so that they consider the needs and rights of others. Kohlberg (1969, 1973), in a discussion group context in which youngsters reason at differing levels of morality, has demonstrated that exposing youngsters to a series of moral dilemmas arouses cognitive conflict, the resolution of which will frequently advance a youngster's moral reasoning to that of peers in the group who reason at a higher level.

A 10-week sequence is recommended as a core curriculum with three sessions per week, one each of skillstreaming, anger control training, and moral education. ART has been found to be effective in promoting skills acquisition and performance, improving anger control, decreasing the frequency of acting-out behaviors, and increasing the frequency of constructive, prosocial behaviors (Goldstein, Glick, Irwin, McCartney, & Rubama, 1989; Goldstein, Glick, Reiner, Zimmerman, & Coultry, 1986; Jones, 1990).

RESPONSE OPTIONS TO REDUCE AGGRESSIVE OR VIOLENT REACTIONS WHEN DEALING WITH DIFFICULT BEHAVIOR

Hyman offers the following recommendations to defuse potentially violent situations.

- Keep a safe distance between you and the student. If you are strong enough, stay between the student and the door so that he or she does not run out of the class or out of the school. If the student is too strong, don't get backed into the wall. Often after a blowup, the student wants to get out of the situation; when calmed, the student may be glad to go to a counselor, psychologist, or other helping person.
- Do not threaten punishments until the student calms down. Certainly do not make threats that you cannot enforce on your own such as, "If you try to knock over one more desk, I am going to stop you."
- Keep your hands off the student unless he or she attacks you or others. It is better to move away than to try to grab a student unless you are trained in physical restraint techniques. Even then, the last thing you ever want to do is to physically engage an enraged student who may be out of control.
- Anger is self-limiting, and therefore your strategy should be to wait it out if possible (Hyman, 1997, p. 251).

Using confrontational and deprecatory remarks tends to increase the possibility of violent reactions from students. Instead, teachers should

1. Acknowledge the student's right to have strong feelings
2. Offer assistance
3. Inform students of the consequences for their behavior
4. State that they do not want the student to choose these consequences (e.g., "I know you're angry, but we can work this out. Would you like me to meet with the two of you?"). The teacher also may add, "You know that if you throw punches in this school you will be suspended and will have to return with your parents. I really would like you to be able to stay at school today." If two students are involved it is usually most effective to speak directly to the student you know best and to personalize your statement (e.g., "Jerry, I really want you to be involved in our debate tomorrow and I hope you'll solve this peacefully so you can be in our class tomorrow").

Ways to Replace Anger

Dyer (1977) in his chapter entitled "Farewell to Anger" offers some strategies that can be useful to teach adolescents.

1. Defuse anger by doing something for the first 10 seconds, because these first seconds are crucial to gaining control.
   For example, take a deep breath and blow out slowly to the count of 10, describe how you feel and remind yourself that it is a signal to "cool it," and label how the other person might be feeling.

2. Postpone anger explosions.
   Start by postponing them 15 seconds, then 20 seconds, then 30 seconds, and so on. Keep extending your time before exploding. Postponing is learned control; with practice, this eliminates explosions.

3. Remind yourself that 50 percent of what you believe will be rejected by 50 percent of others 50 percent of the time.
   Once you expect others to disagree you'll choose anger less often. So, rid yourself of the unrealistic expectations you have for others—your "shoulds" for them. When they go away, so will much of your anger. Remind yourself that everyone has a right to act as he or she chooses. Demanding that others be and respond as you want them to will only prolong your anger.

4. When you explode or have a temper tantrum (or give someone the silent treatment), speak up and tell someone about your slip—that your goal is to think and behave differently.
   Owning up to your lapses demonstrates that you're working on controlling your anger.

5. Keep a diary or journal.
   Record all angry behaviors you've chosen, and record your successes at anger control. The very act of recording will persuade you to choose anger less often, and reinforce your successes.

Using Support, Empathy, and Truth (SET)

Kreisman and Straus (1989) recommend using a structured approach called SET (Support, Empathy, Truth) to deal with difficult or challenging behavior. The structure can help teachers reduce their own defenses while also addressing the plethora of emotions of troubled youth (i.e., fear, loneliness, feelings of being misunderstood, helplessness, and loss of control). These steps support setting limits, reinforcing boundaries, and enforcing consequences (Richardson, 2001).

Step 1: Communicate Support.   Challenging youths often feel unsupported and alone. Their lifeboat is slowly sinking, and, from their perspective, no one seems to care. So a good starting point is to offer a personal statement of concern.

> *Jerry, I really care about you and right now, I'm very concerned.* (support)

It is important to acknowledge that challenging youths are unaccustomed to legitimate statements of personal concern and may dismiss such statements or challenge them. However, a genuine statement of concern will often be remembered, even when a student's initial reaction suggests otherwise.

Step 2: Empathize or Validate the Youth's Position.   After offering support, it is important to communicate some understanding of the youth's position and what he or she is feeling. Confrontation and empathy are not mutually exclusive. Here the energy is focused on really listening and understanding the youth's feelings and perspective, and communicating this understanding in a brief, empathic, or validating statement.

> *It sounds like you're pretty frustrated with this whole situation.* (empathy)
>
> *If I were in your position, I would probably feel a little frustrated myself.* (validation)

When using the SET model with escalating youth, the empathic statement should be brief and to the point.

Step 3: Reinforce the Reality or the Truth of the Situation.   Understanding a youth's behavior does not mean excusing it. It is not helpful to deny the reality of living in a world with problems, consequences, and limitations. The idea is to find a way to reaffirm the youth's worthiness and also clearly communicate your expectations. When challenging youth, it is important to communicate that you accept them as they are *and* want them to improve. An effective statement of truth communicates what you can and cannot do as a helper, and that ultimately, the youth is responsible. It may also communicate boundaries, limits, and expectations.

> *I want to help you and there's only so much I can do for you. I can . . .*
>
> *What are you going to do?* (truth)

THE CONTEXTS OF SCHOOL VIOLENCE

Because school violence is a multifaceted phenomenon, preventing violence and responding to violent acts that occur within schools require an understanding of the larger community and society. Human behavior is shaped by social and ecological contexts that include individuals with whom we interact daily, as well as broad societal contexts that influence appropriate behavior and relationships among people (Bronfenbrenner, 1979). A widely accepted model (Tolan & Guerra, 1994) of youth and family violence depicts a nested ecological system of individual factors (e.g., low academic skills, substance abuse), close interpersonal relations (e.g., peers and family), proximal social contexts (e.g., school and neighborhood), and societal macrosystems (e.g., media and laws governing gun use). Figure 9.1 illustrates this model.

The problem of school violence is linked to changes within our culture and society, such as significant changes in family structure and in the status of children. Violence in the entertainment and news media has increased dramatically in recent years and contributes to a sense that youth are being negatively influenced by the movies they see, the television they watch, the popular music they hear, and the video games they play (Leone, Mayer, Malmgren, & Meisal, 2003).

A study by the Center of Media and Public Affairs examining the frequency with which violent images are featured in popular entertainment (Lichter, Lichter, & Amundson, 1999) found that, across all forms of entertainment, seriously violent images or scenes were featured on an average of 14 times per hour of viewing. Sixty percent of men on TV dramas are depicted in violent scenes and, in the media in general, the majority of victims are women and children (Grossman, 1998). Although causal effects between viewing violent images and engaging in violent or disruptive behavior in school are difficult to establish, evidence suggests that exposure to television violence does have an effect on violent behavior (American Psychological Association, 1993; Felson, 1996; Reiss & Roth, 1993).

Fewer adults are at home and available to support students during the non-school hours; there is less time available for parents to assist and monitor their children. Poverty and the availability of parents to supervise their children do not directly create or cause school violence or disruption. Nevertheless, poverty is one of a number of factors that place youth at risk for school failure, dropout, and delinquent behavior (Walker & Sprague, 1999). Inadequate monitoring and supervision of children are associated with the development of antisocial behavior and delinquency (Farrington, 1995; Hawkins, Herrenkahl, Ferrington, Brewer, Catalano, Harachi, & Cothern, 2000; Patterson, 1982).

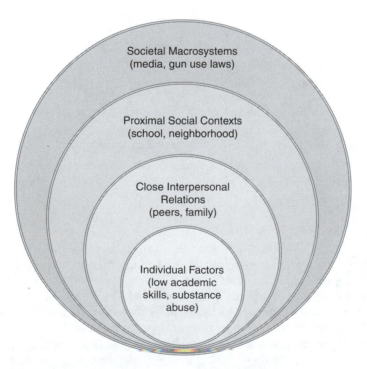

FIGURE 9.1   A Nested Ecological System of Factors Influencing Youth Behavior

RISK FACTORS FOR YOUTH VIOLENCE

INDIVIDUAL RISK FACTORS
- Poor academic skills
- Impulsivity
- Substance use
- Poor social and problem-solving skills
- Inability to understand the perspective of others
- Poor conflict-resolution skills
- Difficulty in understanding the moral consequences of actions

PEER RISK FACTORS
- Low social status
- Rejection by peers
- Gang involvement
- Shared deviant peer norms
- Association with delinquent peer groups

FAMILY RISK FACTORS
- Inconsistent discipline
- Harsh or abusive discipline
- Limited monitoring of activities
- Insecure attachments
- Deviant shared values
- Frequent negative interactions
- Low levels of emotional closeness

SCHOOL AND COMMUNITY RISK FACTORS
- Lack of parent involvement
- Low academic achievement
- Lack of social support
- Few opportunities for recreation
- Unemployment
- High levels of community crime
- Availability of firearms

Source: Adapted from *A Program Planning Guide for Youth Violence Prevention* (1996), by N. G. Guerra and K. R. Williams (Boulder, CO: Center for the Study and Prevention of Violence).

Here are some additional statistics related to school violence. According to various surveys,

- In the United States, about 2 million teenagers carry guns, knives, clubs, and razors (National Institute for Dispute Resolution [NIDR], 1999).
- One in five students says that he or she personally knows a classmate who has brought a gun to school (Langer, 1999).
- Twenty percent of suburban high school students endorse the idea of shooting someone "who has stolen something from you" (Grossman, 1996).
- Nearly one-third of students have heard a classmate threaten to kill someone (Langer, 1999).
- Forty percent of high school students say there are potentially violent cliques at their school (Langer, 1999).

- Half of all violence against teenagers occurs in school buildings, on school property, or on the street in the vicinity of the school (NIDR, 1999).
- More than 525,000 attacks, shakedowns, and robberies occur per month in public secondary schools in the United States (Weinhold & Weinhold, 1998).
- Every day, 160,000 students miss school, totaling 28 million missed days per year, because of fear of attack or intimidation by a bully (Fried & Fried, 1996).

The U.S. Department of Education and the Department of Justice have published a guide for schools (Dwyer, Osher, & Warger, 1998) that contains a list of early warning signs that can alert teachers to a student's potential for violence, as well as signs that violence is imminent.

Early and Imminent Warning Signs of Violence
Early Warning Signs
- Social withdrawal
- Excessive feelings of isolation and being alone
- Excessive feelings of rejection
- Being a victim of violence
- Feelings of being picked on and persecuted
- Low school interest and poor academic performance
- Expression of violence in writings and drawings
- Uncontrolled anger
- Patterns of impulsive and chronic hitting, intimidating, and bullying behaviors
- History of discipline problems
- Past history of violent and aggressive behavior
- Intolerance for differences and prejudicial attitudes
- Drug use and alcohol use
- Affiliation with gangs
- Inappropriate access to, possession of, and use of firearms
- Serious threats of violence

Imminent Signs of Violence
- Serious physical fighting with peers or family members
- Severe destruction of property
- Severe rage for seemingly minor reasons
- Detailed threats of lethal violence
- Possession or use of firearms and other weapons
- Other self-injurious behaviors or threats of suicide

YOUTH VIOLENCE: MYTHS, TRENDS, PATHWAYS, AND PREVENTION

The following sections are based on a recent Surgeon General's report on youth violence (U.S. Department of Health and Human Services, 2001).

Myths about Youth Violence

Recent research findings challenge false notions and misconceptions about youth violence. These are examples of myths about violence and violent youth:

Myth 1: Most future offenders can be identified in early childhood.
Myth 2: Child abuse and neglect inevitably lead to violent behavior later in life.
Myth 3: African American and Hispanic youths are more likely to become involved in violence than other racial or ethnic groups.

Myth 4: A new, violent breed of young superpredators threatens the United States.

Myth 5: Getting tough with juvenile offenders by trying them in adult criminal courts reduces the likelihood that they will commit more crimes.

Myth 6: Nothing works with respect to treating or preventing violent behavior.

Myth 7: Most violent youths will end up being arrested for a violent crime.

Trends in Youth Violence

- Violent crime committed by children and teenagers has declined substantially since 1993 and is at the lowest rate since 1986 (Glassner, 1999).
- The number of school-associated violent deaths has decreased 40 percent, from 43 in 1998 to 26 in 1999 (Portner, 2000b).
- The proportion of schools in which gangs are present continued to increase after 1994 but had declined by 1999. However, evidence shows that the number of youths involved with gangs has not declined and remains near the peak levels of 1996 (U.S. Department of Health and Human Services, 2001).
- Surveys consistently find that about 30 to 40 percent of male youths and 15 to 30 percent of female youths report having committed a serious violent offense by age 17 (U.S. Department of Health and Human Services, 2001).

Pathways to Youth Violence

- There are two general onset trajectories for youth violence: an early one, in which violence begins before puberty, and a late one, in which violence begins in adolescence. Youths who become violent before about age 13 generally commit more crimes, and more serious crimes, for a longer time. These young people exhibit a pattern of escalating violence through childhood, and they sometimes continue their violence into adulthood.
- Most youth violence begins in adolescence and ends with the transition into adulthood.
- Most highly aggressive children or children with behavioral disorders do not become serious violent offenders.
- Serious violence is part of a lifestyle that includes drugs, guns, precocious sex, and other risky behaviors. Youths involved in serious violence often commit many other types of crimes and exhibit other problem behaviors, presenting a serious challenge to intervention efforts. Successful interventions must confront not only the violent behavior of these young people, but also their lifestyles, which are teeming with risk.
- The differences in patterns of serious violence by age of onset and the relatively constant rates of individual offending have important implications for prevention and intervention programs. Early childhood programs that target "at-risk" children and families are critical for preventing the onset of a chronic violent career, but programs must also be developed to combat late-onset violence.
- The importance of late-onset violence prevention is not widely recognized or well understood. Substantial numbers of serious violent offenders emerge in adolescence without warning signs in childhood. A comprehensive community prevention strategy must address both onset patterns and ferret out their causes and risk factors.

Preventing Youth Violence

1. A number of youth violence intervention and prevention programs have demonstrated that they are effective; assertions that "nothing works" are false.

2. Most highly effective programs combine components that address both individual risks and environmental conditions, particularly building individual skills and competencies, parent effectiveness training, improving the social climate of the school, and changes in type and level of involvement in peer groups.

3. Rigorous evaluation of programs is critical. While hundreds of prevention programs are being used in schools and communities throughout the country, little is known about the effects of most of them.

4. At the time this report was prepared, nearly half of the most thoroughly evaluated strategies for preventing violence had been shown to be ineffective—a few were known to harm participants.

5. In schools, interventions that target change in the social context appear to be more effective, on average, than those that attempt to change individual attitudes, skills, and risk behaviors.

6. Involvement with delinquent peers and gang membership are two of the most powerful predictors of violence, yet few effective interventions have been developed to address these problems.

7. Program effectiveness depends as much on the quality of implementation as on the type of intervention. Many programs are ineffective not because their strategy is misguided, but because the quality of implementation is poor.

INTERVENING WITH POTENTIALLY OUT-OF-CONTROL STUDENTS: NONVIOLENT CRISIS INTERVENTION

Often the best a teacher can do is damage control when a situation has escalated into a crisis. The following section describes some specific intervention strategies to help teachers deescalate rather than escalate potentially dangerous situations.

Nonviolent Crisis Intervention is a nonharmful crisis management system designed to aid educators in maintaining the best possible care and welfare of agitated or out-of-control students—even during their most violent moments (National Crisis Prevention Institute, 1994). It presents basic preventative techniques necessary to defuse potentially violent situations while maintaining the safety and security of all who are involved in interventions.

Crisis Development Behavior Levels

In any crisis development situation, there are four distinct and identifiable behavior levels. Each behavior level demands a specific response to provide the maximum chance of defusing the crisis development.

Crisis Development Behavior Levels with Effective Interventions

BEHAVIORAL LEVEL	CRISIS DEVELOPMENT	INTERVENTION
Level 1	**Anxiety** At the Anxiety level there is a noticeable change in behavior. Some of the minimal cues may be finger drumming, pencil tapping, and other nonspecific gestures. The student still has enough reasoning ability to respond.	**Supportive** The teacher is nonjudgmental, empathic, and attempts to alleviate the anxiety the student is experiencing.

Level 2	**Defensiveness**	**Directive**
	At the Defensive level the student becomes less rational, disrespectful, and possibly belligerent. He or she begins to challenge the teacher and the teacher's authority.	The teacher setting simple and reasonable limits appropriate to the misconduct involved will generally stop the behavior from accelerating.
Level 3	**Acting-Out**	**Nonviolent Physical Crisis Intervention (NPCI)**
	At the Acting-Out level, the student has a complete loss of control. Verbal aggression turns into assault.	The teacher uses safe, noninjurious prevention or restraint techniques. Physical restraint is recommended only when all verbal techniques have been exhausted, and when the student presents a danger to self or others.
Level 4	**Tension Reduction**	**Therapeutic Rapport**
	Tension Reduction occurs as a result of the high expenditure of energy after an acting-out episode. Tension Reduction is characterized by a regaining of rationality as the student "runs out of steam." The student may be embarrassed, fearful, or apologetic in his or her own way.	Here the teacher establishes communication when the student is in tension reduction. This is one of the best moments to attempt to communicate with the student.

Verbal Escalation Continuum

Stage 1

> **Questioning.** The student asks nonproductive questions, with the intent to draw the teacher into a power struggle. The student questions anything, testing the teacher's authority.

> **Intervention.** Avoid nonpertinent questions; set limits if the student persists.

Stage 2

> **Refusal.** Refusal is the ultimate challenge. At this stage, the student will say no to almost anything.

> **Intervention.** Set clear, reasonable, and enforceable limits. It is important that the student be made aware that the teacher is not going to force him or her to do anything. The student is responsible for choosing the consequences of his or her behavior.

Stage 3

> **Release.** This is the moment when the student verbally loses control, unloading or venting a tremendous amount of internal energy. The student may curse, rant, or even scream unintelligibly. The student has completely lost rational control and is unfocused.

> **Intervention.** The teacher needs to avoid the trap of raising his or her voice to match the student's. The energy being expended is at such a high level that the student most likely cannot hear what is being said anyway. When there is a lull in the energy level, the teacher should continue setting limits and stating directives that are nonthreatening.

Stage 4

Intimidation. The student is now threatening the personal safety of the teacher through verbal taunts and nonverbal gestures.

Intervention. Do not take the intimidation lightly. Intimidation can be the last stepping stone of verbal aggression. The teacher should get assistance if possible. As a last resort, the teacher needs to be prepared to use Nonviolent Physical Crisis Intervention.

Stage 5

Tension Reduction. The verbal explosion has expended the student's energy and the subsequent tension reduction is both physical and emotional. The student is turning to rational behavior.

Intervention. The teacher should establish Therapeutic Rapport. During any tension reduction, the student is in a very emotional state. This can be one of the best opportunities for productive communication to complete the intervention process.

Key Points for Successful Verbal Intervention
1. Maintain control of your own behavior. If a student detects that you are not in control, he or she will naturally assume that you cannot calm anyone else down.
2. Be prepared to set and enforce limits. Students can be profoundly shrewd when it comes to testing your limits.
3. Isolate the student. It is difficult, if not impossible, to defuse a student who has to save face in front of peers.
4. Keep it simple. Complicated limits and diagnostic, technical jargon tend to confuse the student and intensify the escalation process.
5. Avoid power struggles. An escalating student will often attempt to push your buttons. Do not get into a nonproductive power struggle.

Nonviolent Crisis Intervention: Critical Aspects of Nonverbal Communication

A key factor in intervening with a potentially disruptive or assaultive student is an awareness of nonverbal communication. Because much of the message we deliver is nonverbal, this is an essential point to keep in mind when intervening with the potentially out-of-control student.

Proxemics (Personal Space). Invasion or encroachment of personal space tends to heighten or escalate a student's anxiety level. The encroachment of personal space is often perceived as a threat, or a facedown in front of peers. Being trapped or blocked in increases the tendency of a student to act out. Invading a student's personal space during a crisis development situation tends to minimize the teacher's chances of defusing the situation and maximize the chances of escalating it. As a general rule, personal space is 1½ to 3 feet in length. The teacher should respect the student's personal space to avoid escalating a crisis development.

Kinesics (Body Posture and Movement). Body language, or kinesic behavior, also conveys a message. Moving too quickly can be menacing to some students, as can finger pointing. The teacher's position in relation to a potentially aggressive youth is critical to the message the student perceives. Face-to-face, shoulder-to-shoulder generally is perceived as a challenge or a threat, especially by a youth who is in a highly anxious state. This dynamic becomes even more intensified when peers are present.

Supportive Stance.   Instead of a confrontational, face-to-face posture, the teacher should use a supportive stance. The supportive stance is approximately one leg length away from the student, on an angle, off to the side. This stance not only avoids encroaching personal space, it ensures the personal safety of the teacher.

Paraverbal Communication.   This is the manner in which verbal messages are delivered. Voice inflection determines how a message is perceived through nuances in tone, volume, cadence, or rate. Keep in mind that only a small percentage of messages delivered are perceived by the words used; the most effective responses in crisis development use appropriate paraverbals. These assist in maintaining a professional, calm approach.

A RISING CONCERN: BULLYING IN SCHOOLS

Recent school tragedies directly or indirectly tied to bullying have resulted in increased attention on the part of administrators, teachers, and fellow students to the issue of bullying in schools. According to the National Association of School Psychologists, one in seven school children is a bully or a victim. Bullying directly affects about 5 million elementary and junior high school students in the United States. As mentioned previously, it's estimated that nearly 160,000 students stay home every day because of bullying (Fried & Fried, 1996).

Some of the conclusions regarding the known long-term effects of bullying of the Olweus (1993, 1994) studies are listed here.

Studies on those who are bullied (Olweus, 1993):

- Being bullied during middle school is predictive of low self-esteem 10 years later.
- By age 23, children who were bullied in middle school were more depressed and had lower self-esteem than their peers who had not been bullied.
- Bullied children feel more isolated than their peers, who often reject them out of fear that they, too, will become a target of bullies if they are seen with targeted students.
- Being bullied can lead to suicide.
- Some victims of bullies resort to eventual violent retaliation against the bully.

Studies on the bullies themselves (Olweus, 1994):

- By age 23, about 60 percent of the boys identified as bullies in middle school had at least one conviction of a crime, and 35 percent to 40 percent had three or more convictions.
- Fifty percent of all identified school bullies became criminals as adults.
- Bullies at age 8 are three times more likely to be convicted of a crime by age 30.
- Bullies are less likely than nonbullies to finish college or find a good job.

Bullying differs from grade to grade (Olweus, 1994):

- Bullying occurs in every grade, but most frequently in grades 4 through 8.
- Bullying usually starts as teasing and put-downs with younger bullies, becoming more physical and more violent as bullies get older.
- Bullies can be easily identified in each grade by the sixth week of the school year.
- Potential bullies can be easily identified as early as preschool by recognizing the early warning signs.

Additional facts:

- Children from violent homes are three to four times more likely to become bullies. Contrary to popular belief, most of the violence directed at young children in the home comes from the mother and older siblings (Strau & Gelles, 1988).
- Bullies often have attachment disorders (Weinhold, 1999).

Why do children bully and put down others? There is a clash between the old and the new thinking on the causes of bullying and school violence. The new thinking is based on the recent research findings cited in this chapter. The following chart presents a summary.

Conventional versus Current Thinking about Bullying

CONVENTIONAL THINKING	CURRENT THINKING
Bullying is genetic. Bullies are born that way.	Bullying is shaped by early childhood experiences.
Bullies should just be expelled.	Bullying is a cry for help.
Bullying is normal childhood behavior.	Bullying is a symptom of untreated trauma.
Bullying is harmless.	Bullying is traumatic for those being bullied.
Bullies will grow out of it.	Without intervention, bullying leads to further violence.
Bullies are influenced by peer modeling.	Bullies are influenced more by media and family modeling.
Watching violence on TV or in movies is harmless.	TV and movie violence can traumatize kids.

Source: Adapted from *School Violence and Children in Crisis* (2003), by J. Miller, I. R. Martin, & G. Schamess (Denver, CO: Love Publishing).

Children today face bullying that is more intense in frequency and seriousness. While in the past girls relied mostly on verbal forms of bullying, such as taunting and shunning, they are now becoming more physical in their aggression. Difference has always been an excuse for bullying, and today we live in a more diverse society.

Bullying often goes unnoticed because bullies tend to hurt or abuse others when adults aren't around to see it, or they act in ways that adults don't notice. Parents, teachers, and administrators don't take action because they aren't sure what to do. Some feel overwhelmed. Some don't know how to recognize bullying, let alone prevent it or intervene. Worse yet, some people blame the victim. Bullying goes unreported because victims are ashamed of being bullied, fear retaliation, or worry that adults can't or won't help them. Witnesses don't want to get involved or they don't interpret what they're seeing as bullying, but instead as teasing, normal, or "kids being kids" behavior. Bullying starts as early as preschool, peaks during the middle school years, and declines slightly during high school. In colleges and universities, bullying continues as hazing, sexual harassment, and assault. In adulthood, bullying behavior can be seen in abusive spouses, parents, coworkers, or bosses.

Strategies for Addressing Bullying

Bullies don't just grow out of their abusive behavior unless they learn better ways of relating to others. Because bullying behavior is learned, it can also be unlearned. Teachers need to show children that bullying is not acceptable, that victims can take more control of their lives, and that bullies can and must change their behavior. Beane (1999) suggests that teachers designate their classrooms bully free—places where people accept, value, and treat each other with kindness and respect. He also recommends teaching children what to do on their own about bullying by teaching them that they can reduce a bully's power over victims in the following ways:

1. Refuse to join in or watch (joining in or watching gives the bully permission to continue abusive behavior).
2. Speak out (say, "Don't do or say that. It's not right.").
3. Report any bullying they know about or see to a trusted teacher or adult.
4. Stand up for the person being bullied and gather around him or her (there's safety in numbers).
5. Make an effort to include students who are normally left out.
6. Distract the bully so he or she stops the bullying behavior.

A Schoolwide Approach to Reducing Bullying

Garrity and colleagues (1996, 2000) have developed a comprehensive approach to reducing bullying that involves the entire school (students, teachers, administrators, staff) as well as students' families. Staff receive training in response procedures and teachers implement the program within their classes. All school personnel are involved in staff training to learn about the different manifestations of bullying (e.g., physical aggression, name calling, gossiping, intimidating phone calls, verbal threats, locking in confined spaces). They learn ways to address both the victim and the bully. Teachers generate "antibullying" curricula, such as selecting literature on bullies and victims or creating skits or artwork with similar themes.

Students are taught rules to eliminate bullying, strategies for reacting to bullying, and steps to follow if they see bullying occurring. The following rules are recommended:

Rules for Bully Proofing Our Classroom
1. We will not bully other students.
2. We will help others who are being bullied by speaking out and by getting adult help.
3. We will use extra effort to include all students in activities at our school.

Teasing: A Dimension of Bullying

A common and often difficult problem that many children face is coping with teasing and name calling. There are no specific characteristics that are focused on by teasers, although students with academic problems and those who are overweight seem to be the targets of teasers more often than others. Teasing, often occurring on a daily basis, is highly stressful and students can exhibit a variety of symptoms including poor achievement, anxiety, physical symptoms (stomachache, headache), aggressive behaviors, and school phobia, as well as depression and suicidal feelings (Rothschild, 1994).

A Cognitive-Behavioral Strategy for Helping Students Deal with Teasing. Helping a child to truly ignore teasing by not taking it seriously and increasing "tease tolerance" is a successful long-term strategy (Bernard, 1989; Vernon, 2004). Although many teachers and parents view the problem of teasing as relatively inconsequential compared to other problems, from a child's perspective it is a major difficulty.

As in dealing with other problems, strengthening a student so he or she can cope with teasing begins with developing the understanding that much of his or her disturbance comes not from the teasing itself but from their point of view about it. Once students accept this, they also begin to understand that they can alleviate their distress about teasing and not take it so seriously. The process involves helping children and adolescents understand that realistically, teasing at worst is annoying, irritating, frustrating, and saddening. It is not terrible or "can't stand-able, curl up and dieable."

Much of the anger generated by those teased comes from blaming or self-righteous indignation about the teaser. Rothschild (1994) notes that teasers often operate because of problems they have, but this doesn't make a teaser a totally bad person. They may tease because they want to be liked, want to appear smart, or feel inadequate, so that putting others down makes them feel temporarily better about themselves. Some teasers report that they hate to be teased and often get teased and pushed around by older siblings. Some victims report that they tease others. Thus, it appears that those doing and those receiving the teasing often have the same problems. Their emotional reactions are like the two sides of a coin—what helps one often helps the other.

Once students have a different perspective about teasing and the teaser, then teachers can help victims practice thinking rational self-statements. Instead of thinking things that anger or upset them, like "I can't stand being teased," when the teasing happens, teachers can help them to practice thinking things like, "I don't like being teased but I'm tough and I can stand it"; "I won't like it but I won't curl up and die if it continues"; or "Teasing can't hurt me unless I let it."

Students can also be encouraged to think things about the teaser when teased, such as, "I wonder what Jamal's problem is today. I'm not gonna take his teasing seriously and make it my problem," or "Lucinda wants to put me down for the fun of it. I'm not gonna play her game and give her what she wants."

Because the victim's emotional reaction reinforces the teaser's behavior, overt reactions are what teasers want. If the victim stops taking it seriously and does not get upset (cry, get mad, tease back, yell, or fight), and continues this demeanor even when the teaser keeps trying, the teasing will likely lessen or may even stop entirely. Based on the principle of reinforcement, teasers tease to get a response, to catch a fish. When they don't get a response, they'll have to go to another pond (that is, find someone else to tease).

TEACHER EMOTIONAL ESCALATION IN REACTING TO CHALLENGING STUDENT BEHAVIORS

Although teachers can't control how students act and react, they can exercise control over their own actions and reactions to students' behavior. Often teachers automatically react to a student's inappropriate behavior rather than consciously deciding how best to respond to the student or the situation. Teachers can get drawn into situations with students that quickly escalate into no-win episodes. By becoming more aware of how students can, and do, push their emotional buttons, teachers can develop more supportive and effective strategies to deescalate conflicts.

Dealing with Student Defiance

Responding to direct student defiance is an especially difficult situation for teachers to deal with effectively. Such situations are usually emotional encounters for both teachers and students. Colvin (1988) notes that teacher defiance involves a sequential chain of events that are relatively trivial early in the chain (questioning, arguing), but that culminate in very serious behaviors at the end (verbal and physical abuse, threats). He has developed a procedure for anticipating and preventing direct teacher defiance that relies on careful situational analysis and teacher self-control. The key is to anticipate and exercise control during the trivial behaviors early in the chain, so that escalation does not occur and you prevent more serious behaviors.

Situations that are likely to escalate quickly often begin when the student is in an agitated emotional state (angry, frustrated) and engages the teacher in a confrontational interaction through a question-asking strategy in response to the teacher's requests or directives. Once the engagement process begins, the teacher and student are usually log-jammed in a power struggle that quickly escalates into explosiveness and defiance.

The typical sequential chain of events proceeds in this way.

- Student is in agitated state
- Teacher makes request or issues a directive
- Student asks resisting question
- Teacher repeats directive
- Student gives excuse, argues, or complains
- Teacher continues to press for compliance
- Student loses emotional control resulting in verbally or physically aggressive behavior

This chain is summarized in Figure 9.2.

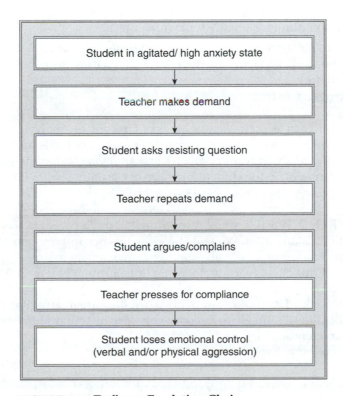

FIGURE 9.2   Defiance Escalation Chain

Here is a dialogue illustrating the chain (Walker & Walker, 1991).

Example of Teacher–Student Escalation Chain.   Context: Eric comes into Mr. Damon's tenth-grade history class 10 minutes late and in a surly mood. He takes his time getting to his desk and engages several students in conversation along the way. An argument develops with one of the students who resents Eric's intrusion. Angry words are exchanged.

(Student is in agitated state.)

> **Mr. Damon:**   *Eric, go to your desk, now! You're always trying the patience of this class and you're running out of rope with me, fast.*
> (Teacher gives a direct terminating command.)
>
> **Eric:**   *Jason borrowed my history book yesterday and he left it home. So what am I supposed to do? I can't work.*
> (Student asks question in an attempt to deflect teacher command.)
>
> **Mr. Damon:**   *Bringing your work materials and books to class is not Jason's responsibility or mine. It's yours! I'm telling you for the last time to sit down!*
> (Teacher reissues command.)
>
> **Eric:**   *Look, I can't work if I don't have the materials to work with, now can I? Any fool can see that.* [Under his breath to a peer, Jason refers to Mr. Damon as a stupid jerk, which Mr. Damon overhears.]
> (Student offers an excuse.)

Context: Mr. Damon ignores the insult but continues to insist that Eric sit down, stop disturbing the class, and occupy himself. He approaches Eric in an authoritative manner. Both are very angry and have the attention of the most of the class.

> **Mr. Damon:**   *For the last time, Eric, you'd better sit down if you know what's good for you! If you want to stay in my class, you'd better do what I say.*
> (Teacher continues pressure for compliance.)
>
> **Eric:**   *I don't give a _____ about this class. _____ you!* [Eric storms out and slams the door. Mr. Damon calls the office and reports the incident.]
> (Student has tantrum and defies the teacher.)

As readily can be seen, the teacher is not in control and has lost the opportunity to teach the student. The student rather than the teacher is in control of the situation. As long as the teacher responds in a stepwise fashion to each increment (question, argument) in the student's pattern of escalating behavior, the interaction is very likely to result in the student exploding.

The Basic Rule.   When a student in an agitated state begins to actively resist teacher demands and attempts to engage the teacher in an interaction about the directive, the teacher immediately should begin disengaging.

To avoid this chain reaction, there are three ground rules.

1. Do not make demands on students when they are in an agitated state.
2. Do not allow yourself to become engaged in the student's question-and-answer agenda.
3. Do not attempt to force the student's hand.

The teacher should attempt to wait out the mood before initiating a direct demand. A student in this state will likely interpret a teacher demand as a provocative event, especially when it is delivered with an audience of peers. In certain situations it might be appropriate to inquire about what's going on with the student, but it should not be followed with a demand at the time.

It is especially important for teachers to recognize the student's engagers, such as questions, disagreements, contradictions, arguments, and counterarguments. The teacher needs to refrain from responding to the student's questions and, above all, not get caught up arguing with the student. Instead the teacher should ignore the student's bait and restate what the student needs to do. If the student refuses, the teacher should leave the student alone while the student is in the agitated state. The teacher should not try to coerce the student through such tactics as hovering and waiting, using social punishment (glaring, verbal reprimands, social intimidation), or making threats about future consequences. Never touch the student in this state; leave the student's presence, and end the interaction. If there is a set consequence for this type of behavior, such as loss of points or privileges, it should be applied promptly with a minimum of verbalization.

Dealing with Students under Stress

The conflict cycle paradigm developed by Long (1996) offers a way to understand why and how competent teachers can find themselves in self-defeating struggles. Students under stress behave emotionally because they are controlled more by feelings than by logic. They will protect themselves from pain and perceived or actual attack by being defensive and regressive. When the teacher reacts to this type of behavior with righteous indignation, a power struggle ensues in which the teacher's primary objective becomes winning rather than resolving the conflict.

According to the conflict cycle paradigm, the interaction between a student and a teacher follows a circular pattern in which the attitudes, feelings, and behaviors of the teacher and the student influence each other to create the conflict cycle. Once this cycle is set in motion, the negative interplay between the teacher and the student is very difficult to interrupt. When teachers react emotionally, they invalidate the feelings and deny the issues behind the student's behavior and become part of the problem rather than part of the solution.

As shown in Figure 9.3, the conflict cycle depicts the circular and escalating nature of student–teacher conflict and how troubled students create counteraggressive feelings in teachers that frequently lead to a mutually self-defeating power struggle. Enacting the cycle serves to reinforce the student's irrational beliefs. (Irrational beliefs as well as strategies for helping students deal with them also are discussed in Chapter 7.)

The Conflict Cycle Paradigm
- A stressful incident occurs that activates student's irrational belief (e.g., all adults are hostile).
- These negative thoughts determine and trigger the student's feelings.
- The student's negative feelings drive inappropriate behavior.
- The inappropriate behavior incites the teacher.
- The teacher mirrors the student's behavior.
- This adverse reaction increases the student's stress and triggers more intense feelings and drives more inappropriate behavior.
- More severe inappropriate behavior causes even more teacher anger and denunciation.
- The student's irrational belief (all adults are hostile) is reinforced.
- The student has no reason to change either the irrational belief or the inappropriate behavior.

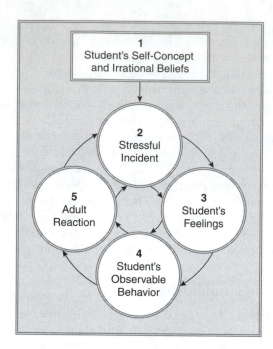

FIGURE 9.3   The Conflict Cycle

Even if the student loses the initial battle by the teacher winning and dispensing punishment, the student wins the psychological war. The irrational belief is perpetuated and serves as a self-fulfilling prophecy.

It is important to note that in this model, a stressful incident is an event that the student perceives as threatening and serves to activate the student's irrational belief. The student's internal process for deciding whether an event is stressful is based on the meaning the student attributes to the event. An ordinary request to share an answer could be the stressful triggering event, if it brings up an irrational belief such as "If I don't get it right everyone will think I'm stupid."

The cycle begins with a student's eroded sense of self-esteem; this plays a central role in determining how the student thinks about him- or herself, relationships with others, and beliefs about what will happen in the future (i.e., self-fulfilling prophecy). Developmentally, a child's sense of self is formed by the nature of relationships with significant adults and, later, peers in the child's life who provide ongoing feedback about the child's character and behavior. When a child receives primarily negative feedback that tells the child he or she is difficult, stupid, hopeless, or weak, over time the child internalizes a deprecating self-perception. How a child learns to think about him- or herself becomes the prevailing element in determining feelings and, ultimately, behavior. In other words, the child's behavior will be consistent with this internalized self-image, regardless of the real data or facts.

In addition to developing a set of personal beliefs, the child also develops beliefs about the world and other people. If the adults in the child's world are hostile, rejecting, and hopeless, the child learns to mistrust adults. Personal beliefs and beliefs about the way the world works merge some time in the early elementary school years and form the child's emerging personality. Now the child has a characteristic way of perceiving, interpreting, feeling, behaving, and responding to life events.

As Long notes, troubled children need to explain why they were abused, neglected, or rejected. The search for an explanation does not take place in reality;

rather, irrational beliefs form to explain their painful life experiences. This means all life events are filtered and evaluated by the student's belief system, activated by the student's irrational thoughts. Initially, the student's negative beliefs about others represent an accurate assessment of the student's experiences. What moves these reality-based beliefs to irrational status is the projection to all situations and relationships in the future. The following is an example of how an irrational belief forms.

My mother neglected me [fact].

I can't count on her to meet my needs [fact].

All adults I'll ever meet will neglect me and my needs [irrational belief].

These irrational beliefs are maintained because they provide troubled students with a sense of security and control by making their world predictable. But most importantly, these irrational beliefs protect students from experiencing the underlying feeling of rage. They maintain these beliefs by projecting their internal worldview on others and engaging them in endless power struggles. This process of getting others to confirm their irrational beliefs becomes the student's self-fulfilling prophecy.

The following case illustrates the self-fulfilling prophecy of a student who is passive-aggressive.

Student belief	*Showing I'm mad is dangerous so I'd better disguise my feelings. If the teacher ever finds out how I really feel, terrible things will happen.*
Learned behavior	Student learns to express anger in passive-aggressive, or indirect, ways.
Classroom behaviors	When the teacher asks student to do something he doesn't like, the student does it in a way that disappoints and frustrates the teacher.
	When he's angry at the teacher, he will get back at her by stealing her keys or messing up the room when she's gone.
Impact on teacher	As all the little things add up, the teacher over time experiences emotional overload. But the teacher is unaware of the accumulated anger toward the student.
Precipitating incident	At the end of a particularly tiring day, the student falls out of his chair, "accidentally" ripping off part of the teacher's new bulletin board display. When the student ignores the first two requests to get back in his seat, the teacher "loses it" and yells, threatens the student, and throws a tantrum.
Student response	*Gee, I didn't mean to do it.*
Teacher thought	*Boy, I shocked myself by the amount of anger I expressed. Maybe I did overreact. That's not like me, I owe him an apology.*
Teacher statement	*I'm sorry I yelled at you.*
Student statement	*That's okay.*
Student thought	*Look at how crazy people get when they show their anger. It's a good thing I don't act like that! Ms. Lee needs to change, not me.*
Result	The student's self-fulfilling prophecy stays in place.

One of the most significant insights gained by understanding the conflict cycle is how a student can recreate his or her own negative feelings in the teacher.

Aggressive students create counteraggressive feelings, depressed students create feelings of helplessness, and so forth. The teacher usually acts on these feelings by mirroring the student's behavior. For example, if the student yells, the teacher yells. Once the teacher behaves like the student, the cycle is set in motion. The teacher feels unjustly attacked by an aggressive student act and becomes flooded by feelings of outrage. Because the teacher feels totally justified in a retaliatory reaction, he or she doesn't acknowledge a role in escalating the conflict, which makes the cycle extremely difficult to stop. Teachers do not have control over how students behave and react, but they do have control over how they react to students. As teachers become more aware of how students push their emotional panic buttons, they can use more effective strategies to interrupt the conflict cycle. They can do significant *damage control* when they respond in a calm, yet decisive manner.

Breaking the Cycle of Reacting

It is important to remember that once a conflict escalates into a power struggle, there are no winners. At this point, there is very little chance that the student is going to act more maturely while in such an intense state of arousal. The greatest hope for change lies in the teacher's ability to respond in a way that can break the cycle. When teachers know how students in conflict think and feel, and understand how students can provoke them into acting in hostile and rejecting ways, they recognize that managing student behavior begins with self-control. But teachers also have to move beyond understanding the dynamics that suck them into mirroring the student's behavior to learning to avoid such power struggles.

In order to help students, teachers need to identify and address the important and underlying issues in a student's life, rather than allow mere knee-jerk reactions to provoking behavior. Teachers can use the insight the conflict cycle offers to recognize and accept the counteraggressive feelings often evoked in conflicts with students and refrain from sending blaming you-messages such as the following.

> *Don't you dare do that with me!*
>
> *Can't you ever use your head?*
>
> *Why don't you act your age for a change?*

The blaming you-messages the student receives only serve to support the student's view of him or herself and confirm the student's self-fulfilling prophecy. Receiving these negative you-messages fuels the fire by creating more stress, leading to more inappropriate behavior and greater teacher disgust. For the student, the teacher is now part of the problem, and for the teacher, having the last word and winning overrides all else.

Situations in which the teacher feels upset and angry in response to student behavior that is aggressive, hostile, and defiant call for an authentic message that expresses the teacher's feelings. When the message is about the teacher's feelings, not about the student's shortcomings, it will be delivered in I-language, not blame-attributing you-language, as the following message illustrates.

> *I really get angry when you come into my room, kick stuff around, and yell in my face. I can see you're upset, but that kind of behavior doesn't help me understand why you're angry or make me want to help you.*

Such an honest response also helps limit the teacher's impulse to retaliate and keeps the focus on what the student needs to do to regain control. When the response doesn't imply right or wrong, it keeps the communication channels open.

Most importantly, such responses model exercising control over angry feelings while simultaneously accepting and acknowledging the teacher's right to experience and express negative feelings. (Using I-language is also discussed in Chapter 4; other strategies for confronting students are discussed in Chapter 8).

When teachers consciously choose to express their anger, it helps them replace destructive words about the student with constructive words about what needs to happen. Being able to identify why student behaviors may trigger your reactions can help you begin to make better choices as you work with students.

■ ■ ■ ■ ■ ■ ■ ■

CRITICAL REFLECTION ON PRACTICE: BECOMING PROACTIVE AND BREAKING THE CYCLE OF REACTING

Activity Directions: Working with a partner, take turns sharing answers to the following questions.

What behaviors push your buttons?

_____

_____

_____

Which of the following behaviors frustrate you or make you angry?

☐ Hoarding materials	_____	☐ Talking all the time	_____
☐ Sulking	_____	☐ Demanding attention	_____
☐ Talking back	_____	☐ Bullying smaller students	_____
☐ Constantly asking questions	_____	☐ Showing anger	_____
☐ Not beginning work on time	_____	☐ Always moving around	_____
☐ Taking others' things	_____	☐ Disrupting the group	_____
☐ Not following directions	_____	☐ Challenging you	_____

For those you identified, put them in priority order.

For your top priority, consider why this behavior might be difficult for you. List reasons that come to mind for why this behavior causes you to react.

_____

_____

_____

REFLECTIVE QUESTIONS

Do you react overtly or do you usually try to hold yourself in check?

What are some ways you can separate your own issues from what your expectations are for your students?

Abel, M. H., & Sewel, J. (1999). Stress and burnout in rural and urban secondary school teachers. *Journal of Educational Research, 92* (5), 287–293.

Alan Guttmacher Institute (1999). *Teen sex and pregnancy.* Washington DC: Author.

Albert, L. (1996). *Cooperative discipline.* Circle Pines, MN: American Guidance Service.

Albert, R. D. (1983). The intercultural sensitizer or culture assimilator: A cognitive approach. In D. Landis & R. W. Brislin (Eds.), *Handbook of intercultural training* (vol. 2). New York: Pergamon.

Alberto, P. A., & Troutman, A. C. (2003). *Applied behavior analysis for teachers.* Columbus, OH: Merrill.

Albion, F. M. (1983). A methodological analysis of self-control in applied settings. *Behavior Disorders, 8,* 87–102.

Allen, J. (1980). Jogging can modify disruptive behaviors. *Teaching Exceptional Children, 12,* 66–70.

American Psychological Association. (1993). *Violence and youth: Psychology's response.* Washington, DC: Author.

Anderson, L. M., Evertson, C. M., & Brophy, J. E. (1979). An experimental study of effective teaching in first-grade reading groups. *Elementary School Journal, 79,* 193–223.

Argyris, C. (1990). *Overcoming organizational defenses.* Boston: Allyn & Bacon.

Aronson, E., & Patnoe, S. (1997). *The jigsaw classroom: Building cooperation in the classroom* (2nd ed.). New York: Longman.

Artesani, A. J. (2001). *Understanding the purpose of challenging behavior: A guide to conducting functional assessments.* Upper Saddle River, NJ: Merrill Prentice Hall.

Astor, R. A., Meyer, H. A., & Behre, W. J. (1999). Unowned places and times: Maps and interviews about violence in high schools. *American Educational Research Journal, 36* (1), 3–42.

Bandura, A. (1977). Self-efficacy: Toward a unifying theory of behavioral change. *Psychological Review, 84,* 191–215.

Bandura, A. (1997). *Self-efficacy: The exercise of control.* New York: W. H. Freeman.

Bandura, A. (1993). Perceived self-efficacy in cognitive development and functioning. *Educational Psychologist, 28* (2), 117–148.

Barker, P., & Graham, S. (1987). Developmental study of praise and blame as attributional cues. *Journal of Educational Psychology, 79,* 62–66.

Barkley, R. (1987). *Defiant children: A clinician's manual for parent training.* New York: Guilford Press.

Barton, P. E., Coley, R. J., & Wenglinsky, H. (1998). *Order in the classroom: Violence, discipline, and student achievement.* Princeton, NJ: Educational Testing Service.

Battistich, V., Solomon, D., Kim, D., Watson, M., & Schaps, E. (1995). Schools as communities, poverty levels of student populations, and students' attitudes, motives, and performance: A multilevel analysis. *American Educational Research Journal, 32,* 627–658.

Beane, A. L. (1999). *The bully free classroom: Over 100 tips and strategies for teachers K–8.* Minneapolis, MN: Free Spirit.

Beck, L. (1994). *Reclaiming educational administration as a caring profession.* New York: Teachers College Press.

Bennett, P. (1988). The perils and profits of praise. *Music Educators Journal, 75*(1), 22–24.

Berkey, R., Curtis, T., Minnick, F., Zietlow, K., Campbell, D., & Kirschner, B. W. (1990). Collaborating for reflective practice. *Education and Urban Society, 22* (2), 204–232.

Bernard, M. E. (1989). *Increasing your child's tease tolerance. Unpublished paper,* University of Melbourne, Australia.

Bernard, M. E. (2001). *Program achieve: A curriculum of lessons for teaching students how to achieve and develop social-emotional-behavioral well-being* (Vols. 1–6). Laguna Beach, CA: You Can Do It! Education.

Bernard, M. E., & DiGiuseppe, R. (1994). *Rational-emotive consultation in applied settings.* Hillsdale, NJ: Lawrence Erlbaum Associates.

Bernard, M. E., & Joyce, M. R. (1984). *Rational-emotive therapy with children and adolescents.* New York: Wiley.

Bernstein, D. A., & Borkovec, T. D. (1973). *Progressive relaxation training: A manual for the helping professions.* Champaign, IL: Research Press.

Berreth, D., & Berman, S. (1997). The moral dimensions of schools. *Educational Leadership, 54* (8), 24–26.

Bibou-Nakou, I., Stogiannidou, A., & Kiosseoglou, G. (1999). The relation between teacher burnout and teachers' attributions and practices regarding school behavior problems. *School Psychology International, 20* (2), 209–217.

Blase, J., & Kirby, P. (1991). *Bringing out the best in teachers: What effective principals do.* Newbury Park, CA: Corwin.

Bleich, J., Ingersoll, S., & Divine, J. (2000). *National campaign against youth violence.* (Academic Advisory Council report). Boston: Harvard University, John F. Kennedy School of Government.

Bocchino, R. (1999). *Emotional literacy: To be a different kind of smart.* Thousand Oaks, CA: Corwin Press.

Boggiano, A., Main, S., & Katz, P. (1988). Children's preference for challenge: The role of perceived competence and control. *Journal of Personality and Social Psychology, 54,* 134–141.

Bolle, J., & Duncan, A. (1992). *Focus: Facilitating organized change with unconventional strategies.* West End Special Education Local Plan Area, San Bernardino County Schools. San Bernardino, CA.

Bornstein, P. H. (1985). Self-instructional training: A commentary and state of the art. *Journal of Applied Behavior Analysis, 18,* 69–72.

Bower, S. A., & Bower, G. H. (1991). *Asserting yourself: A practical guide for positive change.* Reading, MA: Addison-Wesley.

Bowlby, J. (1982). *Attachment and loss* (vol. 1). New York: Basic Books.

Boyer, E. (1983). *High school: A report of the Carnegie Foundation for the Advancement of Teaching.* New York: Harper-Collins.

Boyer, E. (1995). *The basic school. A community for learning.* Princeton, NJ: The Carnegie Foundation.

Boyle, G. J., Borg, M. G., Falzon, J. M. & Baglioni, Jr., A. J. (1995). A structural model of the dimensions of teacher stress. *British Journal of Educational Psychology, 65,* 49–67.

Brandt, R. (1988). On students' needs and team learning: A conversation with William Glasser. *Educational Leadership, 45* (6), 38–45.

Brendtro, L. K., Brokenleg, M., & Van Bockern, S. (1990). *Reclaiming youth at risk: Our hope for the future.* Bloomington, IN: National Educational Service.

Brendtro, L., & Ness, A. (1983). *Re-educating troubled youth: Environments for teaching and treatment.* New York: Aldine du Gruyter.

Brendtro, L., & Seita, J. (2002). *Kids who outwit adults.* Longmont, CO: Sopris West.

Brendtro, L., & Van Bockern, S. (1994). Courage for the discouraged: A psychoeducational approach to troubled and troubling children. *Focus on Exceptional Children, 26* (8), 1–16.

Brendtro, L., & Wasmund, W. (1989). The peer culture model. In R. Lyman, S. Prentice-Dunn, & S. Gabel, *Residential and inpatient treatment of children and adolescents.* New York: Plenum Press.

Bright, B. (1996). Reflecting on "reflective practice." *Studies in the Education of Adults, 28* (2), 162–184.

Brislin, R. W., Cushner, K., Cherrie, C., & Yong, M. (1986). *Intercultural interactions: A practical guide.* Newbury Park, CA: Sage.

Brock, B. L. (1999). Perceptions of teacher burnout in Catholic schools. *Catholic Education: A Journal of Inquiry and Practice, 2,* 281–293.

Brock, B. L., & Grady, M. L. (2000). *Rekindling the flame: Principals combating teacher burnout.* Thousand Oaks, CA: Corwin Press.

Broussard, C. D., & Northup, J. (1995). An approach to functional analysis of disruptive behavior in regular education classrooms. *School Psychology Quarterly, 10,* 151–164.

Bronfenbrenner, U. (1979). *The ecology of human development: Experiments by nature and design.* Cambridge, MA: Harvard University Press.

Brookfield, S. D. (1995). *Becoming a critically reflective teacher.* San Francisco: Jossey-Bass.

Brophy, J. (1979). Teacher behavior and its effects. *Journal of Educational Psychology, 71,* 733–750.

Brophy, J. (1981). Teacher praise: A functional analysis. *Review of Educational Research, 51,* 5–32.

Brophy, J. (1983). Classroom organization and management. *Elementary School Journal, 83,* 265–285.

Brophy, J. (1987). Synthesis on strategies for motivating students to learn. *Educational Leadership, 45,* 40–48.

Brophy, J. (1988). Educating teachers about managing classrooms and students. *Teaching and Teacher Education, 4* (1), 1–18.

Brophy, J. (1996). *Teaching problem students.* New York: Guilford Press.

Brophy, J. (1998). *Motivating students to learn.* Boston: McGraw-Hill.

Brophy, J. (1999). Perspectives of classroom management: Yesterday, today, and tomorrow. In H. J. Freiberg, *Beyond behaviorism: Changing the classroom management paradigm.* Boston: Allyn & Bacon.

Brophy, J., & Evertson, C. (1974). *Process-product correlations in the Texas Teacher Effectiveness Study: Final report* (Research Report No. 74–4). Austin: University of Texas, Research and Development Center for Teacher Education (ERIC ED 091 094).

Brophy, J., & Evertson, C. (1981). *Student characteristics and teaching.* New York: Longman.

Brophy, J., & Good, T. (1974). *Teacher-student relationships: Causes and consequences.* New York: Holt, Rinehard & Winston.

Brophy, J., & Good, T. L. (1986). Teacher behavior and student achievement. In M. C. Wittrock (Ed.), *Third handbook on research on teaching* (pp. 328–375). New York: Macmillan.

Brophy, J., & McCaslin, M. (1992). Teachers' reports of how they perceive and cope with problem students. *Elementary School Journal, 93,* 3–68.

Brophy, J. E., & Putnam, J. C. (1978). *Classroom management in the elementary grades.* ERIC ED 167, 537.

Brouwers, A. & Tomic, W. (2000). *Disruptive student behavior, perceived self-efficacy, and teacher burnout.* Paper presented at the annual meeting of the American Psychological Association, Washington, DC.

Brown, M. W. (1949). *The important book.* New York: Harper & Row.

Bryk, A., & Driscoll, M. (1988). *The high school as community: Contextual influences and consequences for students and teachers.* Madison Wisconsin Center for Education Research, University of Wisconsin-Madison.

Bullough, R. V. (1994). Digging at the roots: Discipline, management, and metaphor. *Action in Teacher Education, 16* (1), 1–10.

Burbules, N. C. (1993). *Dialogue in teaching. Theory and practice.* New York: Teachers College Press.

Burbules, N. C., & Rice, S. (1991). Dialogue across differences: Continuing the conversation. *Harvard Educational Review, 61,* 264–271.

Burch, N., & Miller, K. (1979). *Teacher effectiveness training workbook.* Solana Beach, CA: Effectiveness Training.

Caffyn, R. (1989). Attitudes of British secondary school teachers and pupils to rewards and punishments. *Educational Research, 31,* 210–220.

Caine, R. N., & Caine, G. (1997). *Unleashing the power of perceptual change: The potential of brain-based teaching.* Alexandria, VA: Association for Supervision and Curriculum Development.

Caine, R. N., Caine, G., McClintic, C., & Klimek, K. (2004). *Kaleidoscope: Dynamic teaching for a new generation.* Thousand Oaks, CA: Corwin Press.

Cameron, J., & Pierce, W. D. (1994). Reinforcement, reward, and intrinsic motivation: A meta-analysis. *Review of Educational Research, 64* (3), 363–423.

Camp, B. W., & Bash, M. A. (1981). *Think aloud: Increasing cognitive skill, a problem-solving program for children.* Champaign, IL: Research Press.

Cangelosi, J. S. (1999). *Classroom management strategies: Gaining and maintaining students' cooperation* (4th ed.). White Plains, NY: Longman.

Cannella, G. S. (1986). Praise and concrete rewards: Concerns for childhood education. *Childhood Education, 62,* 297–301.

Canter, L., & Canter, M. (1976). *Assertive discipline: A take-charge approach for today's educator.* Seal Beach, CA: Lee Canter and Associates.

Canter, L., & Canter, M. (1992). *Assertive discipline: Positive behavior management for today's schools* (rev. ed.). Santa Monica, CA: Lee Canter and Associates.

Cantrell, M. (1992). Guns, gangs and kids [Special Issue]. *Journal of Emotional & Behavioral Problems, 1* (1).

Capra, F. (1983). *The turning point: Science, society, and the rising culture.* New York: Bantam.

Carducci, D., & Carducci, J. (1984). *The caring classroom.* Palo Alto, CA: Bull Publishing.

Carlson, J. (1978). *The basics of discipline.* Coral Springs, FL: CMTI Press.

Carpenter, R. L., & Apter, S. J. (1987). Research in integration of cognitive-emotional interventions for behavioral disordered children and youth. In M. C. Wang, H. J. Walberg, & M. C. Reynolds (Eds.), *Handbook of special education: Research and practice.* Oxford, England: Pergamon.

Cautela, J. R., & Groden, J. (1978). *Relaxation: A comprehensive manual for adults, children, and children with special needs.* Champaign, IL: Research Press.

Center, D. B., & McKittrick, S. (1987). Disciplinary removal of special education students. *Focus on Exceptional Children, 20* (20), 1–9.

Chandler, L. K., & Dahlquist, C. M. (2002). *Functional assessment: Strategies to prevent and remediate challenging behavior in school settings.* Upper Saddle River, NJ: Merrill Prentice Hall.

Chandler, T. (1981). What's wrong with success and praise? *Arithmetic Teacher,* 10–12.

Charles, C. M. (2002). *Building classroom discipline* (7th ed.). White Plains, NY: Longman.

Child Development Project (1996). *Ways we want our class to be: Class meetings that build commitment to kindness and learning.* Oakland, CA: Development Studies Center.

Children's Defense Fund (2001). *The state of America's children yearbook 2001.* Washington, DC: Children's Defense Fund.

Cicchetti, D. (1989). How research on child maltreatment has informed the study of child development: Perspectives from developmental psychopathology. In D. Cicchetti & V. Carlson (Eds.), *Child maltreatment. Theory and research on the causes and consequences of child abuse and neglect* (pp. 377–431). New York: Cambridge University Press.

Cicchetti, D., & Toth, S. L. (1998). The development of depression in children and adolescents. *American Psychologist, 53* (2), 221–241.

Cohen, E. G. (1994). *Designing groupwork: Strategies for the heterogeneous classroom* (2nd ed.). New York: Teacher College Press.

Cohen, E. G. (1998). Making cooperative learning equitable. *Educational Leadership, 56* (1), 18–21.

Cole, A. L., & Knowles, J. G. (2000). *Researching teaching: Exploring teacher development through reflexive inquiry.* Boston: Allyn & Bacon.

Cole, M., & Cole, S. R (1989). *The development of children.* New York: Scientific American Books.

Coles, A. D. (2000, June 14). Lately, teens less likely to engage in risky behaviors. *Education Week,* 6.

Coloroso, B. (1999). *Parenting with wit and wisdom in times of chaos and confusion.* Littleton, CO: Kids Are Worth It!

Colvin, B. (1988). *Procedures for preventing serious acting out behavior in the classroom.* Unpublished manuscript, Lane Education Service District. Eugene, OR.

Colvin, G., Kameenui, E. J., & Sugai, G. (1993). School-wide and classroom management: Reconceptualizing the integration and management of students with behavior problems in general education. *Education and Treatment of Children, 16,* 361–381.

Combs, A. W. (1991). *The schools we need: New assumptions for educational reform.* Lanham, MD: University Press of America.

Condry, J., & Chambers, J. (1978). Intrinsic motivation and the process of learning. In M. R Lepper & D. Greene (Eds.), *The hidden cost of reward: New perspectives on the psychology of human motivation.* Hillsdale, NJ: Erlbaum.

Cooperman, M. (1975). Field-dependence and children's problem-solving under varying contingencies of predetermined feedback. *Dissertation Abstracts International, 35,* 2040–2041.

Cormier, W. H., & Cormier, L. S. (1997). *Interviewing strategies for helpers.* Monterey, CA: Brooks/Cole.

Coughlin, D., & Shanahan, D. (1991). *Boys Town family home program training manual* (3rd ed.). Boys Town, NE: Father Flanagan's Boys' Home.

Crocker, R. K, & Brooker, G. M. (1986). Classroom control and student outcomes in grades 2 and 5. *American Educational Research Journal, 23,* 1–11.

Csikszentmihalyi, M. (1993). *The evolving self: A psychology for the third millennium.* New York: Harper-Collins.

Curtis, J. D., & Detert, R. A. (1981). *How to relax: A holistic approach to stress management.* Mountain View, CA: Mayfield.

Curwin, R. L. (1992). *Rediscovering hope: Our greatest teaching strategy.* Bloomington, IN: National Educational Service.

Curwin, R. L., & Fuhrmann, B. S. (1975). *Discovering your teaching self: Humanistic approaches to effective teaching.* Boston: Allyn & Bacon.

Curwin, R. L., & Mendler, A. N. (1988). *Discipline with dignity.* Alexandria, VA: Association for Supervision and Curriculum Development.

Curwin, R. L., & Mendler, A. N. (1997). *As tough as necessary: Countering violence, aggression, and hostility in our schools.* Alexandria, VA: Association for Supervision and Curriculum Development.

David and Lucille Packard Foundation (2002). *Children, youth and gun violence. The future of children, 2002.* Los Altos, CA: Author.

Davis, G., & Thomas, M. (1989). *Effective schools and effective teachers.* Boston: Allyn & Bacon.

Davis, M., McKay, M., & Eshelman, E. R. (1982). *The relaxation and stress reduction workbook* (2nd ed.). Oakland, CA: New Harbinger.

Day, H. M., Horner, R. H., & O'Neill, R. E. (1994). Multiple functions of problem behaviors: Assessment and intervention. *Journal of Applied Behavior Analysis, 27,* 279–289.

De Charms, R. (1976). *Enhancing motivation: Change in the classroom.* New York: Irvington.

Deci, E. L. (1976). *Intrinsic motivation.* New York: Plenum.

Deci, E. L. (1978). Applications of research on the effects of rewards. In M. R. Lepper & D. Greene (Eds.), *The hidden costs of reward: New perspectives on the psychology of human motivation.* New York: Erlbaum.

Deci, E. L., Koestner, R., & Ryan, R. M. (1999). A meta-analytic review of experiments examining the effects of extrinsic rewards on intrinsic motivation. *Psychological Bulletin, 125,* 627–668.

Deci, E. L., Koestner, R., & Ryan, R. M. (2001). Extrinsic rewards and intrinsic motivation in education: Reconsidered once again. *Review of Educational Research, 71* (1), 1–27.

Deci, E. L., & Ryan, R. M. (1985). *Intrinsic motivation and self-determination in human behavior.* New York: Plenum.

Deci, E. L., & Ryan, R. M. (1987). The support of autonomy and the control of behavior. *Journal of Personality and Social Psychology, 53,* 1024–1037.

Deiro, J. A. (1996). *Teaching with heart. Making healthy connections with students.* Thousand Oaks, CA: Corwin Press.

Dewey, J. (1963). *Experience and education.* New York: Collier Books. (Original work published 1938.)

Dickinson, A. M. (1989). The detrimental effects of extrinsic reinforcement on "intrinsic motivation." *The Behavior Analyst, 12,* 1–15.

DiGiuseppe, R. (1999). Rational emotive behavior therapy. In H. T. Prout & D. T. Brown, *Counseling and psychotherapy with children and adolescents: Theory and practice for school settings* (pp. 252–293). New York: John Wiley & Sons.

Dill, V. S., & Haberman, M. (1995). Building a gentler school. *Educational Leadership, 52* (5), 69–67.

Dinkmeyer, D., & McKay, G. D. (1989). *The parent's handbook* (3rd ed.). Circle Pines, MN: American Guidance Service.

Dinkmeyer, D., McKay, G. D., & Dinkmeyer, D. Jr. (1980). *Systematic training for effective teaching: Teacher's handbook.* Circle Pines, MI: American Guidance Service.

Doyle, W. (1986). Classroom organization and management. In M. C. Wittrock (Ed.), *Third Handbook of research on teaching* (pp. 392–431). New York: Macmillan.

Dreikurs, R. (1968). *Psychology in the classroom: A manual for teachers* (2nd ed.). New York: Harper & Row.

Dreikurs, R., & Cassel, P. (1972). *Discipline without tears.* New York: Hawthorn.

Dreikurs, R., and Grey, L. (1968). *Logical consequences: A new approach to discipline.* New York: Plume. Reprinted 1993.

Dreikurs, R., Grunwald, B., & Pepper, F. (1982). *Maintaining sanity in the classroom.* New York: Harper & Row.

Duke, D., & Meckel, A. (1984). *Teacher's guide to classroom management.* New York: Random House.

Dunham, J. (1984). *Stress in teaching.* New York: Nichols.

Dunlap, G., White, R., Vera, A., Wilson, D., & Panacek, L. (1996). The effects of multi-component, assessment-based curricular modifications on the classroom behavior of children with emotional and behavioral disorders. *Journal of Behavioral Education, 6,* 481–500.

Dwyer, K., Osher, D., & Warger, C. (1998). *Early warning, timely response: A guide to safe schools.* Washington, DC: U.S. Department of Education.

Dyer, W. (1977). *Your erroneous zones.* New York: Avon Books.

Ellis, A. (1974). *Humanistic psychotherapy: The rational-emotive approach.* New York: McGraw-Hill.

Ellis, A., & Bernard, M. E. (1984). *Rational-emotive approaches to the problems of childhood.* New York: Plenum.

Ellis, A., & Dryden, W. (1997). *The practice of rational-emotive therapy.* New York: Springer.

Ellis, A., & Harper, R. A. (1975). *A new guide to rational living.* No. Hollywood, CA: Wilshire Book Company.

Ellis, J., & Magee, S. K. (1999). Determination of environmental correlates of disruptive classroom behavior: Integration of functional analysis into public school assessment process. *Education and Treatment of Children, 22* (3), 291–316.

Emery, G., Hollon, D. S., & Bedrosian, R. D. (1981). *New directions in cognitive therapy.* New York: Guilford Press.

Emery, R., & Marholin, D. (1977). An applied behavior analysis of delinquency: The irrelevancy of relevant behavior. *American Psychologist, 32,* 860–873.

Emmer, E. T., Evertson, C. M., & Anderson, L. M. (1980). Effective classroom management at the beginning of the school year. *Elementary School Journal, 80,* 219–231.

Erikson, E. H. (1980). *Identity and the life cycle.* New York: Norton.

Erikson, E. H. (1991). *Childhood and society.* New York: Norton.

Evertson, C. M. (1985). Training teachers in classroom management: An experimental study in secondary school classrooms. *Journal of Educational Research, 79,* 51–58.

Evertson, C. M. (1989). Improving elementary classroom management: A school-based training program for beginning the year. *Journal of Educational Research, 83,* 82–90.

Evertson, C. M., Anderson, C. W., Anderson, L. M., & Brophy, J. E. (1980). Relationships between classroom behaviors and student outcomes in junior high mathematics and English classes. *American Educational Research Journal, 17,* 43–60.

Evertson, C. M., & Emmer, E. T. (1982). Effective management at the beginning of the school year in junior high classes. *Journal of Educational Psychology, 74,* 485–498.

Evertson, C. M., Emmer, E. T., Clements, B. S., & Worsham, M. E. (2003). *Classroom management for elementary teachers* (6th ed.). Boston: Allyn & Bacon.

Evertson, C. M., Emmer, E., Sanford, J., & Clements, B. (1983). Improving classroom management: An experiment in elementary classrooms. *Elementary School Journal, 84,* 173–188.

Evertson, C. M., & Weade, R. (1989). Classroom management and teaching style: Instructional stability and variability in two junior high English classrooms. *Elementary School Journal, 89* (3), 379–393.

Faber, A., & Mazlish, E. (2002). *How to talk so kids will listen and listen so kids will talk.* New York: Avon Books.

Fagen, S. (1979). Psychoeducational management and self-control. In D. Cullinan & M. Epstein (Eds.), *Special education for adolescents: Issues and perspectives.* Columbus, OH: Merrill.

Fagen, S. A., & Hill, J. M. (1977). *Behavior management: A competency-based manual for in-service training.* Burtonville, MD: Psychoeducational Resources.

Fagen, S., Long, N., & Stevens, D. (1975). *Teaching children self-control.* Columbus, OH: Merrill.

Farber, B. A., & Miller, J. (1981). Teacher burnout: A psychoeducational perspective. *Teachers College Record, 83* (2), 235–243.

Farrington, D. P. (1995). The challenge of teenage antisocial behavior. In M. Rutter, *Psychological disturbances in young people: Challenges for prevention* (pp. 83–130). New York: Oxford University Press.

Feindler, E. L., & Ecton, R. B. (1986). *Adolescent anger control.* New York: Pergamon Press.

Farson, R. (1977). Praise as a motivational tool. In D. E. Hamachek (Ed.), *Human Dynamics in Psychology and Education* (3rd ed.). Boston: Allyn & Bacon.

Feindler, E. L., & Fremouw, W. J. (1983). Stress inoculation training for adolescent anger problems. In D. H. Meichenbaum & M. E. Jaremko (Eds.), *Stress reduction and prevention.* New York: Plenum.

Feindler, E. L., Marriott, S. A., & Iwata, M. (1984). Group anger control training for junior high delinquents. *Cognitive Therapy and Research, 8,* 299–311.

Felson, R. B. (1996). Mass media effects on violent behavior. *Annual Review of Sociology, 22,* 103–128.

Flink, C., Boggiano, A., Main, D., Barrett, M., & Katz, P. (1992). Children's achievement related behaviors: The role of extrinsic motivational orientations. In A. Boggiano & T. Pittman (Eds.), *Achievement and motivation: A social-developmental perspective* (pp. 189–214). Cambridge: Cambridge University Press.

Forehand, R., & McMahon, R. (1981). *Helping the noncompliant child.* New York: Guilford Press.

Forman, S. G. (1980). A comparison of cognitive training and response cost procedures in modifying aggressive behavior of elementary school children. *Behavior Therapy, 11,* 594–600.

Forness, S. R. (1973). The reinforcement hierarchy. *Psychology in the Schools, 10,* 168–177.

Forum on Child and Family Statistics (2002). *America's children 2002: Key national indicators of well-being, 2002.* Federal Interagency Forum on Child and Family Statistics. Washington, DC: Government Printing Office.

Foster-Johnson, L., & Dunlap, G. (1993). Using functional assessment to develop effective, individualized interventions for challenging behaviors. *Teaching Exceptional Children, 25,* 44–50.

Frieberg, H. J. (1999). *Beyond behaviorism: Changing the classroom management paradigm.* Boston: Allyn & Bacon.

Freiberg, J. (1996). From tourists to citizens in the classroom. *Educational Leadership, 54,* 32–36.

Freire, P. (1993). *Pedagogy of the oppressed* (rev. ed.). New York: Continuum.

Fried, S., & Fried, P. (1996). *Bullies and victims: Helping your child survive the schoolyard battlefield.* New York: M. Evans & Co.

Friedman, I. A. (1995). Student behavior patterns contributing to teacher burnout. *Journal of Educational Research, 88* (5), 281–289.

Frieman, B. B. (2001). *What teachers need to know about children at risk.* Boston, MA: McGraw Hill.

Friesen, D., Prokop, C., & Sarros, J. (1988). Why teachers burn out. *Educational Research Quarterly, 12* (3), 9–19.

Froyen, L. A., & Iverson, A. M. (1999). *Schoolwide and classroom management: The reflective educator-leader.* New York: Merrill.

Gable, R. (1999). Functional assessment in school settings. *Behavioral Disorders, 24,* 246–248.

Gage, N. (1978). *The scientific basis of the art of teaching.* New York: Teachers College Press, Columbia University.

Gallagher, P. A. (1995). *Teaching students with behavior disorders: Techniques and activities for classroom instruction* (2nd ed.). Denver, CO: Love.

Gardner, H. (1993). *Multiple intelligences: The theory in practice.* New York: Basic Books.

Garmezy, N. (1984). Children vulnerable to major mental disorders: Risk and protective factors. In L. Grinspoon (Ed.), *Psychiatric update* (vol. 3, pp. 91–104, 159–161). Washington, DC: American Psychiatric Press.

Garner, H. (1982). Positive peer culture programs in schools. In D. Safer, *School programs for disruptive adolescents.* Baltimore: University Park Press.

Garrity, C., Jens, K., Porter, W., Sager, N., & Short-Camilli, C. (1996). Bully-proofing your school: A comprehensive approach. *Reclaiming Youth and Children, 5* (1), 35–39.

Garrity, C., Jens, K., Porter, W., Sager, N., & Short-Camilli, C. (2000). *Bully-proofing your school: A comprehensive approach* (2nd ed.). Longmont, CO: Sopris West.

Gast, D., & Nelson, C. M. (1977a). Legal and ethical considerations for the use of timeout in special education settings. *Journal of Special Education, 11,* 457–467.

Gast, D., & Nelson, C. M. (1977b). Time out in the classroom: Implications for special education. *Exceptional Children, 43,* 461–464.

Gathercoal, F. (1997). *Judicious discipline* (4th ed.). San Francisco, CA: Caddo Gap Press.

George, P. S. (1980). Discipline, moral development, and levels of schooling. *Educational Forum, 45,* 57–67.

Gersten, R., Woodward, J., & Darch, C. (1986). Direct instruction: A research-based approach to curriculum design and teaching. *Exceptional Children, 53* (1), 17–31.

Gesten, E. L., Weissber, R. P., Amish, P. L., & Smith, J. K. (1987). Social problem-solving training: A skills-based approach to prevention and treatment. In C. A. Maher & J. E. Zins (Eds.), *Psychoeducational interventions in the schools* (pp. 26–45). New York: Pergamon.

Ginott, H. (1965). *Between parent and child.* New York: Avon.

Ginott, H. (1969). *Between parent and teenager.* New York: Macmillan.

Ginott, H. (1972). *Teacher and child.* New York: Macmillan.

Glasser, W. (1965). *Reality therapy: A new approach to psychiatry.* New York: Harper and Row.

Glasser, W. (1969). *Schools without failure.* New York: Harper & Row.

Glasser, W. (1974). A new look at discipline. *Learning, 3* (4), 6–11.

Glasser, W. (1977). 10 steps to good discipline. *Today's Education, 66,* 60–63.

Glasser, W. (1978). Disorders in our schools: Causes and remedies. *Phi Delta Kappan, 59,* 331–333.

Glasser, W. (1986). *Control theory in the classroom.* New York: Harper & Row.

Glasser, W. (1998a). *The quality school. Managing students without coercion.* New York: Harper & Row.

Glasser, W. (1998b). *The quality school teacher.* New York: HarperCollins.

Glasser, W., & Dotson, K. (1998). *Choice theory in the classroom.* New York: HarperCollins.

Glassner, B. (1999, August 13). School violence: The fears, the facts. *The New York Times,* p. A21.

Glenn, H. S. (1982). *Developing capable people* (Learner's guide). Fair Oaks, CA: Sunrise Press.

Glenn, H. S., Nelsen, J. (2000). *Raising self-reliant children in a self-indulgent world.* Rocklin, CA: Prima Publications.

Gmelch, W. (1983). Stress for success: How to optimize your performance. *Theory Into Practice, 22* (1), 7–14.

Golanda, E. (1990). *The importance of the source of power in an educational setting.* Paper presented at the annual meeting of the Southern Regional Conference of Educational Administration, Atlanta, GA.

Gold, Y. (1988). Recognizing and coping with academic burnout. *Contemporary Education, 59* (3), 142–145.

Goldstein, A. P. (1988). *The prepare curriculum: Teaching prosocial competencies.* Champaign, IL: Research Press.

Goldstein, A. P. (1991). *Delinquent gangs. A psychological perspective.* Champaign, IL: Research Press.

Goldstein, A. (1994). *Student aggression: Prevention, management, and replacement training.* New York: Longman.

Goldstein, A. P., & Conoley, J. C. (1997). *School violence intervention.* New York: Guilford Press.

Goldstein, A. P., & Glick, B. (1994). Aggression replacement training: Curriculum and evaluation. *Simulation & Gaming, 25* (1), 9–26.

Goldstein, A. P., Glick, B., Irwin, M. J., McCartney, C., & Rubama, I. (1989). *Reducing delinquency: Intervention in the community.* New York: Pergamon.

Goldstein, A. P., Glick, B., Reiner, S., Zimmerman, D., & Coultry, T. (1986). *Aggression replacement training.* Champaign, IL: Research Press.

Goldstein, A. P., Sprafkin, R., Gershaw, N.J., & Klein, P. (1980). *Skillstreaming the adolescent.* Champaign, IL: Research Press.

Goldstein, A. P., Sprafkin, R. P., Gershaw, N.J., & Klein, P. (1983). Structured learning: A psychoeducational approach for teaching social competencies. *Behavioral Disorders, 8* (3), 161–170.

Goleman, D. (1995). *Emotional intelligence.* New York: Bantam.

Goleman, D. (1998). *Working with emotional intelligence.* New York: Bantam.

Good, T., & Brophy, J. (2002). *Looking in classrooms* (9th ed.). New York: HarperCollins.

Goodlad, J. (1990). *Teachers for our nation's schools.* San Francisco: Jossey-Bass.

Gootman, M. E. (2001). *The caring teacher's guide to discipline: Helping young students learn self-control, responsibility, and respect.* Thousand Oaks, CA: Corwin Press.

Gordon, T. (1974). *T. E. T. Teacher effectiveness training.* New York: David McKay.

Gordon, T. (1989). *Teaching children self-discipline at home and at school.* New York: Times.

Gossen, A. C. (1996). *Restitution: Restructuring school discipline.* Chapel Hill, NC: New View Publications.

Gothelf, C. R., Rikhye, C. H., & Silberman, R. K (1988). *Working with students who have dual sensory impairments and cognitive disabilities: Handbook for special education teachers and related services personnel.* Albany: New York State Education Department, Office for Education of Children with Handicapping Conditions, Title VI-C.

Grant, G. (1988). *The world we created at Hamilton High.* Cambridge: Harvard University Press.

Grossman, H. (1985). *Educating Hispanic students: Cultural implications for instruction, classroom management, counseling, and assessment.* Springfield, IL: Charles C. Thomas.

Grossman, H. (1990). *Trouble free teaching: Solutions to behavior problems in the classroom.* Mountain View, CA: Mayfield.

Grossman, D. (1996). *On killing: The psychological cost of learning to kill in war and society.* New York: Little, Brown & Co.

Grossman, H. (2003). *Classroom behavior management for diverse and inclusive schools* (3rd ed.). Lanham, MD: Rowman & Littlefield Publishers.

Guerra, N. G., & Williams, K. R. (1996). *A program planning guide for youth violence prevention.* Boulder, CO: Center for the Study and Prevention of Violence.

Gunter, P. L., Denny, R. K., Jack, S. L., Shores, R. E., & Nelson, C. M. (1993). Aversive stimuli in academic interactions between students with serious emotional disturbance and their teachers. *Behavioral Disorders, 18,* 265–274.

Hall, J. (1971). Decisions, decisions, decisions. *Psychology Today, 5* (6), 51–54, 86, 88.

Hall, R. V., & Hall, M. (1980). *How to use time out.* Lawrence, KS: H & H Enterprises.

Halliger, P., & Murphy, J. (1986). The social context of effective schools. *American Journal of Education, 94,* 328–355.

Hamburg, D. A. (1992). *Today's children: Creating a future for a generation in crisis.* New York: Times Books.

Hartner, S. (1978). Effective motivation reconsidered: Toward a developmental model. *Human Development, 21,* 34–64.

Harvey, J. (1988). *The quiet mind: Techniques for transforming stress.* Honesdale, PA: Himalayan International Institute.

Hatton, N., & Smith, D. (1995). Facilitating reflection: Issues and research. *Forum of Education, 50,* 49–65.

Hawkins, J. D., Catalano, R., & Miller, J. Y. (1992). Risk and protective factors for alcohol and other drug problems in adolescence and early adulthood: Implications for substance abuse prevention. *Psychological Bulletin, 112* (2), 64–105.

Hawkins, J. D., Herrenkohl, T. I., Farrington, D. P., Brewer, D., Catalano, R. F., Harachi, T. W., & Cothern, L. (2000). Predictors of youth violence. *Juvenile Justice Bulletin.* Washington, DC: U.S. Department of Justice, Office of Juvenile Justice and Delinquency Prevention.

Haycock, K. (1998). Good teaching matters . . . a lot. *Thinking K–16, 3* (2), 1–14.

Heider, J. (1985). *The tao of leadership.* New York: Bantam Books.

Herman, J. L. (1992). *Trauma and recovery.* New York: Basic Books.

Hitz, R., & Driscoll, A. (1988). Praise or encouragement? New insights into praise: Implications for early childhood teachers. *Young Children 43*(5), 6–13.

Hobbs, N. (1982). *The troubled and troubling child.* San Francisco: Jossey-Bass.

Hollister-Wagner, G. H., Foshee, V. A., & Jackson, C. (2001). Adolescent aggression: Models of resiliency. *Journal of Applied Social Psychology, 31* (3), 445–466.

Holt, P., Fine, M. J., & Tollefson, N. (1987). Mediating stress: Survival of the hardy. *Psychology in the Schools, 24,* 51–58.

Hoover, R. L., & Kindsvatter, R. (1997). *Democratic discipline: Foundation and practice.* Columbus, OH: Merrill.

Hoyert, D. L., Anas, E., Smith, B. L., Murphy, S. L., & Kochanek, K. D. (2001). *Deaths: Final data for 1999.* National Vital Statistics Reports 49 (8). Hyattsville, MD: National Center for Health Statistics.

Hughes, J. N. (1988). *Cognitive behavior therapy with children in schools.* New York: Pergamon.

Hyman, I. A. (1990). *Reading, writing, and the hickory stick.* Lexington, MA: Lexington Books.

Hyman, I. A. (1997). *School discipline and school violence: The teacher variance approach.* Boston: Allyn & Bacon.

Individuals with Disabilities Act Amendments of 1997, 20 U. S. C. §1400 *et seq.*

Jackson, N. F., Jackson, D. A., & Monroe, C. (2002). *Getting along with others: Teaching social effectiveness to children.* Champaign, IL: Research Press.

Jakubowski, P. A. (1977). Assertive behavior and clinical problems of women. In D. Carter & E. Rawlings (Eds.), *Psychotherapy with women.* Springfield, IL: Charles C. Thomas.

Jakubowski, P., & Lange, A. J. (1978). *The assertive option: Your rights and responsibilities.* Champaign, IL: Research Press.

Jalongo, M. R (1991). *Creating learning communities. The role of the teacher in the 21st century.* Bloomington, IN: National Educational Service.

Jenkins, S., & Calhoun, J. F. (1991). Teacher stress: Issues and intervention. *Psychology in the Schools, 28* (1), 60–70.

Johns, B. H., & Keenan, J. P. (1997). *Techniques for managing a safe school.* Denver, CO: Love.

Johnson, J. M. (1996). Distinguishing between applied research and practice. *The Behavior Analyst, 19,* 35–47.

Johnson, S. M. (1990). *Teachers at work.* New York: Basic Books.

Johnson, D., & Johnson, R. (1987). *Learning together and alone: Cooperative, competitive, and individualistic learning.* Englewood Cliffs, NJ: Prentice-Hall.

Johnson D. W., & Johnson, R. T. (1995). Why violence prevention programs don't work—and what does. *Educational Leadership, 52* (5), 63–67.

Johnson, D., Johnson, R., Holubec, E., & Roy, P. (1984). *Circles of learning: Cooperation in the classroom.* Alexandria, VA: Association for Supervision and Curriculum Development.

Jones, F. (1987). *Positive classroom discipline.* New York: McGraw-Hill.

Jones, V. F., & Jones, L. S. (2004). *Comprehensive classroom management: Creating communities of support and solving problems* (7th ed.). Boston: Allyn & Bacon.

Jones, Y. (1990). *Aggression replacement training in a high school setting.* Unpublished manuscript. Brisbane, Australia: Center for Learning & Adjustment Difficulties.

Joseph, R. (2001). *Stressfree teaching: A practical guide to tackling stress in teaching, lecturing, and tutoring.* London, UK: Kogan Page Limited.

Kagan, S. (1990). *Cooperative learning. Resources for teachers.* San Juan Capistrano, CA: Resources for Teachers.

Kamii, C., Clark, F. B., & Dominick, A. (1994). The six national goals: A road to disappointment. *Phi Delta Kappan,* 672–677.

Kanouse, D., Gumpert, P., & Canavan-Gumpert, D. (1981). The semantics of praise. In J. H. Harvey, W. Ickes, & R. F. Kidd (Eds.), *New Directions in Attribution Research* (Vol. 3). Hillsdale, NJ: Erlbaum.

Kaplan, C. (1992). Teachers' punishment histories and their selection of disciplinary techniques. *Contemporary Educational Psychology, 17,* 258–265.

Kaplan, J. S. (1995). *Beyond behavior modification: A cognitive behavioral approach to behavior management in the school* (3rd ed.). Austin, TX: Pro-Ed.

Kasl, E., Dechant, K., & Marsick, V. (1993). Living the learning: Internalizing our model of group learning. In D. Boud, R. Cohen, & D. Walker (Eds.), *Using experience for learning.* Bristol, PA: Open University Press.

Kast, A., & Connor, K. (1988). Sex and age differences in response to informational and controlling feedback. *Personality and Social Psychology Bulletin, 14,* 514–523.

Katz, N. H., & Lawyer, J. W. (1994). *Preventing and managing conflict in schools.* Thousand Oaks, CA: Corwin Press.

Keane, R. (1987). The doubting journey: A learning process of self-transformation. In D. Boud & V. Griffin (Eds.), *Appreciating adults' learning: From the learners' perspective.* Toronto: Ontario Institute for Studies in Education Press.

Kendall, P., & Braswell, L. (1984). *Cognitive behavioral therapy for impulsive children.* New York: Guilford Press.

Kendall, P., & Braswell, L. (1985). *Cognitive behavioral therapy for impulsive children.* New York: Guilford Press.

Kennedy, R. L., & Morton, J. H. (1999). *A school for healing: Alternative strategies for teaching at-risk students.* New York: Peter Lang Publishing.

Kerr, M. M., & Nelson, C. M. (1998). *Strategies for managing behavior problems in the classroom* (3rd ed.). Upper Saddle River, NJ: Merrill.

Kijai, J., & Totten, D. L. (1995). Teacher burnout in small Christian school: A national study. *Journal of Research on Christian Education, 4,* 195–218.

Killion, J., & Todnem, G. (1991). A process of personal theory building. *Educational Leadership, 48* (6), 14–17.

King, P. M., & Kitchener, K. S. (1994). *Developing reflective judgment.* San Francisco: Jossey-Bass.

Kirschenbaum, H. (1995). *100 ways to enhance values and morality in schools and youth settings.* Boston: Allyn & Bacon.

Knowles, J. G., Cole, A. L., & Presswood, C. S. (1994). *Through preservice teachers' eyes: Exploring field experiences through narrative and inquiry.* New York: Merrill.

Knowles, M. (1975). *Self-directed learning: A guide for learners and teachers.* New York: Cambridge.

Knowles, M. (1992). *The adult learner: A neglected species* (4th ed.). Houston, TX: Gulf.

Kohlberg, L. (1969). Stage and sequence: The cognitive-developmental approach to socialization. In D. A. Goslin (Ed.), *Handbook of socialization theory and research* (pp. 347–480). Chicago: Rand McNally.

Kohlberg, L. (1973). *Collected papers on moral development and moral education.* Cambridge, MA: Harvard University, Center for Moral Education.

Kohlberg, L. (1975). The cognitive-developmental approach to moral education. *Phi Delta Kappan, 56,* 670–677.

Kohlberg, L. (1984). *The psychology of moral development.* San Francisco: Harper & Row.

Kohlberg, L., & Gilligan, C. (1972). The adolescent as a philosopher: The discovery of the self in a postconventional world. In J. Kagan & R. Coles (Eds.), *12 to 16: Early adolescence* (pp. 144–179). New York: Norton.

Kohn, A. (1993). *Punished by rewards: The trouble with gold stars, incentive plans, A's, praise and other bribes.* New York: Houghton Mifflin.

Kohn, A. (1996). *Beyond discipline: From compliance to community.* Alexandria, VA: Association for Supervision and Curriculum Development.

Kottler, J. A. (2002). *Students who drive you crazy: Succeeding with resistant, unmotivated, and otherwise difficult young people.* Thousand Oaks, CA: Corwin Press.

Kounin, J. S. (1970). *Discipline and group management in classrooms.* New York: Holt, Rinehart & Winston.

Kreidler, W. J. (1984). *Creative conflict resolution: More than 200 activities for keeping peace in the classroom.* Glenview, IL: Scott, Foresman.

Kreisman, J. J., & Straus, H. (1989). *I hate you—don't leave me: Understanding the borderline personality.* New York: Avon.

Kroth, R. L. (1985). *Communicating with parents of exceptional children* (2nd ed.). Denver, CO: Love.

Kyriacou, C. (1987). Teacher stress and burnout: An international review. *Educational Research, 29,* 146–150.

Lackoff, G., & Johnson, M. (1980). *Metaphors we live by.* Chicago: The University of Chicago Press.

Ladson-Billings, G. (1994). *The dreamkeepers: Successful teachers of African American children.* San Francisco: Jossey-Bass.

Ladson-Billings, G. (1995). Toward a theory of culturally relevant pedagogy. *American Educational Research Journal, 32* (3), 465–491.

Lange, A. J., & Jakubowski, P. (1976). *Responsible assertive behavior.* Champaign, IL: Research Press.

Langer, E. J. (1989). *Mindfulness.* Reading, MA: Addison Wesley.

Langer, G. (1999, April 26). Students report violent peers. *ABCNEWS.com,* April 26, 1999, pp. 1–2.

Larrivee, B. (1985). *Effective teaching for successful mainstreaming.* New York: Longman.

Larrivee, B. (1991). Social status: A comparison of mainstreamed students with peers of different ability levels. *Journal of Special Education, 25,* 90–101.

Larrivee, B. (1992). *Strategies for effective classroom management: Creating a collaborative climate.* Boston: Allyn & Bacon.

Larrivee, B. (1995). Reconceptualizing classroom management. In B. G. Blair & R. Caine (Eds.), *Integrative learning as the pathway to teaching for holism, complexity and interconnectedness.* Lewiston, NY: Edwin Mellen Press.

Larrivee, B. (1996). *Moving into balance.* Santa Monica, CA: Shoreline.

Larrivee, B. (1997). Restructuring classroom management for more interactive and integrated teaching and learning. In T. Jennings (Ed.), *Restructuring for integrated education: Multiple perspectives, multiple contexts.* In the Henry A. Giroux Critical Studies in Education and Culture Series, Westport CT: Bergin & Garvey.

Larrivee, B. (2000a). Transforming teaching practice: Becoming the critically reflective teacher. *Reflective Practice, 1* (3), 293–307.

Larrivee, B. (2000b). Creating caring learning communities. *Contemporary Education, 71* (2), 18–21.

Larrivee, B. (2002). The potential perils of praise in a democratic interactive classroom. *Action in Teacher Education, 71* (2), 18–21.

Lasley, T. J. (1992). Inquiry and reflection: Promoting teacher reflection. *Journal of Staff Development, 13* (1), 24–29.

Lazarus, A. (1997). *Brief but comprehensive psychotherapy: The multimodel way.* New York: Springer Publishing.

Lee, J. L., Pulvino, C. J., & Perrone, P. A. (1998). *Restoring harmony: A guide for managing conflicts in schools.* Columbus, OH: Merrill.

Leone, P. E., Mayer, M. J., Malmgren, K., & Meisel, S. M. (2000). School violence and disruption: rhetoric, reality, and reasonable balance. *Focus on Exceptional Children, 33* (1), 1–20.

Lepper, M. (1983). Extrinsic reward and intrinsic motivation: Implications for the classroom. In J. Levine & M. Wang (Eds.), *Teacher-student perceptions: Implications for learning.* Hillsdale, NJ: Erlbaum.

Lepper, M. R., & Greene, D. (Eds.). (1978) *The hidden costs of reward: New perspectives on the psychology of human motivation.* New York: Erlbaum.

Lewis, W., & Lewis, B. (1989). The psychoeducational model: Cumberland House after 25 years. In R. Lyman, S. Prentice-Dunn, & S. Gabel, *Residential and inpatient treatment of children and adolescents.* New York: Plenum Press.

Lichter, S. R., Lichter, L. S., & Amundson, D. (1999). *Merchandising mayhem: Violence in popular culture.* Washington, DC: Center for Media and Public Affairs.

Lieberman, A. & Miller, L. (1984). The social realities of teaching. In A. Lieberman (Ed.), *Teachers: Their world, their work* (pp. 1–16). Alexandria, VA: Association for Supervision and Curriculum Development.

Lightfoot, S. (1984). *The good high school.* New York: Basic Books.

Lipsey, M. W., & Wilson, D. B. (1993). The efficacy of psychological, educational, and behavioral treatment: Confirmation from meta-analysis. *American Psychologist, 48,* 1181–1209.

London, T., & Monjes, A. (1999). *Rough spot training: A manual for helping children develop emotional control, self-soothing and behavioral management.* Goose Printing.

Long, N. (1996). The conflict cycle paradigm on how troubled students get teachers out of control. In N. Long & W. Morse (Eds.), *Conflict in the classroom: The education of at-risk and troubled students* (5th ed., pp. 244–265). Austin, TX: Pro-Ed.

Long, N., & Morse, W. (1996). *Conflict in the classroom: The education of at-risk and troubled students* (5th ed.). Austin, TX: Pro-Ed.

Long, N., Morse, W., & Newman, R. G. (1976). *Conflict in the classroom: The education of emotionally disturbed children* (3rd ed.). Belmont, CA: Wadsworth.

Long, N. J., & Newman, R. G. (1961). A differential approach to the management of surface behavior of children in school. *Bulletin of the School of Education* (Indiana University, Bloomington), *37,* 47–61.

Lortie, D. C. (1975). *Schoolteacher: A sociological study.* Chicago: University of Chicago Press.

Lucic, K. S., Steffen, J. J., Harrigan, J. A., & Stuebing, R. C. (1991). Progressive relaxation training: Muscle contraction before relaxation? *Behavior Therapy, 22,* 249–256.

Luria, A. R. (1961). *The role of speech in the regulation of normal and abnormal behaviors.* New York: Liveright.

Lynch, J. (1989). *Multicultural education in a global society.* London: Falmer Press.

Lynch, M., & Cicchetti, D. (1992). Maltreated children's reports of relatedness to their teachers. In R. Pianta (Ed.), *Beyond the parent: The role of other adults in children's lives* (pp. 81–108). San Francisco: Jossey-Bass.

Madden, L. (1988). Do teachers communicate with their students as if they were dogs? *Language Arts, 65,* 142–146.

Marshall, H. H. (1992). *Redefining student learning: Roots of educational change.* Norwood, NJ: Ablex.

Martin, J. R. (1992). *The schoolhome.* Cambridge: Harvard University Press.

Marzano, R. J. (2003). *Classroom management that works: Research-based strategies for every teacher.* Alexandria, VA: Association for Supervision and Curriculum Development.

Maslach, C. (1982). *Burnout: The cost of caring.* Englewood Cliffs, NJ: Prentice Hall.

Maslow, A. (1968). *Toward a psychology of being.* New York: Van Nostrand Reinhold.

Masten, A., & Garmezy, N. (1985). Risk, vulnerability, and protective factors in developmental psychopathology.

In B. B. Lahey & A. E. Kazdin (Eds.), *Advances in clinical child psychology* (vol. 8, pp. 1–52). New York: Plenum.

McCaslin, M., & Good, T. L. (1992). Compliant cognition: The misalliance of management and instructional goals in current school reform. *Educational Researcher, 21* (3), 4–17.

McCaslin, M., & Good, T. L. (1998). Moving beyond management as sheer compliance: Helping students to develop goal coordination strategies. *Educational Horizons, 76,* 169–76.

McCroskey, J. C., & Richmond, V. P. (1983). Power in the classroom I: Teacher and student perceptions. *Communication Education, 32,* 175–184.

McCroskey, J. C., Richmond, V. P., Plex, T. G., & Koarney, P. (1985). Power in the classroom V: Behavior alteration techniques, communication training, and learning. *Communication Education, 34,* 214–226.

McEwan, B. (1998). Contradiction, paradox, and irony: The world of classroom management. In R. E. Butchart & B. McEwan (Eds.), *Classroom discipline in American schools: Problems and possibilities for democratic education.* Albany: SUNY.

McEwan, B. (2000). *The art of classroom management: Effective practices of building equitable learning communities.* Upper Saddle River, NJ: Merrill-Prentice Hall.

McEwan, B., Gathercoal, P., & Nimmo, V. (1997). *An examination of the applications of constitutional concepts as an approach to classroom management: Four studies of judicious discipline in various classroom settings.* Paper presented at the American Educational Research Association Conference, San Francisco.

McGinnis, E., & Goldstein, A. P. (1984). *Skillstreaming the elementary school child: A guide for teaching prosocial skills.* Champaign, IL: Research Press.

McGinnis, E., & Goldstein, A. P. (1990). *Skillstreaming the elementary school child.* Champaign, IL: Research Press.

McKay, M., David, M., & Fanning, P. (1981). *Thoughts and feelings: The art of cognitive stress intervention.* Oakland, CA: New Harbinger.

McLaughlin, H. J. (1994). From negation to negotiation: Moving away from the management metaphor. *Action in Teacher Education, 16* (1), 75–84.

McLaughlin, M. (1991). *Strategic sites for teachers' professional development.* Paper presented at the annual meeting of the American Educational Research Association, Chicago, IL.

McLaughlin, M. (1993). What matters most in teachers' workplace context? In J. Little & M. McLaughlin (Eds.), *Teachers' work.* New York: Teachers College Press.

McLaughlin, M. W., & Talbert, J. (1990). Constructing a personalized school environment. *Phi Delta Kappan, 72* (3), 230–235.

McMillan, D., & Chavis, D. (1986). Sense of community: A definition and theory. *Journal of Community Psychology, 14,* 6–23.

McNabb, W. H. (1990). *The developing capable people parenting course: A study of its impact on family cohesion.* Unpublished doctoral dissertation, Pepperdine University, Malibu, CA.

McWhirter, J. J., McWhirter, B. T., McWhirter, A. M., & McWhirter, E. H. (2004). *At-risk youth: A comprehensive response* (3rd ed.). Pacific Grove, CA: Brooks/Cole.

Medley, D. (1977). *Teacher competency and teacher effectiveness.: A review of process product research.* Washington, DC: American Association of Colleges for Teacher Education.

Meichenbaum, D. (1975). Self-instructional methods: How to do it. In A. Goldstein & F. Kanfer (Eds.), *Helping people change: Methods and materials.* Elmsford, NY: Pergamon.

Meichenbaum, D. (1977). *Cognitive behavior modification: An integrative approach.* New York: Plenum.

Meichenbaum, D. (1979). Teaching children self-control. In B. B. Lahey & A. E. Kazdin (Eds.), *Advances in clinical child psychology* (vol. 2). New York: Plenum.

Meichenbaum, D. (1980). Cognitive behavior modification: A promise yet unfulfilled. *Exceptional Education Quarterly, 1* (1), 83–88.

Meichenbaum, D. (1985). *Stress-inoculation training.* Elmsford, NY: Pergamon.

Meichenbaum, D. (1993). Changing conceptions of cognitive behavior modification: Retrospect and prospect. *Journal of Consulting & Clinical Psychology, 62* (2), 202–204.

Meichenbaum, D., & Cameron, R. (1983). Stress-inoculation training: Toward a general paradigm for training coping skills. In D. H. Meichenbaum & M. E. Jaremko (Eds.), *Stress reduction and prevention.* New York: Plenum.

Meier, D. (1995). *The power of their ideas.* Boston: Beacon Press.

Merrell, K. W. (2001). *Helping students overcome depression and anxiety: A practical guide.* New York: The Guilford Press.

Merzfeld, G., & Powell, R. (1986). *Coping for kids: A complete stress-control program for students ages 8–18.* West Nyack, NY: Center for Applied Research in Education.

Meyer, W. U., Bachmann, M., Bierman, U., Hempelmann, M., Plager, F. O., & Spiller, H. (1979). The information value of evaluative behavior: Influences of praise and blame on perceptions of ability. *Journal of Educational Psychology, 79,* 259–268.

Meyer, W. (1992). Paradoxical effects of praise and criticism on perceived ability. In W. Stroebe & M. Hewstone (Eds.), *European review of social psychology* (vol. 3, pp. 259–283). Chichester, England: Wiley.

Miller, D. & Hom, H. (1997). Conceptions of ability and the interpretation of praise, blame, and material rewards. *The Journal of Experimental Education, 65,* 163–177.

Miller, J., Martin, J. R., & Schamess, G. (2003). *School violence and children in crisis.* Denver, CO: Love Publishing.

Mills, R. A., Powell, R. R, & Pollack, J. P. (1992). The influence of middle level interdisciplinary teaming on teacher isolation: A case study. *Research in Middle Level Education, 15* (2), 9–25.

Morgan, D. P., & Jenson, W. R. (1988). *Teaching behaviorally disordered students: Preferred practices.* Columbus, OH: Merrill.

Morgan, S. R., & Reinhart, J. A. (1991). *Interventions for students with emotional disorders.* Austin, TX: Pro-Ed.

Morganett, R. S. (1990). *Skills for living: Group counseling activities for young adolescents.* Champaign, IL: Research Press.

Morganett, R. S., & Bauer, A. M. (1987). Coping strategies in mainstreaming educable mentally handicapped children. *Indiana Counsel for Exceptional Children Quarterly, 36,* 20–24.

Morrow, G. (1987). *The compassionate school. A practical guide to educating abused and traumatized children.* Englewood Cliffs, NJ: Prentice Hall.

Morse, W. C. (1985). *The education and treatment of emotionally impaired children and youth.* Syracuse, NY: Syracuse University Press.

Moskovitz, S. (1983). *Love despite hate: Child survivors of the Holocaust and their adult lives.* New York: Schocken.

Mueller, C. M., & Dweck, C. S. (1998). Praise for intelligence can undermine motivation and performance. *Journal of Personality and Social Psychology, 75,* 33–52.

Murdick, N., & Gartin, B. (1993). How to handle students exhibiting violent behavior. *The Clearing House, 66,* 278–280.

Nafpaktitis, M., Mayer, G., & Butterworth, T. (1985). Natural rates of teacher approval and disapproval and their relation to student behavior in intermediate school classrooms. *Journal of Educational Psychology, 77,* 362–367.

National Campaign to Prevent Teen Pregnancy (2001). *Emerging answers: Research findings on programs to reduce teen pregnancy.* Washington, DC: Author.

National Center for Children in Poverty (2002). *National Center for Children in Poverty: A program report.* New York: Columbia University School of Public Health.

National Center for Educational Statistics (2001). *Nonfatal teacher victimization at school:* Teacher reports. Washington, DC: U.S. Departments of Education and Justice.

National Center for Injury Prevention and Control (NCIPC, 2001). *Web-based injury statistics query and reports system.* (WISQARS). Retrieved March 11, 2004, from www.webapp.cdc.gov/sasweb/ncipc/nfirates.html.

National Crisis Prevention Institute (1994). *Nonviolent crisis intervention.* Brookfield, WI: NCPI.

National Institute for Dispute Resolution (1999). Conflict resolution education facts. Retrieved September 23, 2003, from www.CRFnet.org.

Natriello, G., & Dornbusch, S. (1985). *Teacher evaluation standards and student effort.* New York: Longman.

Nelsen, J., Lott, L., & Glenn, H. S. (2000). *Positive discipline in the classroom: Developing mutual respect, cooperation, and responsibility in your classroom.* Roseville, CA: Prima Publishing.

Nelson, J. R., Roberts, M., Mathur, S., & Rutherford, R. B. (1999). Has public policy exceeded our knowledge base? A review of the functional behavior assessment literature. *Behavioral Disorders, 24,* 169–179.

Noblit, G. (1993). Power and caring. *American Educational Research Journal, 30,* 23–38.

Noddings, N. (1992). *The challenge to care in schools.* New York: Teachers College Press.

Noguera, P. A. (1995). Preventing and producing violence: A critical analysis of responses to school violence. *Harvard Educational Review, 65* (2), 189–212.

Novaco, R. W. (1975). *Anger control: The development and evaluation of an experimental treatment.* Lexington, MA: Lexington Books.

O'Donnell, J., Hawkins, D., Catalano, R, Abbott, R. D., & Day, L. E. (1995). Preventing school failure, drug use, and delinquency among low-income children: Long-term prevention in elementary schools. *American Journal of Orthopsychiatry, 65,* 87–100.

Oldfather, P. (1993). What students say about motivating experiences in a whole language classroom. *The Reading Teacher, 46* (8), 672–681.

Ollendick, T., & Shapiro, E. (1984). An examination of vicarious reinforcement process in children. *Journal of Experimental Child Psychology, 37,* 78–91.

Olweus, D. (1993). Victimization by peers: Antecedents and long-term consequences. In K. H. Rubin & J. B. Asendorf (Eds.), *Social withdrawal, inhibition, and shyness in childhood.* Hillside, NJ: Erlbaum.

Olweus, D. (1994). *Bullying at school: What we know and what we can do.* Oxford, UK: Blackwell Publishers.

O'Neill, R. E., Horner, R. H., Albin, R. W., Sprague, J. R., Storey, K., & Newton, J. S. (1997). *Functional assessment and program development for problem behavior: A practical handbook.* Pacific Grove, CA: Brooks/Cole.

O'Rourke, S. L., Knoster, T. & Llewellyn, G. (1999). Screening for understanding: An initial line of inquiry for school-based settings. *Journal of Positive Behavior Interventions, 1* (1), 35–42.

Patterson, G. R. (1982). Coercive family process. Eugene, OR: Castalia.

Peck, M. S. (1987). *The different drum.* New York: Simon & Schuster.

Pederson, E., Faucher, T. A., & Eaton, W. W. (1978). A new perspective on the effects of first grade teachers on children's subsequent adult status. *Harvard Educational Review, 48,* 1–31.

Peele, S. & Brodksy, A. (1991). *The truth about addiction and recovery.* Lexington, MA: Lexington Books.

Perkins, D. (1995). *Outsmarting IQ: The emerging science of learnable intelligence.* New York: The Free Press.

Perls, F. (1976). *The Gestalt approach and eyewitness to therapy.* New York: Bantam.

Piaget, J. (1961). *The psychology of intelligence.* New York: International Press.

Piaget, J. (1965). *The moral judgment of the child.* New York: Free Press.

Pittman, T., Davey, M., Alafat, K., Wetherill, K., & Kramer, N. (1980). Informational versus controlling verbal rewards. *Personality and Social Psychology Bulletin, 6,* 228–233.

Pittman, T., Boggiano, A., & Ruble, D. (1982). Intrinsic and extrinsic motivational orientations: Limiting conditions on the undermining and enhancing effects of reward on intrinsic motivation. In J. Levine & M. Wang (Eds.), *Teacher-student perceptions: Implications for learning.* Hillsdale, NJ: Erlbaum.

Polsgrove, L. (1979). Self-control: Methods for child training. *Behavioral Disorders, 4,* 116–130.

Portner, J. (2000a). Complex set of ills spurs rising teen suicide rate. *Education Week, 19* (31), 1, 22–25.

Portner, J. (2000b). School violence down, report says, but worry high. *Education Week, 19* (31), 3.

Purkey, S. C., & Smith, M. S. (1983). Effective schools: A review. *Elementary School Journal, 83,* 427–452.

Queen, J. A., Blackwelder, B. B., & Mallen, L. P. (1997). *Responsible classroom management for teachers and students.* Columbus, OH: Merrill.

Rak, C., & Patterson, L. E. (1996). Resiliency in children. *Journal of Counseling and Development, 74,* 368–373.

Randolph, C. H., & Evertson, C. M. (1994). Images of management for learner-centered classrooms. *Action in Teacher Education, 16* (1), 55–63.

Randolph, C. H., & Evertson, C. M. (1995). Managing for learning: Rules, roles, and meanings in a writing class. *Journal of Classroom Interaction, 30* (2), 17–25.

Raschke, D. (1981). Designing reinforcement surveys: Let the student choose the reward. *Teaching Exceptional Children, 14,* 92–96.

Reagan, T. G., Case, C. W., & Brubacher, J. W. (2000). *Becoming a reflective educator: How to build a culture of inquiry in the schools.* Thousand Oaks, CA: Corwin Press.

Redfering, D. L., & Bowman, M. J. (1981). Effects of meditative relaxation exercise on non-attending behaviors of behavioral disturbed children. *Journal of Clinical Child Psychology, 10,* 126–127.

Redl, F. (1966). *When we deal with children.* New York: Free Press.

Redl, F., & Wattenberg, W. (1959). *Mental hygiene in teaching* (2nd ed.). New York: Harcourt, Brace and World.

Redl, F., & Wineman, D. (1957). *The aggressive child.* New York: Free Press.

Reiss, A. J. & Roth, J. A. (1993). *Understanding and preventing violence.* Washington, DC: National Academy Press.

Repp, A. C. (1999). Naturalistic functional assessment with regular and special education students in classroom settings. In A. C. Repp & R. H. Horner, *Functional analysis of problem behavior: From effective assessment to effective support* (pp. 238–258). Belmont, CA: Wadsworth.

Repp, A. C., & Horner, R. H. (1999). *Functional analysis of problem behavior: From effective assessment to effective support.* Belmont, CA: Wadsworth.

Rhodes, W. C. (1992). Empowering young minds (Special issue on Life-Impact Curriculum). *Journal of Emotional & Behavioral Problems, 1* (2).

Richardson, B. (2001). *Working with challenging youth: Lessons learned along the way.* New York: Taylor & Francis Group.

Richmond, V., & McCroskey, J. (1984). Power in the class room II: Power and learning. *Communication Education, 33,* 125–136.

Robb, L. (2003). *Literacy links: Practical strategies to develop the emergent literacy at-risk children need.* Portsmouth, NH: Heinemann.

Robin, A., Schneider, M., & Dolnick, M. (1976). The turtle techniques: An extended case study of self-control in the classroom. *Psychology in the Schools, 13,* 449–453.

Rodis, P., Garrod, A., & Boscardin, M. L. (2001). *Learning disabilities and life stories.* Boston: Allyn & Bacon.

Rogers, C. (1969). *Freedom to learn.* Columbus, OH: Merrill.

Rogers, C., & Freiberg, H. J. (1994). *Freedom to learn* (3rd ed.). New York: Merrill.

Rosenberg, M. B. (1999). *Nonviolent communication: A language of compassion.* Encinitas, CA: PuddleDancer Press.

Rosenshine, B. (1979). Content, time, and direct instruction. In P. Peterson & H. Walberg (Eds.), *Research on teaching: Concepts, findings, and implications.* Berkeley, CA: McCutcheon.

Rosenshine, B., & Berliner, D. C. (1978). Academic engaged time. *British Journal of Teacher Education, 4,* 3–15.

Rosenshine, B., & Stevens, R. (1984). Classroom instruction in reading. In D. Pearson (Ed.), *Handbook of research on teaching.* New York: Longman.

Rosenshine, B., & Stevens, R. (1986). Teaching functions. In M. C. Wittrock (Ed.), *Third handbook on research on teaching* (pp. 376–391). New York: Macmillan.

Rosenthal, R., & Jacobson, L. (1968). *Pygmalion in the classroom: Teachers' expectations and pupils' intellectual development.* New York: Holt, Rinehart & Winston.

Ross, D. D. (1990). Programmatic structures for the preparation of reflective teachers. In R. T. Clift, W. R. Houston, & M. C. Pugach (Eds.), *Encouraging reflective practice in education: An analysis of issues and programs* (pp. 97–118). New York: Teachers College Press.

Ross, D., Bondy, E., & Kyle, D. (1993). *Reflective teaching for student empowerment: Elementary curriculum and methods.* New York: Macmillan.

Ross, M. (1976). The self-perception of intrinsic motivation. In J. H. Harvey, W. J. Ickes, & R. F. Kidd (Eds.), *New directions in attributional research* (vol. 1). Hillsdale, NJ: Erlbaum.

Rost, J. C. (1991). *Leadership for the twenty-first century.* New York: Praeger.

Rothschild, M. (1994). A rational perspective on the problems of students. pp. 149–185.

Roush, D. (1984). Rational-emotive therapy and youth: Some new techniques for counselors. *Personnel and Guidance Journal 62,* 414–417.

Rowan, B. (1990). Commitment and control: Alternative strategies for the organizational design of schools. *Review of Research in Education, 16,* 353–385.

Rowe, M. (1974). Relation of wait-time and rewards to the development of language, logic, and fate control: Part II—rewards. *Journal of Research in Science Teaching, 11,* 291–308.

Ryan, B. (1979). A case against behavior modification in the "ordinary classroom." *Journal of School Psychology, 17* (2), 131–136.

Ryan, R. (1982). Control and information in the intrapersonal sphere: An extension of cognitive evaluation theory. *Journal of Personality and Social Psychology, 43,* 450–461.

Ryan, R., Mims, V., & Koestner, R. (1983). Relation of reward contingency and interpersonal context to intrinsic motivation: A review and test using cognitive evaluation theory. *Journal of Personality and Social Psychology, 45,* 736–750.

Sanders, W. L., & Horn, S. P. (1994). The Tennesse value-added assessment system (TVAAS): Mixed-model methodology in educational assessment. *Journal of Personnel Evaluation in Education, 8,* 299–311.

Sapon-Shevin, M. (1995). Building a safe community for learning. In W. Ayers (Ed.), *To become a teacher: Making a difference in children's lives.* New York: Teachers College Press.

Sapon-Shevin, M. (1999). *Because we can change the world: A practical guide to building cooperative, inclusive classroom communities.* Boston: Allyn & Bacon.

Sasso, G. M., Conroy, M. A., Stichter, J. P., & Fox, J. J. (2001). Slowing down the bandwagon: The misapplication of functional assessment for students with emotional and behavioral disorders. *Behavioral Disorders, 26,* 269–281.

Schon, D. A. (1995). The new scholarship requires a new epistemology. *Chance, 27*(6), 27–34.

Schumaker, J. B., Hazel, J. S., & Pederson, C. S. (1988). *Social skills for daily living.* Circle Pines, MN: American Guidance Service.

Schwab, R. L., Jackson, S. E., & Schuler, R. S. (1986). Educator burnout: Sources and consequences. *Educational Research Quarterly, 10,* 14–30.

Schwartz, B. (1990). The creation and destruction of value. *American Psychologist, 45*, 7–15.

Schwieso, J., & Hastings, N. (1987). Teacher's use of approval. In N. Hastings & J. Schwieso (Eds.), *New directions in educational psychology: 2. Behaviour and motivation in the classroom* (pp. 115–136). London: Falmer.

Scott, T. M., & Nelson, C. M. (1999a). Functional behavioral assessment: Implications for training and staff development. *Behavioral Disorders, 24* (3), 249–252.

Scott, T. M., & Nelson, C. M. (1999b). Using functional behavioral assessment to develop effective intervention plans: Practical classroom applications. *Journal of Positive Behavior Interventions, 1* (4), 242–251.

Seligman, M. (1995). *The optimistic child: A revolutionary program that safeguards children against depression and builds a lifelong resilience.* New York: Houghton Mifflin.

Senge, P. M. (1990). *The fifth discipline.* New York: Currency Doubleday.

Sergiovanni, T. (1992). *Moral leadership.* San Francisco: Jossey-Bass.

Sergiovanni, T. (1994). *Building community in schools.* San Francisco: Jossey-Bass.

Shapiro, S. B., & Reiff, J. (1993). A framework for reflective inquiry on practice: Beyond intuition and experience. *Psychological Reports, 73*, 1379–1394.

Shipman, W. M. (1984). Emotional and behavioral effects of long-distance running on children. In M. L. Sachs & G. W. Buffone (Eds.), *Running as therapy: An integrated approach.* Lincoln: University of Nebraska Press.

Shores, R. E., Jack, S. L., Gunter, P. L., Ellis, D. N., DeBriere, T. J., & Wehby, J. H. (1994). Classroom interactions of children with behavior disorders. *Journal of Emotional and Behavioral Disorders, 1* (1), 27–29.

Silberman, M. L., & Wheelan, S. A. (1980). *How to discipline without feeling guilty: Assertive relationships with children.* Champaign, IL: Research Press.

Sizer, T. (1984). *Horace's compromise.* Boston: Houghton Mifflin.

Slavin, R. E., Karweit, N. L., & Madden, N. A. (1989). *Effective programs for students at risk.* Boston: Allyn & Bacon.

Smead, R. (1981). *A comparison of counselor administered and tape-recorded relaxation training on decreasing target and non-target anxiety in elementary school children.* Unpublished doctoral dissertation, Auburn University.

Smith, S. L. (1989, April). The mask students wear. *Instructor, 27–28*, 31–32.

Soar, R., & Soar, R. (1975). Classroom behavior, pupil characteristics, and pupil growth for the school year and summer. *JSAS Catalog of Selected Documents in Psychology, 5*, 873.

Sokol, A. V., & Cranton, P. (1998, Spring). Transforming, not training. *Adult Learning*, 14–16.

Sparks-Langer, G., & Colton, A. (1991). Synthesis of research on teachers reflective thinking. *Educational Leadership, 48* (6), 37–44.

Spiel, O. (1962). *Discipline without punishment.* London: Faber and Faber.

Stahelski, A., & Frost, D. (1987). *Modern managers move away from the carrot-and-stick approach.* Paper presented at the annual meeting of the Western Psychological Association, Long Beach, CA.

Stallings, J. (1975). Implementation and child effects of teaching practices in Follow Through classrooms. *Monographs of the Society for Research in Child Development, 40*, 7–8.

Staus, M. & Gelles, R. (1988). How violent are American families? Estimates from the national family violence resurvey and other studies. In G. Hotaling et al. (Eds.), *Family abuse and its consequences: New directions in research.* Beverly Hills, CA: Sage.

Steffy, B. E., Wolfe, M. P., Pasch, S. H., & Enz, B. J. (2000). *Life cycle of the career teacher.* Thousand Oaks, CA: Corwin Press.

Sternberg, R. J. (1988). *The triarchic mind: A new theory of human intelligence.* New York: Viking.

Sunburst Communications. *Student workshop: Mediation skills.* Pleasantville, NY: Author.

Sutherland, S. (1993). Impoverished minds. *Nature, 364*, 767.

Teaching Tolerance (1999). *Responding to hate at school: A guide for teachers, counselors and administrators.* Montgomery, AL: The Southern Poverty Law Center.

Thompson, C., & Poppen, W. (1972). *For those who care: Ways of relating to youth.* Columbus, OH: Merrill.

Tierney, J., Dowd, T., & O'Kane, S. (1993). Empowering aggressive youth to change. *Journal of Emotional & Behavioral Problem, 2* (1), 41–45.

Tolan, P. H., & Guerra, N. G. (1994). Prevention of delinquency: Current status and issues. *Applied & Preventive Psychology, 3*, 251–273.

Travers, C. J. & Cooper, C. L. (1996). *Teachers under pressure: Stress in the teaching profession.* New York: Routledge.

U.S. Department of Health and Human Services. (2001). *Youth Violence: A Report of the Surgeon General—Executive Summary.* Rockville, MD: U.S. Department of Health and Human Services, Centers for Disease Control and Prevention, National Center for Injury Prevention and Control.

U.S. Department of Health and Human Services, Children's Bureau (2002). National child abuse and neglect data system (NCANDS). *Summary of key findings from calendar year 2002.* Washington, DC: Government Printing Office.

Usher, R. S., & Bryant, I. (1989). *Adult education as theory, practice and research: The captive triangle.* New York: Routledge, Chapman and Hall.

Vernon, A. (2002). *What works when with children and adolescents: A handbook of individual counseling techniques.* Champaign, IL: Research Press.

Vernon, A. (2004). *Counseling children & adolescents.* Denver, CO: Love Publishing.

Vernon, A. (1998a). *The Passport program: A journey through emotional, social, cognitive, and self-development, grades 1–5.* Champaign, IL: Research Press.

Vernon, A. (1998b). *The Passport program: A journey through emotional, social, cognitive, and self-development, grades 6–8.* Champaign, IL: Research Press.

Vernon, A. (1998c). *The Passport program: A journey through emotional, social, cognitive, and self-development, grades 9–12.* Champaign, IL: Research Press.

Vernon, A. (2004). Applications of rational emotive behavior therapy with children and adolescents. In A. Vernon (Ed.), *Counseling children and adolescents* (3rd ed.) (pp. 164–187). Denver, CO: Love Publishing.

Vorrath, H., & Brendtro, L. (1985). *Positive peer culture* (2nd ed.). New York: Aldine du Gruyter.

Vygotsky, L. (1962). *Thought and language.* New York: Wiley.

Walen, S. R., DiGiuseppe, R., & Wessler, R. L. (1980). *A practitioner's guide to rational-emotive therapy.* New York: Oxford University Press.

Walker, H. (1979). *The acting out child: Coping with classroom discipline.* Boston: Allyn & Bacon.

Walker, H. M., Colvin, G., & Ramsey, E. (1996). *Antisocial behavior in school: Strategies and best practices.* Pacific Grove, CA: Brooks/Cole.

Walker, H. M. & Sprague, J. R. (1999). The path to school failure, delinquency, and violence: Causal factors and some potential solutions. *Intervention in School and Clinic, 35* (2), 67–73.

Walker, H. M., & Walker, J. E. (1991). *Coping with noncompliance in the classroom.* Austin, TX: Pro-Ed.

Wang, M. C., Haertel, G. D., & Walberg, H. J. (1993). Toward a knowledge base for school learning. *Review of Educational Research, 63* (3), 249–294.

Watson, T. S., Ray, K. P., Sterling-Turner, H., & Logan, P. (1999). Teacher-implemented functional analysis and treatment: A method for linking assessment to intervention. *School Psychology Review, 28* (2), 292–302.

Watson, D. L., & Tharp, R. G. (2002). *Self-directed behavior: Self-modifications for personal adjustment.* Pacific Grove, CA: Brooks/Cole.

Weiner, B. (1979). A theory of motivation in some classroom experiences. *Journal of Educational Psychology, 71,* 3–25.

Weinhold, B. (1999). Bullying and school violence. *Counseling Today, 42* (4), 14.

Weinhold, B. & Weinhold, J. (1998). Conflict resolution: The partnership way in schools. *Counseling & Human Development, 30* (7), 1–12.

Weinstein, C. S. (2003). *Secondary classroom management: Lessons from research and practice.* New York: McGraw-Hill.

Weinstein, C. S., & Mignano, A. J. (2003). *Elementary classroom management. Lessons from research and practice.* New York: McGraw-Hill.

Werner, E. E. (1990). Protective factors and individual resilience. In S. J. Meisels & J. P. Shonkoff (Eds.), *Handbook of early childhood intervention* (p. 109). Cambridge, UK: Cambridge University Press.

Werner, E. E., & Smith, R. S. (1992). *Overcoming the odds: High risk children from birth to adulthood.* Ithaca, NY: Cornell University Press.

Wheatley, M. J. 1992. *Leadership and the new science.* San Francisco: Berrett-Koehler.

Williams, M. (1981). *The velveteen rabbit, or, how toys become real.* Philadelphia: Running Press.

Wolfgang, C., & Brudenell, G. (1982). The many faces of praise. *Early Child Development and Care, 9,* 237–243.

Wood, M. (1986). *Developmental theory in the classroom.* Austin, TX: Pro-Ed.

Wright, S. P., Horn, S. P., & Sanders, W. L. (1997). Teacher and classroom context effects on student achievement: Implications for teacher evaluation. *Journal of Personnel Evaluation in Education, 11,* 57–67.

York-Barr, J., Sommers, W. A., Ghere, G. S., & Montie, J. (2001). *Reflective practice to improve schools.* Thousand Oaks, CA: Corwin Press.

Zehm, S. J., & Kottler, J. A. (2000). *On being a teacher. The human dimension.* Newbury Park, CA: Corwin Press.

Zimrin, H. (1986). A profile of survival. *Child Abuse and Neglect, 10,* 339–349.